CITY ON A HILLTOP

CITY ON A HILLTOP

American Jews and the Israeli Settler Movement

SARA YAEL HIRSCHHORN

Harvard University Press

Cambridge, Massachusetts
London, England
2017

Library of Congress Cataloging-in-Publication Data
Names: Hirschhorn, Sara Yael, 1981– author.
Title: City on a hilltop : American Jews and the Israeli settler
movement / Sara Yael Hirschhorn.
Description: Cambridge, Massachusetts : Harvard University Press,
2017. | Includes bibliographical references and index.
Identifiers: LCCN 2016044711 | ISBN 9780674975057 (alk. paper)
Subjects: LCSH: Jews, American—Palestine—History. | Zionists. |
Liberalism—Palestine—History. | Palestine—Colonization—History. |
Arab-Israeli conflict. | Israel—Emigration and immigration.
Classification: LCC DS125 .H56 2017 |
DDC 305.892/405695309045—dc23
LC record available at https://lccn.loc.gov/2016044711

Contents

CITY ON A HILLTOP

Introduction

MALKA (MARILYN) CHAIKEN met me at the bus stop in the Avraham Avinu (Abraham Is Our Forefather) neighborhood of the city of Hebron as I disembarked from the armored Egged public bus from Jerusalem on a dusty, hot August morning. As the motor coach creaked to a stop at the top of a sharp curve, I caught a glimpse of the hulking stone edifice of the Tomb of the Patriarchs/Ibrahami Mosque, a holy site to both Judaism and Islam. In 1994 Baruch Goldstein, an American-Israeli settler terrorist and the legal guardian of the Chaikens' children, gunned down twenty-nine Palestinian supplicants bowed in early morning prayer—his shocking and deplorable act set off months of rioting and helped doom the Oslo peace process. The historic city center nearby was once a bustling hub before the closure of the casbah during the second intifada in 2003. A decade and a half earlier, during the first Palestinian uprising in the West Bank, Chaiken's husband Yona had been stabbed in one of its narrow alleyways by a Palestinian assailant while out shopping. On the August day of my visit the area was eerily deserted, apart from IDF soldiers on patrol. To my mind it looked like the film set of a Wild West town: I could almost imagine tumbleweed rolling down the abandoned main street. Racist graffiti was scrawled on the rusting metal awnings of shuttered Palestinian shops. Some bore a Jewish star with slogans like "Kahane Tzadak" (Kahane Was Right), referring to the violent xenophobic views of the American-Israeli rabbi, radical agitator, and Knesset representative Meir Kahane. Yet Hebron once had a rich history as a multiethnic municipality where religious populations lived in harmony. This rapport was shattered with the Arab riots of 1929 during the British mandate in Palestine, when most of the city's Jewish community was expelled or murdered. After Israel's conquest of the West Bank from the Kingdom of Jordan during the Six Day War, a small coterie of settlement activists led by future Gush Emunim (Bloc of the Faithful) founder Rabbi Moshe Levinger and his Bronx-born wife, Miriam, temporarily resettled the downtown area in the spring of 1968 and later established a permanent enclave in 1977. Today Hebron is the highly segregated home to a majority population of 170,000 mostly Sunni Muslim Palestinians and a fluctuating population of 500 to 800 Israeli Jewish settlers and yeshiva students. Although it is one of the smallest settlements in the occupied territories, Hebron has been a flashpoint for tensions for almost five decades.

Malka and her husband arrived in Hebron in 1984 when the Jewish quarter housed only a few dozen families. However, they were hardly the only Americans in town—one report suggested that 65 percent of the settlement's initial population were immigrants from the United States.[1] Yona, then known as John, hailed from Springfield, Massachusetts, a former industrial center in the western part of the state. (I grew up in its most heavily Jewish populated suburb.) He likely entered the covenant of the faith at the synagogue where my grandfather served as president, he graduated from the same high school as my aunt and uncle, and he was only a few years younger than my father. His upbringing was likely filled with many of the same landmarks and legacies as my childhood. So how did this man and his wife from my own small Jewish community end up living in one of the most contentious settlements in the occupied territories?

Malka had agreed to speak with me about her family's story. A petite woman with a big smile, she dressed modestly but moved brusquely, ushering me into a dilapidated apartment building in the old Jewish quarter of Hebron. We came inside the cramped flat that she once shared with her now-deceased husband and their eight children, which was filled from wall to wall with the family's two main sources of sustenance: holy books and massive refrigerators. I could hear the call of the muezzin through the open window, which she had lined with sandbags to protect her salon from snipers during the second intifada. We sat together at her dining room table for hours, where she told me the story that traced their arc from Springfield to settlement.

Marilyn Chaiken was born in 1954 in Philadelphia, Pennsylvania, and was raised in the home of traditional American Jews who affiliated with Conservative Judaism. The family attended synagogue, kept a kosher home, observed holidays, and her parents enrolled their eldest daughter in Hebrew school and a Zionist youth movement. "I was always fascinated by being Jewish," she rhapsodized, "it was a very serious curiosity for me. . . . I was searching for a sense of belonging and attachment." As a teenager, she discovered a spirit of solidarity in the drama of the Six Day War, spending each day of the crisis meticulously clipping *New York Times* articles about the unfolding events. When her Hebrew school teacher decamped for a kibbutz shortly thereafter, it struck her as "a very powerful statement" for her future life.[2] As a high school student Marilyn deepened her commitment to Jewish and Zionist ideals as a *baalat teshuvah* (returner to the faith). After graduation she spent a gap year in Israel as part of the Young Judea program before the Yom Kippur War. Like many Jewish-American settlers who had their first exposure to the occupied territories as students, volunteers, and tourists, she briefly visited the West Bank during her course, including an excursion to the Tomb of the Patriarchs in Hebron, if it never crossed her mind that she would later make her adult home there. Upon her return to the United States, she was inspired by her faith but struggled to find a religious and educational path in New York City. She first enrolled at the Conservative movement's Jewish Theological Seminary, but later dropped out to explore the German Modern Orthodox Jewish community of Washington Heights, attend Rabbi Shlomo Riskin's lectures on Zionism at Lincoln Square Synagogue, and consider non-Zionist ultra-Orthodoxy. A new chapter of her personal journey commenced when she met her future husband, Yona.

John Chaiken was born in 1949 in the predominantly Christian Five-Mile Pond neighborhood of Springfield, the son of a navy veteran and "proud Jews."[3] He had little exposure to Judaism or Zionism growing up, although some early experiences with anti-Semitism stirred in him inchoate feelings of peoplehood.[4] Following his graduation from Classical High School, where he won several prizes in science and mathematics, Chaiken attended the Massachusetts Institute of Technology (MIT).[5] Like his future wife, he became a returner to the faith, finding a Jewish community in Cambridge and taking a year off from college to study in Israel. After completing a bachelor's degree in physics, he met Marilyn, and the couple married in 1975.

The Chaikens resided in a Victorian mansion in an affluent section of Boston for several years after their marriage. John ran a lucrative computer consulting business and pursued a PhD at MIT (which he never completed) while his wife taught at local Jewish academies, including the prestigious Maimonides School.[6] Yet early in their courtship both Yona and Malka had expressed their interest in immigrating to Israel and longed to consummate their Zionist dream as a couple. Their parents, however, vocally disapproved of this idea. Arthur Chaiken mournfully admitted to a reporter that he couldn't dissuade his headstrong son, as "we told him many a time that it's a dangerous place. But he knew the story there—that it's like running into a lion's mouth. That's the way he is."[7] Malka also drifted farther from her family over her Jewish and Zionist commitments—only recently, she has reconnected with her sister, a lesbian peace activist in Philadelphia. Nevertheless, they were undeterred by the growing family rift and Yona, Malka, and their five children (aged 8, 6, 4, 2, and a newborn) relocated to the West Bank settlement of Kiryat Arba in late summer 1984.

Weeks earlier, the American-Israeli ultra-nationalist Meir Kahane had been elected to the Knesset as the lone parliamentarian for the Kach (Thus) party, an electoral surprise that shook the Israeli polity. (A *Boston Globe* reporter later confirmed that the couple were members of the movement.[8]) Meanwhile the country was wrestling with the political fallout of the disastrous Lebanon war and confronting rising Palestinian nationalism under occupation. Since the death of the first Israeli settler in the occupied territories in its own casbah in 1981, Hebron had been in the cross-hairs of the Israeli-Palestinian conflict.

While they were ideologically supportive of settlement in the occupied territories, the Chaikens ended up in temporary accommodation in the area because their preferred absorption center selection in Mevaseret Zion, a small city outside Jerusalem, was full. At that point, Kiryat Arba was a place that "sounded nice and there were some other Americans," yet they had little understanding of its significance within the Israeli settler project and "we didn't know that Hevron [even] existed."[9] They were open to the idea of settling over the Green Line, but the couple had never imagined living out their American-Israeli dream in urban surroundings. Malka chuckled years later, "Our image was that we would end up in some nice community with some grass and trees and a backyard. We didn't expect to end up living in an apartment building in the middle of a very large city populated by Arabs."[10]

What later seemed to Malka like destiny came much by happenstance. While she and her husband explored employment and residency options on both sides of the Green Line, Rabbi Levinger got word of the new American couple in the nearby absorption center and sent his emissaries to welcome them. They arrived unannounced one frantic dinnertime as the Chaikens struggled to feed, bathe, and put five children to bed, describing the settlement in downtown Hebron above the din. A few days later they called to set up a tour of the downtown area for the entire family to help persuade the Chaikens that the urban settlement could be their new home. According to Malka, "We didn't know we were being set up for the kill."[11] Later that week the couple and their children were entirely confounded by what they observed on their outing to the city center. "It was like being on the scene of [the film] *Casablanca*," Malka reminisced in an Orientalist revelry. "[We were] just in complete shock, looking to the right, looking to the left. . . . We saw Mercedes on the street. . . . We saw these stores with fancy up-to-date European fashions. And then we saw peasants on donkeys and camels. . . . We saw people putting sheep into station-wagons . . . it was a real menagerie, it was just like a very crazy combination of modern and sort of like, pre-modernity. . . . The bottom line is we went back to Kiryat Arba and we were in complete and utter shock."[12]

A few days later, on the eve of the high holy day of Rosh Hashanah, false rumors of a Palestinian terrorist attack against the Jewish settlement in downtown Hebron filtered back to Kiryat Arba. Gripped by panic, the absorption center quickly transformed into a "boiling pot of insanity." Just as the hysteria reached its climax, one of Rabbi Levinger's disciples turned up on Malka's doorstep. Ignoring the atmosphere of acute tension, "he says, 'Hi, how are you? How would you like to move to Hevron on Sunday?' And my husband says, 'Oh yes, great!' and I started bursting into tears." They moved that weekend on the condition that Malka could veto her husband's decision at any time. The couple was cautiously optimistic, even though the director of the absorption center "thought we were completely insane" and saved their empty apartment predicting an imminent return.[13]

The Chaikens were couple no. 24—replacing a family that had decided to leave the settlement. They initially moved into a prefabricated caravan in the courtyard of Beit Romano, a crumbling structure built by Turkish Jew Avraham (Haim) Romano in the old Jewish quarter in 1879. They furnished their flat with handouts from the neighbors, which included several other American-Israeli households. For Malka, the first weeks and months in Hebron were the fulfillment of lifelong ambitions. She later maintained, "As a child I had three big dreams: I wanted to marry a serious Orthodox Jew who learned Torah, I wanted to have a large family, and I wanted to live a pioneering life in Eretz Yisrael. That was my goal—and I had all those things by the time I was thirty." Yet, at the time, she did not foresee that her Zionist fantasy might have flaws, seeing her new settlement only as "a nice community, you would be rebuilding Judea and Samaria, restoring the Jewish community in Hevron." In retrospect she ruefully confided, "Now, did I really understand what we were getting into? Not really."[14]

Weeks later, as the community braced for another rumored wave of Palestinian attacks, her Israeli neighbor and ultra-nationalist activist Orit Shtruck sat the couple down on her couch for a heart-to-heart chat.[15] "Before you moved here, did anyone tell you that you could get hurt?" "No," the Chaikens responded with naiveté. "Did anyone tell you that you could get killed?" "No!" the couple chorused in confusion and consternation. By the end of the conversation, the new American-Israeli settlers were "totally shell-shocked, our mouths hanging open, and we're white with fear."[16] Yet despite potential dangers, the couple quickly regained their sense of purpose. They purchased a set of pistols and prepared to make a permanent commitment to the community.

In the months and years that followed, Yona Chaiken rededicated himself to his personal mission. As he proselytized to a visiting reporter, "You have to decide what you want to do with your life. I know a lot of people couldn't hack this. I have a unique opportunity for a Jew. This is something where you don't only study Jewish history, you make Jewish history." He averred, "This land will never go back to the Arabs"—anyway, he and his family would not leave. He claimed to have "no fear whatsoever" and would stake a physical claim to the land and contribute to Hebron's Jewish community because "it is important to be here."[17]

Nevertheless, he seemed stunned by how others saw his activities, speculating, "I'm supposed to be a fanatic because I live here?"[18] Malka

Chaiken recalled her shock when during a reunion in Israel alumni of the Young Judea program she had attended in her gap year castigated her for her life choices. "Here I had come from an Orthodox community in America . . . and now we were living in Hevron, suffering from stones, the occasional Molotov cocktails, and stabbings, and things weren't always so idyllic," she recollected, evincing visible indignation, "and here all these people were telling me that I'm the racist? I'm the fascist? I'm the one who is violent?" Afterward, "I went home and I thought a lot about where I had grown up—I was a bit shaken." To her mind, "the question is: what do you do with it? When you start to see reality, you can either adapt your ideology to the reality, or you can try to ignore the reality and go with the ideology. . . . I saw that." Ultimately she concluded, "I think that liberalism in very many ways is in denial that some people have more rights than others . . . all the liberals are extremely racist against the Arabs because they don't hold them to the same standards of behavior that they hold the Jews and they hold most Western people."[19] Feeling a renewed sense of purpose, she recommitted herself to settlement activism.

Yet journalist Robert I. Friedman from the *Village Voice,* who visited the family in Hebron in 1985, was under no illusion about the Chaikens' liberal pretensions. In his portrait of the couple, whom he considered "zealots for Zion" in the occupied territories, he completely dismissed their progressive protestations about the Hebron project.[20] He quoted Yona Chaiken proclaiming, "You may say the fact that Jews lived here 2,000 years ago is no reason for Jews to live here now—that it's an Arab city and it's not ethical to force them out. Well, I say Western European values are bullshit. The Messiah will come. There will be a Jewish kingdom . . . [and] you can't create a messianic Jewish state with 1.9 million Arabs! . . . We came to Hebron out of a sense of adventure and outrage. The adventure is building a Jewish kingdom. The outrage is that Arabs still live here!"

Friedman illustrated not only the Chaikens' radical ideas but their militant deeds. He described how the couple regularly provoked Palestinian residents of Hebron, which not only embittered their daily lives but was intended to persuade locals to abandon their city altogether. He recounted how Yona and other male settlers' supposedly participated in a terrorist attack at a local mosque, where they broke into and vandalized the sanctuary. The reporter also claimed to observe Malka scream at and slap a Palestinian child in the casbah. "The Arabs are worse than the niggers," she allegedly told Friedman, "but not by much." In her eyes, to dwell in the whole of the land of Israel "you have to live in the realm of perfect faith."[21]

The Chaikens vigorously disputed the faithfulness of Friedman's account and sued the reporter and the *Village Voice* in state and federal court for defamation and emotional distress. (Their claims were later dismissed.[22]) The couple were also at pains to provide a counternarrative of their activities to other members of the international media. Yona Chaiken insisted to an American journalist, "I have Arab friends . . . I have no hatred toward the Arabs. I understand them. To them, Judaism is an affront to Islam. The Arabs are scared, not of the soldiers but of the PLO."[23] He hoped that animosity between Jews and Muslims would diminish and meanwhile claimed to engage in his own acts of dialogue like meeting a Palestinian neighbor for coffee and shopping in the casbah. Malka Chaiken later extolled her husband's extraordinary efforts to integrate into the city, which included joining the Hebron library, paying taxes at city hall, and attempting to enroll in a course at the Hebron polytechnic—although she scoffed that the local community college didn't have much to teach an MIT graduate. Mostly the couple longed for a normal life in the city. Malka fondly recalled how in summertime they put their children to bed early to take long strolls together through the streets of Hebron, holding hands and eating kosher ice cream cones. These (literal) walks in the park were her idea of coexistence.[24]

This fragile—if perhaps imaginary—harmony was shattered by the arrival of the first Palestinian *intifada* (uprising) in Hebron in late 1987. A few months later, Yona was involved in a street brawl with local Palestinians, supposedly defending a group of settler women ambushed on their way to a demonstration in Jerusalem. In Malka's telling, Chaiken leaped from his car (leaving his four-year-old daughter unattended), began shooting in the air, and held a Palestinian passerby hostage until the stoning ceased. The event was apparently video-recorded by Meretz, a left-leaning political party, although her husband was never arrested.[25] After playing hero, Yona Chaiken himself became a victim of the intifada in 1988 when he was jumped and grievously injured in a stabbing one Friday morning while shopping in a hardware store in the casbah. He managed to fend off his attacker, chasing him down the street while firing repeatedly from his pistol. Chaiken shot his assailant in the shoulder before the gun jammed. He finally collapsed near death from severe blood loss outside a building inhabited by other Israeli settlers.[26] Malka's narration of the events sounded like a scene in a spaghetti Western film, with her husband with his "big peyus, curly hair, red from shoulder to shoes with blood . . . walking holding up his gun down the street slowly . . . these Arabs looking, thinking they are seeing this apparition."[27] As he was being rushed into surgery, Chaiken managed to offer both a string of profanities about Palestinians and political analysis, opining, "My stabbing is a result of the American pressure on Israel not to take strong measures against the Arabs."[28]

The Chaikens chose to remain in Hebron after Yona's release from the hospital, but his health never recovered. He was subsequently diagnosed with a brain tumor and died in 1991 at the age of forty-two, leaving behind his wife and eight children, including a daughter born after his death. Some counseled the new widow to leave Hebron, but Malka decided to remain living in the settlement in spite of her family's tragedy. "I know a lot of people have said to me, 'Why are you staying?,'" considering, "Look, this is a community that I know, I have a lot of friends here, I have a lot of love here, a lot of support here, I found a job, where am I going to go?" Ultimately, even after her children grew up and left the home, "I realized that I felt very connected to this place."[29] Malka has weathered the more than two decades since as a warrior for the ideals she and her husband shared. Since her husband's death, she has protested the Oslo peace process, witnessed Baruch Goldstein's shocking act of settler terrorism, endured the second intifada, and continued to live intimately with the cycle of violence in the city. Malka is a true survivor: a vulnerable woman who has persevered in the face of family tragedy and the vagaries of daily life in the midst of the political maelstrom she calls home.

After more than three decades in Hebron, Malka Chaiken has firm views about the future of the Israeli-Palestinian conflict. She pronounced the two-state paradigm a failure and advocates for the full annexation of the occupied territories by the State of Israel. While she would encourage local civilian control for Palestinians under Israeli sovereignty, she is also not opposed to population-transfer policies with economic compensation. She supports uncompromising measures against Palestinian terror and is proud to send her children to the military. At the end of the day, she believes that "God gave us this country . . . [and] the fact of the matter is that it belongs to us," and she recognizes that "this is a process of redemption . . . to live here is to live with miracles."[30] Considering her role within the Israeli

settlement enterprise, she reflected, "I raised a good family here, contributed to a Jewish presence in the community, in Maarat Ha-Mahpela." As
a woman born on the week of the Torah reading cycle that discusses the
Tomb of the Patriarchs, she feels that her legacy in Hebron has been to live
out "my birthright."[31]

As Malka walked me back to the bus stop several hours later, I couldn't
help but wonder: How did Yona Chaiken—a man from my own hometown—
choose this path, which diverged so completely from my own?

The Chaikens' life story epitomizes many of the themes and contradictions of Jewish-American settlement in the occupied territories, combining
tropes of messianic redemption with modern-day pioneering, hawkish ter-
ritorialism with Jewish history, sacred promise with suburbanization, ultra-
nationalism with utopian idealism, and most importantly, liberal values
with an illiberal project.[32] The couple's self-conception as idealistic, progressive American-Israelis is not a cynical propaganda tool. Rather, it is a
reflection of how both they and their peers understand themselves and their
activities within the Israeli settler enterprise. While they may have seen it
as their historical destiny, many of these Jewish-American immigrants made
profound personal sacrifices (with sometimes deadly consequences) in de-
voting their lives to this political project.

The Chaikens' saga also personifies the political and moral tightrope
that many Jewish-American settlers beyond the Green Line have traveled
in staking their territorial claims. Like many American-Israeli immigrants
in the occupied territories (although not all, including perhaps her own
husband), Malka Chaiken is not an apocalyptic maniac, bloodthirsty vigilante, or uneducated thug, although she holds ultra-nationalist views that
she willingly admits aren't "politically correct" and that others consider
radical, violent, and dangerous.[33] She hasn't killed anyone, torched property, or engaged in underground activity—most of her time seems to be
spent eking out a living, caring for her family, and observing her faith—
even though she owns a gun that she has trained to use in self-defense and
has sworn to use civil disobedience to resist the Israeli Defense Forces
should her settlement be evacuated in the future. She professes that she
doesn't hate Palestinians, yet she would deny them sovereignty in their own
independent state and citizenship in the State of Israel.

For all intents and purposes, Malka is a nice person engaged in a not-so-nice political program. A grandmother for Greater Israel. A kindly neighbor for ultra-nationalism. Malka Chaiken is not a monster: she's a very mild-mannered middle-aged woman who reminds me a little of my Mom.

This is a portrait that some, including many fellow academics, are unable or unwilling to abide. Surely it is easier to frame Malka as a messianic fanatic than as a fully realized person. It is more comfortable to regard her as a political heretic and psychologically unhinged propagandist than as a peer who actually shares a similar background to many American Jews of her generation. It is easier to conceive of her activities as the work of a single-minded ideologue than as those of a woman with a cosmopolitan intellectual and emotional worldview. The fact that Malka cannot be reduced to the caricature of crazed zealot and must be acknowledged as a human being with complex, if, to my mind, cognitively dissonant motivations makes it all that much more difficult to understand her role, along with over 60,000 other Jewish-American immigrants, within the Israeli settler movement today. It also poses particular challenges to a historian to write about this topic.

In many ways, I identify with and admire Malka's family background, her passionate idealism, her Zionist commitments and sacrifices, her pursuits in the interest of Jewish peoplehood, and her daily struggles as a woman in difficult circumstances. Yet, both professionally and personally, I am deeply concerned by the consequences of the ideological project in which she has invested her life. As the member of a family that considered immigrating to Israel, I am also chagrined that she has come from a life of comfort in the United States to contribute to making the Zionist project a less liberal, democratic, inclusive enterprise. Neither she nor I are naive to the limits of liberalism, the nightmares of nationalism, or the instability of Israel's neighborhood in the Middle East today. Yet for a historian it's often discomfiting to abandon conventional wisdoms and popular stereotypes to write about Jewish-American settlers. I know it will be even harder for my audience to read this book without thinking that I have penned either a spirited defense of the settler enterprise or a vitriolic condemnation of the entire Zionist proposition. Despite my best efforts to provide an objective, rigorous, scholarly account, I am under no illusions: this work may be instrumentalized to support various political agendas in the public debate over Israel/Palestine, including positions and policies I personally do not share. Nonetheless, I believe it is important—both as a scholar and as a Jewish Zionist—to offer the nuanced understanding of this historical phenomenon that is lacking in the current narrative today.

YOU MAY NEVER HAVE sat in Malka Chaiken's salon in Hebron, been to the occupied territories, or even traveled to Israel/Palestine, but this book is going to require you to embark on a metaphorical—if not physical—journey. It is likely that you will leave your comfort zone. At the very least, readers must come to these chapters equipped with historical empathy and the willingness to distinguish it from sympathy.[34] Yet you have likely picked up this book because this is a constituency within the conflict today that you've wondered about, or may even have a personal connection to, as a reader. There has been much speculation about the role of Jewish-American settlers, the subjects of this study, within the Israeli settlement enterprise. The American-Israeli settler has even become a recognizable character in popular culture—you have probably turned on television news only to see media spokespeople with fluent English (sometimes tinged with a thick Brooklyn accent and American slang) offering insights from a windswept hilltop of the West Bank. Two common—and contradictory—caricatures characterize this constituency today.[35] One prevalent representation is the immigrant-suburbanite of "occupied Scarsdale," a settler stripped of ideological significance who for all intents and purposes is nothing more than a New Age yuppie living the American dream over the Green Line or a back-to-the-land pioneer on the West Bank frontier.[36] In contrast, there is the representation of Jewish-American settlers as the quintessential "zealots for Zion," the most fanatical ideologues within the movement. Yet despite much interest—and even suspicion—about this group's role within the settlement project in the occupied territories over the past five decades, neither of these viewpoints offers a satisfying or sufficiently complex study of this constituency.

This book builds upon a small but robust interdisciplinary literature on Jewish-American immigration to Israel, the process of social and ideological acculturation, and the translation of concepts of frontiers across borders.[37] Within the Israeli context, this study also follows on the extant scholarship on the Six Day War and the origins of the Israeli settler enterprise, which places particular emphasis on its first two decades.[38] There are also a few, but important, accounts by settlement activists themselves.[39] This book also expands upon theoretical conceptualizations of the Israeli settler movement, a particular deficiency of this scholarly literature to date. My study rejects much of the popular terminology used to characterize this phenomenon, including fundamentalism (which does not capture the broad and sometimes nonreligious "imagined community" of adherents to the settler agenda[40]), "right-wing" (which obscures the contributions of groups who draw from liberal-democratic backgrounds), and the vague ideological and operational labels of "radicalism," "extremism," and "zealotry."[41] Rather, this work is based upon Charles S. Liebman's model of Israeli ultranationalism, measured as the convergence of three axes: territorial maximalism, exclusionary ethnonationalism, and cultural hegemony.[42] This project is also deeply indebted to Ehud Sprinzak, the founder of the scholarly field on the post-1967 Israeli right,[43] and other writings on religious, cultural, and immigrant enclaves.[44]

This study seeks to occupy a new space in the scholarly debate on settlements. As a deeply researched, rigorous, academic book, it departs from the often polemical treatises published on this topic in recent years. While it is primarily a work of contemporary history, this narrative also seeks to intervene in the existing literature by integrating several interdisciplinary approaches to answer questions at the intersection of immigration and ultra-nationalism. It is also the first account of the Israeli settler movement to adopt a transnational framework, illuminating its origins and context on two continents.

The ethnic and religious makeup of the settlements, the interest of the media (with its twenty-four-hour news cycle) in Israel/Palestine, and the realities on the ground in the occupied territories have also changed dramatically since the publication of earlier studies in this field. With this project I aspire to pioneer a second generation of scholarship, emphasizing the multiple ideologies, discourses, and constituencies within the settler enterprise after five decades in existence. It recognizes the waning influence of the national-religious sector in the settlements and how the state's suburbanization agenda for the occupied territories has radically transformed its population and worldview. The book also underscores the increasingly belligerent and bloody situation in the West Bank today and the two Palestinian intifadas as key turning points in the radicalization of both populations. Finally, the occupation can no longer be written about as a merely provisional situation in the aftermath of a war, given the exponential growth, large financial investments, and semipermanency of the settlements today.

While the settler movement was once a footnote on the international agenda, today the Israeli-Palestinian conflict has a high priority in global politics and even figures prominently in U.S. and European leadership campaigns. However, this work moves beyond traditional diplomatic history to consider the quadrilateral relationship between Jewish-American settlers, the State of Israel, the native Israeli settler movement, and the Palestinians, with an awareness of the dichotomies between insiders and outsiders in this dynamic. It introduces new voices and perspectives into the canon, challenging classic notions of history from below. Unlike many other studies in this field, my findings draw upon not only new archival material but also periodical press, media, literature, film, music, Internet resources, and oral histories never before brought to light, to provide a fuller understanding of this phenomenon.

Last but not least, I hope this book builds a bridge between professors, foreign policy makers, and public stakeholders on Israel / Palestine. I deeply believe it is imperative—for historians, humanists, and all who who desire harmony in this region—that there be informed, objective, historical, and readable accounts available not only to our peers in the professoriate but to professionals and interested parties beyond academia. This book is not a work of advocacy, nor does it make practical recommendations, but I do strive to provide new historical and scholarly insights that will inspire both academic and public dialogue after five decades of settlement in the occupied territories.

Despite great interest in Jewish-American settlers, to date we have not been able to answer even the most fundamental questions about them: Who are they? How many live in the occupied territories? Where did they come from and settle? Which roles have they played within the Israeli settler movement over the past five decades and what has motivated this activity? Why are they disproportionately represented within the ranks of both American-Israeli migrants and settlers? Can we understand their participation in the settler project as a particular brand of Jewish-American activism? Does this constitute a new and important chapter in both the history of American Jewry (and American Studies) as well as Israel / Palestine?

This book provides some explanations for this phenomenon. Having evaluated several sources of data, I estimate that Jewish-American immigrants comprise approximately 15 percent (upward of 60,000 individuals) of the roughly 400,000 Israeli citizens in the occupied territories today.[45] These figures show that this group is strikingly overrepresented both within the settler movement itself and among the total population of Jewish-American immigrants in Israel.[46] A demographic profile further disputes popular presumptions about Jewish-American settlers—including that they were the mediocrities of their milieu in America, that they were uniformly Orthodox and strictly observant, and that they were universally committed to right-wing or neoconservative politics—as patently false. In contrast, I contend that most of these new arrivals were usually young, single, highly educated, upwardly mobile, and traditional but not necessarily Orthodox in their religious practice, voted for Democratic Party candidates, and were politically supportive of and active in the liberal and leftist politics of the 1960s and 1970s, including the civil rights movement and the anti–Vietnam War struggle prior to their immigration to Israel. Thus, the portrait that emerges is one of a group of youthful, idealistic, intelligent, and seasoned liberal American Jewish Zionist political activists who were eager to apply their values and experiences to the Israeli settler enterprise.[47]

Drawing on archival sources from the Israel State Archive and the Jewish Agency, periodical press and other media, and interviews never before brought to light, this book reconstructs the history and politics of the participation of these Jewish-American settlers and the discourses that surround their project.

As a work of transnational history, this narrative's point of departure in Chapter 1 is the decade of the 1960s in the United States, exploring how political change at home (the civil rights and anti-Vietnam movements) and abroad (the Six Day War) transformed American Jewry of its era against a backdrop of Holocaust reckoning, ethnic revival, and the changing role of Jewish activists within the New Left. Taken together, the "1967 moment" had a profound significance for this specific cohort of Jewish-Americans and would later propel their migration to Israel and the occupied territories. As tourists, students, and volunteers during and after the Six Day War, these individuals often made their incipient contacts with the nascent Israeli settler enterprise. Some American-Israelis also took part in the two major settlement projects of the immediate postwar period at Kibbutz Kfar Etzion and Hebron and planned a short-lived scheme for the large-scale immigration of Jewish-Americans to Shalom City, Israel. Though these initiatives met with varying degrees of success, a moment became a movement for these individuals and families in less than a decade. Moreover, their settlement activities introduced new models for collective immigration projects after the 1973 war. These early attempts also introduced uniquely American rights-based discourse combining religio-political imperatives with utopian suburban pioneering that came to characterize Jewish-American settlement in the occupied territories. Early tensions between liberalism and Zionism foreshadowed future dilemmas this constituency would confront over the Green Line.

The centerpiece of this project is three in-depth chapters on American-Israeli settlements in the occupied territories: Yamit, along the coast of the Sinai Peninsula (Chapter 2); Efrat, in the Gush Etzion region of the West Bank (Chapter 3); and Tekoa, on the Eastern West Bank (Chapter 4). These case studies tell the story of these well-known communities established by and for American-Israeli settlers and examine their shifting alliances and tensions with the Israeli government, the native Israeli settler movement, and the Palestinians over the past five decades. The successes and failures of Jewish-American settlers as both leaders and cadres constitute their historical legacy.

Chapter 2 chronicles the rise and fall of Garin Yamit, a cooperative organization of Jewish-American immigrants founded in Cincinnati, Ohio. Alongside a Russian contingent, these immigrants from the United States can be considered the founding fathers and mothers of Yamit, their settlement on the sea in the Sinai Peninsula. Although these American-Israelis comprised approximately half of the city's initial population and brought innovation, entrepreneurialism, and dogged determination to life in a remote locale, their fortunes were built on shifting sands. After nearly a decade building their castles by the seashore, the settlement of Yamit was evacuated and destroyed as part of the Israeli-Egyptian peace treaty in 1982. In the end, the Jewish-American immigrants at Yamit chose to leave the city peacefully, yet they pined for a paradise lost. Their project may have been effaced, but its historical saga endures. Today it is remembered as a beachhead for a uniquely American-Israeli narrative and discourse, which is reconstructed here for the first time.

While Jewish-American settlers at Yamit saw their homes bulldozed on national television, the immigrants from the United States who had recently arrived in the new West Bank settlement of Efrat in the early 1980s heralded that "for a Jew, it's home." Chapter 3 profiles this "city on a hilltop"— perhaps the most recognizable Jewish-American settlement in the occupied territories. An upscale suburban paradise stereotyped as "Central Park West Bank" and "occupied Scarsdale," Efrat proffers million-dollar mansions alongside messianic redemption for its yuppie population. The personal friendship and professional partnership between Efrat's founders, native settler activist Moshe Moshkowitz and New York–based Orthodox spiritual leader Rabbi Shlomo Riskin, created a hybrid model for Jewish-American settlement in the occupied territories as well as a blended historical rights-based discourse combining prophetic fulfillment with ideas of pioneering ("with a bit of luxury") on the West Bank frontier. At the center of this settlement project is the quixotic and controversial rabbi, who has led its community across two continents. A self-described "passionate moderate," the hardening of Riskin's views—and those of the larger community—since the first intifada have come to dominate the history and future of their settlement.

Unlike Efrat, which has enjoyed a privileged place within the "national consensus" of Israeli settlements, the Jewish-American founders of the West Bank settlement of Tekoa (Chapter 4) explicitly saw themselves as guarantors of a Jewish presence in the "heart of Zion" in the midst of the Camp David Accords. "Turn left at the end of the world," as one of its founders once described their settlement, mapped not only the settlement's remote location but the landscape of 1960s American activism in which their community took root. However, more than any other Jewish-American community in the occupied territories profiled in this book, their aspirations came into profound conflict with the Palestinians since the first intifada. The settlement also experienced direct confrontation with the native Israeli settler movement over the religious dialogue project of Tekoa's rabbi Menachem Froman, who died in 2013. Tekoa's fate hangs in the balance of any future final status agreement between Israelis and Palestinians, therefore its untold history brought to light here will continue to unfold.

Finally, Chapter 5 explores the evolving role of Jewish-American immigrants within the Israeli settler enterprise since the 1990s. While heinous and high-profile attacks committed by American-Israeli settler terrorists have dominated news headlines, these events have often overshadowed the sustained engagement of this group as press experts who have used their English-language skills and media savvy to revolutionize the public relations of the Israeli settler movement. This chapter focuses on the divergent roles of this constituency and the broader clash between liberal values and settler realities that have helped determine these disparate paths. Today these larger tensions between moderates and extremists continue to develop as the Israeli settler enterprise matures after five decades.

Borrowing from anthropologist Kevin Avruch's description of his own work, this book too is "half about 'Jewishness' in contemporary America, and half about 'Americanness' in contemporary Israel."[48] Traditionally, scholars of immigration and diasporas point to either "push" forces of hardship[49] or "pull" factors of personal choice[50] to account for the motivations of migrants—yet these paradigms obscure the particular dilemma of the subjects of this study. I argue that the case of *aliya* (lit. ascendance, Jewish immigration to Israel) should be classified (and normalized) within the broader canon of ethnic return migration, and I seek to position the Jewish-American settler constituency as a subcategory of this immigration pattern.[51] This definition also allows a more capacious historical understanding of the challenges this cohort faced in fully realizing their hyphenated identities in the United States in the 1960s and 1970s. As the New Left became increasingly radical and hostile to Israel, Jewish-Americans were confronted with painful choices about their identities in America. For some, this political quandary even raised the imperative of immigration. As historian Matthew Frye Jacobson explained, "the question was asked: 'Given *who* I am, where do I belong?' "[52]

For a select group, their answer was in the settlements beyond the Green Line. Whereas emancipation in Europe had raised the so-called Jewish problem of full integration in liberal democracies centuries earlier, these partisans saw their immigration from the United States to Israel on more personal terms, as "my problem as a Jew."[53] One migrant even confirmed that "by coming to Israel, I solved the Jewish Question."[54] Only in the settlements—which they considered the heartland of Jewish peoplehood—did their core Zionist and Jewish hermeneutics find a home.

Yet in moving to Israel/Palestine, these individuals did not leave their identities as activists behind, nor did they entirely abandon the liberal values and tactics that had imbued their lives in the United States. In fact, like previous generations of U.S. immigrants who came before them, they confronted a new conundrum: how to be a progressive American in a Middle Eastern milieu.[55] Facing profound challenges assimilating into Israel's military-bureaucratic complex and often cast as the *freier* (sucker) of Israeli popular culture, many of these immigrants entrenched—and idealized—their identities as Americans.[56] They celebrated the perceived advantages of U.S. society, appointing themselves as agents of "progress," "development," "rationality," and "change."[57] Many even saw their role as American-Israeli activists as a bulwark against the encroaching "Levantinization" of Israeli civilization and spoke of a "white man's burden" incumbent upon immigrants from the United States in their host country.[58] Some Jewish-American settlers came to identify as "true radicals" in Israel, committed to reform long after their American peers settled into lives of contented suburbanism back home. For some, this desire to "make a difference" inspired them to establish their own communities beyond the Green Line.

Further, for many, settlement in the occupied territories mapped both ideological and social motivations. While neither urban anomie nor kibbutz collectivism appealed to the needs of capitalist, community-minded Jewish-American immigrants to Israel, the Israeli settler movement often afforded new opportunities for inclusion. While some American-Israelis felt alienated by the Israeli establishment and unable to fully acculturate into both the political and social circles of *sabras,* the settlements seemed to offer a suitable alternative: an enclave culture (often of fellow English speakers or migrants), small communities, face-to-face interaction, and new locales that desperately welcomed both manpower and capital. In sum, communities beyond the Green Line may have appeared more accessible, pluralistic, and inviting to immigrants. Further, as brand-new settlements, Jewish-American immigrants often saw a chance to mold their community in the image of what they left back home.

Hence, this book explores the history of Jewish-American participation within the Israeli settler enterprise through the prism of a complex interplay of ideological, associational, and lifestyle factors that formed a total settlement experience—if each impetus was inherently political. I argue that their investment in the settler movement not only was impelled by biblical imperatives to live in the whole of the land of Israel, but also was inspired by a deeply and uniquely American discourse of pioneering and building new, utopian, suburbanized communities in the occupied territories that would serve as a kind of "city on a hill(top)" to both Israel and the United States.[59] This vision, which was justified by a liberal, progressive, rights-based political vocabulary, drew heavily on their American background and history to defend what they perceived as their human and civil rights to fulfill their Jewish destinies. This rhetoric is both a reflection and a refraction of how American-Israeli settlers continued to frame their psyches, activities, and discourses as Jewish-American Zionists, liberal activists, and Israeli immigrants. While I consider this an authentic internal understanding and not merely a propaganda tool, Jewish-American settlers have also pioneered a new public relations campaign to justify, normalize, and promote the Israeli settlement enterprise to the international community.

The central theme of this book is the clash between Jewish-American settlers' liberal personas and their illiberal project. By examining key historical turning points in their participation within the Israeli settler movement, one can trace the radicalization of this cohort as Israel's political spectrum itself has slowly shifted rightward over the past five decades. While this narrative neither ignores nor downplays the routine aggression and high-profile acts of terror committed by American-Israeli settlers against Palestinians (and the reciprocal impact of Palestinian terror on these communities), this discourse analysis challenges popular views that Jewish-American settlers are uniformly inspired by messianism or violence. This narrative allows for the complexity of competing worldviews in the minds of its subjects and engages with the cultural encounter between their American liberal identities and the realities on the ground in the occupied territories.[60] Most importantly, it explores the cognitive dissonances inherent in this confrontation and its consequences for this group's historical legacy. By analyzing how this group applies liberal ideas to illiberal programs and mobilizes the language of the left to realize the ambitions of the ultra-nationalist right, this book challenges conventional political paradigms to offer new perspectives on this ideological project.

From a wider angle, this book is about the liminality of liberalism, the plasticity of progressivism, and the resilience of rights discourses in both the

United States and Israel. From its origins, the Zionist movement sought to reconcile tensions between universalism and particularism in the making of the state of the Jews, a matter that took on new meaning and urgency with the 1967 war and its aftermath. The history of American-Israeli settlers lends new insight into the controversy over the settler enterprise's culpability for the crisis of liberal Zionism today. From the perspective of the regional panorama, it also prompts questions, especially in the wake of the Arab Spring, about the unintended consequences of importing liberalism into the Middle East since World War I. This study underscores that the participation of Jewish-American immigrants within the Israeli settler project is part of a larger narrative of Israel and its neighborhood.

Given its transnational scope, this study is also about the limits of liberalism in American Jewish life, especially as the political landscape of the United States has been redrawn since the decade of the 1960s. However, rather than reifying Jewish-Americans, this book recognizes them as a new kind of foreign policy actor in the age of the religious turn. Thus, this book situates American-Israeli settlers within the larger attitudes and activities of Americans abroad. I will comment more fully on some of these themes in the Conclusion.

While one book alone cannot settle this debate, we now begin our journey over the Green Line to the origins of the "city on a hilltop."

CHAPTER ONE

From Moment to Movement

Jewish-American Immigration to the Occupied Territories

" L ET ME PUT IT this way," Dr. Jay Shapiro resolved of his life decision to immigrate to Israel in the midst of the Six Day War, "the first thing I said to myself is what . . . if 30 years from now, my children said to me, where were you when the State of Israel was in danger? At the time I was on a path or trajectory that was very common for young America Jews. . . . I could say to them I had a great position and a good salary. And somehow that wouldn't cut it. . . . In the final analysis you have to answer to yourself: God forbid the State of Israel was destroyed, thirty years later, I look in the mirror and say, 'Why wasn't I involved somehow?' "[1]

For a generation of Jewish-American activists like Jay Shapiro, the 1967 war "moment" was the genesis of a transformative journey that has mobilized the participation of over 60,000 American-Israelis within the Israeli settler movement over the past five decades. As a demographic profile reveals, many of his peers were just like him: highly educated, upwardly mobile young professionals who strongly identified with both their Jewish heritage and the liberal social movements of the heady 1960s and 1970s. As Jay Shapiro articulated, this background was bolstered by their lived experience of the 1967 war and its aftermath in America, which foregrounded six frantic days of unprecedented activism against a backdrop of concurrent trends including a Holocaust reckoning, ethnic revival, and the changing role of Jews within the New Left in 1960s and 1970s. For many men and women like Jay Shapiro, a comfortable life of career success in America was no longer an option with the fate of the State of Israel and the occupied territories at stake.

While Jay Shapiro immigrated to Israel in 1969, later moving to the West Bank settlement of Karnei Shomron where he became a spokesperson for the Israeli settler lobby, the path from moment to movement was more commonly one of circular routes and historical detours. In many cases, it was initial contacts as tourists, volunteers, and students with Israel and the occupied territories after the 1967 war that inspired some to join the incipient Israeli settler movement. Although there was limited settlement activity before the 1973 war, a few intrepid American-Israelis joined the nascent Israeli settler enterprise in its major projects of the period at Kibbutz Kfar Etzion and Hebron in the West Bank. There were also those "who had a dream" of larger-scale settlement of Jewish-American immigrants beyond the Green Line, including the short-lived plan for "Shalom City, Israel."

For early American-Israeli settler activists like Jay Shapiro, the interwar period provided both a framework for future activities and models for later collective immigration projects. It also introduced a unique rights-based discourse combining biblical imperatives with modern-day pioneering and utopian promise that would come to define the American-Israeli city on a hilltop in the occupied territories. In less than a decade, a moment would truly become a movement for a cohort of Jewish-American immigrants at the center of this highly contested enterprise.

From Data to Destiny? A Statistical and Demographic Profile of Jewish-American Settlers

First, it must be noted just how exceptional Jay Shapiro and his colleagues are: less than 5 percent of Jewish-Americans have immigrated to the State of Israel since its founding.[2] American-Israeli migrants—and the even smaller group that have settled beyond the Green Line—are only a minuscule proportion of American Jewry, who themselves are a small minority in the United States.[3] Nonetheless, they have played an outsized role in the occupied territories over the past fifty years.

The two decades between the 1967 war and the first intifada witnessed the highest number of Jewish-Americans decamping from the United States to fulfill their Zionist dreams. Before the establishment of the State of

Israel in 1948, a mere trickle of 6,000 American Jewish immigrants moved to Palestine, constituting only 1.5 percent of new migrants in the *Yishuv* (the pre-state Jewish community under the British mandate).[4] To put these numbers in some perspective, nearly 6,000 immigrants transplanted themselves to Israel in 1969 alone.[5] Jay Shapiro joined more than 30,000 potential and actual immigrants from the United States who journeyed to Israel between 1967 and 1973.[6] Since the 1970s the rate of immigration decelerated dramatically, dropping below the annual average of the pre-state period. However, in recent years, the rate of Jewish-American immigration has started to accelerate again and a steady stream of these new arrivals have joined earlier generations in settling beyond the Green Line.[7]

Of the approximately 400,000 settlers who live beyond the Green Line today, a statistically significant percentage—which I estimate at 15 percent—are of Jewish-American origin and hold citizenship in the United States.[8] While it must be acknowledged that the available data sources are limited and possibly politically tainted—I call upon statisticians to conduct a comprehensive, objective, and accessible survey for scholars—this figure indicates that Jewish-American immigrants are a large and overrepresented cohort both within the general settler population and among American-Israeli citizens in Israel/Palestine.

Even though numbers alone convey their significant historical contribution to the Israeli settler movement, this cohort's demographic profile illuminates some of the forces that put them on a path from moment to movement. In his study of Jewish-American migrants to Israel after 1967, Gerald Berman surmised that "[the] question of why people migrate is not so easily distinguishable from the question of who migrates."[9] If the central question for these men and women was "Given who I am, where do I belong?," a closer examination of their backgrounds and lived experiences helps clarify why the answer for many of these Jewish-American activists could be found over the Green Line.[10] Gary Mazal described the group he joined to settle the Sinai as "We were all different, we came from different states. Most were married, about half had kids, and two of us were single guys. We ranged from secular to very observant. We had different levels of education and divergent interests, except when it came to Yamit. There we were all united." Yet this diversity belied the larger congruities among his cohort.[11] In fact, looking more closely, Mazal's generation over the Green Line had much in common.

Perhaps predictably, the vast majority of Jewish-American migrants to Israel came from major urban population centers with large concentrations of American Jews on the East Coast (66.2 percent), the Midwest (12.8 percent), and California and the West (11.3 percent).[12] Many of the Jewish-American settlers profiled in this book hailed from the New York City area, although some had moved to Israel from places as far-flung as Cincinnati, Ohio, San Antonio, Texas, and Miramar, Florida. Certainly the surroundings in which they were reared in the United States shaped the kind of communities they hoped to create in the settlements. Settlement founders like Shlomo Riskin and Bobby Brown, residents of Manhattan, were eager to escape urban life for "religious pioneering on the suburban frontier" in the occupied territories.[13] Others, like Malka Chaiken from Philadelphia, and David Wilder from Paterson, New Jersey, had grown up in American cities that had experienced ethnic friction, which was formative to their understanding of the conflict at Hebron. Others hoped to replicate relished attributes of their upbringing in the United States, as Robert Smallman from California and Carole Rosenblatt from Florida continued to enjoy the coastal lifestyle at Yamit.

It seems probable that the geographic dimension of immigration was a self-reinforcing trend. Individuals were more likely to move if they had migration infrastructure (such as Israel Aliya offices or branches of an immigration-promotion movement) in their cities, an American social network in Israel, and the promise of a lifestyle that comported with what they had in the United States. More than half of the subjects of scholar Chaim I. Waxman's small study of Jewish-American settlers in the 1980s cited "associational" considerations, not just ideological convictions, in their choice to migrate. This group who moved over the Green Line tended to "like [the] type of community" (35%) especially if it resembled their lifestyle back home, explained it was "convenient, had friends here, it was available" (18%), and established new settlements as they "wanted to be a pioneer and wanted [the] challenge of starting a new community" (5%). Sharon Katz expressed how she was drawn to the settlement of Efrat not only out of deeply-held religious principles but the dream of a suburban paradise where she could still eat a New York–style bagel on a Sunday morning.[14] For Shmuel Sackett, the proximity to friends, family, and an English-speaking community in the tony residential neighborhood of Neve Aliza of Karnei Shomron was part of what convinced him to settle beyond the Green Line.[15] In contrast, for native New Yorker Bobby Brown, both his adherence to notions of Greater Israel and the desire to escape the American suburban experience of having his neighbors tell him "how high his grass could grow" inspired him to found the counter-cultural township of Tekoa in a far corner of the Gush Etzion bloc.[16] Drawn to antiestablishment enclave cultures, suburban communities, and upstart settlements that desperately required both manpower and capital, many American-Israelis mobilized both the literal and metaphysical geography of their lives in the United States in moving beyond the Green Line.

There is currently some evidence that the cost of living for Jews in America's major urban centers has encouraged a new wave of economic migration to Israel and the West Bank.[17] Although some settlements do offer the possibility of putting a higher quality of life within middle-class financial reach, most Jewish-American settlers today are not prompted to immigrate solely for financial reasons.[18] Further, the price of real estate in many of the most popular settlements with Jewish-American immigrants is competitive with urban parts of the United States—for example, housing values in the West Bank settlement of Efrat often exceed $1 million for an average single-family home. Rather, Jewish-Americans are propelled to the occupied territories by a complex interplay of ideological, associational, and lifestyle factors, which they import to Israel/Palestine.

In fact, most of the 1967 war cohort of U.S. migrants to Israel (70 percent) were born in the United States and were second- or even third-generation Americans.[19] These idealists were young—nearly half were under age twenty-five and more than two-thirds were below age thirty-five at the time of immigration.[20] Many, including more than half of female immigrants to Israel, were single and transplanted themselves, at least in part, to seek a Jewish spouse.[21] Jewish-American settlers were more likely to come as married couples than were their migrant peers, but young bachelors like Gary Mazal and Yisrael Medad and divorcees like Robert Smallman and Carole Rosenblatt saw the settlements as sites of both ideological and social opportunity.

Since the 1970s the generational data on Jewish-American immigrants to Israel and the occupied territories has changed dramatically. Today's migrant is older, with a mean age of thirty-seven, and almost a quarter of individuals moving to Israel are now over the age of forty-five. Most immigrants (73 percent) are attached to a family unit.[22] Israelis have recorded the highest rates of child-bearing within the Organization for Economic Cooperation and Development (OECD)[23] and Jewish-American residents beyond the Green Line tend to have very large families that surpass these statistics. Several individuals I interviewed had six to ten children including many who were born in Israel and constitute successive generations of American-Israeli settlers.

What is particularly striking about this data is that even as second- and third-generation Americans, these settlers seemingly felt far less socially rooted in the United States than their contemporaries. However, other elements of this profile explain why they were restless to fulfill their Jewish destinies—even at an older age with more family obligations as the years went on—than many of their peers in the United States.

Although the stereotype of Jewish-American settlers as ne'er-do-well wanderers persists, their migration was not for want of economic opportunity in the United States. Goldscheider found that 84 percent of Jewish-American immigrants had some college education in the United States and at least 80 percent of those who entered the workforce in Israel were employed in the white-collar sector. These qualifications vastly exceeded those of their contemporaries in the United States and especially in Israel in this era.[24] While the educational and occupational credentials of American-Israelis have declined somewhat over time, a recent Nefesh B'Nefesh survey indicates that nearly 50 percent immigrate to Israel with a bachelor of arts (including those from Ivy League institutions) and an additional 25 percent have advanced degrees.[25] However, many struggle to find suitable work after immigration and more than half are classified as unemployed in Israel.[26]

Jewish-American immigrants who joined the Israeli settler enterprise were the academic and professional elite of their larger immigrant cohort. Waxman's 1984 sample revealed that nearly half graduated with a bachelor's degree, more than a quarter had earned a master's, and almost a tenth held a doctorate.[27] The group I interviewed were even more impressive: all but one was a college graduate, twelve held a master's or an advanced professional degree, and three had earned a doctorate. They held positions in uniformly white-collar professions: rabbi, aeronautics engineer, attorney, IT specialist, social worker, theater director, journalist, librarian, entrepreneur, cantor, and other esteemed positions. Most were gainfully employed at the time of interview and many had or were currently pursuing further training or degrees in their respective fields in Israel.

Even though the subjects of this study had educational and occupational opportunities in the United States that most of their peers on either continent did not, their immigration can largely be explained by subjective factors, especially their perceived inability to fulfill religious and Zionist aspirations in America.

Prior to their immigration, the 1967 generation of immigrants were high Jewish identifiers and vigorous participants in American Jewish communal life—but it should be noted that they were pluralistic in their Jewish practice, with only 37 percent of the subjects of Goldscheider's study identifying as strictly Orthodox. Those who moved to the occupied territories were more likely to be (although were not universally) affiliated with East Coast modern Orthodoxy and its institutions, such as Yeshiva University, although many were among the more religiously progressive of their peer group and later established halakhically radical institutions including Rabbi Riskin's educational network in Efrat and mixed secular-religious enclaves like Tekoa. What is more significant than their denominational identification, however, is that an overwhelming majority of Jewish-American immigrants of the post-1967 generation indicated that they were "religious" (attributed in part to the atmosphere of the parental home) and 75 percent characterized themselves as "strongly Jewish."[28] Most had received Jewish education (85 percent), attended a synagogue (83 percent), and observed Jewish dietary laws (53 percent).[29] More than 70 percent had joined a Jewish organization in the year prior to their immigration and stated that almost all their friends were fellow Jews.[30] This profile was highly atypical of Jewish-American households at the time, which mostly self-identified in denominational terms as Conservative (40.4 percent) or Reform (30 percent)[31] and were only marginally engaged in learning, ritual, and community.[32]

Over time the religious classification of Jewish-American immigrants to Israel—and correspondingly, those who move over the Green Line—has changed. These findings track closely with the fast-growing shift to observant immigrants: today some 70 percent identify as Orthodox (85 percent consider themselves active participants in prayer and ritual) and the remaining 15 percent label themselves as Conservative (40 percent actively observant), 3 percent as Reform, and the rest as unaffiliated.[33] Yet despite popular perceptions, very few were *Baalai Teshuva* (Returners to the Faith)[34] and many had received high levels of childhood Jewish education, with over 35 percent having studied at the secondary level.[35] Further, although some 60 percent of Waxman's sample embraced the millenarian vision of the premier native Israeli settler group Gush Emunim (Bloc of the Faithful), not all Jewish-American settlers considered an imminent redemption probable or saw messianism as a primary motivation for settlement.[36] In my own study, I found similar support for Gush Emunim, but most of the settlers I interviewed did not identify as messianic or see the prospect of an apocalyptic event occurring in their own lifetime.

In addition to their Jewish identification, immigrants to Israel had strong Zionist attachments from an early age. One study by Aaron Antonovsky and Avraham David Katz revealed that 60 percent of the post-1967 generation were members of a Zionist group and 39 percent were members of organizations that explicitly promoted immigration to Israel.[37] Waxman's study of Jewish-American settlers found that 70 percent had been active in Zionist youth movements, including those with religious Zionist agendas such as Bnai Akiva (36 percent).[38] Bobby Brown and Yisrael Medad cited their exposure to ideas of immigration and settlement in Greater Israel in BETAR, the Revisionist Zionist youth movement, and both later served as its national executive. Though later rejected by some of her peers, Malka Chaiken credited her participation in Young Judea for finding Judaism and Zionism as a teenager. Gary Mazal's enrollment in the World Union of Jewish Students program literally brought him to the sandy shore of Yamit for the first time.

In sum, their religio-ethnic heritage ranked highest in their hierarchy of identifications and performed dialectically as both the "push" and the "pull" toward immigration.[39] Life beyond the Green Line offered opportunities absent in the United States to fulfill Jewish and Zionist ambitions like "[I] wanted to be part of an important aspect of Jewish history" and "[I] want Territories to remain under Jewish control." In settlements like Yamit, Efrat, and Tekoa, their core Zionist and Jewish hermeneutics found a home.

Perhaps it is predictable that Jewish-American immigrants were committed Zionists who cherished their Jewish backgrounds. The most interesting and surprising aspect of this demographic profile is the political background of Jewish-American settlers in the United States prior to their immigration to Israel. Contrary to popular perceptions that these future immigrants were card-carrying Republicans or members of the nascent neoconservative movement, their party affiliation and ideological principles lay on the opposite end of the political spectrum. In fact, it was their primary identity as liberal or left-wing activists, especially being sympathetic to and engaged in the major movements of 1960s and 1970s social protest, that later led them to deepen their commitments to Jewish particularist campaigns at home and inspired their struggle for what they perceived as Jewish human and civil rights in the occupied territories abroad.

Jewish-American immigrants of the post-1967 generation followed the voting patterns of their peers who remained in the United States—over half (57 percent) were registered Democrats, 41 percent were independents mostly leaning toward the Democratic Party, with a mere 2 percent identified as registered Republicans.[40] Waxman's study of Jewish-American settlers in particular revealed an even greater propensity to lean left: 95 percent were affiliated with the Democratic Party and 40 percent had participated in demonstrations against the Vietnam War.[41] My own sample produced only one participant who identified as a Republican, Marc Zell, an international attorney who lives in the West Bank settlement of Alon Shvut and is the leader of the GOP in Israel. At least half of my group had active exposure to the civil rights movement and anti–Vietnam War struggle in their early years. Both their affiliations and attitudes suggested that these American-Israelis saw settlement activity as a reflection and expression of American Jewish liberalism. It is clear that this group was profoundly shaped by the politics of their time in the United States and transferred their activist tendencies to their settlement projects in the occupied territories.

Upon their arrival in Israel, these Jewish-American activists did not abandon the ideals of their home country and they continued to harbor positive characterizations of the political culture of the United States (80 percent). The majority believed that America offered "a great and good society," which they found "generally positive" and toward which they felt "a strong sense of gratitude." Many also indicated that Israel would benefit from the introduction of American-style behaviors and reforms.[42] Jewish-American settlers in particular remained disciples of democracy.

Some 50 percent "strongly supported" this framework, with another 29 percent affirming its value with various qualifications, including a limited democracy prioritizing Israel's "Jewish character" and/or Jewish law with fewer rights for Palestinians and Israeli Arabs. Nearly 70 percent of those in Waxman's study were categorically opposed to the racist platform of the Kach Party in Israel, which campaigned for Palestinian population transfer, although the remainder confessed some interest in (or implicit agreement with) its ideology but were not willing to endorse its tactics or join the movement.[43]

Given their overwhelmingly positive attitudes toward their country of origin and readiness to implement American-style reforms in Israel, why did this group leave the United States?

As Waxman argued, these settlers seemed ambivalent about social change in the United States in the 1960s, as the majority agreed with conservative statements such as "Blacks in America have gone too far in their demands" and "Everything considered, life in the U.S. was better ten years ago."[44] Some who had been active in left-wing politics shifted their focus to Jewish particularist activism in the late 1960s and early 1970s. On both religious and political grounds, they didn't envision their future living in America and were committed to a campaign for Jewish human and civil rights beyond the Green Line. I now turn to examine how the lived experience of the 1967 moment helped these individuals find their futures in the Israeli settler movement.

The 1967 Moment: A Retrospective

This year, 2017, marks the fiftieth anniversary of the 1967 war and the inauguration of Israel's administration of the occupied territories. It should be a period of reflection for both Israeli and Diaspora Jews—previous milestones have similarly prompted a reevaluation of the significance of the 1967 moment to American Jewry. As one Jewish studies scholar and peace activist wrote in commemoration, "Israel's Six Day War ... marked a sea change in the life of the U.S. Jewish community." Others regarded it a "rollercoaster of emotions" and even "a rabbit hole down which we could flee the social traumas of the 1960s."[45] Abraham Foxman, the longtime national director of the Anti-Defamation League (ADL), suggested a "transformative" turn toward Israel where "the Six Day War made us all Zionists." Further, "American Zionism was not the only winner," he argued, "so too was Jewish self-confidence."[46] These commentators all acknowledge that the war prompted a profound reorientation of American Jewry's appreciation of Israel and of themselves. Yet how do we put these reflections in their relevant context?

Before 1967, Zionism was a minority movement in American Jewish political life.[47] While some prominent Jewish-American religious leaders and distinguished professionals actively advocated for a Jewish state during World War II, most of the community were passive spectators to the campaign.[48] (The old joke was that the American Zionist was an individual who gave money to a second partisan who passed on the donation to a third supporter who actually settled in Israel.) While the founding of the State of Israel was celebrated by American Jewry and the influence of a so-called Jewish lobby may have contributed to U.S. recognition of the State of Israel in the United Nations, that support was not always universal.[49] As public intellectual Norman Podhoretz reminded fellow American Jews after the Six Day War, "once upon a time, there were anti-Zionist Jews in America, there were non-Zionist Jews in America, and there were Jews in America indifferent to the whole issue of Jewish statehood."[50]

Not only were some American Jews ambivalent about Israel, both establishment leaders and the rank and file were slow to recognize Jewish sovereignty as part of the communal agenda.[51] In 1950 the American Jewish Committee, the official organ of organized American Jewry, released a public memorandum known as the Blaustein-Ben-Gurion understanding which proclaimed that "the Jews in the United States, as a community and as individuals, have only one political attachment and that is the United States of America. They owe no political allegiance to Israel."[52] Despite some Jewish-American interest in current events and the Suez Campaign over the state's first two decades, there was little sustained engagement. In fact, in a 1966 hundred-page *Commentary Magazine* symposium titled "State of Jewish Belief," Israel was mentioned only twice by thirty-one leaders of the day[53] and most were keen to distance themselves from the "parochialism" and "chauvinism" of the Zionist movement.[54] On the eve of the 1967 war, scholar Morris Kertzer confessed that "American Jews, try as they may, find difficulty in feeling the peoplehood of Israel, the mystical bond that unites them with their co-religionists outside the United States . . . the boundaries of America are the limits of their creative Jewish concerns."[55]

The 1967 war made its debut in the United States as what intellectual Leonard Fein described as the "standing-room only hit show of our Jewish time," a cosmic drama played out over transistor radios, televisions, and synagogue pulpits within the American Jewish community.[56] Despite the fact that Israel's victory in battle was largely assured by a preemptive strike against the Egyptian air force and her superior military capabilities over the combined Arab armies, the six days in June occasioned an extreme emotional response among American Jews. As Fein conceded, "[in 1967] we lost our cool completely." Imitating the atonement prayer of the Yom Kippur liturgy, he chronicled, "We begged, we pleaded, we demanded, we insulted, we threatened, we promised, we were aggressive, petulant, temperamental."[57] So unsettled by his anxieties, one American Jew in the Midwest even reported "psychosomatic symptoms" to scholar Marshall Sklare![58]

"How does one explain this eruption of feeling?" mused scholar Melvin I. Urofsky, explaining that "emotions of such magnitude are not created in matter of days or weeks. The Six Day War did not *manufacture* this sentiment, but *awakened* it [from almost two decades of slumber since the founding of the State of Israel]."[59] In the longer term, American Zionist scholar and spiritual leader Rabbi Arthur Hertzberg attested that from mid-May 1967, "the mood of American Jewry underwent an abrupt, radical, and possibly permanent change."[60] Although such all-consuming engagement inevitably diminished in the years after the war, those six days profoundly reconfigured the emotional concerns of those who would migrate to Israel and the occupied territories.

This affective response also roused the American Jewish public into action in the arena of fundraising, the most important and visible communal activity of the 1967 war. As Edward Shapiro observed, "I am because I give" became the existential definition of American Jewishness and over the course of a week American Jews gave on a "sacrificial level."[61] One scholar commented that donating was even seen as a "religious act" and attendance at fundraising events may even have surpassed that at services on the High Holy Days.[62] Ultimately, $323 million were raised in 1967, $179 million in the Emergency Appeal alone ($150 million in cash), more than double the funds solicited in 1948.[63]

Astonishing gestures of grassroots generosity were reported from across Jewish America: $15 million ($1 million per minute) brought in from benefactors during a brief fundraising bid in New York City, $3 million collected in one day in Cleveland, $2.5 million funded by five Boston families alone, and $5,000 secured in St. Louis, the entire life savings of a Holocaust survivor.[64] Elderly Jews without bank accounts came to bring funds in cash, secretarial staff dropped off donations on their lunch hours, children proffered up their piggy banks, Boy Scout troops raided their treasuries, soldiers serving in Vietnam sent money from abroad, and one group in Chicago even organized a three-night performance of belly dancing to obtain funds for the Emergency Appeal.[65] Competition between local Jewish congregations to solicit donations was so intense that the rabbi of one Midwestern town sarcastically chided his impassioned Emergency Fund director, "We'll even get you a guest speaker who died in the war!"[66] Interestingly, many heavily assimilated Jews with no connection to local Jewish communities contributed for the first time—12,000 previously unaffiliated donors were recorded on the rolls in Chicago alone.[67]

Those who could not pledge funds took out loans or contemplated other ways to contribute. Cash-poor but asset-rich, the owner of a New York gas station chain turned over the deeds for his properties to the United Jewish Appeal (UJA).[68] Ruby's Dry Cleaners of Pittsburgh offered to donate the proceeds from the cleaning of every incoming item to the Emergency Appeal.[69] One father arrived at the New York Jewish Agency office with two young men in tow, telling officials, "I have no money to give but here are my sons. Please send them over immediately."[70] Corporations also joined the effort: Manhattan department store S. Klein shipped a fifty-foot trailer filled with linens for battleground hospitals in Israel and the American headquarters of El Al airlifted a pair of human eyes to save a soldier's vision.[71] In addition to opening their pocketbooks, thousands of people came out to participate and volunteers were put to work making phone calls for pledge drives, assembling media kits, and even persuading executives to use their private airplanes to shuttle UJA officials and the Israeli mission to meetings across the country. Hostilities ended so quickly that little of the funds raised went to serve the war effort itself, although it seems that few givers were aware or overly concerned how their funds were distributed. For those who would later settle in the occupied territories, wartime charity may have inculcated the notion of immense personal and financial sacrifice in the interest of Zionist commitments.

Another arena of mobilization around the 1967 war was in the political realm. A striking 99 percent of American Jews stood in solidarity with Israel.[72] Thousands of Jewish-Americans sent telegrams and letters to U.S. president Lyndon B. Johnson and members of Congress in support of Israel during the war.[73] At a national leadership emergency meeting organized by the Conference of Presidents of Major Jewish Organizations on June 7–8, breaking news of a ceasefire was met by the cheers of over 40,000 leaders, congressmen, trade unionists, and average citizens. Postwar, a July rally held at the Hollywood Bowl in Los Angeles was attended by politicians including California governor Ronald Reagan. Smaller assemblies were also very successful: one at the St. Louis Jewish Community Center caused a three-mile traffic jam. As Hertzberg observed, 1967 inspired individuals who were "at present largely inactive as Jews [but who] had within them some kind of Jewish involvement, dormant but powerful, which came out in a moment of crisis and moved them to radical action."[74] For American-Israelis over the Green Line—even those too young to participate themselves—these memories galvanized their future political activism.

The Six Day War also inaugurated a major theological awakening. In the immediate moment of crisis, synagogue attendance skyrocketed, welcoming even those who had never stepped foot in a house of worship before. Rabbi Arthur Hertzberg related how a room of New York Jewish leaders wept upon hearing the *Shehehiyanu* (Who Has Granted Us Life) benediction, recognizing that "the sense of belonging to the Jewish people, of which Israel is the center, is a religious sentiment, but it seems to persist even among Jews who regard themselves as secularists or atheists. There are no conventional Western theological terms with which to explain it."[75] Indeed, there was a newfound interest—or reliance—on divine intervention to save the Jewish people from disaster. As Milton Himmelfarb put it, "with the Israeli war, there was a reassertion of an old Jewish feeling about God and Providence."[76] It is perhaps with this sentiment in mind that Norman Podhoretz affirmed, "Thus did Israel now truly become the religion of American Jews."[77] For future American-Israeli settlers, the new role of Israel at the center of religious life may have revived the meaning of biblical imperatives to live in the whole of the land of Israel and motivated them to take part in what they perceived as a miracle in their times.

There is little doubt that the Six Day War was a "watershed" moment for American Jewry. Yet how did they describe this transformation of their worldview at the time?

In the immediate aftermath of the war, both Jewish leaders and average individuals articulated a fundamental shift in American Jewish life. "Has the Six Day War produced a change in my weltanschauung?" considered Holocaust survivor and public intellectual Elie Wiesel at a symposium on U.S.-Israel relations after the war, "I would go even further and say that the change was total, for it involved my very being as both a person and as a Jew."[78] Another American Jew ventured to Golda Meir on her visit to the United States, "I don't know how to explain it to you, Mrs. Meir, but I do know one thing. My life will never be the same again."[79] New Yorker Nancy Weber famously opined in the New York *Village Voice* a week after the war, "The Arab-Israeli collision was a moment of truth. . . . Two weeks ago, Israel was a they, now Israel is a we."[80] As Rabbi Arthur Hertzberg himself concluded only two months after the war: "The main outlines of the effect that the Middle East crisis had . . . are then, relatively clear. It has united those with deep Jewish commitments as they have never been united before, and it has evoked such commitments in many Jews who previously seemed untouched by them . . . very large numbers of American Jews now feel their Jewish identity more intensely than they have for at least a generation . . . [and] they are much less worried than ever before about what the rest of the world might be thinking."[81]

For future Jewish-American settlers, their thoughts were increasingly turning to Israel and the occupied territories.

Holocaust, Hippies, and Hawks: The Transformation of American Jewish Identity after 1967

Although it is important not to exaggerate the lasting impact of the Six Day War for the entirety of American Jewry, this momentous event had special significance to many future U.S. settlers.[82] This was especially true as this cosmic drama played out against a backdrop of other contemporaneous processes in American Jewish life at the time, including a reckoning with the horror of the Holocaust, ethnic revival in the United States, and the changing role of American Jews within the politics of the New Left.[83]

One major shift was the increasing saliency of Holocaust discourse during and after the 1967 war. Despite the fact that Israel's victory in the 1967 war was all but assured, the crisis brought the fear and fatalism of the Holocaust back to the fore.[84] Indeed, as Elie Wiesel heralded, "[In that moment] I became a child again, astonished and vulnerable, threatened by nightmare . . . I had the feeling of having witnessed it once before . . . whether we wanted it or not, a parallel was drawn with the Holocaust-era: all Jews had suddenly again become children of the Holocaust."[85] Further, Rabbi Arthur Hertzberg saw 1967 wartime mobilization in part as "moral reparation for the memory of the passive victims of mass murder."[86] The Jewish-American historian Lucy Dawidowicz even surmised that the outpouring of American Jewish philanthropy was guilt money that served as "expiation for their indifference 25 years earlier."[87] Israel's definitive conquest against Middle Eastern regimes was also interpreted by American Jews as a kind of redemptive myth.

For future American-Israeli settler Jay Shapiro from Philadelphia, the analogues he perceived between the Holocaust and the Six Day War helped propel his immigration to Israel and participation within the Israeli settler movement. Despite the fact that he had recently earned a PhD in aeronautics from the University of Pennsylvania and had just been promoted to a prestigious position at General Electric when the war broke out, he felt called to participate personally in the fight for Israel's future. "Let me put it this way," he explained, "The first thing I said to myself is . . . what if 30 years from my now, my children said to me, where were you when the State of Israel was in danger? At the time I was on a path or trajectory that was very common for young America Jews. . . . I could say to them I had a great position and a good salary. And somehow that wouldn't cut it. . . . In the final analysis you have to answer to yourself: God forbid the State of Israel was destroyed, thirty years later, I look in the mirror and say, 'Why wasn't I involved somehow?' "[88]

Shapiro and his family immigrated to Israel in 1969 and later moved to the West Bank settlement of Karnei Shomron, where he became an English-language spokesperson for the YESHA Council (the umbrella nongovernmental settler lobby), a radio host for right-wing Arutz 7 radio, an author of popular histories, and a translator. Shapiro joined many other future settlement founders who argued that the perceived apathy and inaction of their parents' generation spurred their activism beyond the Green Line.

Not only did the 1967 war mobilize American Jewry, it marked a historical break with the past. Scholar Peter Novick described this moment as a "radical discontinuity between the bad old days of Jewish vulnerability and the new era of Jewish invincibility."[89] This ascendant Jewish self-regard was representative of and reinforced by the era of "hyphen nation" in the late 1960s, when many "white ethnics" rediscovered their roots.[90] The 1967 war required American Jews not only to reimagine their past but also to determine their own destiny in the future. As Charles Silberman underscored, "the Six-Day war was a watershed between two eras—one in which American Jews had tried to persuade themselves, as well as Gentiles, that they were just like everybody else, only more so, and a period in which they acknowledged, even celebrated, their distinctiveness."[91] Now, as Lucy Dawidowicz explained, their pride was in the experience "of being victorious . . . in being Jewish in the aura of General Moshe Dayan, his ruggedness, vigor, determination . . . no longer seen as a victim or historic typification of a persecuted people."[92] Newfound Jewish pride even led one journalist to dub 1972 as "the Year of the Jew."[93] As Bobby Brown, a Jewish-American activist who later became the co-founder of the West Bank settlement of Tekoa, attested, 1967 taught him "the idea that Jews would protect themselves . . . [that] the solution was not always 'don't go down that block, there are a lot of tough goyim [gentiles]' . . . that was a very important lesson to learn."[94]

While ethnic revival was fostered in part by American Jewry's heavy participation within the civil rights movement. Their involvement in political struggle and the New Left in the 1960s and 1970s also inserted Jewish identity into a fraught age of social tensions. American-Jewish counterculture figure Jerry Rubin, who had spent time in Israel in his youth, remarked, "[I] personally felt terribly torn about being Jewish . . . I know it made me feel like a minority or outsider in Amerika [sic] from my birth and helped me become a revolutionary . . . yet Judaism no longer means very much to us because the Judeo-Christian tradition has died of hypocrisy."[95] Others—like some Jewish-American activists who later became involved in the Israeli settler movement—wondered why their Jewishness didn't matter to them more. As Eli Birnbaum, a co-founder of the West Bank settlement of Tekoa, articulated, "I started thinking, wait a minute, you are willing to demonstrate for the Eskimos, you are willing to demonstrate for civil rights, is there a reason why you won't demonstrate for something Jewish?"[96]

By the late 1960s, as Jewish-American activists reckoned with their re-awakened Jewish identities, they became keenly aware that their role within the movement was changing. Many Jewish-Americans saw their participation in the civil rights struggle as the natural product of their liberal self-image or the prophetic tradition within Judaism. Yet they were dismayed that other minorities increasingly considered them, in the words of Chicana writer Cherrie Moraga, simply as "a colored kind of white people."[97] Growing ambivalence for and about American Jews in the New Left could not be ignored in the aftermath of Six Day War.[98] Indeed, 1967 signaled the end of the "liberal hour" and the dawn of a new era of liberation movements that self-consciously rejected the politics and tactics of earlier generations of activists.[99] American Jews of the New Left, who had cheered Israel's victory in the 1967 war, suddenly realized that Zionism was no longer seen as the national liberation movement of the Jews, rather as a colonial and oppressive anathema. The thirty-two-point resolution published by the Student Nonviolent Coordinating Committee (SNCC) in the summer of 1967 condemning Israel, which included a now-famous provocative photo of a "Zionist army" lining up and shooting Palestinians against a wall captioned "This is the Gaza Strip, Palestine, not Dachau, Germany," conveyed this message and proved to be a pivotal moment for Jewish-Americans within the civil rights struggle. Not only did American Jews find themselves increasingly marginalized within the movement's new Black Power agenda and internationalist outlook alongside other white peers, many perceived a climate of overt hostility toward Jews and, especially, Jewish Zionists.[100] For both the African-American and the Jewish-American community, the 1967 war mostly ended a honeymoon period of civil rights cooperation and heralded a shift toward parochial campaigns.

Jewish-American activists diverged in their approach to this identity crisis. For some, what had once been an outward expression of Jewish pride now presented as a partisan retreat into parochialism and militancy. In some cases, the turn inward was manifested in the new Jewish neoconservative movement spearheaded by Norman Podhoretz, an intellectual outlet for pro-Israel, pro-capitalist, anti-Communist former liberals and socialists—however, it did not seem to interest most of the settlers I interviewed.[101] However, many future Jewish-American settlers did move further into radical spheres of Jewish activism. Some future settlement founders such as Bobby Brown, Shlomo Riskin, and Yisrael Medad gravitated to the Student Struggle for Soviet Jewry (SSSJ), a grassroots campaign for the release of Jews behind the Iron Curtain, which grafted an explicitly Jewish cause with the tactics and framework of civil rights era protest.[102] Other American-Israeli settlers like Shmuel Sackett, Mike Guzofsky, and Yehiel Leiter joined Meir Kahane's Jewish Defense League (JDL), which was mobilized as a self-styled militia to protect Jews against anti-Semitism in New York City in 1968 and saw itself as a kind of Jewish liberation movement, but soon acquired a reputation for violence, hooliganism, and vigilantism.[103]

Some Jewish-American activists tried to reconcile their liberal personas and Zionist principles after 1967 in a process where "many Jewish radicals now became, quite self-consciously, *radical Jews.*"[104] Some of these so-called New Jews (riffing on the idea of the New Left)[105] applied the spirit of the counterculture to domestic spheres of Jewish prayer, ritual, sexuality, and feminism.[106] Others rededicated themselves to Israel activism by appropriating Black Power, such as the Radical Zionist Alliance, which appealed for "the liberation of the Jewish people."[107] Most of these ad hoc groups soon collapsed, although some of these short-lived initiatives inspired Zionist activists who later settled in the occupied territories.[108]

Just like the civil rights crusade, the war in Vietnam gave rise to another social movement in which young Jews stood in solidarity with other activists in service of Jewish traditions. Yet the antiwar movement's impassioned calls for pacifism abroad were suddenly challenged by the 1967 war: Were American Jews content to forgo the use of force with the fate of Israel at stake?[109] Scholar Michael E. Staub considered Vietnam and the Six Day War to be twin generational battles in the American Jewish consciousness that fractured the community into factions of hawks and doves.[110]

These intellectual clashes had the most significant consequences for those Jewish-Americans who were actually fighting abroad and motivated a small group of servicemen to immigrate over the Green Line.[111] These veteran-settlers had often experienced pervasive anti-Semitism in the United States and found their Holocaust memories and hyphenated identities put to the test in combat in Vietnam. Yet it wasn't the wartime hostilities these men endured overseas but the country they came home to that proved to be the true battleground for their identities and impelled their immigration to the occupied territories. David Ramati, a Marine Corps officer from Chicago who later moved to Kiryat Arba, railed against the rejection of returning Vietnam veterans, as "We never left America. America left us. We never stopped loving America. America stopped loving us. We didn't reject America, America rejected us. We fought and we died and we bled for America and we were rejected by America."[112] He came to idealize Israel for what he perceived as its spirit of pioneering and simplicity, considering that it represented cherished values he felt had vanished in the United States. "Israel's like America in the fifties. . . . In terms of their concepts of right and wrong, family duty, duty to country, and things like that," he concluded, venturing of his immigration decision that "Israel's like living in America before Vietnam."[113] Upon his arrival in Israel however, he criticized the Israeli Defense Forces (IDF) for its "timidity" and advocated for a more aggressive stance against the Palestinians. He declared bluntly, "We're the Israeli fascists. We're the Israeli imperialists. We're the Israeli expansionists. We're looking for an opportunity to go there and kill more Arabs and take their land. That's our belief."[114] For others like Kuzriel Meir, a three-tour medical officer who later joined Ramati in Kiryat Arba, it seemed as if Vietnam nightmares had been psychologically superimposed upon Zionist sentiments: "I don't like living in a ghetto. I don't like living behind fences. And I don't like running and hiding from an enemy, when all it takes is a little bit of a show of bravery to back him down and chase him away. . . . Let's put it this way: there's a lot of us here in Kiryat Arba who hold that Meir Kahane was left-wing. Maybe it's because I've always been a rightist—I believe very strongly in Eretz Yisrael. That it belongs to us. If I want it, I'm gonna have to fight for it. If I want my children to grow up with pride and with dignity as Jews, and not with the ghetto mentality, then I have to make a fight."[115]

Few Jewish-American Vietnam veterans immigrated to Israel or the occupied territories, but many of those who did move over the Green Line joined ideologically radical settlements, including those that rejected the liberal worldview that most of their Jewish-American settler colleagues shared.

Many more future Jewish-American settlers were involved in the anti–Vietnam War struggle than those who fought overseas. When Sharon (Shifra) Blass participated in the March on Washington against the Vietnam War in 1968, she pronounced her activism a moral imperative: "How can you not go? How can you stand by? You're alive, you know what's happening, how can you not get involved? . . . If you love the place [where] you are, and you think there is a right way, and you are willing to do it, how are you going to make anything change if you are not willing to do something?"[116] These estimations were later echoed in her justifications for joining Gush Emunim as a founder and the first Jewish-American woman in the West Bank settlement of Ofra and for serving as an English-language spokeswoman for the YESHA Council.

As anthropologist Kevin Avruch argued, "many of the immigrants spoke of their experiences in the civil rights movement . . . as 'clearing the way' for an investment in Jewishness . . . American society was seen to be . . . an inappropriate (if not quite hostile) environment for that identity. The question was asked: 'Given *who* I am, where do I belong?' "[117] For many, the path from a moment to movement proceeded from initial contacts that later matured into lifetime commitments.

First Contact: Jewish-American Tourists, Volunteers, and Students beyond the Green Line

While the war was over in less than a week, the significance of the 1967 moment lingered in the minds of many American Jews. Some satisfied their interest as armchair activists by reading new literature or attending lectures in the United States, while other Jewish-Americans longed to see the land of Israel and its new territories for themselves.[118] Today tourism, volunteerism, study abroad, and even immigration to Israel have become institutionalized within American Jewish culture, but these trends emerged only after the Six Day War.

Even before 1967, Jewish-American tourism to Israel was a blossoming enterprise, bolstered by the popularity of cruise vacations along the Mediterranean coastline. After the war, the State of Israel was eager to welcome back tourists from the United States, if mostly for revenue and public relations benefits.[119] Tourism Minister Moshe Kol impressed this point upon 150 travel agents flown to Israel in the fall of 1967, imploring his guests to "encourage tours to Israel" and "dispel rumors of tension allegedly prevailing in the country."[120] These efforts were apparently effective: in a single year's time from 1967 to 1968, the number of Jewish-American tourists doubled from 70,000 to 140,000 individuals.[121] The Israeli government also gave special subsidies to the tourism industry, some of which were used to sponsor travel beyond the Green Line. For example, *Israel Digest* vaunted in 1968 that "new tourist attractions" at the Dead Sea and Jericho in the West Bank were "now being brought up to an international standard" worthy of foreign visitors.[122] Home stays in villages and kibbutzim, including at Kibbutz Kfar Etzion in the West Bank, also became a popular new attraction promising an educational "English-speaking . . . home away from home."[123] In the fall of 1968, a 450-member UJA fact-finding delegation from the United States was escorted to the newly captured Golan Heights and East Jerusalem and met with Defense Minister Moshe Dayan, who stressed the necessity to "hold the line, the front line—the Suez canal line, the Jordan line, and the Golan line," and to substitute the cease-fire agreement for "permanent borders."[124] Throughout that year more than 2,000 "key leaders" on UJA missions visited Israel, where they not only met Israeli dignitaries, got to "hobnob with the Israeli Prime Minister over cocktails," and were briefed by intelligence officials, but also had the opportunity to tour across Israel and the occupied territories, including "an inspection of the Golan Heights or some other border area" and a "trip to the hills of Judaea, from which hostile guns could easily shell Jerusalem."[125] New programs were promoted to college students and adults and major Jewish organizations and religious denominations planned their own conferences.[126] Once back home, many American Jewish leaders redoubled their support for the occupied areas—one rabbi from Paterson, New Jersey, even announced that his community had "adopted" the village of El-Al in the Golan Heights in 1969.[127]

Organized tourism to the occupied territories also accelerated in the early 1970s. "Who has not heard of Gush Etzion, its valiant fighters and their destiny? Who has not visited Etzion?" enquired the *Jerusalem Voice* newsletter of the Association of Americans and Canadians in Israel (AACI) in September 1973, advertising an outing for senior citizens ("friends and houseguests" too) appointed in style with "experienced" English-speaking tour guides, round-trip coach transport, and refreshments to the Kibbutz Kfar Etzion museum, synagogue, and field school, as well as the adjoining new settlements of Alon Shvut and Rosh Tsurim in the Gush Etzion region of the West Bank.[128] AACI also announced a scheduled trip to the newly occupied Sinai in late October, which was presumably canceled due to the 1973 war.[129]

Intrepid future Jewish-American settlers like Rabbi Jonathan and Shifra Blass also intently explored areas beyond the Green Line as individuals.

The couple dedicated much of the summer of 1972 to these excursions after Shifra naively suggested a series of day trips to her husband. With scant knowledge of the occupied territories but inspired by religious sentiment, she suggested, "I had my little Sunday school map—that was Israel, as far as what interested me at the time."[130] They managed to navigate across unfamiliar terrain, but the couple was greatly discouraged by the conditions they found at supposed biblical sites. "We went to see Kever Yosef [the Tomb of Joseph, in Nablus]," their first stop on the tour, and found "it was a garbage dump . . . [with] potato chip bags and rusted Coke cans. This is Kever Yosef? . . . It's an *atar*—a holy site—why is it like this?" They pressed onward to Shilo, the supposed plot of the biblical tabernacle, but "there was nothing there . . . we got off somewhere the driver said according to our map [that] would have been right . . . [but] it was nothing. I said, how could this be Shilo?" Next was Beit El, the locale mentioned in the Book of Genesis as the site of Jacob's dream, which they found similarly desolate, with only a few abandoned Jordanian army buildings. "I couldn't believe it," she blustered, but resolved, "well, if these people don't know how to appreciate [it] we're going to live it." Within two years, the Blass family became the first Jewish-Americans to join a Gush Emunim settlement as founders of Ofra in the West Bank.

Another category of Jewish-American visitors who came to Israel and the occupied territories were the 1,355 individuals from the United States (of over 8,000 Westerners) who spent time as volunteers during and after the 1967 crisis.[131] Though most were intent to serve at the front lines, few, if any, saw combat—instead they were sent to replace native male residents either still on active duty or who had been killed or injured during the war in the fields, hospital floors, and factories of Israel.[132] As one *Haaretz* reporter wryly observed, "they came on a rescue mission and were sent to pick plums."[133] Prime Minister Levi Eshkol seized not only on the practical utility but the public relations dividends in Jewish-American service, reporting to his generals, "I have read beautiful letters from America, written by young men who have visited here . . . now they have calluses on their hands and stories to tell in America."[134] The only volunteers who got to the front were those Jewish-American veterans dispatched by the IDF to the newly occupied Sinai region to aid in demobilization efforts. Midwesterner Michael Zimmerman, a former U.S. army officer, was assigned to command an international brigade charged with recovering military equipment around the abandoned United Nations army base at El-Arish. When he received his job description reading "we would wear plain fatigues with no insignia. We should avoid journalists. The pay was zero. Rations would be mediocre, and we would be billeted, well, it was not clear how, but I should expect the facilities to be raw," his "heart rose." In addition to exploring the Sinai and Eilat in the course of his volunteer service, he marveled at how the occupied territories had been transformed from the "end of the world" to new tourist and living destinations on "hastily printed maps."[135] Although the opportunities for volunteerism in the occupied territories were limited, Sarah Feifel was moved by her sister's mission to Israel after the 1967 war to later settle at Yamit in the Sinai.

A third contingent of young Jewish-Americans who embarked to Israel and the occupied territories in the late 1960s were foreign-exchange students.[136] Over 5,000 individuals attended Israeli universities and other institutions of learning such as yeshivot, seminaries, and professional training programs across the country in the late 1960s, and American rabbinical schools also instituted a year-abroad in Israel as a degree requirement during this time.[137] By the 1980s, upward of 125,000 high school and college students had enrolled in higher education courses in Israel since the Six Day War.[138]

Sociologist Simon Herman conducted several important studies on Jewish-American foreign-exchange students to Israel, including a group who matriculated at the Hebrew University of Jerusalem during and after the Six Day War.[139] Some powerful vignettes exemplifying the Zionist commitment of the 1967 cohort emerged: On the campus of the Hebrew University, the American students' society held a meeting to convince (or even coerce) colleagues to stay in Israel during the war. At the Jewish Agency's Institute for Youth Leaders from Abroad, only two students from a class of 200 left for America—notably, one woman whose parents physically dragged her onto the tarmac at Sde Dov airport. All sixty students who had just completed the academic year at the Greenberg Institute canceled their flights and petitioned for wartime volunteer assignments.[140] Herman estimated that many foreign-exchange students experienced a deep sense of solidarity with Israeli society and the formative summer of 1967 had a significant effect on their settlement plans in Israel.

For future American-Israeli settler Yisrael Medad, his junior year overseas from Yeshiva University at the Jewish Agency's Institute for Youth

Leaders from Abroad in 1966–1967 proved to be a decisive factor in his later immigration to the occupied territories. After classes ended in Jerusalem that spring, Medad opted to stay in Israel during the war and volunteered at Moshav Amatzia as a self-trained cowboy and onion planter. The prospect of settlement in the newly captured territories became part of his thinking "immediately" after Israel's victory, especially as Medad had already been exposed to the vision of "both banks of the Jordan" through his national leadership role in the Revisionist youth movement BETAR in New York City. He soon calculated that "there was no way back," visiting the Western Wall and Hebron only weeks after the conclusion of hostilities.[141] Reflecting upon his year as a student, Medad reckoned, "That was quite a framing experience and I cannot emphasize that enough . . . in essence, I had become Israeli, and made up my mind to return quickly and contribute to assuring [that] the gains of that war would be assured [to] the Jewish people."[142] Medad officially immigrated to Israel in 1970, where he later became a founder of the West Bank settlement of Shilo, an aide to right-wing political activist and Knesset representative Geula Cohen, and a journalist and English-language spokesperson for the Israeli settler movement.

Tourism, volunteerism, and student foreign exchange were important stepping stones toward Jewish-American settlement in the occupied territories. Soon some American-Israelis began to contemplate plans to claim the territory for themselves.

Forward Movement: Jewish-American Settlement in the Occupied Territories, 1967–1975

Although there was limited settlement activity in the occupied territories before the Yom Kippur War, Jewish-American immigrants were active participants in the settler enterprise from its inception. The life stories of the first two Jewish-American settlers who joined the nascent movement during this period—Sandy Sussman at Kibbutz Kfar Etzion and Miriam Levinger at Hebron—allow a unique insight into settlement in the interwar era.

Kibbutz Kfar Etzion, one of four Jewish collective agriculture settlements founded in the West Bank during the British mandate that were destroyed in the days before the 1948 war, was reestablished with the approval of the Eshkol administration in September 1967.[143] These tidings were greeted with "enthusiastic applause" at a convention of Western volunteers, where several vowed to join the settlement on the spot.[144] Jewish Agency chair Arye Pincus later affirmed to journalists that one-third of Kfar Etzion's inhabitants would be new arrivals from the United States affiliated with the Bnai Akiva (Sons of Akiva) youth movement.[145]

It seems that only one Jewish-American woman was true to her word: Sandy Sussman, age twenty-one, an active member in the Los Angeles chapter of Bnai Akiva. She was already serving as a volunteer in Israel in 1967 when she "heard the call" to settle in the occupied territories.[146] Sandy then approached her immigration representative, Land of Israel Movement activist and journalist Israel Harel, about her aspiration to start a new life beyond the Green Line, who apprised her, "Kfar Etzion is a new kibbutz but they are making history."[147] In fact, she already knew a bit about the settlement from her Bnai Akiva training, having even struck up a pen-pal relationship with pre-1948 residents in the youth movement. With her mind made up, she showed up with only a suitcase in hand a mere six weeks after the kibbutz was reestablished. Kfar Etzion veteran and future Gush Emunim founder Hanan Porat, who met Sussman on the road that October morning disembarking from a taxi, skeptically admonished her "It's not Bnai Akiva summer camp."[148] But Sussman soon settled in, making friends while washing dishes in the kibbutz dining hall, sharing Zionist dreams with other idealistic mates including her future husband Avinoam Haimovitch (Amichai), the son of an original member of the pre-1948 kibbutz. Only a few months later the couple married in a ceremony broadcast over the radio to the entire country. Sandy wore a wedding dress belonging to one of the settlement's founding members and attendants performed a song they composed themselves, singing, "Life again is thriving in Etzion . . . we'll take revenge upon our enemies/by building and planting and rejoicing."[149] Sandy shared the sentiment her husband whispered in her ear on their wedding day: "You are now witnessing a miracle in our generation."[150]

In November 1969 the AACI approached Sandy Amichai for an interview for their monthly bulletin. When asked by the journalist about her experience living in the occupied territories, she averred, smiling, "It's a Jewish area occupied by Jews." The reporter was less sanguine, stressing "this is occupied territory" and commented that Amichai's characterization of her new life "seems a bit chauvinistic" for his tastes.[151]

Amichai's honeymoon period at Kibbutz Kfar Ezion was tragically in-
terrupted when her husband was killed in the 1973 war, leaving Sandy a
widow with three young children. Yet she remained at Kibbutz Kfar Etzion
even after her children grew up "because God gave it to us." Over the years,
her viewpoint on the Israeli-Palestinian conflict has hardened from the
early days when she made history as the first Jewish-American in the occupied territories. She now recommends that "the Arabs [would] be better
off under our rule."[152] Reflecting on her legacy in a 2010 interview, Amichai left little room for doubt about her Zionist resolve: "My message: this
is our country, there is no other place for our people, and we have to do
everything we can to defend it, to support it, and to be part of it."[153] Sandy
Amichai has lived at Kibbutz Kfar Etzion for fifty years where she works
as a docent in its museum and has edited a history of the region.[154] She is
most proud that all of her children and grandchildren followed in her footsteps by making their lives in the Etzion Bloc.

The same AACI correspondent who approached Sandy Amichai also
paid a visit to some Jewish-Americans in Hebron in the fall of 1969, a little
over a year after a group led by Rabbi Moshe Levinger and his Bronx-born
wife Miriam began squatting in the historic locale.[155] Born in 1939, Levinger grew up in the home of Hassidic Zionists in the South Bronx where
she encountered anti-Semitism as a child and was deeply influenced by the
events of the Holocaust. "Eighty-percent of my family went up the chimney
[at Auschwitz], and I grew up with that. That is what makes me tick," she
testified, describing settling at Hebron as "I am fulfilling a mission for all
those who died."[156] Despite receiving both religious and secular education,
Levinger professed, "I had my priorities. I took my Jewish background seriously." She joined the Bnai Akiva youth movement as a teenager and
immigrated to Israel shortly after graduating from Hunter College High
School in 1956.[157] Upon completing the nursing school program at Shaarei
Zedek Hospital, she wed native Jerusalemite Moshe Levinger in 1959. She
later disclosed her marital philosophy, which would come to define fifty-
five years of joint activism, as "My duty is to make it easier for my husband
and to fulfill the role given to me by the Torah."[158]

In 1967 the couple and their children had left Jerusalem for Moshav
Nehalim in the Galilee, where Moshe Levinger held a pulpit. When her
husband was called up for reserve duty in the paratrooper unit that captured the Old City of Jerusalem, Miriam Levinger was forced to weather

the 1967 war alone with her family. She described herding the children into ditches during aerial bombardments of the north, chronicling her wartime experience as "emuna bli brera [faith without a choice]." Yet when the tide of the war changed, "everyone was delirious, it was as if the *moshiah* [messiah] had come."[159] To her, "the Six-Day war was of the Arabs' doing, so for me it's a sign from God. All this land where my forefathers trod suddenly came into our possession again. My husband said, 'God did His; so we have to do ours!'"[160]

In a curious act to catalyze momentum for the Hebron project in the summer of 1967, Rabbi Levinger cooperated with the secular leadership of the newly formed Land of Israel Movement to organize trips to the area and make contacts within the tentatively encouraging Eshkol administration.[161] Though Miriam Levinger claimed to be "busy at home with four children"[162] while her husband contemplated the resettlement of Hebron, other sources put her at the center of the process. As Moshe Levinger impatiently awaited a government decision in the spring of 1968, she instructed him, "The government won't send you there. Go settle, and things will work out."[163] In April he announced his intention to move the family to Hebron, giving his wife twenty-four hours to accede to his request. Citing her American upbringing, she complied enthusiastically, maintaining, "I remember when I was in Bnai Akiva when I read all the Zionist history and the stories about the pioneers, etc. . . . when I came in the '50s, I had this feeling that I missed out."[164] The theme of modern-day pioneering would later emerge as a trademark of Jewish-American settlement in the occupied territories.

That Passover, Levinger took matters into his own hands by hosting a *seder* (ceremonial meal) in Hebron. Posing as a Swiss tourist to a Muslim innkeeper, he rented out the Park Hotel in the city center for ten days and placed an ad in Israeli newspapers inviting guests to "resettle the ancient city of Hebron." Some thirty families, including at least one other American-Israeli couple, came to celebrate the holiday. Then, they decided to lodge in the city center for the long term. After the holy day, Moshe Levinger dispatched a cheeky telegram on behalf of his group to cabinet minister Yigal Allon, reading, "Blessings for Festival of our Freedom to You from Hebron City of Patriarchs from First of Those Returning to Settle in It."[165]

Miriam Levinger vigorously backed her husband in the Hebron venture, famously bringing not only their four children but a refrigerator and washing machine in tow. To her, spending Passover at the Park Hotel symbolized "a historical breakthrough, and we felt deeply moved and excited."[166] When the government moved the group from the hotel to cramped and unsanitary conditions at nearby military headquarters, she took charge, shopping and cooking for up to 120 people per day, running an on-site kindergarten, and serving as a medic. Miriam was also a role model for other Jewish-American women contemplating their own settlement in the occupied territories. On her first trip over the Green Line during her year as a foreign-exchange student at the Hebrew University in 1970–1971, Shifra Blass spent a Sabbath with the settlers in Hebron, later reminiscing, "I was completely blown away by the people there, by what they were willing to do, by the way they were willing to live . . . [and] it left a deep impression . . . that they were changing Israeli history."[167] Levinger also supported her husband in his struggle to maintain the morale of the settler community in the face of stiff resistance from the Muslim population. "People tell us it isn't safe in Hebron," she remarked to a visiting *New York Times* reporter in 1971, "but I'd rather be killed by an Arab in Hebron than by some nut in New York City."[168] As tensions escalated, she coped by evoking the popular Disney film *Peter Pan* of her American childhood, explaining, "It was like living in Never, Never Land, you didn't know what's going to be tomorrow."[169] By 1971, with 149 settlers (including several other American-Israeli families) crammed into military headquarters in Hebron, Levinger longed for permanency and "a normal life."[170] That fall, in what she described as a democratic decision by the group's majority, the government relocated the Levingers and their disciples to the new adjoining development of "upper Hebron" or Kiryat Arba.[171]

After seven years of religious pioneering on the West Bank frontier—though in those days Kiryat Arba was more of a rustic outpost than the sprawling township of today—the Levingers vowed to return to downtown Hebron. This time an American-Israeli woman would lead the way.[172] At 3 a.m. one early morning in March 1979, Miriam Levinger smuggled a group of twenty women (some pregnant) and thirty children concealed on the floor of a flatbed truck past an IDF checkpoint into the Hebron city center, ushering the group up a ladder and through a broken window into the abandoned medical clinic called Beit Hadassah in the Jewish quarter. Levinger later described occupying the building as "wip[ing] out the shame of 1929."[173] After a cold night without electricity, heat, or sanitation, the children awoke at daybreak and began singing, quickly attracting the attention of the stunned and angry IDF command. Authorities who questioned the youth were informed "they had been led there by Abraham, Isaac, and Jacob,"[174] although perhaps more accurately they had been chaperoned by modern-day matriarchs Miriam (Levinger) and Sarah (Nachshon).

Military and political authorities made no immediate move to evict the group, aiming to sap their willpower by preventing reentry to the building, barring visits from family members, and providing only the most basic food and sanitary items. Levinger's medical training and leadership qualities proved critical to the group's perseverance over the next six months. Ultimately the Begin administration relented, normalizing relations and allowing Jewish residents to occupy other sections of downtown Hebron over the strong resistance of the local Palestinian population. Miriam Levinger was unconcerned by her neighbors' hostility, contending, "We decided to re-establish the Jewish community in Hebron [and] we don't care that it's the center of town. . . . We see ourselves in a link in the chain of return. . . . This site is biblical Hebron [and] for us has spiritual value. The crux is 'are we sovereign' . . . I believe we are . . . [and in the Middle East] there's no such thing as compromise."[175]

After 1978 the Levingers were often at the center of the cycle of violence. Miriam stood by her husband as he supported the Jewish Underground and was convicted and sentenced to jail time for committing deadly terrorist acts against local Palestinians.[176] In the 1990s she herself spent three months in prison for assaulting a police officer.[177] Miriam's training as a medic was often put to the test as a first responder to terrorist attacks against Hebron's settlers during the first intifada. Later, they joined the community at Hebron in resisting the Oslo peace process and largely condoned fellow Jewish-American immigrant Dr. Baruch Goldstein's massacre at the Tomb of the Patriarchs in 1994. Together they protested the implementation of the Hebron Protocol in 1997, survived the second intifada, and continued to nurture the growth of the settler community in the downtown area. Reflecting on her legacy in the mid-1990s, Miriam Levinger considered her life's work as part of a new historical chapter, claiming, "It is a victory of the Jewish people . . . the Messiah hasn't arrived yet, but . . . this is the beginning of a new era."[178] In recent years, after almost five decades as leaders of the settler movement, the elderly couple receded from public view. Rabbi Moshe Levinger died in May 2015.

Although only a few American-Israelis settled beyond the Green Line before the 1973 war, the Israeli government began collaborating with one American-Israeli Zionist on the first plan for large-scale Jewish-American immigration in the occupied territories a mere six months after 1967.

Far away from the West Bank on the West Coast of the United States, a creative consul-general in Los Angeles named Moshe Yegar circulated an internal memo to the prime minister's office in November 1967 with the subject heading: "American Project for Aliya."[179] The diplomat wrote of a new plan to bring several thousand Jewish-American immigrants to Israel, an urgent proposal he considered "greatly strengthened as a consequence of this war." Yet his diplomatic consultations in California impressed upon him that "our problem isn't the need to preach to them about Aliya." Rather, "those who will immigrate to the land will do so on the condition that they will have the feeling that it presents them a challenge, and that they are required and necessary to the State of Israel." He advised that future immigration initiatives must contain "an idealistic element"—likening it to the American Peace Corps[180]—and that potential recruits must feel they could fulfill "a personal and Jewish challenge" where "this is your project."

In Yegar's eyes, his proposition to establish an enclave for Jewish-American immigrants in the Hebron area could actualize all these objectives. "There's nothing bad in that a project like this will be 'American' in its character," Yegar concluded, while cautioning against the creation of a "closed ghetto." Most importantly, the consul urged that "what must be made to stand out is the necessity that *everything* will be done by the settlers from the United States."[181] In conclusion Yegar pronounced, "There is no doubt in my mind that there was no other way to bring Aliya from the United States" and asked that his proposal be forwarded to the prime minister.[182]

Fortuitously (at least for Yegar), his file was quickly followed by a petition from Rabbi Norman Samson, a self-described Zionist, graduate of Yeshiva University, Baltimore-area suburban housing developer, and short-term resident of Israel sent to the prime minister's office in December.[183] Samson's cover letter introduced the eight-part "A Prospectus of an American City in Israel," which he believed conceptualized "the correct formula" for achieving "mass Aliya from America."[184] This appears to be the first known program for the mass migration of American-Israelis to the occupied territories and is also the earliest articulation of the ambitions of Jewish-American settlers to pursue religio-political imperatives alongside a utopian, suburban pioneering project over the Green Line.

Samson produced his proposal in light of serious soul-searching in the postwar moment, suggesting that "the divine deliverance of Israel of the past summer [sparked] renewed dedication on the part of many of us . . . and the time has come for these feelings of devotion on the part of American Jews to be translated into more specific acts of creation in Israel itself." The author averred, "[I myself had] thought hard about the need of the moment, American Aliya . . . and probed my own conscious for the reasons that have kept me and others like me from undertaking [it]." Samson then called for the creation of a new urban community of 100,000 immigrants primarily from the United States and Canada. He stressed the importance of location, observing that potential settlers were not only put off by the rural agricultural communities of a kibbutz or moshav, but also dissuaded by urban destinations because "as they are constituted [they] are not geared to receive, let us say, a new couple from Detroit, U.S.A." and these cities strike immigrants as "a completely strange environment." In contrast, Samson endorsed a new strategy to build settlements in the "hitherto barren and unpopulated area of Israel or the occupied territories" in accordance with "the overall Israel Master Plan for the Development of Greater Israel," despite the fact that no such program existed in Israel at the time and the Eshkol administration made settlement decisions on an ad hoc basis. Samson suggested three locations: the West Bank city of Hebron, the Gaza Strip, and the town of Megiddo in the Galilee. Of the two sites in the occupied territories, Samson saw the appeal both of their historical significance and their suburban potential and did not make any substantive distinction between areas within or beyond the Green Line. To Samson's mind, parcels beyond the Green Line were of particular interest to immigrants as they offered the potential to "involve prospective and actual American olim [immigrants] in the physical creation of a new environment" who would "be invigorated by the challenge and high excitement of participation." This trope of self-realization, coupled with the erasure of legal and metaphysical boundaries between territorial Israel and the occupied territories, would later resonate among the major themes of American-Israeli settlement projects. Samson himself did not betray any recognition of the political sensitivities of settlement in the occupied territories; in fact, he recommended naming the new township "Shalom City, Israel," as a message of peace from settlers he envisioned as progressive pioneers.

Certainly its U.S.-born architects were encouraged to imbue their new settlement with a uniquely American tenor. Shalom City should be a community where the American Jew's "particular genius, as well as financial contributions will be realized." He envisioned a kind of city on a hilltop that would be a living exhibit or "showplace of American know how, ideas, and institutions on the local level . . . [which] is anticipated . . . [to] be copied, refined, and adapted on a national level in the unfolding of Greater Israel." Their colony would be a "new city that is creating a bit of America on the Israel landscape."

In fact, evoking the establishment of the original American colonies, Samson hoped to fund his project through a kind of joint-stock corporation whose major stakeholders would be sworn to a "written Aliyah pledge." The city's economy would be based in light industry for export to foreign markets and would specialize in servicing the defense and space industries with American expertise. Interestingly, Samson also suggested that American Christian talent should also be tapped as an "incentive on [their] part . . . to contribute to the transplanting of a bit of the American Dream and Promise to the Holy Land." Shalom City would provide an unparalleled professional experience and it was predicted that "such a city indeed should attract skilled idealistic American Jewish workmen, professionals, and business men by the thousands."

Most importantly, Shalom City should prove a "welcome mat" to Jewish-American immigrants in their personal lives. He sketched an urban utopia without traffic or noise, where honking car horns and motorcycles would be outlawed, "dirty car exhausts are strictly penalized," and "a heavy fine is imposed . . . [for] the creation of disturbance on the Sabbath." Adults would stroll and children could cycle freely in the streets of this carefully designed suburban space. The city's main street would mimic the fixtures of suburban life in United States, featuring businesses such as a pharmacy, deli, bookstore, gift-shop, public library, bakery, hair-dresser, and dry-cleaners. At the open air neighborhood café, patrons could order "felafel as well as hot dogs and hamburgers, which you could wash down with either Mitz [juice], Gazoz [seltzer], Pepsi or Coke." He even fantasized that Israelis would flock to town to "try out the new Drive In Bank" which would use "the latest automatic equipment providing efficient and courteous service to customers arranged in orderly waiting lines." (Certainly, queuing was an original idea in Israel!)

In their free time, residents might frequent leisure facilities imported from suburban America at "sand-lot baseball diamonds, tennis and basketball courts, football fields, bowling alleys, and even a golf course," or participate in familiar pastimes like "chess-clubs, Little Leagues, and bowling tournaments." For indoor activities, Samson rhapsodized, "I see movie houses featuring American films with subtitles in Hebrew, uninterrupted by commercials, being shown to quiet and appreciative audiences," or "Broadway plays performed in English by the local theatre group." At home, families could enjoy housing "pre-wired for color and VHF TV reception" or read the local newspaper, a "free press beholden to no group . . . motivated by an educational impulse and dedicated to social action." In fact, there would be ample time for leisure, as Shalom City would be the first township in Israel to adopt the Western workweek. He also romanticized American democracy in his representation of city government, which would be "very responsive to public opinion . . . conscious of receiving their power from the consent of the governed . . . [and] act as the servant of the citizen." In Samson's vision, not only had the Green Line been erased, verily any substantive difference with life at home in the United States. Some of these very commercial, recreational, and bureaucratic amenities were later actualized in the American-Israeli settlements at Yamit, Efrat, and Tekoa, which helped obscure the ideological dimensions of immigration to the occupied territories.

Further, Shalom City would be a model for a new heterogeneous and tolerant spiritual movement. For example, Samson wrote at great length about the importance of retaining the American secular holiday of Thanksgiving (although "in Hebrew it's called Yom Hodu [lit. Turkey Day]") each year at Shalom City, complete with an annual high-school football match, an "ecumenical service [which] takes place in Kennedy Hall [where] Christians as well as Moslems and members of the Bahai faith participate," and even the customary meal, "yes, there is turkey too. But in the Israeli version of turkey schnitzel." For religious observance, Samson envisaged one synagogue where Jews of all denominations would pray together, men and women sitting separately wearing appropriate head coverings, with the liturgy in Hebrew and a sermon typically delivered in English. All residents would enroll their children in the new school system, where pupils of varying levels of Jewish observance would learn side by side and their parents would select a curriculum appropriate for their family, with the Orthodox specializing in Bible and Talmud instead of secular subjects like Hebrew literature. A noncoercive and pluralistic religious community would later become a hallmark of future Jewish-American settlements.

Above all, these various political, economic, commercial, recreational, religious, and educational ventures should reflect the core values of the American settlement where "Shalom City is a friendly place to live. There is an underlying 'live and let live' philosophy that permeates all its institutions. There is a healthy respect for the views, prejudices, and idiosyncrasies of others. There is a basic acceptance of Divine Providence in the affairs of man. This idea underlies both the educational and civil philosophy. At the same time there is acceptance of ritual differences and variations in customs."

To Samson, Shalom City represented a "revolutionary project" that would "mark a giant step forward in American Jewish involvement in Israel." Only there, "American Jews would share responsibility as an equal partner with the people of Israel in the building of Greater Israel and the fulfillment of the Jewish destiny." To him, "the creation of an American City in Israel would be fulfilling the needs of the hour." Evoking John F. Kennedy's 1961 inaugural address of "ask not what your country can do for you, but what you can do for your country," Samson concluded, "We can no longer discharge our full responsibilities to our people, our country, and to mankind—if you like—by the mere dispatch of our financial contributions . . . it is time we made our presence felt in Israel . . . the time for enlarging ourselves by creating, transplanting, and fusing the best of our heritage and our traditions in a fulfilled image on the soil of the ancient homeland."

Despite Samson's fervor, the file languished on the desks of Israeli bureaucrats until it was finally dispatched for review to Harry M. Rosen, a prominent Canadian businessman and Zionist, in mid-February 1968. Only two days later, Rosen posted a scathing confidential report to Jewish Agency chair Arye Pincus.[185] He bluntly dismissed the plan as either "highly presumptuous" or "very naïve." "The project simply is not feasible," wrote Rosen, pronouncing that "many of Mr. Samson's basic premises are false," including his reliance on the precedent of Levittown, Pennsylvania, as a prototype for an American city in Israel.[186] While he agreed in theory that many Jews in the United States would immigrate if they could "live American," he judged that "it would be wellnigh impossible, however, to create and sustain in Israel the carbon copy or even a reasonable facsimile of the American dream city which is the basis of Mr. Samson's proposal." Moreover, Rosen despaired that the Shalom City model was a contentious, even threatening, challenge to U.S.-Israeli relations, speculating that "Mr. Samson's 'Americans know best' theme would antagonize many Israelis," and that the native population would not "accept kindly a campaign—let alone an actual city— whose second major goal is to teach Israelis how to live and do things in the American way." Rosen's brief was circulated within the Jewish Agency and then forwarded to the prime minister's office in March.[187] No further discussion is recorded in the archival file.

ALTHOUGH SHALOM CITY, ISRAEL, never came to fruition, it germinated a new model for American-Israeli settlement in the occupied territories after the Yom Kippur War called the *garin* (seed colony) that brought together young Jewish-American families (and sometimes singles) in non-hierarchical, self-governing, cooperative immigration associations for settlement in the occupied territories. Samson's plan also marked the debut of a new rights-based discourse combining biblical promise with a utopian pioneering project that mobilized the commitments and contacts of the 1967 war "moment" generation as the Israeli settler movement got under way after 1973. Despite the fact that Shalom City struck its critics as a preposterous fantasy, integral parts of this vision were later realized by the Jewish-American settlers of Yamit, Efrat, and Tekoa over the past five decades.

CHAPTER TWO

City of the Sea

The Rise and Fall of Garin Yamit

T HE TIDES OF HISTORY have not been kind to the settlement of
Yamit in the Sinai: this is a narrative of crests and troughs over the
course of the decade between the city's establishment in 1973 and
its destruction in 1982.

The members of Garin Yamit, a cooperative association of Jewish-
American immigrants founded in Cincinnati, Ohio, in 1972 were among
the founding fathers and mothers of this settlement in the Sinai Peninsula.
Joining Russian immigrants and native Israelis, American Jews comprised
approximately half of the city's initial population. Leaving the United States
for a remote, isolated, brand-new seaside locale, they brought an American
spirit of pioneering, entrepreneurialism, and determination to life in their
new city on a hilltop of sand dunes.

However, their hopes and dreams failed to take root in the sandy soil at
Yamit. From its earliest days, Garin Yamit found itself stuck in the quick-
sand of Israeli bureaucracy, considered only as token participants rather
than as a true partner in the project for the first centrally planned city in
the occupied territories. The group also clashed with both the native Israeli
leadership of the city and the Israeli settler movement over the future of Yamit.
In contrast, they found calmer waters in negotiating their relationship with
the local Bedouin and Palestinian community in the area. Yet despite many

changes in course, the Jewish-American settlers thrived during their short existence in the city.

In 1977 the sands shifted in the Sinai. Shortly following the ninth Knesset elections, Prime Minister Menachem Begin initiated a process that would culminate in the historic Egyptian-Israeli peace accords and a full-phased civilian and military withdrawal from the Sinai Peninsula. On April 23, 1982, after a long and vociferous campaign to save the city—although one in which most of its American-Israeli founders declined to participate— Yamit was evacuated and destroyed by the Israel Defense Forces. The Jewish-American garin saw their decade-long project effaced, much like pounding waves upon sandcastles along the seashore.

Since then the story of Garin Yamit has lived on mostly in the memories of its American-Israeli residents. This chapter represents the first attempt in the scholarly literature to document their important narrative through the use of archival materials, the periodical press, and interviews never before brought to light. This section also examines the unique discourse of Garin Yamit, which was envisioned as a secular beachhead for a uniquely American vision to become contemporary pioneers on a Zionist frontier. In their city on the sea, these Jewish-Americans hoped to create an oasis of ecological, fiscal, and social harmony. By making the desert bloom, they hoped that both their personal and Zionist dreams could flourish. This stream of rhetoric, which was devoid of the religio-political imperatives characteristic of the other case studies profiled in this book, set them apart from both other Jewish-American settler groups and their native Israeli peers. In the end, this was the legacy of Garin Yamit, who left a unique and indelibly American watermark upon their city of the sea.

Historical Background: Sinai and City of the Sea, 1956–1973

The Sinai Peninsula is a 23,000-square-mile desert land-bridge with an inhospitable arid climate and few natural resources to sustain settlement. The area was named for Mt. Sinai, the supposed locale of the revelation to the Jews, although it was never considered part of the biblical land of Israel and had been incorporated into Arab lands from ancient Egyptian times. Since the dawn of Christianity, a small community of monks has also lived in the slope of the mountain. For the next 1,500 years, the region was captured by successive Roman, Byzantine, and Muslim empires, although there was little attempt to develop the desert. Beginning in 1517, the peninsula came under the rule of the modernizing Ottoman empire, although it remained an administrative backwater. Capitalizing on weak ties to Constantinople, Muhammad Ali asserted his autonomous reign over Egypt, including the Sinai hinterland, in the mid-nineteenth century. The British occupation of Egypt in 1882 saw the peninsula fall under foreign rule once again. While potential oil deposits and mineral resources were discovered during this period, the terrain remained only sparsely populated by nomadic Bedouin tribes and little attempt was made to extract precious materials. Later, El-Arish became a battleground between Great Britain and the Ottomans in World War I. The region was returned to Egyptian sovereignty following independence from Britain in 1922 and the adjoining Gaza Strip was added to areas under the monarchy's rule after the 1948 war. The peninsula first became a battleground between Israel and Egypt during the Sinai Campaign (1956) and remained contested throughout the War of Infiltration (1956–1967), although a shaky status quo held in place until 1967, when President Gamal abd-al Nasser closed the Straits of Tiran, creating a *casus belli* for regional conflagration. At the beginning of the Six Day War, Israel launched a ground assault into the land mass and captured the entirety of the Sinai Peninsula on 8 June 1967, the fourth day of battle.

The Sinai Peninsula emerged as a central element of Israel's postwar strategic thinking both as a territorial buffer zone and as a means to control access to the important economic and military assets of the Suez Canal, the Straits of Tiran, and the Gulf of Aqaba. Yet the idea of Israeli settlement in the area was not a postwar innovation—plans for a city surrounded by agricultural settlements in the northern Sinai were drawn up as early as 1961.[1] After the 1967 war, an administrative unit known as the Eshkol District (named for the sitting prime minister) was created. The Jewish Agency Settlement Division then produced its first development plan for the region in early 1969.[2] By May of that year, a seventy-three-member Noar Haluzai Lohem (NAHAL) military unit comprised of former Bnai Akiva youth group members established an outpost deep in the Sinai at Dekel (named for the nearby oasis of palm trees), which was quickly joined by Moshav Sadot and the town of Ofirah near Sharm el-Sheikh. In 1972 General Ariel Sharon ordered the forced population transfer of thousands of Bedouin from the Gaza Strip and Rafah Plain to make way for large-scale Jewish settlement in the area.[3]

That year, Defense Minister Moshe Dayan championed the creation of "the new Jezreel Valley" in the Sinai region, which would be anchored by a major port city of 230,000 people along the Mediterranean coast that would rival Ashdod and Haifa.[4] (It was rumored that the real strategic aim of a deep-water port was to conceal, or perhaps service, the building of a nuclear weapons depot near the site.[5]) In early 1973 the Jewish Agency Settlement Division outlined plans to develop fifteen agricultural communities, a town, and a regional urban center called Yamit (lit. of the sea) in the Eshkol District.[6] The Israeli political establishment was internally divided over the retention of territory in the Sinai in general, and the construction of the city-settlement in particular, yet Dayan refused to abandon the project, leveraging government approval for Yamit to remain in the Rafi party in the 1973 elections. A scaled-down version of Sinai settlement plans was approved by the Knesset in a 78–0 vote in August, although the agreement was overtaken by the 1973 war.[7] Later that fall, construction at Yamit began in earnest, awaiting its first residents in 1975.

From Cincinnati to the Sinai: Garin Yamit's Coalescence, 1972–1975

In the early 1970s, Yamit was but a sandcastle in the sky for a young married couple living in Cincinnati, Ohio. Chaim Feifel, a cantor in the Conservative movement, grew up in a Zionist home in Brooklyn, New York, and first came to Jerusalem as a foreign-exchange student in 1958–1959, vowing to immigrate to Israel immediately after a short visit home. Fate got in the way when he met and married Sarah, a nutritionist and fellow ardent Zionist from Boston, Massachusetts, who had been intrigued by life in Israel from her early memories of watching films at Hebrew school. The couple soon became active in American Zionist leadership, later assuming the co-presidency of the Association of Americans and Canadians for Aliya (AACA). Deeply influenced by the 1967 war and Sarah's sister's move to Israel, the Feifels revisited their personal and professional aims to immigrate themselves. As Chaim Feifel explained, "I'm not a spectator, I'm a ballplayer, I want to be where the action is . . . in the back of my mind, if I was going to make a move, a really big move, it was to come to live in Israel."[8]

Their timing was auspicious, as the Jewish Agency representative in Cincinnati at the time was involved in the initial planning of Yamit. Sarah Feifel's imagination was stirred when "One day, Uzi [Haimovich] came to us and said, 'Do you want to join the *halutzim* [pioneers]?'" Her husband Chaim also saw the potential for a liberal-progressive, utopian, self-realization project that evoked early pioneering on the frontier at Yamit, as "The idea of coming to Israel was in my head all the time . . . but as Yamit came into the picture, that really turned me on. To be a *halutz,* to be new, to build something from scratch, to be part of that."[9] The couple quickly began to coordinate with Joseph Shadur at the Israel Aliya Office in New York and were given official authorization and an expense account to advertise an amorphous, if aspirational American aliya initiative for Yamit.

While early planning for Yamit was kept from the press, the entirety of the emerging relationship between the Israeli government and the Jewish-American group has been preserved in a thick file at the Israel State Archives, Jerusalem. Initial correspondence between Israeli officials and the inchoate Garin Yamit illustrates the bewilderment, frustration, and conflict, mixed with hope and idealism, that came to characterize the relationship between the state and the American-Israeli contingent in the city. From the very beginning, the Jewish-American group had big dreams and demanded a meaningful role in shaping the future of Yamit, but they were often derided and dismissed by the Israeli government who saw them strictly as a source of manpower and capital for the state's strategic agenda in the Sinai.

This clash was evident from the very first item of correspondence between Chaim Feifel and Jewish Agency chair General Uzi Narkiss and his deputies Moshe Yakir, director of the Immigration and Absorption Division, and Abraham Rozeman, head of the Settlement Division, in January 1973. Feifel's letter opened with his declaration of intent to immigrate to Israel and organize a large Jewish-American contingent to join him in settling in the Sinai. He eagerly related dazzling potential immigrants with the prospect of new-age pioneering in the peninsula at meetings across the United States, where "believe it or not, all I had to do was show them camels, palm trees, sand, and the sea [and] the groups were very enthusiastic and motivated by the pioneering concept, the challenge, and being new settlers—the first in town." Yet the practical-minded Americans wanted more details— Feifel reproduced in his letter specific queries about location, housing, employment, and education—particularities that went to the core of the Yamit project.

Feifel's questions not only were an attempt to gather information but betrayed a deep anxiety about the exclusion of Jewish-Americans from their destiny in the new city-settlement. "I know that planning for Yamit is not static, that every day decisions are being made for the future of Yamit," imploring, "We want to share in these plans. We want to know that there is a great trust between Yamit officials and our garin. We should like to see a cooperation and synchronization of our efforts toward the development of Yamit. We want to feel we are partners in this project." Feifel decried the fact that as his departure date for Israel approached, his group felt neglected and mistrusted, and "we have yet to hear someone say to us, 'we don't know where Yamit is going, but if it is to succeed, we would like to share our projections with you.' No one has said to us, 'We really want you Americans in Yamit. We want you to be an integral part of this project.'" He then cautioned, "I am not stating this as a threat but rather as a statement of FACT. The Israeli government is going to have to show and indicate to us that it cares about the American contingent for Yamit. We need ATTENTION. We need CONCRETE ANSWERS. We need to be PARTIC-IPANTS in sharing the town's growth." "I am tired of boxing with shadows," Feifel groused and threatened to resign as the group's American organizer if improved communication and material assistance were not forthcoming from the Israeli government.[10]

Had he been privileged to the internal discussion of this letter, all of his greatest fears would have been substantiated. "Who today can provide detailed and accurate answers to Chaim Feifel's specific questions?" immigration officials pondered, as plans for Yamit remained fluid and had not yet received official government approval. Further, there was great skepticism about this sincere, but naive American group, especially as it was clear to immigration representative Joseph Shadur that "their ideas about what Yamit will be, if and when it will ever materialize, are vague . . . [and] at present there is nothing serious in 'K'vutzat Yamit' as a group settlement project." Nonetheless, Jewish Agency bureaucrats decided to keep them hanging, even though "it is clear that we have no obligations in regards to the city of Yamit and that they must be prepared for other suggestions."[11]

Totally unaware of the Israeli government's ambivalence about them, the Feifels made their first trip to Israel to meet government officials and tour Yamit in the summer of 1973. Sarah Feifel chuckled in recollection, "It was all sand. There was nothing! There was absolutely nothing except [mimicking officials' hand-gestures] 'over there, over there.'" They also met members of the Russian-Israeli garin living at Moshav Sadot, who would later join them, and a third population of native Israelis at Yamit. They found this group to be well organized and well received by the Israeli government, an absence of support that the couple keenly felt. The Feifels also celebrated receiving a letter from the Minister of Housing promising Garin Yamit forty apartments in the new city—only later, they learned it was an empty promise when the Minister of Agriculture subsequently told Sarah "it isn't worth a piece of toilet paper."[12] Yet, at the time, the Feifels were buoyant about their trip and eager to share their experience with potential immigrants at meetings across the United States.[13]

The couple also penned an intimate account inspired by their visit, which made an inauspicious public debut in the weeks before the 1973 war, for the AACA newsletter *Aliyon,* describing "beautiful hills of sand on one side, and the palm trees, green foliage, and the sea on the other!" Their attempts to portray the area as "peaceful," "calm," and "serene" were intended not only to accentuate the land's natural beauty but to assure readers of the tranquility of the political situation in the Sinai as well.[14] A follow-up article sought to assuage any nagging doubts, stressing that "the settlement is not liable to affect any option for a peace settlement" and that major figures like Pinchas Sapir (who, they failed to disclose, was a dovish minister not at all sympathetic to the Yamit project) and Abba Eban (a diplomat especially well known to Jewish-American audiences, but who, the Feifels declined to mention, was a firm opponent to settlement building) were supposedly in agreement about the "acceptability" of settling beyond the Green Line.[15] Mostly, as self-consciously evoked in the headline "Yamit: Chalutz Aliyah of the Mid. '70s," the Feifels sold Yamit as an opportunity for modern-day pioneering on the Israeli frontier. "Right now, it is not much more than a site, a plan, and some dreams," the organizers admitted, but emphasized that settlement in the Sinai was a superior choice for new Jewish-American immigrants, as "Many people who have given serious consideration to aliyah and to building their lives in Israel have been put-off by the costs of housing, the difficulties of settling in as individuals, and also by some of the social and cultural problems of Israel as they affect lifestyles and integration. It also seemed to many that places like Tel Aviv or

Haifa may not provide any challenge or grip the imagination. . . . Yamit however, does precisely offer the feeling of real participation and of personal involvement in setting up a new community with a promising future. It is a pioneering chalutz venture in the 1970s."[16]

Later, Chaim Feifel returned to these themes of adventures in modern-day pioneering, building a utopian community, and opportunities for liberal-progressive self-realization within the Yamit project, writing of life in the United States "in a society of automation and impersonality where most people feel frustration and futility because they have little to say about shaping their society. In a way they have lost touch with reality." In contrast, "Yamit in the onset offers a sense of reality which allows each individual the opportunity to shape his life and his community," alongside "opportunities for self-education, creativity, and adventure." While Feifel acknowledged "the price for this opportunity will demand a change of lifestyle—and looking at daily living in a different way," he encouraged interested parties to apply to Garin Yamit as "a special opportunity that comes perhaps once in a lifetime."[17] By fulfilling the Zionist aspiration of making the desert bloom in the Sinai Peninsula, personal dreams too could flourish.

In the weeks before the Yom Kippur War, Feifel bragged to Uzi Narkiss about the success of these early outreach efforts, describing how organizers had received many letters from potential members and that the garin had begun screening applicants.[18] Even in the midst of the Yom Kippur War, Settlement Division head Abraham Rozeman confirmed to Feifel that progress was still being made on the ground at Yamit, including an important bureaucratic step transferring administrative authority for the development of the site to the Housing Ministry. In light of the wartime moment, he expressed the first words of comradeship to Garin Yamit, writing, "In these great days that pass over us as a part of the Jewish people, we are engaging in activities that contain the possibility of contributing—each to his own abilities—to the victory that will come even before you receive this letter."[19]

Despite the massive disruption of the 1973 war, the garin dispatch in December was upbeat, reporting that 75 to 100 families would depart for Yamit in nine months' time—although, as Chaim Feifel later admitted in an interview, this figure required a bit of creative mathematics, where, "We had a list of names, fictitious names, all kinds of names, we had to do that, you know."[20] He also sought to reassure Jewish-Americans of the Israeli government's continued commitment to the project.[21] While Feifel conceded,

"The Yom Kippur War has created doubts in the minds of many of us as to the future of Yamit," he vowed, "Together we shall succeed."[22]

While Feifel continued to publicly sell the Israeli government's active involvement with Garin Yamit after the 1973 war, privately he was pained by the group's "nebulous position" and absence of "meaningful dialogue" with native officials.[23] Yet Garin Yamit evinced little understanding of the massive strategic and economic dislocation that certainly distracted the Israeli government. They also chose to ignore Israeli insiders' advice about how to work more effectively within the system, including an important recommendation to accelerate their own immigration efforts in the Israeli manner of creating facts on the ground.[24] Instead the Feifels chose to confront Israeli politicians with a cross-continental correspondence campaign, unabashedly working their way up the chain of command by first writing Moshe Dayan ("No one has talked to us . . . why doesn't someone officially tell us the straight story") and then Prime Minister Golda Meir ("This lack of communication has caused me much concern") to demand further updates about Yamit's progress.[25] Bureaucrats wrung their hands at this behavior, wondering why the Americans didn't take more active measures on their own.[26] By May 1974, Jewish Agency chair Uzi Narkiss had had enough of the exchange of letters. "I am happy you have been travelling all over the States during the past year developing the Yamit project," he expressed, "however, I am disappointed with your campaign to get the whole world here to focus on your efforts. Difficulties cannot be overcome by those methods." Narkiss then asked pointed—and likely embarrassing—questions about how many immigration files had been opened and the number of members with confirmed plans for immigration. He closed, "The ball is now in your court. . . . I hope we have finished with the talking phase and that in August we'll be meeting with your group in an absorption center somewhere in Southern Israel. See you soon."[27] Surely it was stunning wake-up call to Chaim Feifel, the self-described "ballplayer" back in Cincinnati.

Two weeks after receiving Narkiss's letter, Feifel wrote back, apologetic and somewhat chagrined, having finally internalized Israeli modes of operation. "I can only say that we are a serious group of capable people who will now be tested to see if we have the material to be pioneers and become part of a new way of life," he wrote the Jewish Agency head, "we want to succeed and I believe we will." While taking the opportunity to reiterate his frustrations, he admitted, "You are right, now we have to enter from the talking phase into the action phase of development. I do hope that all of us will work in a cooperative way, that we will all grow from this experience." He concluded his letter by announcing one active measure on the part of the Jewish-American garin: the Feifels' imminent immigration in mid-July 1974.[28]

Trying to move the proverbial ball along, Feifel also arranged for the fledgling group to meet face-to-face for the first time at a convention held in a Philadelphia hotel a few months later in mid-March 1974. There Garin Yamit coalesced, officially incorporated, and signed a charter.[29] The inaugural conference drew an eclectic group of individuals and families from across the United States seeking a life-changing opportunity.

One new member of the garin was twenty-seven-year-old bachelor Gedaliah Mazal (formerly Gary Meisels), an accountant for the Amalgamated Bank of New York who later became its first Jewish-American representative in Israel and the group's treasurer. Born in Los Angeles, Mazal was a lifelong Zionist who had first vowed to move to Israel at the age of thirteen. Before signing up with Garin Yamit, Mazal had worked extensively with the Israel Aliya Office to locate an appropriate destination for himself in Israel, insisting only, "I want to go to something new. And I don't want anything else."[30] Mazal was put in touch with the Feifels through a relative and joined the group on the spot at the weekend gathering.

Carole Rosenblatt, a thirty-four-year old single mother of three who later became the president of Garin Yamit, came to the convention with a very different story. A first-generation American and daughter of a kosher butcher who had deep ties to the local Jewish community in Long Island, she grew up in a semi-observant non-Zionist family. However, after divorcing her husband in her early thirties, Rosenblatt was desperate for a change for herself and wanted to give her children a better life than she could provide in Miramar, Florida, where they experienced anti-Semitism in their neighborhood and she could not afford to send her kids to Jewish schools. "I threw my husband out and I want to go now!" Rosenblatt explained to the local Jewish Agency representative, who sarcastically replied, "They're really waiting for you there. A young woman, with three little kids, who doesn't know the language—you'll starve in the streets!" She quickly apprehended her limited aliya options, which her *shaliah* (immigration representative) summed up as "They won't take you on a kibbutz without a husband to work, you have no money for a moshav, just stay in touch." A year and half later, the official informed her of a new development town in the Sinai. Initially, she wasn't particularly sold on the opportunity, but "it was the only offer he had given me [and] I'll tell you I wanted to try it . . . for my kids . . . and I figured I'd manage . . . so I said, what do I have to lose?" She began corresponding with Chaim Feifel, who invited her to the conference in Philadelphia. She found her weekend companions to be "really nice, down to earth people" and became so enamored with the whole project that "I wasn't going to go right away, but they said we need the first people to go in August [1974] and they said, 'Who's ready?' and I said, 'Me!' "[31]

Mazal and Rosenblatt were joined at the conference by future Garin Yamit vice president Howard (Zvi) Arenstein (age twenty-four), a freelance producer for National Public Radio in Philadelphia, along with his new bride Jennifer (age twenty-three), an English teacher.[32] Dov Segal (age thirty-four), another Floridian by way of two years on a kibbutz who owned a car repair shop and his wife Hedda (age thirty-two), a stay-at-home mother, came with their two children. Donald Swerdlov (thirty-six), his wife Mazal, and their child arrived from Staten Island, New York, where he had been working as a film editor at NBC news and hoped to open a media studio with Zvi Arenstein at Yamit. Trudi and Irv Pushkin, a building contractor from Culver City, California, were joined by another Golden State native, Robert Smolen (Smallman), a forty-seven-year-old divorcé from Desert Hot Springs. Gedaliah Mazal observed, "We were all different, we came from different states. Most were married, about half had kids, and two of us were single guys. We ranged from secular to very observant. We had different levels of education and divergent interests, except when it came to Yamit. There we were all united: We would create a completely unique community, one where anyone, from any walk of life, would be welcome."[33] "It was a fresh start for all of us," he reflected, "every one of us had a story behind us, a past, and we wanted to leave it on aliya." Through their Zionist project of making the desert bloom, Garin Yamit also hoped to have the opportunity for personal blossoming and self-realization.

Their indefatigable leader Chaim Feifel considered the conference a critical turning point for Garin Yamit. Sixteen families and six individuals committed to immigrating in summer 1974 and an additional sixty-five candidates subsequently opened files at Jewish Agency offices across the

United States.[34] He judged the group "people of high caliber with good educations and with enough flexibility to fit into whatever job is necessary in the area."[35] (Unemployment would later emerge as a central problem in the city.) Moreover, the membership had begun to consolidate, where "we arrived on a Friday with a mixed group of people who did not know each other—by the end of the convention, we were a solid group of Americans ready to make Aliyah to Yamit this summer."[36]

Yet as participants dreamed of their future homes and finally took active steps to immigrate to the Sinai, the Israeli government was simultaneously formulating criteria for garin membership that would exclude many of them from the project.[37] "We had signed in our constitution, our *aguda*, [that] we considered everybody equal," explained Gedaliah Mazal, a single man who would be rejected under these new rules, "[but] the government didn't . . . they only wanted whole families, they felt that would be a better survival set-up here."[38] Fellow bachelor Bob Smolen, who hoped to open a beachfront hotel at Yamit, even wrote to the Housing Minister expressing his "extreme shock, indignation, and outrage at the recent regulations passed down . . . [which gives] 'single' American Jews the feeling that they are not wanted," yet reaffirmed, "We intend to arrive on Aliyah as planned and will continue protesting to all and any levels of government this discrimination which is a miscarriage of the ideals of our Jewish state." (Internal correspondence between Israeli officials reveals that they were inclined to bend the rules for Smolen, but seemingly not for Mazal, on the grounds that they believed the Californian would bring assets upward of $100,000 to the city-settlement, further indication that Garin Yamit was strictly seen as a source of capital and manpower.)[39] Single parents like Carole Rosenblatt and childless couples such as Trudy and Irv Pushkin were also concerned about possible disqualification under these new restrictions.[40] The Israeli government seemingly backpedaled on a strict prohibition against unmarried members in June, but the group continued to struggle over candidacy guidelines as Garin Yamit prepared to arrive in Israel that summer.[41]

Meanwhile, as a participant in the World Union of Jewish Students (WUJS) program in Arad in the spring of 1974, Gedaliah Mazal became the first member of the Jewish-American garin to witness progress on the ground since the Yom Kippur War. Visiting Moshav Dekel only a few kilometers from his future home on an Israeli Independence Day outing, Mazal begged supervisors to take his group to Yamit: "When I went there the first day with WUJS that April day, nothing, there was nothing, the bulldozers were just flattening the ground waiting for the prefab houses to go up. It was just amazing. I was sitting there in awe. I sat on the hillside, I took pictures of [it]. . . . And I said, 'this is where I'm going to live.' I couldn't believe it in another year later it won't be just a grain of sand."[42] In addition to providing early reconnaissance for the group back in the United States, Gedaliah Mazal also oversaw budgets at the Israeli Ministry of Finance branch office in Pitkak Rafah near Yamit. He glamorized the adventurist aspects of accounting for the Israeli government, suggesting that his professional work allowed him to play the role of an "undercover agent" for the garin. Among the fiscal files and tables, he tabulated, "[I had] already gotten my feet where I should be."[43]

While Mazal planted himself in the budget office that summer, the first eight families of Garin Yamit were literally getting their feet wet at the sandy beach at Yamit.[44] Mere moments after arriving at the Beersheba absorption center from Florida in early August 1974, Carole Rosenblatt and her three children were informed that the Jewish Agency planned to take the garin on their first tour of their future home that morning. "We dumped our bags and got on the bus," marveling at the site, finding "nothing at all was built there yet, just that exquisite beach, blue water, and white sand."[45] "It was really like a movie," she later added, instantly falling in love with the place, "I put my foot in the Mediterranean and said, 'You know, we're here, we'll make do, we'll do it!'"[46] Trudi Pushkin concurred, offering her own description of her future home: "Yamit—the name doesn't give a clue about what our new address looks like. So close your eyes and imagine the blue sky, endless blue water and pure white beach, surrounded by sand dunes. Date palms stretch their trunks high while the fronds give shade and hide the clusters of dates. Everywhere you look, you are startled by the beauty of this spot. Sound romantic? Sound unreal? Well, it is real, it is romantic, it's Yamit."[47]

Seeing their future home for the first time reinforced their utopian vision for the land. In an article pointedly titled "Pioneering—1975" in November 1974's *Israel Digest* magazine, the Pushkins, the oldest couple in the group, dreamed of a life that would allow them to leave behind the materialism of the United States, where "We were brought up with all American values [and] worked hard to get these things . . . yet when we finally got all those things, they weren't what we were looking for; we wanted something more, more lasting . . . we think people our age should think about this. It will give them a new lease on life." Similarly, the Lawrence family, a middle-aged couple from Miami, saw Yamit as "an opportunity to make [our] mark by actually being in there and getting my hands in it." In a complementary vein, David Kaminsky, a conservation engineer in the United States, saw the possibility to safeguard the Sinai environment, as "I've seen a definite need for someone to clean up the cities and . . . I want to make people feel conscious of the way they handle the land. Yamit [is] a city that's fresh and people are living there without their old hang-ups." His wife Sandy added, "It's a new community. . . . We'd like to see the area kept beautiful for everyone to enjoy and respect." The Arensteins from Philadelphia had a longer-term vision and "imagined looking back in 70 years at the city we had built. Something young people our age don't get a chance to do." Carole Rosenblatt summed up the sentiments of the group by exclaiming, "I had always wanted to be a pioneer!" Interestingly however, she was the only member of the garin who also seized on the strategic aspect of settlement in the Sinai, seeing their contribution as "something different, Israel needs new immigrants in the administered areas which our government won't be able to keep unless they have population there."[48] Years later, Rosenblatt admitted, "we had no idea as Americans about the politics. We were *so* naïve. They said, 'someday if there is peace with Egypt . . . we'll be there as the buffer between Egypt and Israel, and this whole string of settlements and El-Arish would be the border' . . . and I believed it!"[49]

Despite the idealized image the Jewish-American garin presented to North American audiences back home, the group was losing faith that the government would help them achieve the goal of their immigration project. "I am writing this letter with a feeling of disappointment," Chaim Feifel informed Jewish Agency chair Uzi Narkiss in early September 1974, "One and a half months ago our garin, 23 adults and their children came to Israel to settle in Yamit . . . [where] we were informed upon our arrival we would be dealt with in a meaningful way . . . to move toward our goal if we would stop talking and start working." In fact, "we have been indeed working, knocking ourselves out for the betterment of our group [and] we bounce like a ball from office to office"—a petition submitted by Feifel the ballplayer and his deputy Zvi Arenstein for mileage reimbursement revealed they had covered some 1,800 kilometers of travel in repeated visits to Jerusalem and Tel Aviv—yet "we feel as though we have accomplished nothing."[50] Through these trials, they had come to understand that "we have been thrown a bone to abate our hunger—we need more than a budget; we need a sponsor. . . . In essence, the 'Abba' [father] we need seems nowhere to be found and we are nothing until we find him, until we have a permanent address, a 'bayit' [house]." Further, "I do not enjoy writing you this way but I feel that we are being duped—fooled and kidded. . . . Who will come forward and extend a hand in the faith that our success will aid the future of aliya?" "You and your office sit quietly and let this unique opportunity slip away," Feifel fulminated, pointedly informing officials, "If not one wants to help us then let them come out and tell us so. Then at least we will know where we stand." Turning Narkiss's earlier advice on its head, he concluded, "The ball is back in your hands. It is high time to stop talking and start acting. . . . Together we can build something that would have only been a dream. . . . We hope you also have the strength necessary to follow through."[51]

Feeling that their missive was ignored, the Feifels resorted to a second correspondence crusade, first writing to the Israel Aliya Center in New York ("How much running and hassling will we have to do before some agency will come along and remove some of the stumbling blocks on our road to success?"), the Ministry of Housing ("We did not expect to be left out of the picture—as if we don't exist. We want to help . . . WE DON'T WANT TO FALL IN BETWEEN THE CHAIRS"), and finally the president, prime minister, and all ministers of the Israeli government ("We want to help. We want to be part of the total picture. We want to build a city—Yamit—that we will be proud to live in.").[52] Yet they had few bargaining chips to offer beyond garin recruitment and their cries for attention and assistance mostly fell upon deaf ears.[53]

Meanwhile the Jewish-American group tried to start their lives as new immigrants in the Negev. They began learning Hebrew at the absorption center and some also found work in Beersheba. Others, like Carole Rosenblatt, struggled to get their children settled in local schools. The Feifels began scouting suppliers for the store they planned to open in Yamit. Other individuals formed partnerships for small businesses like the Segal/Kaminsky grocery store, the Arenstein/Swerdlov media studio, and the Smolen/Rosenblatt beachfront development. The group also intensified efforts to work with the Russian contingent at Moshav Sadot. One Jewish-American recalled a chance encounter with Prime Minister Yitzhak Rabin at a Beersheba restaurant as the two *garinim* celebrated their first "mixed marriage" between the membership, "[Rabin was] shocked as we went around the table and told him where we were from . . . 'Moscow' . . . 'Riga' . . . 'Cincinnati' . . . 'Ukraine' . . . 'Philadelphia.' "[54] Besides forming social ties, the group cooperated with the Russians to design plans for heavy industries at Yamit, a critical collaboration as the entrepreneurially minded Americans had few technical skills to work in the government's preferred businesses. They also jointly labored to attract intensive media interest to Yamit, citing radio and television reports broadcast in multiple languages.[55]

In December 1974, four months after their arrival in Beersheba and nearly a year and half after their initial exchange of letters, Garin Yamit scored a small victory on the bureaucratic front when it signed a letter of obligation with the Jewish Agency.[56] In early January 1975 the Jewish-American group also officially incorporated themselves as an *aguda shitufi* (cooperative association) self-consciously named the "Association of Pioneers of Yamit," wrote a charter, and claimed to receive government recognition by the Ministry of Housing, the Ministry of Immigration and Absorption, and the Ministry of Defense.[57] In a particularly exciting moment for Garin Yamit, Defense Minister Shimon Peres even took an aerial tour of the city and met with some representatives of the American-Israeli group in February 1975. The Ministry of Housing also appointed a designated representative for Yamit named Rafi Leshem who began working directly with the two immigrant populations in developing the city.

Meanwhile the Jewish-American garin continued to build capacity on its own, as male members of the group, almost all of whom had been white-collar professionals in their previous lives in the United States, began working to construct prefabricated houses at the site. Sarah Feifel conceded their lack of experience, but suggested it "was just like an adventure for them."[58] As Chaim Feifel rejoiced to recruits in North America, "The action is here in Yamit and we love it!" His wife, now the rotating president of Garin Yamit, also concurred on the bureaucratic front, "Now we are seeing a little more action. We are no longer falling between the chairs as the saying goes in Israel. . . . The horizon is changing. We have a new name, a new board, and more positive attention from the powers that be." A new recruitment form for Chalutzei Yamit (Pioneers of Yamit) shared a similar sentiment: "We feel that we have in our hands a fresh ball of clay ready to be molded. We need your help to sculpt Yamit into a living vibrant city. The area is beautiful and the potential great, but success will only come with people who are sure of their future. We need people who despite attractive incentives on all sides will continue to be tenacious on the long hard road to Yamit. We know the road is tough but we are not afraid to fight. Together we will build a city of beauty, a city of culture . . . an exciting place to live."[59] For those seeking to take part in a pioneering initiative to build a new, utopian, liberal-progressive community in the Sinai, Yamit could be the adventure of a lifetime.

Yet when an intrepid reporter from the Israeli daily *Maariv* came down to visit Yamit in the spring of 1975, he found Chaim Feifel on a break from home-building at the lone beach kiosk, openly grumbling about the garin's situation after nine months of uncertainty in the Beersheba absorption center. Dubbing himself the "foreign minister of the group," Feifel bemoaned the fact that he had worked "until it broke me!" He complained to the correspondent, "You know Israeli bureaucracy. It's not normal. . . . I ran around like a crazy person between offices and authorities. One sends you to the next. They send you to a third. Everyone smiles politely, but nothing happens. You run around all week long and in the end, you realize that you are in the same position in which you started. At first, I thought I would prevail, but I have to admit, they beat me. I put up my hands [in surrender]." Yet Feifel soon brightened, characterizing the situation as "an abnormal balagan [lit. chaos, a slang term usually used to describe difficulties with the Israeli bureaucratic-complex]. But a happy balagan . . . because what could be better for a human being than to live in a new city, with clean air, with . . . the sea on the one hand, and clean, beautiful beaches on the other."[60]

Feifel's cheerful suffering notwithstanding, the morale of the Jewish-American group was in sharp decline as the days and weeks at the Beersheba absorption center seemed to lengthen toward the horizon. As Zvi Arenstein wrote in Chalutzei Yamit's spring newsletter, "Nothing is definite. You will notice how many times I have used the words 'probably,' 'should,' 'has been promised,' 'we believe,' 'we have been told,' or 'planning and development.' In Israel, we find that talk is cheap but action is expensive. Over the last nine months, we have heard much talk but seen very little action. Our group suffers, both physically and mentally, for this indecisiveness."[61] The situation was quickly reaching a boiling point.

Feeling increasingly isolated and excluded, both the Russian and the American immigrants took their case to the Israeli public in a special Passover edition of the Hebrew daily *Maariv*. In a stunning exposé, both populations sat down with the press to attack the "monopoly of the Housing Ministry" and its policy regarding bachelors, an issue they considered "a blow to the city of the future, a squandering of potential." Seemingly, the strategy worked, as a Housing Ministry directive revealed that Israeli officials bowed to pressure to absorb these men.[62] Yet as their summer move-in date drew near—the archival record even contained a few handwritten notices assigning the first house numbers at Yamit that April—new complications arose regarding the distribution of apartments to the Jewish-American group.[63] "We, the undersigned members of Chalutzei Yamit wish to express our deep disappointment and anger with our treatment concerning the allotment of housing in Yamit," the group declared in an open letter signed by the entire group in May 1975, "We have been sitting in the Merkaz Klita [absorption center] in Beersheva for almost one year with the assurance of high ministry officials that we would be given priority in location and type of housing when it was assigned." (The annotated archival copy shows question marks written in pencil next to this statement, noting the reader's skepticism.) They continued, "We have helped build these houses [and] are aware that they are almost ready," reaffirming "WE feel the time has come for us to speak out and demand answers and action . . . not promises. . . . We should not and WILL not be on the bottom after all this time." The group then indignantly issued an ultimatum to resolve the issue in a week's time, reminding the Israeli government that "We have committed ourselves to living in Yamit in good faith and request that the ministries do the same, by helping us settle Yamit as dignified human beings not having to beg for normal assistance toward our common goal of building a city for all of Israel to be proud."[64] Despite their righteous anger, Garin Yamit clearly failed to appreciate Israeli government priorities, which viewed the development of the Sinai primarily as a military and strategic asset and had correspondingly decided to give housing preference to the native Israeli IDF families who would work at nearby military bases and the future heavy-vehicle garage at Yamit while joining the two immigrant groups at the site.

When this petition and a subsequent "position paper" to the Ministry
of Absorption were ignored, the situation exploded.[65] First the Jewish-
American garin traveled to Tel Aviv to campaign outside the offices of the
Ministries of Housing and Absorption. According to Chaim Feifel, "After
the protest, we got the houses."[66] Despite emerging divisions between the
future populations at Yamit by June 1975, all three groups chose to band
together and collectively turn to the press to vent their frustrations and
embarrass the Israeli government into further action later that summer.
"The Minister of Defense is destroying seed colonies for settlement," opined
Maariv in an exclusive interview with Jewish-American, Russian, and Israeli members, promising the scoop on "the bitter experience" of those who
"are asking to take root at Yamit and are now clashing with the foolish
policy of the Ministry of Housing." In addition to interviewing leaders of
all three communities, the journalist even trailed their representatives to
meetings with Israeli bureaucrats, reporting that they emerged looking like
"beaten dogs" upon encountering the "brick wall from the side of the
Housing Ministry." The reporter surmised that the government "does not
value or take care of seed colonies for immigration, and even worse—it
doesn't have any interest in them. It cuts off their oxygen tank, puts the
brakes on their growth momentum, and plays with, and disintegrates, their
vigorous enthusiasm." The reporter had particularly damning conclusions
about the treatment of the Jewish-American garin by Israeli officials, citing
remarks from Jewish Agency head Uzi Narkiss (as related secondhand by
Ministry of Defense representative Elhanan Yishai), who was reported to
maintain, "Leave it alone. There is no immigration from America, it is difficult to bring them. I don't believe in these ideas." When Chaim Feifel reiterated to the reporter his timeworn complaint that "there isn't anyone to
talk to and no one wants to listen to us," his words seemed to ring true.[67]

Later Feifel met Narkiss in person for the first time in a closed-door
meeting that quickly erupted into a screaming match. "'Who are you?'"
Feifel was asked by means of introduction despite the dozens of letters they
had exchanged, then "'Uzi says 'yeah you're the one who wrote the article
[in *Maariv*]—you're a liar!'" and hurled a torrent of obscenities at him.
Feifel quickly retorted, "I'm a liar? You're a liar! I'll tell you, one day in
heaven you'll get your just rewards." Years later Feifel admitted, "I had a
big mouth in those days . . . because we were in charge of the group, we

promised them, we brought them from America, we have this responsibility of doing something for them."[68]

Carole Rosenblatt, who took over as garin president a few months later, more readily embraced Israel's informal official culture and therefore was somewhat more successful than Feifel in advancing the garin's agenda. In a recent interview, she mischievously related barging into meetings at the prime minister's office to make progress. She even resorted to subterfuge when necessary, recalling that when she once needed to attend a critical interdepartmental meeting but could not secure an invitation from either ministry (each of which claimed that the other was responsible), she employed a ruse. "I just went to the meeting and they both thought that the other had invited me!" she chuckled, but added on a serious note, "That's how the bureaucracy was—they were going to discuss all about us and we weren't even going to be there."[69] The Jewish-American garin could only hope that the tides would change once they moved to Yamit in the fall of 1975.

"And Here We Are, Really Living in This Place!": Yamit, 1975–1977

After enduring months of delays, the Jewish-American garin—thirty-four adult couples, two single men, and twenty-four children—finally moved to Yamit in late summer 1975. The group quickly settled into single-family houses and apartments in the sole completed quartile of the city. Garin Yamit president Carole Rosenblatt worked with the Jewish Agency up until the last minute to ensure that the American-Israeli contingent would have the most basic provisions like cots to sleep on and brooms to sweep out the perpetually accumulating sand from their new living spaces. When she first arrived with her children as the ninth family in Yamit, she found that the houses were standing but plumbing hadn't been hooked up, the fence around the city had yet to be installed, and resident parking lots were still sand dunes. The Feifels were the eleventh family in town and their store's payphone was the new settlement's only telecommunication link to the outside world. Their earliest memory was that "there was sand in our beds, sand in our soup, sand in everywhere!"[70] Gedaliah Mazal, who as a single man was only allowed to join the group a month after families moved in, found bachelor housing primitive at best. "I lived in an *eshkubiah* [prefabricated caravan], a 23-meter one room flat," without running water, electricity, indoor plumbing, or other amenities and "didn't have anything . . . [but] my own water bottle, a canteen, a little oven you just put the match to light it, and a [place where I] went out [to use a latrine] . . . for the first six weeks." Undaunted, Mazal nostalgically recollected, "I felt like a chalutz [pioneer], I felt like a Bedouin. I appreciated life more than anything else because of what I did at that point."[71] For him and the others, "thus, for the first six weeks, living in Yamit was really pioneering: We roughed it, but it was definitely worth it."[72] Yamit's initial population was only about one hundred people in the settlement's first months. More than half of the constructed units in the completed section of the city remained unoccupied. Despite initial difficulties, daily life began to take shape. Empty apartments were soon commandeered to house a post office, a branch of the Amisra gas company, and the Feifels' general store. "We sold *everything*," they explained of their eclectic *kol-bo* (lit. everything in it), including household items, baby goods and toys, writing implements, electrical supplies, agricultural and gardening tools, hardware, books, gifts, keys, *toto* (football lottery tickets), and newspapers, all in "the American style" of open shelves and a shop-keeper behind the counter. Business was often slow, but the store served as an outlet to the rest of the country in the first weeks and months. The Feifels recollected of the first residents that "they used to line up like crazy like it was the last day for the newspapers!" Shopping at Kol-Bo Feifel also became a way to pass the time in the sleepy Sinai settlements, as Sarah once overheard one *moshav* resident explain, "'Ani holehet l-hanut Feifel l-hizdangev [I go to Feifel's shop as if to promenade along Dizengoff Street (the main commercial thorough-fare of Tel Aviv)].'" She quickly gathered, "We were kind of like the entertainment."[73] (This parallel, among others, also reinforced a historical vision linking the first Zionist settlement of Tel Aviv to Yamit in the occupied territories.[74]) In their ample spare time, the Feifels enjoyed the sea—walking, swimming, and sailing at Yamit's pristine beach.

Another source of recreation was Carole Rosenblatt's beachfront kiosk—at first only a wagon with soda cans on ice—which attracted local Bedouins and other passersby curious to witness progress in the city. By 1976 her shack had grown into a rustic 125-seat restaurant. "In the beginning, it was very hard—nobody really wanted to go there," Rosenblatt reminisced, although she soon convinced some idealistic Israeli suppliers "who had faith in us" to lend her equipment and commodities. She also began importing fresh food from the Gaza Strip, laughingly recalling that, trained as a secretary in Florida, "me and my partner, we're going to have a fish restaurant [and] neither of us knew how to cook a fish! . . . We were up all night cleaning the fish [the first time]. . . . I'll never forget that!" As the business grew, Rosenblatt began hiring workers from the Palestinian city and refugee camp of Rafah, employing twelve staff members at the height of her business in the late 1970s when visitors flocked to the seashore. Rosenblatt even recounted tall tales about life at Yamit to tourists dining at the restaurant, which awed her visitors.[75] While Gedaliah Mazal initially felt astounded that "they outnumbered us" when busloads of Israelis began cavorting at their coastline each weekend, he took great pride in the fact that "they thought it was an experience for them to come out to us from the big cities of Tel Aviv, Rehovot, or whatnot to come to our beach."[76]

Meanwhile, Mazal too had entrepreneurial ambitions and became the famed "meat-man of Yamit," owning a wildly popular side business that took orders from local residents who craved a taste of home. Yet, like many of Yamit's residents, he kept his day job in Beersheba at the Ben-Gurion University library and organized a carpool for himself and two doctors who worked at the BGU-Soroka Medical Center, a difficult commute that took an hour by car or two-and-a-half hours by public transportation. (Mazal even showed me a yellowed copy of the first Egged bus schedule listing once-daily service to Yamit.) Sometimes "transportation broke down—I used donkey carts, horses, I even rode a camel for eight kilometers," although he fondly recollected, "I was young, and it was exciting."[77]

In addition to serving the city, Mazal's entrepreneurialism brought him—and by extension, the entire settlement—into more regular contact with local Bedouin tribes who wanted to buy his product to start their own business as a competitor to Carole Rosenblatt's restaurant. He began making weekly deliveries to El-Arish, becoming friendly with many of its villagers, who even offered protection for his services! Mazal, like all of Yamit's residents, also routinely drove through the Gaza Strip because the closest Israeli bank branches, medical facilities and health insurance departments, government and bureaucratic offices, markets, restaurants, gas stations, and car repair shops were located there. "We went to Gaza *every day!* All the time!" the Feifels reminisced, "we used to eat *ful* [a traditional fava-bean dish] at the restaurants . . . we had a guy at the bank who taught me Arabic . . . we rode our bicycles from Gush Katif and back . . . we didn't feel threatened or anything, not at all, the relations with the Arabs was good, the relations with the Bedouins even better. . . . We had a good life there."[78] Although the relationship between Yamit's residents and their Bedouin and Palestinian neighbors was mostly transactional, Mazal expressed no hostility. "All these things, it's so intertwined, it's so stupid," he explained, "Since Yishmael we already grew together, so why fight each other. Just try to live with each other. That was the whole thing in Yamit. That was what I was doing. I didn't have anything against anybody. Just to live together with our brothers. . . . [The politicians] really didn't get the idea. The government was tied up in the . . . processes . . . and it really kills [peace]."[79]

While the American community at Yamit embraced coexistence with its neighbors, they prioritized bonding within the city itself. As more families moved into town, the Jewish-American garin got to know their Russian and Israeli neighbors, forming communal ties and business enterprises together. They shopped in each other's stores, ate in each other's homes and at the beachfront restaurant, and planned social occasions and outings. Rosenblatt, as a single divorcée, reported that sexual escapades were also an important part of daily life in the Sinai—embracing the free-love spirit of the 1970s, singles actively dated each other and there was even a swingers circle for married couples at Yamit![80]

The *Yamiton*, the city's weekly newspaper, is an essential historical source about daily life, local affairs, and internal debates at Yamit from the autumn of 1975 until the evacuation of the Sinai in 1982. Media professional Zvi Arenstein of the Jewish-American garin initially served as its editor, although much of his American group and the Russian population struggled to read in Hebrew.[81] For several years, Garin Yamit continued to have a separate column written in English that printed news and events of particular interest to the Jewish-American contingent. For example, a special six-month anniversary issue announced a meeting for all American-Israelis where schooling, the industrial area, car repair garage, and a hotel would be discussed, an outing to Beersheba to meet with a visiting expert

about filing U.S. income tax returns, news of upcoming international dele-
gations to Yamit including new recruits from the United States, Jewish-
American tourists on an Israel Bonds trip, and a group of Jewish Defense
League members, and finally, a reminder about the upcoming Yamit Purim
Party ("Don't forget to come in costume!") later that month.[82]

Nine months after moving into Yamit, Carole Rosenblatt also wrote
to the *Aliyon* in the United States to confirm, "We finally did make it." By
February 1976 the members of the Jewish-American, Russian, and Israeli
garinim already settled in the city eagerly awaited the arrival of new members in *Shlav Bet* (phase B). Rosenblatt described how the economic foundations of the city were taking shape, including the plans for an American-run
beachfront hotel/country club (envisioned complete with two swimming
pools and a whirlpool spa), the Feifels' general store, and the joint Russian-
American cabinetry shop, car repair garage, computer laboratory, and
industrial park. Rosenblatt also boasted of various social and cultural
achievements in the city including the founding of the *Yamiton,* weekly
movie nights, lectures, and parties.

The report expressed an idealized view of city life where a diverse population lived in peace and harmony. As a mother of three, she emphasized
youth welfare, highlighting "no traffic" neighborhoods where the settlement's children bicycled freely in the streets. She noted that youngsters of
various backgrounds got along, preferring to communicate with each other
in Hebrew, much to the pride (and sometimes chagrin) of parents who could
not speak the language.

In fact, the two main problems Rosenblatt outlined in their first year
related to the communication barrier. The new immigrants still struggled to
learn Hebrew—while there was no *ulpan* (language-training facility) in the
city, the settlement was trying to organize classes in Hebrew, English, and
notably, Arabic, for its residents in the evenings. Yet Yamit's diverse populations were keen to communicate: Rosenblatt triumphantly related how
she overcame linguistic and cultural difficulties to convince the Russian
grocery to stock the American culinary staple of pancake mix. "Sometimes
our party and city meetings are like Tower of Babel meetings," she described,
but "we all get along." More troublingly, all three *garinim* still experienced
difficulties speaking the language of Israeli bureaucracy. For example, the
problem of singles remained a sore point. According to Rosenblatt, "The

entire government has a 'Jewish Mother' complex. 'Everyone should get married!' " Despite these difficulties, she was optimistic about the recruitment of a second wave of members from the United States.[83]

What Rosenblatt did not mention to her American audience was Yamit's unemployment crisis. While the motto on Chaim Feifel's general store business card was Herzl's "Im Tirzu, Ein Zo Agada" (lit. If you will it, it is not a dream, which he cleverly translated as "If you want it, we will get it")[84] no amount of tenacity or entrepreneurialism on the part of Garin Yamit could overcome an endemic problem in the city. Many who sought work within the settlement were under- or unemployed.[85] In January 1976, about six months after the first residents moved in, Yisrael Nir, a Russian immigrant and chair of the Yamit Citizen's Council Committee, charged the Ministry of Housing with "ineptness" and an "utter lack of coordination" in providing residents with jobs. Israeli Housing Ministry representative Rafi Leshem was utterly unsympathetic, suggesting to one unemployed family at a citywide meeting, "Didn't you know what the situation was before you came here?"

Further, the Jewish-American garin's attempts to develop industry and small business were also met with delays and discouragement. For example, while Robert Smolen's beachfront hotel, Carole Rosenblatt's shoreline campground and recreational facility, and the Donald Swerdlow/Zvi Arenstein media studio had reached interim stages of approval by the Israeli government by mid-1976, officials continued to favor the development of heavy industry over local entrepreneurship. Further, though the garin sponsored its own members' plans for the Yamit commercial center, including such American-inspired enterprises as a clothing boutique, a garden and pet food supply outlet, a bakery ("for pita and American style bagels"), a beauty parlor/barbershop/cosmetician business, a furniture showroom, a children's emporium, a shoe store, a hardware and appliance depot, and a gift shop for Israeli crafts, Israeli bureaucrats refused to consider business plans until after the building had been built.[86] Once construction was finally completed, some small-business people complained that the government dragged its feet with utility hookups and other services required for them to open their stores. Meanwhile, the government worked assiduously to promote its preferred industries including a metalworking shop, a carpentry floor, and a garage for repairing IDF vehicles and equipment—workplaces that would also employ military men. Although officials billed these operations as joint enterprises of the Russian and Jewish-American garinim, very few American-Israelis had the manual labor skills to work in these industries.[87] Nir warned that the situation would only deteriorate as new immigrant families arrived and threatened Israeli officials that residents would stage a protest if their concerns were not addressed.[88]

While reluctant to discuss the situation with Yamit's citizens, Israeli bureaucrats acknowledged the severe unemployment problem in internal memos, admitting that "the opportunities for employment are completely unclear. At the moment, we can only say that there is work in the [general] area." Nonetheless, they continued to press the government's agenda of populating the city.[89] By the spring of 1976, the government began to respond more vigorously—notably, the Ministry of Defense formulated an innovative scheme to employ a large number of town residents as civilian employees of the IDF, presumably in connection with the garage.[90] Later the Ministry of Absorption floated the idea of opening an immigrant absorption center in Yamit, although the plan was quickly shot down by Jewish Agency chair Uzi Narkiss, who dryly remarked that he didn't have a spare ten million lira for the project.[91] (Israel at the time was in the midst of a massive recession and immigration had slowed.) While some of these ideas were promising in the long term, the government underscored that "right now, there are no plans for employment in Yamit itself."[92]

Meanwhile Garin Yamit did its best to recruit essential manpower for the city-settlement's future development, including doctors for understaffed medical facilities and engineers for the deepwater port project. The group stressed the positives and possibilities in the city, as Rosenblatt wrote to one potential recruit, "Your letter of interest in Yamit was exciting. Yamit is such a beautiful city with such potential that I hope you fall in love with it."[93] Yet as Garin Yamit members approached their first anniversary in the city, they grew sober about employment prospects.

The professional and personal impact of the unemployment crisis on members of Garin Yamit is well illustrated by the plaintive correspondence between one American-Israeli couple and native officials in the fall of 1976. Dorit Nudel, a teacher who had been unemployed for nearly a year, wrote in simple Hebrew, "I'm not working and I sit at home and this is very difficult. And it's not healthy that I don't work. I don't know what will happen next? . . . I don't have feel I have strength . . . what will cause me to stay in Yamit if I'm not working? How can I spend the year in this manner?"[94]

"I really don't understand what is going on here," added her husband Jerry, a fellow teacher soon to be discharged from active service in the IDF, "we've been in Garin Yamit 10 months already . . . and now you are writing [us] that we can't work in Yamit? I'm embarrassed to live like this! . . . What can we do without work? This isn't acceptable! . . . But it doesn't bother you at all!" He then accused the government of corruption, suggesting that only those with "protexia" [connections] were able to se-cure employment in the city and that the government took no action to remedy the situation for the common citizen.[95] The Nudels hinted at plans to abandon Yamit and move back to Beersheba.

Other Americans echoed their concerns about corruption at Yamit. As her restaurant and beachfront parking concession became highly profitable, Carole Rosenblatt alleged that Israeli officials tried to force her into a tourist cooperative with native Israelis, demanding to use her enterprise as collat-eral until other businesses were established. Refusing to give up her rights as an entrepreneur (despite her lack of an official business contract) or pay a bribe, she alleged that an army man was given her restaurant concession in a corrupt process to favor military families. When local government tried to forcibly take over her restaurant, Rosenblatt informed officials, "You'll take me out of there over my dead body." For months she fought local authorities tooth and nail when they came to shut off her utilities (she brought in a generator and water tank instead), sent in health in-spectors to withdraw her license, and even put out a warrant for her arrest. According to Rosenblatt, the situation deteriorated to the point where "they sued me so often, I'd walk into court, and the judge would say, 'What did you do now?' I wasn't about to go quietly."[96] "Israelis can be really nasty sometimes," Rosenblatt reflected, recalling that the same city secretary who was intent on destroying her business once came into her restaurant and asked to be served a cup of coffee, which she threw in his face. To her mind the whole situation "was a dirty [corrupt] thing," but she mostly blamed herself, as "[being an] an American, stupidly, I fought it [through the courts] and lost."[97]

As fellow small-business people, the Feifels also complained about the problem of "taxation, but no representation" and corruption at Yamit. De-spite their desire to be "ballplayers," they concluded that "we didn't know how to play the game" compared to more savvy Russian immigrants and native Israelis.[98] Reflecting on these troubles, Gedaliah Mazal suggested,

"We were economists. We were Westernized thinkers. . . . They [the Israeli government] are Middle Eastern, it's as simple as that. And the Russians came from Communism. . . . We were really looking at it from another angle."[99]

During their first year, continuing concerns about employment, corruption, and cultural differences in a new, isolated city eroded the American-Israeli group's cohesiveness. By May 1976 a Jewish Agency official observed that "this garin certainly isn't crystallized," and "it is very doubtful if the majority of them are interested in and are capable of joining in cooperative activities."[100] Another report suggested that the group was comprised of "problem families" and lacked "high-level leadership."[101] Despite the fact that the garin had been unified in their desire to immigrate collectively, Chaim Feifel confirmed that "the minute we moved to Yamit, there really wasn't anything solid between the people . . . [we had] nothing in common." Ultimately, he admitted that "my relationships with the Israelis were much better than with the Americans."[102]

In May 1976 tensions at Yamit spilled onto the pages of the *Yamiton*. In a public airing of grievances, Garin Yamit president Carole Rosenblatt devoted her English-language column to condemning Ministry of Housing representative Rafi Leshem, calling for him to be fired and replaced with a more competent city manager who would address the settlement's problems.[103] Leshem published a riposte pointedly titled "L-Maan Shituf Peula [For the Sake of Cooperation]" in the same issue, condemning "personal ambitions" and "unfounded accusations" that had "tarnished the good public image of Yamit" and allowed a "foul odor to enter the settlement," pleading for patience and cooperation "for the future of Yamit and the good of her residents."[104] By July conditions were so dismal that a visitor who came to explore opportunities to promote the Yamit project to North American audiences felt compelled to write Uzi Narkiss "to point out what I feel is the overall negative atmosphere existent in Yamit" and a "lack of community spirit of any kind" where "almost no-one had a good word to say about the place or about their fellow settlers."[105] By the end of 1976 even Israeli officials privately acknowledged their fundamental failures at Yamit, admitting that "we didn't succeed in realizing their dreams, despite the maximal efforts that the state provided to them."[106]

While Yamit's problems became increasingly serious and complex as the city expanded, some idealism and enthusiasm remained. "For most people Yamit is just a name on the map [but] for us Yamit is a living vibrant force that grows and changes each day," Chaim Feifel wrote back to the United States in August 1976 to celebrate his first anniversary in their new home. He boasted of the 140 families that now lived in the city, the completion of 350 new apartments, and the opening of a twelve-room schoolhouse for a growing population of children. While Feifel openly acknowledged that "the beautiful picture . . . is only one-sided. The other side reminds us that coming to a new country and a development city presents problems in living," he also sought to downplay tensions within the community as "the citizens all have their share of gripes and complaints, but they also take matters into their own hands to try and effect positive change." All and all, their central idea had been realized, "and here we are—really living in this place!"[107] Carole Rosenblatt echoed this sentiment in the anniversary issue of the *Yamiton,* concluding her essay about the brief history of the American garin with "this first year at Yamit, we give a special thanks to all of the crazy people who believed in the dream—and helped make it a reality."[108]

"My Own Personal Holocaust": The Fall of Yamit, 1977–1982

By 1977 Yamit was beginning to thrive. The city had doubled in size again in only six months' time, now housing approximately 250 families. That spring and summer also brought some of Garin Yamit's last happy moments. Gedaliah Mazal and his Israeli fiancée, Gila, a reporter for *Time* magazine, were married on the grounds of Yamit's new schoolhouse—it was the first wedding in the new city and the entire community participated in the event. Yamit's beach also continued to attract a large number of visitors. New construction authorization for Robert Smolen's luxury resort had the potential to transform the city into a tourism mecca. Residents hoped that Yamit would emerge as the shining star of the Israeli south.

On 17 May 1977, the residents of Yamit joined their compatriots across Israel in going to the polls to cast ballots for the ninth Knesset. According to Gedaliah Mazal, who ran an ad hoc electoral commission for his garin, about 90 American-Israelis turned out, splitting their votes between the centrist Democratic Movement for Change (30), the right-leaning Likud

(27), the leftist Alignment (22), the National Religious Party (5, including Mazal), and other smaller parties.[109] Clearly, Jewish-American immigrants at Yamit did not feel the need for strategic voting to ensure their future in the Sinai. However, with the victory of a Likud government headed by the hawkish settlement proponent Prime Minister Menachem Begin—which broke almost three decades of Labor Party domination in Israel since 1948—continued support for the city seemed all but assured.

If the 1977 elections are often described as an "earthquake" in Israeli political life, the residents of Yamit were about to experience an unanticipated aftershock: the Egyptian-Israeli peace process. Yet there were few public early warnings; five months after the elections, Prime Minister Begin visited Yamit to dedicate its new community center, signing the city's guestbook with the message "Jerusalem Blesses Yamit, which will be built and become the joy of the nation and its pride."[110] Stopping by Moshav Naot Sinai afterward, Begin expressed his desire to retire there following his prime-ministership.[111] Yamit's residents looked forward to future government patronage and continued expansion under the Begin administration.

Little did they know that two weeks before Begin's famed visit, he had authorized Foreign Minister Moshe Dayan to create a covert diplomatic backchannel with Egypt and pass a classified three-line memorandum that gave Israel's consent to exchange the entirety of the Sinai Peninsula for a peace deal.[112] This rapprochement was followed by Egyptian president Anwar Sadat's historic visit to Jerusalem in November 1977. Over the course of the next nine months, Begin continued to publicly reject territorial concessions while his Israeli negotiating team secretly formulated plans for the evacuation of the Sinai. Residents of Yamit were not included in any governmental discussions about the future of their city.

By early 1978 it was clear that the State of Israel's support for Yamit had diminished. On a return visit to the city in January, Foreign Minister Moshe Dayan announced to the assembled crowds, "If you stand in the way of peace, the country is not going to back you."[113] The Jewish-American residents of the Sinai were staggered. Moshav Sadot resident Jeannie Illan, originally from Los Angeles, told the *New York Times*, "Dayan was the father of Sadot, Dayan pushed in the Knesset for settlement here, and now, what is to become of us?"[114] Zvi Arenstein, who reported on Dayan's speech for the *Jerusalem Post*, wrote, "Today, the inhabitants of Yamit are in a state of psychological shock: they simply cannot believe their ears. After years of reassurances and promises, of being lulled into believing that giving the area back to Egypt was absolutely out of the question, they are facing a new reality . . . we didn't come here to live in Egypt." He then outlined two scenarios for the city, opining, "What is the road to take? One will turn Yamit into a Jewish community (complete with a yeshiva) on the border between two developing countries, each helping the other. The other will make the partially completed plans for a city of 100,000 people as worthless as the sand-dunes it was to be built upon."[115] Arenstein and his family chose to leave Yamit in 1978.

The remaining members of the Jewish-American group were both intellectually and emotionally unprepared for profound change. Many expressed unease about their futures but seemed to be in denial about the severity of the situation. Some, like Yamit's postmaster Jeffrey Benjamin, formerly of Albany, New York, simply described the situation as "our depression."[116] Others took an unrealistically optimistic view. "When Begin proposed giving back the Sinai, it just blew our minds,"[117] Gedaliah Mazal acknowledged, but expressed confidence that nothing would change: "As a resident of Yamit, Israel, I am . . . concerned about what will happen to us in the Rafah Salient. . . . I have no thoughts about living in any other place than Yamit. I do not see any panic in our minds and those who are concerned as I am, are living an everyday life, as we always have. We came with government backing in 1974 and continue to have that backing even today. . . . Although the government has been somewhat slow in the past, today we are getting greater attention and support. We are here to stay and will remain always under Israeli administration and sovereignty."[118] Carole Rosenblatt, writing to a group of Floridians who had recently toured Yamit, had a utopian vision, musing, "Many reporters have already asked how we would feel being a real border town—with friendly borders. Frankly, I can't imagine it so I don't know how I'd feel (except it would probably be great for business!) Can you imagine Sadat dropping in for a milkshake!"[119]

These aspirations notwithstanding, the sands were shifting quickly at Yamit. In September 1978 Begin and Sadat attended a ten-day meeting hosted by U.S. President Jimmy Carter at the Camp David retreat in Maryland and signed a "Framework for Peace" (also known as the Camp David Accords) containing a preliminary agreement regarding the peninsula.[120] On 26 March 1979 Egypt and Israel concluded a bilateral peace treaty that definitively called for the full-phased Israeli withdrawal of armed forces and civilians from the Sinai.[121]

Finally, members of the Jewish-American garin recognized that the signatures on the peace accords represented the handwriting on the wall for Yamit. Chaim Feifel lamented the loss of a pioneering dream, where "it was an exciting time. You were building a new community with your own hands. With Camp David, it all came to a stop." Sarah Feifel took the news much harder, telling a journalist, "After Camp David, I walked down to the beach and wept. I went through all the stages of mourning."[122]

When Prime Minister Begin returned to Yamit to talk about the peace treaty in April 1979, he received an angry reception from its radicalized settlers—his security team even placed snipers on city roofs to protect against a potential assassination attempt. As residents denounced him with catcalls of "Liar!" "Crook!" "Traitor!" and "The shame of Israel!"[123] Begin responded, "If you want to curse me, go ahead. I know it hurts—it hurts me too—but everything I did was for peace and the future of the people of Israel."[124] Prime Minister Begin even offered his personal sympathies to Chaim Feifel in an exchange of letters, writing,

> My dear friend . . .
>
> Your words moved me deeply. I wish you to know that the Knesset vote concerning our settlements in the Sinai was one of the most agonizing decisions I have ever shared. It is a pain I will carry with me until the end of my days . . . [yet] I could not, in all good conscience, have acted otherwise. I can understand the uncertainty and confusion you describe. With this, I ask you, dear friend, to be patient. We, the Government, shall not, God forbid, renounce our responsibilities. . . . I do not, for one moment, minimize the difficulties. I can only appeal to your understanding of my national responsibility to do all in my power to bring peace to our nation. I write these lines to you from the heart.[125]

Gedaliah Mazal, who was in attendance at Begin's rally, expressed, "We were shocked. Not one person thought this was real. We just thought that they were talking, but it would never come to be . . . but in the end, it entered our consciousness, we understood that the city no longer had a future."[126] Carole Rosenblatt also internalized the consequences of the disengagement during Begin's visit, suggesting, "When we learned Yamit was going to be turned over to Egypt, we were stunned. All along we'd been assured that it wouldn't happen, and then it did." She soon came to realize that political currents would also bring about material changes, musing to a reporter, "We have a unique standard of living here, I've got a nice three-bedroom house with a 20-foot long living room and a barbeque in the yard. I'd have to be a millionaire to find the same thing in Tel Aviv."[127]

As the details of the Israeli cabinet's $263 million compensation settlement package (an average of about $188,000 per family) became public, it did not alleviate all the concerns of American-Israelis at Yamit.[128] Rosenblatt became quite vocal about perceived mistreatment of entrepreneurs, contending that while homeowners were paid restitution on apartments and villas, the government refused to compensate her for parking and other concessions at the beach that were paid in advance.[129] Meanwhile, Russians and Israelis with closer ties to the government were able to extract additional benefits. Echoing her earlier complaints, Rosenblatt grumbled, "The whole thing was dirty, because people knew how to play the game." In the end she was so aggrieved that "as soon as we had the ok that we were going to get compensation, we took red paint and sprayed the entire house—there was a lot of bitterness."[130]

Moreover, Rosenblatt sensed the animosity of Israeli government officials toward any accommodation for Yamit's residents in their future lives beyond Yamit, suggesting, "The Ministry of Housing were all these little clerks, that hardly made any money, who sat in offices, and they couldn't *stand* the thoughts that maybe we would get compensated." Further, "The bureaucrats were awful, but the hardest part was the way Israelis treated us. Everyone assumed we'd planned this, to come to Yamit, and then be paid to leave. Afterwards, they all thought we were rich—when landlords heard 'Yamit,' the rent went up. For years, my kids refused to admit they were from Yamit. The assumption was we'd scammed the government. The truth was exactly the opposite."[131] Chaim Feifel corroborated these sentiments, recalling that when passersby noticed the Yamit address on his panel truck on a trip to Tel Aviv in the late 1970s, they spit on him, threw stones at his vehicle, and yelled "Thieves! You're stealing all the money from the State!" Sarah Feifel added with profound sadness, "We turned around from being halutzim [pioneers] to *rodfei peza* [reparations chasers]."

While resigned to leaving the city-settlement, remaining members of Garin Yamit felt that the government had given up on their larger pioneering dreams. One Jewish-American working at Ben-Gurion University explained, "We have been living here in limbo for the last year. The government has made no effort to help resettle us anywhere elsewhere. Instead, they just want us here as 'hostages' in case the peace treaty fails." Her husband added that the government needed to find them a creative solution because "we have no desire to live in a development town, and we can't afford to start up again in one of the large cities." "We have been treated as non-entities by the government," Sarah Feifel echoed, "people here are so disheartened and disillusioned. They just don't have the willpower to start over again." Carole Rosenblatt, still the nominal president of Garin Yamit, reminded the Ministry of Absorption of the remaining idealism in the group, observing that "they didn't want to take the money and go." She tried to explain to bureaucrats that while her group had once been untested immigrants, "by the time they were in Yamit for a few years, their babies were born, they spoke Hebrew, they had professions. Now they were viable to be an immigrant anywhere." She begged officials to organize tours to other parts of the country, but with inadequate government response, "these people left [for the United States] . . . and they never looked back. It's a shame . . . they lost a whole generation."[132] While she confirmed her intention to stay in Israel with her children, Rosenblatt lamented to a reporter, "We face the same situation we did five years ago. Only this time, the Zionism is gone."[133]

Most American-Israelis at Yamit were left in limbo in its last year awaiting the reparations payments they needed to start a new life in Israel or to return to the United States. In early 1981 Chaim Feifel made the momentous decision to stop buying inventory for the store, often spending his days aimlessly (if enjoyably) at the beach. Carole Rosenblatt also struggled with the inevitability that overshadowed daily life, recalling, "I had built this most beautiful garden, with all these trees growing, and I'm standing there with the hose saying, 'Do I water, or not? I can't take the trees with me, they're going to bulldoze them for the Egyptians—or maybe the Egyptians will like them?' Nobody knew what was going to happen." For her, the final year was an excruciating wait, "People were leaving, people were crying, people were swearing, it was the most awful feeling."[134]

For many, the eventual payment of fiscal restitution was inadequate compensation for their physical and emotional investment in the city. Sarah Feifel had a psychological crisis, remembering, "It was very difficult. . . .

I took things personally in those years and . . . I got to a point where I was really, really hysterical, you couldn't talk to me, I was *so* angry, *so* angry." Only with the help of a psychotherapy group for Yamit residents, "all of a sudden, I realized my mental health was more important than being hysterical." The couple chose to "turn their energy inward," using their compensation to commission an architect to build a new house (and life) in the northern coastal town of Zichron Yaakov. Yet as Chaim Feifel explained, "Consciously we thought we were detached, but we weren't. The trauma lasted a long time. . . . We'd do crazy things, things that normally you don't do, and we did it without even realizing it was the result of the trauma." While the couple refused to elaborate, it was clearly a sore point to the present day.[135]

The Feifels were not alone in their trauma. Journalist Yocheved Miriam Russo, who revisited the Yamit withdrawal in 2007, suggested that "the pain and disillusionment the residents felt was beyond explaining." In an interview with her decades after the disengagement, Mazal still struggled to put his feelings into words, remembering, "It was horrific . . . you can't imagine the despair . . . we were losing everything we'd dreamed of and worked for. It was very difficult." Psychological trauma hit close to home for Mazal, as his was one of fifty divorces in the city during the period. He refused to speak about the breakup; one reporter speculated that the split was caused by the couple's disagreement over participation in the protest movement at the end of Yamit.[136] Mazal even witnessed one of the eight suicides in the last years at Yamit, when "one day, just after *mincha* [the afternoon prayer], I was sitting in my living room when the guy in the house next to mine—an army guy with three boys—shot himself. The bullet went through his window, through my bedroom window, and lodged in my closet, where the police had to dig it out." Summing up his memories to the reporter, Mazal concluded, "For me, Yamit was my own personal Holocaust."[137]

Partially in response to the Holocaust symbolism of going like sheep to the slaughter,[138] three distinct protest movements appeared in and around the seaside city in its last year. Local farmers and businesspeople separately engaged in direct negotiations with the government as well as joined together in high-profile media and civil disobedience actions in order to protest their compensation packages and the forced withdrawal from the city. Chaim Feifel opined, "Those people who made a big noise . . . they were very smart, because when it came to *pizuim* [reparations], the government gave them more, just to keep them quiet. . . . We didn't know how to play the game."[139] The third collective was a large, nonindigenous movement calling itself Ha-Tenua L-Azirat Ha-Nesiga B-Sinai (The Movement to Halt the Retreat in the Sinai [MHRS], led by longtime Gush Emunim (Bloc of the Faithful) and Tehiya (Renaissance) party activists Hanan Porat, Uri Elitzur, Moshe Merhavia, and Geula Cohen and their ragtag following of party members, yeshiva students, youth group affiliates, and some secular residents of Yamit. MHRS effectively became the face of the protest movement, obscuring local, largely ineffective groups.

In the end, the battle for Yamit was mostly fought by those who had little connection to the city itself and who espoused a religio-political ideology alien to the settlement.[140] Their campaign sat uncomfortably with the Jewish-American immigrants who had struggled to build Yamit. "This was the issue," Sarah Feifel explained, "Everybody in Yamit in '78, after Sadat came, all of us became like a family and all those people who came to protest against giving back Yamit, they were outsiders." Their presence irked locals like Feifel who felt that a foreign contingent had occupied her town and changed the dynamic of daily life, citing, "Like on Friday mornings, you went into the supermarket to get your challah and they had already purchased all the challot—there wasn't any challah for you! . . . I remember in the beginning until people got electricity, until people got telephones, until everything was connected in their homes—and then all of a sudden, these people, they come and they have [it all]? . . . Who gave them? How was it all possible?"[141] Chaim Feifel also took umbrage with the ideology and tactics of the MHRS, which contradicted the loyal opposition of Yamit's own residents. He had a major disagreement with Rabbi Haim Druckman, a sitting Knesset member, over his role in encouraging disobedience toward the IDF. Their son Azi also refused his rabbis' pleas to leave his yeshiva and lead fellow students in the last struggle for Yamit. For the most part, the Jewish-American garin absented itself from the protest movement in Yamit's final days, although some members like Carole Rosenblatt and Zvi Arenstein participated in demonstrations in the years preceding the evacuation.[142] Most Jewish-American immigrants resigned themselves to their fate to evacuate the city and left town as soon as they were provided compensation for their homes and businesses.[143]

Gedaliah Mazal wanted little to do with the protest movement and left Yamit before its scheduled demolition date in April 1982. "I wasn't a protestor," noted Mazal, a newly divorced father of a toddler that feared losing his position at Ben-Gurion University, "I couldn't afford it. I was lucky: I had a good job and I was in Israel for the long haul . . . I didn't want to have anything to do with politics, I came to live in the land, I didn't come here to beat down the bushes."[144] He even pointedly told MHRS leader and settlement activist Hanan Porat that he wanted nothing to do with their battle. His views notwithstanding, activists took over his abandoned residence for use as a command center in the weeks before the withdrawal.[145]

On 8 February 1982, Gedaliah Mazal left Yamit for the last time. He evoked the biblical parable of Lot's wife in recounting the events, chronicling, "I didn't have to go alone. My Rav [fellow Jewish-American immigrant] Rabbi Natan Reisner, came with me. We drove back [from Beersheva], turned in the keys, paid off the last water bill. Then we just drove away. 'Don't look back,' Rav Reisner told me, and I didn't. I didn't turn around. I didn't look back."[146] On 23 April 1982, nine years to the very day that he had first visited Yamit with the WUJS delegation, Mazal watched his home bull-dozed to the ground on national television. "[I] actually saw it happen," Mazal remembered, "It was shocking. It was hard to take. It was worse than an earthquake."[147]

In Yamit's final days in April 1982, MHRS activists employed violent tactics against the IDF, storming road barricades and attempting to reach the city by sea, assaulting military troops with burning tires, stones, rocks, and chemicals, engaging in civil disobedience tactics, and even scaling a war monument, requiring the Israeli army to remove them by crane.[148] Most dramatically, a small suicide cell of followers of American-Israeli radical Rabbi Meir Kahane holed up in an abandoned structure in the city during its last hours, rigging the building with explosives and vowing that one member would kill themselves every half hour if the withdrawal continued.[149] When government pleas and prayers with Israel's Chief Rabbis failed to deter them, Kahane was flown back from meetings in New York and convinced the group to leave on its own volition.[150] On 23 April 1982, the settlement of Yamit was bulldozed to the ground and buried in the sand.[151]

"Yamit disappeared very quickly," wrote Azi Feifel, who came to the city at the age of twelve and left the only home in Israel he had ever known at the age of twenty, but the pain still lingered for him as an adult, adding, "I sometimes feel a shooting pang of longing for our short-lived haven. But the pain is no longer sharp or intense. It's just a delicate tenderness in some remote area of the heart, a scar healed over." Yet, as his father had explained to him, "Yamit was like a puddle of clear water. But when a foot comes and stirs the dirt settled at the bottom, the water remains muddy for quite some time. Yamit may have been a panacea for certain social ills, but the trauma caused by its dismantling was long felt, especially by families with weaker foundations."[152] Both the Feifels and Carole Rosenblatt spoke of how the experience at Yamit had transformed some of their children into troubled youth. It took years for their teenagers to come to terms with their adult parents. For Chaim Feifel himself, the experience in the Sinai changed his entire personality, explaining, "I was very active at Yamit, very social, [but] once I got out of Yamit I became very recessive . . . go slowly with the flow . . . I'm not a pusher anymore, it changed my entire life. So in that sense, until this day, I'm very quiet and I don't have friends." Sarah Feifel "took a long time to get over it," and coped with prolonged psychological strain.[153] Carole Rosenblatt, who suffered financial straits after Yamit, also endured an estranged relationship with one son who moved back to the United States after the withdrawal.[154] In darker moments, the trauma was almost too much to bear for Gedaliah Mazal, who lamented, "In the sand of Yamit, I not only buried my home and my family, but also my life dream. I live now only through the power of inertia, so twenty years have passed."[155] For Garin Yamit members who had spent the best years of their adulthood building the city, it was difficult to cope with their paradise lost.

Yet, for the most part, Yamit's American-Israeli residents look back on their sojourn in the Sinai with warm nostalgia. "Until the end, I never had a sad day in Yamit," Gedaliah Mazal recalled, "I was always happy. It was a paradise. . . . Every day there was a blessing."[156] Carole Rosenblatt felt that her life in the Sinai may have been a blessing in disguise, acknowledging, "If I had to do it today, and with what I understand, maybe I would have tried something else . . . [but] I'm certainly glad I brought my kids to Israel to live. I think Yamit was the only solution for me at that point." Now a great-grandmother, she reflected, "I certainly made a Jewish family." Yamit was also a place of self-realization and exciting exploits for Rosenblatt, as "I think the whole aliya changed me, because all of sudden I had to be a woman sticking up for my own rights . . . I mean, my mother never believed it because I had been a very shy girl, but I could talk to Begin and Rabin! . . . Yamit was just a short experience in my life, part of it, and it helped. I think everything you do helps build . . . makes you see things differently. Life should be an adventure!"[157] As the American-Israel "mother" of Yamit, Sarah Feifel shared in this sense of female empowerment, noting, "In 1973 I was 33 years old, it was a very interesting time in my life. I look back at it—it was very exciting. . . . It was really such a *huge* contrast to being this girl that grew up in America, that lived American values." "From 1974 until 1982, how many years is that?" she mused, "It's a very short time, but it's a very big time, in terms of memories . . . the impression it left on my life . . . for me, it was a wonderful, wonderful experience . . . happy formative times." For Garin Yamit's Jewish-American "father" Chaim Feifel, the endeavor "gave me a chance to understand who and what I am. What I can do and what I can't do. I did things that go *way* beyond what I ever thought I could do . . . it's only after that I said, 'how did I do it? Was I crazy?'" Summing up his experience in the Sinai, he simply stated, "I tell you, it was one of the six and half best years of my life."[158] In the end, the *Yamiton* left the American-Israeli residents of the city with its enduring image—a small sketch on the last page of its final issue of a moving truck slowly driving away.

TODAY THE SAGA of Yamit is often evoked in the context of political debates about future withdrawals from the occupied territories in the interest of peace. The 2005 disengagement from Gaza—a place where some settlers at Yamit had taken up residence only to experience a second dislocation—looked back to the Sinai as a symbol of struggle. In recent years, with a revolution in Egypt and new uncertainty over the status of the Israeli-Egyptian peace treaty, the memory of Yamit once again rushes back to the shoreline of our consciousness.

As this narrative has revealed, the relationship between the Jewish-American garin, the Israeli government, the native Israeli settler movement, and the Palestinian and Bedouin communities was a fluid and dynamic partnership. Most of all, Garin Yamit triumphed in its core objective of living at Yamit and shaping the currents of day-to-day life in the city. It was as active and earnest participants in the local community that Garin Yamit left their lasting watermark.

However, the Jewish-American group could not fight the tides of change. When the Israeli government initiated a top-down peace process with Egypt that culminated in the full military and civil evacuation of the Sinai Peninsula in 1982, local residents were powerless against the tsunami of official policy and public opinion. In the end, the hopes, dreams, and achievements of Garin Yamit were washed away, living on only in their memories.

As the discourse of Garin Yamit reveals, the group envisioned their Zionist settlement experiment in making the desert bloom also as a deeply American opportunity for new-age pioneering, building a utopian community, and engaging in self-realization. Ultimately, members of this Jewish-American group were both idealists and pragmatists, who built their dream city but peacefully allowed it to wash away. Garin Yamit rode the wave but recognized the tide of the future. In the end they abandoned their city of the sea, looking to the horizon of peace between Israel and her neighbors.

CHAPTER THREE

Redemption in Occupied Suburbia?

Rabbi Shlomo Riskin and the West Bank Settlement of Efrat

"For a Jew, It's Home." Thus estimated Rabbi Shlomo (Steven) Riskin of his life's work in establishing the settlement of Efrat (Efrata in Hebrew), an enclave of Jewish-American immigrants in the Gush Etzion (Tree of Zion) region of the West Bank. Serving a population of several thousand American-Israelis today, Efrat is an upscale suburban settlement often stereotyped by both its habitants and its opponents as "occupied Scarsdale," promising million-dollar mansions alongside messianic redemption over the Green Line. In this yuppie paradise, Jewish-American settlers such as Riskin built "the bridge between our origins and our dreams."[1] How did this city on a hilltop become the political "capital of the Gush" since the 1973 war?[2]

Efrat was the product of a marriage of interests between native Israeli settler movement activist Moshe Moshkowitz and the New York–based modern Orthodox spiritual leader Shlomo Riskin. Efrat's unique parentage produced both a new model for settling in the occupied territories as well as a hybridized discourse surrounding the settlement project that combined apocalypticism with American utopianism, strategic imperatives with suburbia, Zionist mythology with modern-day pioneering, and an ultranationalist vision with liberal values. This dual ancestry allowed for a highly successful working relationship with Israel authorities, while imbuing the community with its distinctly American character.

Yet, at various turning points, the Efrat project often felt like a bridge to nowhere between Jewish-American immigrants, the Israeli government, native Israeli settler activists, and local Palestinian communities. While Efrat had the kind of close relationship with top Israeli officials that other Jewish-American settlements lacked, the settlement also challenged the State's agenda during the Camp David and Oslo peace processes. Though its founders shared deep ties with Israeli settler leaders, both Moshkowitz and Riskin broke with Ha-Kibbutz Ha-Dati (the religious kibbutz organization) and Gush Emunim (Bloc of the Faithful) over their community's place and future within the movement. Last but not least, Efrat has been embroiled in conflict with her Palestinian neighbors for almost four decades and could be evacuated as a part of a final status agreement.

This city on a hilltop is a pivotal example of the clash between Jewish-American liberal ideology and settler realities. In particular, this narrative focuses on the persona and politics of Rabbi Riskin, a self-described "passionate moderate," whose views and vision serve as a vantage point into the attitudes of the larger population at Efrat as it has evolved over the past forty years. A quixotic and controversial figure, his contribution to the settlement project is truly unique both within the history of Jewish-American settlement in the occupied territories and the larger Israeli settler project since 1967.

RABBI RISKIN LIKES to tell his version of how Efrat was established in the mid-1970s:

> [In the summer of 1976] he [Moshe Moshkowitz] took me in the car to an empty hill that was someday to become Efrat. He looked at me and said, "You know, they once asked Dizengoff, the first mayor of Tel Aviv, how one could become the mayor of a city in Israel. Dizengoff responded, 'in Israel, if you want to become the mayor of a city, you have to build the city.' . . . A city could be established in this location, with the condition that it be a city founded by new immigrants from countries of plenty like America . . . educated immigrants who were coming out of choice, rather than escaping from poverty or persecution. Let us be partners. You find the new immigrants and I will take care of the Israeli bureaucracy. And you'll see: in a short time, a city will stand on this spot, a city in which I will the mayor and you will be the chief Rabbi." We shook

hands . . . I believed it could happen. My dream of aliya had finally been resurrected.[3]

This carefully honed narrative, which Riskin has perfected in interviews over the past forty years, hearkens back to several historical themes. Evoking Israel Zangwill's trope of "a land without a people for a people without a land," the rabbi mobilized Zionist history to lay the groundwork for the claim that Efrat was built on "empty" state land that did not disenfranchise Palestinians or expropriate any of their territory. The notion that he and Moshkowitz imagined themselves as modern-day Dizengoffs (the city planner and first mayor of Tel Aviv), building a kind of *Ahuzat Bayit* (lit. Homestead Society) beyond the Green Line, placed the two within a hallowed Zionist pantheon and likened Efrat to the utopian renewal project of the first Hebrew city. (Certainly the image of a new "bourgeoisie city" later became closely associated with Efrat.)[4] Further, just as Tel Aviv was envisioned as the crown jewel of the *Yishuv* and a model for Zionist settlement, Efrat too would be a "city on a hilltop" to both Israel and the Diaspora Jewish community. Last but not least, the "resurrection" of Riskin's dream invoked the messianic influences on his suburban ideal. Thus, from the very origins of this city-settlement, its spiritual leader clearly positioned himself within a historical discourse that would play a pivotal role in the literal and figurative construction of the settlement.

Moshe Moshkowitz and the Reimagining of Gush Etzion: Efrat, 1973–1976

Long before Rabbi Riskin first appeared on the scene, native Israeli settlement activist Moshe Moshkowitz envisioned the future settlement of Efrat as the bridge between his origins and his dreams for the occupied territories.

Born in Bratislava, Czechoslovakia, in 1925, Moshe Moshkowitz (commonly known by his nickname "Moshko") was one of four children born to a wealthy industrialist, proud Zionist, and member of the *Mizrachi* religious Zionist movement.[5] Concluding of the dark clouds gathering over the continent that "in Europe there was no chance for Jews," he moved his family to Palestine in 1935, buying property in the Beit Shean valley.[6] His son received a scholarship to the Mikve Yisrael agricultural school and pursued a career as a dairyman. In 1945, Moshe Moshkowitz joined Kibbutz Messuot Yitzhak in Gush Etzion, fulfilling his belief that "the real Land of Israel is between Hebron and Bethlehem."[7]

While their religio-historical claims to the Gush Etzion area are highly contentious, many settler activists over the past fifty years have asserted biblical ties to the region. What can be determined is that several locales in today's West Bank appear in the Hebrew Bible—Efrat is mentioned in the Book of Genesis as the site where the matriarch Rachel died in childbirth—and archaeological excavations reveal successive waves of human settlement and infrastructure until the modern period. Beginning in 1517, the territory was loosely controlled by the Ottoman Empire, until it was incorporated into the *sanjak* (semiautonomous administrative district) of Jerusalem in 1872. Gush Etzion was governed under the British mandate in Palestine after World War I.

The region also played a storied role in early Zionist history as the site of several significant waves of settlement prior to the founding of the State of Israel. Jewish encampment in Gush Etzion was first romanticized in travel writing in the early twentieth century while still under nominal Ottoman rule.[8] Yemenite immigrant members of the Zichron David (Memory of David) organization first settled at Migdal Edar (Watchtower of the Flock) in 1927, although the isolated community was destroyed only two years later during the Hebron riots.[9] In 1933 native Jerusalemite entrepreneur Shmuel Tzvi Holtzmann purchased 5,000 dunams of land—including the holdings of Zichron David at Migdal Edar and its surrounding area—and founded a new settlement company, which he fittingly called El Ha-Har (To the Mountain).[10] In addition to lending his name to the region itself (a translation from the Yiddish *holtz,* meaning tree), Holtzmann and his corporation worked to establish two new settlements, an agricultural kibbutz called Kfar Etzion (Etzion Village) and a tourist compound at Yaar Etzion (Etzion Forest) between 1934 and 1936. Once again, these communities were quickly abandoned during the Arab Revolt (1936–1939). In 1943 a group of religious youth from the Ha-Poel Ha-Mizrachi (the Mizrachi Worker Party) joined together as "Kvuzat Abraham" (Abraham's Group, named after the first Chief Rabbi of Palestine, Rabbi Abraham Isaac Ha-Cohen Kook) to repopulate Kfar Etzion, which was followed by adjoining settlements at Messuot Yitzhak (Beacons of Isaac) in 1945 and Ein Tsurim (Spring of the Rocks) in 1946.[11] A year later, a kibbutz sponsored by the socialist Ha-Shomer Ha-Tsair (Youth Guard) took root at Revadim.[12]

According to some estimates, there were upward of 450 settlers (409 adults and 69 children) living in the Gush Etzion region in 1948, although less than half of its 20,000-dunam land mass was actually owned by the Zionist land management institution Keren Kayemet L-Yisrael (Jewish National Fund).[13]

Three years after Moshkowitz and his family moved to Kibbutz Messuot Yitzhak, the Gush Etzion settlements fell under attack by surrounding Arab forces. Then, in December 1947, the area was beset by a protracted and deadly six-month siege. While most of the women and children were evacuated to Jerusalem—Moshkowitz's own wife was smuggled out in a cattle truck—male residents stayed behind to protect the *kibbutzim* and took part in several battles that later entered the post-war historical mythology.[14] Moshkowitz himself organized one of the last airlifts to the region in April 1948, although his plan to return to the kibbutz to fight on was thwarted when his seat on the tiny Piper airplane was filled with guns, ammunition, and Passover matzah instead.[15] A reduced Jewish force held out, evoking the biblical trope of the many against the few that would later come to define the 1948 war narrative, but the group was cut off from Jerusalem and undersupplied.[16] On May 12, 1948, two days before the birth of the State of Israel, Arab Legion troops assisted by local irregulars surrounded Kfar Etzion shouting "Deir Yassin"—referencing the name of the nearby Palestinian village that was the site of a massacre by Irgun Tsvai Leumi (National Military Organization, IZL) and Lohamei Herut Israel (Fighters for the Freedom of Israel, LEHI) paramilitary forces on 9 April—and launched a final assault on the kibbutzim.[17] They quickly defeated the weakened and isolated Jewish residents, killing most of the 155 male and female Jewish force—the height of battlefield casualties in Zionist history to that date.[18] (Some of the injured were taken as prisoners of war.) Corpses lay in the field until mid-1949 when the Kingdom of Transjordan allowed Israel's chief rabbi Shlomo Goren to collect the bodies. With much pomp and circumstance, they were buried in a ceremony at the state cemetery on Mount Herzl as martyrs to the Zionist cause.[19]

The massacre at Gush Etzion would live on in the fledgling state's collective memory and foundational mythology. Only a year later, the new Israeli government proclaimed its annual day of remembrance for fallen soldiers on the anniversary and Prime Minister David Ben-Gurion penned a poem in honor of the repatriation of Gush Etzion's POWs.[20] The event also emerged as a defining moment of Israeli popular mobilization, as journalist

Gershom Gorenberg suggested, "[there was] no line between the personal and the political; their tragedy belonged to the nation."[21] After 1967, members of the nascent Israeli settler movement who had spent their early years at Gush Etzion were not above exploiting their personal history for political gain. As scholar Michael Feige explained, "For the leaders of Gush Emunim, the story of Gush Etzion was both emotionally moving and ideologically useful . . . they could connect their own narrative of sacred memory and return to the sacred soil of Judea to a consensually accepted heroic story."[22] This theme would emerge as a key element in the establishment of Efrat after the 1973 war.

In the years after 1948, Moshe Moshkowitz suggested that he always hoped to return to Gush Etzion, recalling the nostalgia and deep yearning of its veterans, who "would dream of the day when we would go back and raise our children there, returning them to their heritage." Yet, in the interwar years, "the truth is that, while we dreamed of this, we did not really expect it to happen—not in our lifetimes."[23] Ultimately the collective consciousness of the nation moved on and no Israeli prime minister pursued a revanchist policy prior to the Six Day War.

Like many other displaced residents, Moshkowitz became engaged with other Zionist projects in the early state period. Immediately after the 1948 war he was dispatched to Europe as a Jewish Agency emissary to repatriate Holocaust refugees. In 1949 Moshkowitz returned to the State of Israel to help reestablish Kibbutz Messuot Yitzhak in the Negev. He went on to lead the Sapir Regional Council in the south where his work to integrate new immigrants and develop educational and technical institutions would provide critical expertise for the founding of Efrat. In the meantime, the idea of returning to the Gush remained an elusive fantasy for Moshkowitz and his fellow founders of pre-1948 settlements.

This situation changed dramatically with the 1967 war. The conquest of the occupied territories and the postwar atmosphere radically transformed the worldview of the religious Zionist camp. For Moshkowitz it was "a moment of euphoria [where] we felt that we were in the period of the times of the Messiah." Like many of the sons of Gush Etzion, he immediately contemplated a return to the region.[24] On June 7, the third day of the war, while Israeli forces overran the West Bank but battle was still under way, Moshkowitz supposedly produced a diary entry entitled "Suggestions and Plans for the Rebuilding of Gush Etzion," outlining his ideas for agricultural and urban development in the area with associated economic, educational, cultural, medical, tourism, and recreational facilities.[25] A week after the conclusion of hostilities, Moshkowitz served as the designated representative of the pre-1948 Kibbutz Messuot Yitzhak nominated to tour Gush Etzion with Raanan Weitz, director of the Jewish Agency Settlement Division.[26] "We have an obligation and that is to build the Gush anew," the settlement veteran was said to have lectured the select group, but recognizing current conditions, he advised, "Today, there is no chance to start new kibbutzim here. The ground is not fertile and the kibbutzim are already going out of fashion . . . let us go a bit more to the center of the Gush and establish a large yishuv of . . . families who will do whatever kind of work they want. Some will work here, some in Jerusalem. We will establish educational institutions . . . [and] be a community unto ourselves."[27] Although Moshkowitz had another project in mind at the time, these ideas would come to full fluorescence at Efrat.

Popular momentum supporting renewed settlement in Gush Etzion overtook the Eshkol administration as it debated and dithered over the status of the occupied territories in the summer of 1967.[28] That autumn Moshkowitz approached religious Zionist activist Rabbi Yehuda Amital about his initial project in the area: the establishment of a Yeshivat Hesder (a seminary for religious soldiers in the IDF who studied part-time) in Gush Etzion.[29] "I simply told them that I want to return home," Moshkowitz told a meeting of Israeli cabinet members, a sentiment that was appreciated by the secular-socialist Minister of Labor Yigal Allon as "he saw in the Gush the realization of Zionism as he viewed it—settlement, defense, and education. He said it would help protect Jerusalem."[30] The plan received official approval from the Labor government in 1969.

The themes embodied in this early initiative in Gush Etzion foreshadowed Moshkowitz's proposal for a new urban settlement a few years later. As David Morrison contended, "he emphasized that the story of Gush Etzion is not a war story, a memorial story, it is a story of a vibrant center of Jewish learning intended to reach out to all of Israel, and indeed, all over the world."[31] While the government did not undertake any further development in the Etzion bloc until after the Yom Kippur war, Moshkowitz was soon dreaming of a new project along similar lines: Efrat.

THE FIRST ITEM of correspondence in the archival record about Efrat is a letter between Moshe Moshkowitz and his colleague Prime Minister

Yitzhak Rabin in October 1974, exactly a year after the outbreak of the Yom Kippur War.[32] The settler activist opened his note by introducing his strong Zionist credentials, identifying himself as a member of the pre-1948 Kibbutz Messuot Yitzhak, a son of Gush Etzion, and a member of the Zionist elite who was working to redevelop the region as "a living memorial for our friends that fell in the War of Independence." In an opening salvo betraying a shrewd understanding of Israeli politics and priorities at the time, he cannily pitched his new project in practical terms, casting expansion in the region as a strategic buffer after the catastrophic setbacks of the 1973 war. He pointed especially to the need to establish new settlements and encourage the settler "spirit" in the Etzion Bloc as a way of ensuring the "security of the contiguity and connection with Jerusalem." Switching tacks, he alluded to the depressed postwar socioeconomic climate, arguing that investment in Gush Etzion could provide young native families with affordable housing in the Jerusalem area and also aid in the absorption of new Western immigrants. His proposal to establish an urban settlement could be a low-cost solution to the government's problems as both housing and public services would be covered by independent financing. All he asked was for the government to lend its approval, closing his letter with a request for a quick reply to his petition.[33] As Moshkowitz himself suggested, "This was a whole new concept. Who builds a city? The government. The government built Kiryat Arba, Maale Adumim, Neve Yaacov. I asked them to let me try. I told them: I don't request anything more than you would invest in any city you establish; I promise you we will do better."[34]

Moshkowitz's appealing proposal soon received promising responses from high-level Israeli authorities. Israel Galili, Minister Without Portfolio, was so enthused that he sought an immediate consultation with Yehiel Admoni, settlement division director for the World Zionist Organization (WZO), who heartily wished him "Kol Ha-Kavod [lit. all of the honor, kudos] on this initiative." The WZO seemed to take the idea so seriously that it suggested that the city should house 30,000 to 50,000 individuals.[35] Other officials joined suit, urging the project to be pursued swiftly.

In December 1974 Moshkowitz produced a slick brochure containing a site plan for a new city in Gush Etzion. A name had now been selected for this settlement: Efrat. This program also marked the announcement of the creation of the Corporation for the Development of the Judean Hills (Inc.), billed as "a company established on the initiative of friends and veterans of Gush Etzion and a circle of friends in the United States" with "the goal . . . to establish and develop a unique urban community in the Judean Hills."[36]

The précis to the city plan situated the project in time and space but made no mention of the disputed status of the occupied territories and sought to erase the Green Line at Efrat. Echoing the strategic and economic imperatives of his initial letter to the prime minister, Moshkowitz envisioned a new settlement that would serve a population of young families, pensioners, and new immigrants working in Jerusalem.[37] Seamlessly integrating biblical promise with post-1948 mythology, he expressed his hopes for the future in the flowery statement that "with the assistance of the government and the public . . . a new settlement . . . will thrive on the old road that rises up and connects the city of our fathers [Hebron] with the eternal city [Jerusalem]."[38] The remainder of the pamphlet was devoted to technical details about the development of the settlement. Efrat was to be located on rocky terrain—considered "a hostile environment"—and would therefore require intensive site preparation.[39] One might theorize that Moshkowitz emphasized these topological conditions to exaggerate the emptiness and inhospitableness of the land around Efrat in order to preempt preexisting Palestinian land claims, which emerged as a matter of great controversy in future years. The pamphlet did specifically mention the village of Bayt-Fadjar, described as a community of 2,500 Palestinians mostly employed in the quarrying business, but residents' views were not represented concerning the proposal for an adjoining urban Jewish settlement. The community of al-Khader, the main opponent to the city's development in future years, was not mentioned at all.[40] The original prospectus indicated that the 1,200-dunam plot—the land parcel upon which the city of Efrat would sit—was owned by the state and that an additional 1,000 dunams were "relinquished from the hands of their owners" and had been "checked and found permissible." No verification process was detailed in the archival file, however, which has led some later critics to charge that this was a "fiction" of "official Israeli dogma."[41] Today, Palestinians charge that the settlement of Efrat violates international law and private landholders have filed suit in the Israeli High Court to adjudicate claims to land parcels that were retroactively declared state holdings to allow for further expansion of the city (which will be discussed later in this chapter). However, to date I have not located any legal petitions regarding the original plot. Sketches of the housing, educational, commercial, and light-industry plans for the Efrat project were also included for consideration. Moshkowitz summarized the city as "a settlement where a social framework would be developed whose contribution to the absorption of immigrants and integration of the veteran population will be very unique."[42]

Cabinet-level response to the Efrat plan was a complete success, with the Ministry of Housing expressing the sentiment, "We bless this initiative."[43] An official reply from Galili's office requested that the matter be immediately transferred to the Council of Ministers for approval in order to slate Efrat within the upcoming national five-year plan.[44] In less than three months Moshkowitz had secured the kind of official cooperation and key bureaucratic victories that took other Jewish-American groups years to achieve.[45]

To entice potential immigrants, an English-language version of the Efrat brochure was produced in 1975. A comparison between the Hebrew and English editions is a telling indicator of how Moshkowitz's sales pitch to the Israeli government differed from what he hoped to accentuate to American audiences who had recently become involved with the project.[46] Large parts of the booklet are an exact translation of the material into English, but several important departures in organization and emphasis reveal his efforts to underscore—and even aggrandize—the features of Efrat that would appeal to Jewish-American immigrants. These sections included extensive discussions of new initiatives in education, industry, and recruitment of immigrants that were either absent in the 1974 edition or were significantly condensed and buried several pages into the Hebrew document.[47]

Recognizing "the special needs of new immigrants from the developed countries," including the opportunity to take part in the pioneering "challenge of participating in the construction of a new settlement in Israel," the English pamphlet highlighted quality of life and community at Efrat. The booklet outlined luxury housing options (including the potential for future residents to design and construct single family homes, with the additional perk of mortgages on "special conditions given to new immigrants and settlers of newly developed areas"), a charming bedroom community with an easy commute to big-city employment opportunities, a unique school district catering to the educational needs of immigrant students, and a dedicated local bureaucracy. In their leisure time, families could take part in a myriad of recreational programs, including an American-style community center promising "playing fields and a swimming pool."[48] An appendix to the pamphlet allowed future residents to visualize their new life through architectural renderings of housing units, commercial centers, and educational and recreational areas in the new city that were reminiscent of typical American suburbs. Above all, the brochure sought to create a level of comfort for the Jewish-American immigrant by envisioning a new English-speaking community with American suburban amenities and values. By reassuring them that their familiar modes of life would be replicated, the pamphlet served as an important recruitment tool for "suitable" members.

Yet while Jewish-American immigrants dreamed of their future home, the Israeli settler movement deemed the entire project unsuitable. Serious objections soon arose from within the ranks of Ha-Kibbutz Ha-Dati (the religious kibbutz).[49] Despite the fact that the movement had been deeply involved in the development of Gush Etzion from its early days, a new suburban settlement in the occupied territories represented both an ideological and practical challenge to its kibbutz model, which was in decline by the mid-1970s.[50] The very week Minister Galili reached a verbal agreement with the Housing Authority in March 1975—when plans for Efrat were supposed to be top secret!—Secretary Isaac Kochba sent off a terse letter of protest to the former general.[51] "To our surprise," he wrote, "rumors have reached us in recent days that governmental bodies have agreed to the initiative of Mr. Moshkowitz regarding the establishment of a large urban settlement very close to Gush Etzion." "We don't want to get into the 'policy' of this decision," he continued, "but it is our intent to inform you that under no circumstances and in no way do we agree to this proposal, whose actual implication in the very short term—would change the pastoral character of the entire region." Moreover, Kochba asserted, his organization had already laid claim to the site supposedly in question.[52] While acknowledging the importance of further settlement in principle, he urgently counseled that Efrat be moved to a different location. Not to be shown up by a fellow founding member of his own organization, Kochba added in a snooty aside, "I hereby inform you that Mr. Moshkowitz does not represent the Kibbutz Ha-Dati movement."[53]

About a week later, the secretariat of Kibbutz Rosh Tsurim, a core member of the Ha-Kibbutz Ha-Dati framework in the Etzion Bloc, chimed in as well. Initially they struck a less hostile tone, writing, "We heard a happy rumor about the idea of establishing Efrat, and we also heard about the location that has been found for it," assuring Galili, "we truly hope that this city will be established quickly." Yet they voiced their opinion that "the location *certainly doesn't* appeal to us," preferring to see an additional agricultural kibbutz come into existence at the Efrat site. Nonetheless, they too stressed the importance of a new settlement for defensive purposes. "We still feel that the 'Gush' is alone," they opined, "If we have reached the 'good days' where the government wants to establish two settlements beyond the Green Line, it would be best that they don't compete over the same site . . . and locate each settlement in the correct location."[54]

Moshkowitz immediately attempted to mollify the religious kibbutz movement, even taking their representatives on a scenic tour of the proposed site.[55] When these overtures failed, the government stepped in to provide official mediation.[56] After four months of debates and exchanges, the two parties reached an agreement over Efrat's future location in July 1975.[57] Due in large part to state efforts, Ha-Kibbutz Ha-Dati was transformed from a strong antagonist into an ardent supporter of the Efrat project.

In spite of these challenges, Moshkowitz expressed confidence about the project in a summer 1975 interview with the Hebrew daily newspaper *Yediot Ahronot*. A reporter who got wind of the project that June queried, "Will a new city arise between Gush Etzion and Jerusalem?" Based on his sources, he judged, "if everything progresses in line, and if no unforeseen obstacles pile up, Moshe Moshkowitz will succeed in realizing his dream—and in a short time, a new city, without a name, will be established halfway on the road between Bethlehem and the settlements of Gush Etzion."[58] Though the article lacked specifics—and Moshkowitz proffered several untruths and obfuscations in an apparent attempt to conceal the details of high-level negotiations—it is interesting to note how early the plan reached the press and that it was positively presented to the Israeli public at the time.

While ordinary Israelis got their first impression of Efrat in the newspaper that summer, Galili took the opportunity to tour the site with Foreign Minister Yigal Allon in August 1975.[59] The visit went well but no final decision was reached regarding a plan or location (apparently in contradiction to what had been decided with Ha-Kibbutz Ha-Dati). The Minister of Housing reminded fellow officials that the matter was not for public discussion, presumably encouraging them to keep it out of the newspapers.[60]

Deliberations over Efrat dragged on through the fall of 1975 and consensus built toward selecting a site near the Palestinian village of Bayt-Fadjar.

Rabbi Shlomo Riskin, Garin Raishit Geula, and the Founding of Efrat, 1976–1983

In the new year, Moshkowitz wrote to the Council of Ministers of budding relations with a group of potential Jewish-American immigrants. He relayed their intent to invest in and settle at Efrat once it was built.[61] Who were these American Jews from the Upper West Side of Manhattan so keen on moving thousands of miles away to the West Bank and how did their upbringing in the United States help shape their new settlement in the occupied territories?

In 1976 Efrat was but a dream for a young, dynamic, modern Orthodox spiritual leader named Rabbi Dr. Shlomo (Steven) Riskin and a small cohort of his congregants. Born in Brooklyn in 1940, Riskin was raised in a nonreligious family and only turned to Orthodox Judaism in his teens. Yet he enjoyed a close relationship with his paternal grandfather, an avid communist, and his maternal grandmother, a religious Jew, both of whom inspired Riskin to seek political and religious commitments. According to congregant Edward Abramson, who wrote the only existing study of Riskin's rabbinical career in the United States, his family instilled in him a lifelong quixotic character, or "the fusion within Steven's personality of what might be seen as conflicting forces—the search for pure truth on the one hand, and the intense quality of empathy on the other."[62] His father, a salesman, and his mother, an assimilated Jewish homemaker, provided Riskin with household lessons in marketing his ideas to broader audiences. After attending Brooklyn Talmudic Academy High School as a star pupil, he turned down a full scholarship at Harvard University to enroll at the modern Orthodox educational institution Yeshiva University—it was a formative decision combining elements of intellect and emotion that were later reflected in Riskin's disposition at Efrat.[63] At university, Riskin studied with Rabbi Aaron Lichtenstein, later the dean of Yeshivat Har Etzion in the West Bank. He earned a bachelor's degree as well as rabbinical certification from leading Jewish-American Orthodox thinker Rabbi Joseph Soloveitchik in 1960. During his undergraduate years, Riskin avidly absorbed Yeshiva University's "Torah U'Madda" philosophy combining secular and religious studies. He became so deeply engaged in this educational mission that he joined the faculty upon receiving his doctorate in Jewish history from New York University. Yet Riskin was strangely absent from—and silent on—on the major theological and practical debates that rocked the institution regarding the Holocaust, Israel, and American politics in the 1960s.[64] His apparent political philosophy was "You can't make changes unless you're committed to the fundamental system," which perhaps foreshadowed his approach to conflict at Efrat.[65]

Riskin had his first exposure to Israel as a foreign-exchange student at the Hebrew University of Jerusalem in 1960–1961. He was mentored by intellectual luminary Gershom Scholem, an expert on Jewish messianism, a theme that later emerged as a central element of Riskin's religious Zionism. He also studied with the famed philosopher Martin Buber, although Riskin later reflected that "Buber gave us a theology, but not a lifestyle" at Efrat.[66] While conducting volunteer work in Yemenite immigrant communities during his course, Riskin also gained insights that may have informed his experiences with Palestinians, pointing out, "I learned many lessons that year about understanding different cultures, and the importance of never calling ethnic groups whom we do not understand 'primitive.'"[67] During his trip he also met his future bride in sixteen-year-old Victoria and the couple made "a pact" to move to Israel upon marriage.[68] Unable to find a pulpit in Israel by the end of his study-abroad stint, he returned to the United States to seek a position in New York City.

Riskin entered the rabbinate at a time when the Jewish community in the United States was in a state of transition.[69] Newly married and marginally employed upon his return from Israel, his former mentors encouraged the ambitious young rabbi to take a most unorthodox rabbinical position for a graduate of Yeshiva University: to assume leadership of Lincoln Square Synagogue, a small Conservative movement–affiliated congregation in midtown Manhattan that was operating out of an apartment in a new high-rise development. This suggestion was part of a broader program of *kibush kehilot* (lit. occupying communities) by the Orthodox Union, an interesting presage for Riskin's future project at Efrat.[70] He took the pulpit reluctantly and only as an interim job, refusing to pray with the congregation unless it adopted gender-segregated seating, but Riskin's skillful spiritual leadership convinced the community to move toward greater religious observance. In less than a decade, Riskin nurtured a small congregation of fifteen families into the largest modern Orthodox congregation in New York City. In doing so, he earned a national reputation—even dubbed "Stevie Wonder" by the New York press—for his dynamic religious leadership.

Riskin rose to the rabbinical challenges of the 1960s and 1970s, a critical experiment that would be repeated at Efrat. Lincoln Square Synagogue (LSS) came of age in the period of the "shul with a pool," and Riskin could later be seen as drawing upon the concept of a full-service religious, social, and spiritual center in the settlement.[71] Further, the institutionalization of *havurah* culture (lit. group, from the root of friend, an informal mode of Jewish gathering for prayer and lifecycle events popularized in the 1960s and 1970s) at LSS also provided a precedent for the kind of antiestablishment, do-it-yourself religious community at Efrat.[72] The new settlement project also responded to the interests of some young married couples who hoped to move to suburbia, if in the West Bank instead of Westchester County. Riskin's rise to international prominence as a spiritual leader—including his passionate involvement in the Soviet Jewry movement—also provided critical training for his role as a Zionist activist at Efrat.

Other trends augured Riskin's problematic approach to the Palestinian question. When Riskin introduced new forms of women's participation in ritual life at LSS, more progressive feminists charged that Riskin engaged in "apologetics," a critique later applied to his assessment of Palestinian land claims at Efrat. Broader questions of exclusion also arose in the redevelopment of the Lincoln Towers, which housed LSS, in midtown Manhattan—Riskin and his congregants' willingness to participate in a gentrification project that drove out blue-collar African-American and Hispanic residents in favor of the white middle class also set important precedents for his later involvement at Efrat. Riskin's sympathizers argued that "as always, he has taken a difficult stance; it is always easier to be a complete rejectionist or an extreme inclusionist. But the reasoned middle path continues to be his hallmark."[73]

Despite noteworthy professional success in the United States, Riskin longed to return to Israel and fulfill the couple's immigration pledge. Beginning in 1975 he spent eight consecutive summers as a scholar-in-residence at Kibbutz Ein Tsurim in the south in an unsuccessful attempt to secure a permanent rabbinical position somewhere in the country. "I was the Rabbi of probably what had become the most prominent Orthodox synagogue in America . . . we were written up in Time Magazine," Riskin recalled without great modesty in an interview, "and I could not get a job in Israel."[74] He came to frame his situation as a theological crisis after the 1967 war, as "I cannot say that I wasn't fulfilled as a rabbi and educator in New York. But something was missing. I felt I was letting God down. I wasn't really responding to the great miracle of the generation."[75] In part, he blamed a lack of job opportunities on his most un-orthodox appearance—he was clean-shaven and youthful-looking in his mid-forties—but more likely it was his liberal approach to religious matters, including his attitudes toward women's participation, that did not conform to the bent of Israeli Orthodoxy, both then and now.

While in residence at Ein Tsurim, Riskin and Moshkowitz struck up a friendship that that would change both men's lives.[76] Riskin was entirely enamored with the settler activist, describing him as "a very special individual, a great pioneer . . . he had wonderful government contacts"[77] and even likening him to the prophet Elijah.[78] One Sabbath morning in the spring of 1976, Riskin related how Moshkowitz visited his synagogue in New York City and "came to me [after services] and said, 'What are you doing in America? We need you in Israel.' I said, 'Look, I'm dying to get there and nobody wants to give me a job.'"[79] Later that summer Moshkowitz made his offer to build a new city in Gush Etzion together, an endeavor already under way at the time, which led to their lifelong partnership at Efrat.

The duo began to divide up responsibilities for the Efrat project. While Moshkowitz continued to push the Council of Ministers to reach a final vote on the new city throughout 1976 and 1977, Riskin worked tirelessly to attract immigrants in the United States.[80] As part of his recruitment efforts in those years, Riskin regularly spoke about Israel and the occupied territories at his Wednesday night lecture series and made religious Zionism a critical part of communal life.[81] He even welcomed Yitzhak Rabin to LSS twice, recalling, "[Rabin] was not a man to get excited, but he spoke with a great deal of emotion about Gush Etzion, of the building of Efrat. He was extremely positive and said everyone should follow Rabbi Riskin to Efrat. It would always be an integral part of Israel."[82] Moreover, as congregant Edward Abramson experienced, not only had "the State of Israel play[ed] an active role throughout the synagogue's early years to an extent that was rare in those days (and perhaps becoming rare again)," but that Riskin reframed Zionism as relevant to the living history of his parishioners, as "this role was not only the more typical one of Israel as a recipient of tzedakah [charity], the focus of financial appeals, welfare, and stability. Nor was Israel's role in the synagogue relegated to 'Israel: the Museum'—a place to visit to see the footsteps of Jewish history. Rather, the role highlighted two aspects of Israel that were often downplayed in those years: Israel as a place for Jews to live, and Israel as the center of Torah, the locus from which redemption would sprout."[83]

As the culmination of these initiatives, Riskin and Dr. Ralph (Menachem) Marcus—a self-described ardent Zionist and "follower" of the rabbi—founded Garin Raishit Geula (Seed Colony for the Origins of Redemption), a name taken from the opening line of the Prayer for the State of Israel.[84] However, Marcus's first meeting with Riskin on May 12, 1976, didn't go as planned; the rabbi's initial response to his idea was a dismissive "Gevalt, gevalt!" (Yiddish for "Woe upon me!").[85] Marcus reluctantly approached other New York–area rabbis to lead the garin, at last securing Riskin's agreement to spearhead the initiative later that year, presumably after his meeting with Moshkowitz in Israel.

Garin Raishit Geula's 1977 mission statement shared many themes that were common to Jewish-American settlers in combining politics with pioneering, Torah U'Madda with utopianism, the sacred with the suburban—but what set Garin Raishit Geula apart was its apocalyptic tone, both in name and in practice. Viewing the 1967 war as a messianic harbinger with "clearly redemptive military victories," they cautioned not to let "a singular opportunity to raise Jewish consciousness slip from our grasp" by failing to "develop a program of large scale aliya through which we could provide a crucial impetus to the growth of Torah Judaism in Israel."[86] Therefore, "Confronting these challenges, representatives of a new generation of Jews—born in the shadow of the Holocaust and reared in the light of the miraculous struggle of Israel to survive—have set the foundations for a new Religious Aliya Movement, RAISHIT GEULA. Reaffirming that the Jewish people is united by a single history, a single Torah, and One G-d, our organization will work to transform the religious and social goals of Torah Judaism into a living reality in Eretz Yisrael." Raishit Geula billed itself as "new religious aliya movement" active across the land of Israel, with its flagship settlement at Efrat. The prospectus outlined how the new settlement would combine religio-political imperatives with suburban living, echoing the 1975 English promotional edition. These measures were intended to mitigate "the sundry day-to-day problems that frequently beset new olim in their dealings with Israeli bureaucracy" so that "social adjustment to our new environment will also be predictably much easier." In closing, Raishit Geula appealed to the challenge of its time, declaring that by joining their cohort, "those who have considered aliya but have been discouraged by social, economic, or religious considerations . . . [would have the new opportunity] to help build a model Torah-committed society with a sound economic and social foundation. By confronting the spiritual challenges of Redemption, we will be contributing to the success of the religious community's most meaningful undertaking in our lifetime."

While Garin Raishit Geula sold Efrat as a self-sufficient venture, it was Moshkowitz's access to decision makers that gave Garin Raishit Geula a major advantage over other Jewish-American groups. Riskin's ability to engage in high-level negotiations was evident in his note to Marcus in July 1977: "I'm writing this letter with a great deal of joy, and not without trepidation. We've been in Israel for less than two weeks—and *our* resolve to raise our family here has become immeasurably strengthened. . . . Within the past two weeks I met with Zevulun Hammer (Minister of Education), Arik Sharon (directly responsible for new settlements), and Prime Minister Begin. I cannot tell you the enthusiasm I've been receiving—and I am confident that Efrat will be a reality. Everyone—including the Prime Minister— sees the aspect of *aliya kvutsatit* (group aliya) as charting a new path for aliya in general."[87] Riskin's optimism was not foolhardy: after a long delay, Jewish Agency chair Uzi Narkiss wrote Moshkowitz with word of the government's official authorization for Efrat in October 1977.[88] However, Knesset-approved funding for the new settlement was not released until over a year later in November 1978.

It is no coincidence that the Begin administration's authorization for the Efrat project came in the midst of the Camp David peace process. It is now apparent that the Israeli government was actively approving new settlements in the West Bank during negotiations between Israel and Egypt, although it remains unclear whether this was intended as a strategic hedge or reflected state interest from the outset to dismantle the Palestinian autonomy track. Newly released CIA documents suggest that Prime Minister Begin may have bowed to internal pressure from his right-wing flank who threatened unilateral settlement action.[89] At the same time, officials were keenly aware that a public airing of development plans could have catastrophic consequences both for peace negotiations and international public opinion, especially following a 1977 scandal when word of a plan to build upward of twenty-seven new settlements in the occupied territories leaked to the *New York Times*.[90] Thus, even before it was established, Efrat was a pawn in a larger political-strategic game. Nearly forty years later, Efrat and the Etzion Bloc are commonly raised as obstacles to peace with the Palestinians. The policy at that time, as well as today, seemingly conformed to the sentiment expressed by one bureaucrat: "I suggest that we don't ask questions now about what is liable to change in the future. None of us knows. In regards to changes in the future, Efrat isn't different from any other settlement."[91] Efrat's approval finally leaked to the media in February 1979 as part of a broader plan for settlement expansion, although the cabinet vowed not to build on Arab land.[92] An official gag order, which had long plagued organizers keen to publicize the project, was subsequently lifted.[93] The dovish antisettlement organization Peace Now immediately registered their protest, but plans for Efrat's development continued apace.[94]

Despite being hampered by the publicity ban, Riskin and Moshkowitz quietly made great strides in recruiting potential immigrants for planned residency in 1981. Working closely with the Israel Aliya Center in New York, Garin Raishit Geula's membership rolls reached more than 181 families by 1979.[95] Having achieved this critical mass, organizers held their first national convention on New Year's Day in New York City, an event that was opened by official greetings from Prime Minister Menachem Begin.[96] In an urgent memo to all immigration representatives in February 1979, one Israeli official suggested, "if this group will succeed, it will be a turning point in the development of group aliya to Israel that could be used as a model to other Rabbis and congregations."[97] In May 1980 a second national convention was held in Staten Island and Garin Raishit Geula even sponsored an official float in the Israeli Independence Day parade in New York that June to continue to publicize the Efrat project.[98]

Meanwhile, as Riskin drummed up membership in New York, Moshkowitz worked to oversee construction of housing and the physical plant in Israel. In February 1979 the Ministry of Immigration and Absorption pledged to build 300 dwelling units, two-thirds of which would be set aside for Baneh Beitekh (Build Your Own House) self-financed single family homes and villas (with mortgage loans of up to 110,000 lira) and the remainder as government-built apartments.[99] Preparations proceeded with construction firms to break ground the following winter. Yet as Menachem Marcus recalled of a visit to the site in 1979, "When I went to that hill, there was a forest, a windmill, and a water tower. The Arabs were planting vineyards to show the border. Obviously, there was nothing there before."[100] This emphasis on the emptiness of the land would later embroil Efrat in controversy once it was established.

A cornerstone-laying ceremony was scheduled for February 10, 1980, at 3 p.m.—invitations sent to various dignitaries and supporters requested that participants gather at the Tekoa junction on the Jerusalem-Hebron road a quarter of an hour before the service.[101] However, ten days before the scheduled event, tragedy struck: Swedish immigrant and Kiryat Arba yeshiva student Yehoshua Saloma wandered into the casbah in downtown Hebron—which had emerged as a flashpoint since a group of settlers led by Jewish-American Miriam Levinger reoccupied the downtown area in 1977—and was stabbed to death by a Palestinian terrorist. His murder marked the first fatal attack against an Israeli settler in the West Bank since 1967 and prompted a massive outcry by the Israeli government and general public. According to Riskin, who was en route to Israel when the news broke, the Ministry of Defense immediately called an emergency meeting to cancel the cornerstone-laying ceremony and to suspend construction of all new settlements. Moshkowitz met the rabbi at Ben Gurion Airport "with tears in his eyes," conveying the news that "I came to tell you to turn around, go back to New York . . . I'm sorry, but there won't be corner-stone laying ceremony, not this week, and perhaps—[with] this loss of momentum—not at all!"[102] Riskin was indefatigable, turning to peers to pressure the Ministry of Defense into changing its mind. He first sought out the counsel of his powerful colleague Menachem Mendel Schneerson, the Lubavitch Rebbe who had recently given his blessing to the new settlement of Efrat.[103] He was advised to try to rouse settlement activist Rabbi Chaim Druckman, who had recently suffered a devastating heart attack, to advocate for their cause with the prime minister. According to Riskin's account, the two managed to persuade Druckman to telephone Begin from his sickbed and the prime minister invited them to meet with him at the Knesset.[104] (This kind of intimate access to the highest corridors of power was unthinkable for other Jewish-American immigrants.) With great anticipation at this official audience, the New York rabbi chronicled the five-year saga of Efrat, even producing a list of all the families who had contributed a down payment toward a home in the settlement. Riskin recounted how Prime Minister Begin, with "tears in his eyes," took Herzl's famous tract *Der Judenstaadt* (The Jewish State) off his bookshelf, quoting, "Every congregation will settle in Israel, each congregation with its rabbi," expressing in "an emotionally-charged voice . . . 'you are fulfilling Herzl's prophecy, how can I stop your progress? I will overrule the decision of the cabinet. This Sunday, you may have the cornerstone laying ceremony, but with only two government ministers in attendance and without any publicity whatsoever.' " The ecstatic rabbi "embraced him in gratitude" but shrugged off the publicity ban. More than 3,000 individuals attended the event that weekend.[105]

Perhaps unsurprisingly, news broke to the *New York Times* a month later that the Israeli government had formally seized a parcel near Bethlehem to build Efrat. Palestinian land claims to the area, which had been papered over in discussions with government officials and the Israeli media, were immediately raised by nearby residents. According to unnamed sources, unequivocally "the land belonged to the Arab village of al-Khader" and Palestinian villagers told the reporter that they planned to take their case directly to the Israeli High Court in protest.[106] To date, I have not been able to locate this docket number, but if suit was brought, it would be the first in a series of legal challenges to the territory of Efrat that continue to be adjudicated up until today.

Conflict over territorial claims calls attention to the triangular relationship between Rabbi Riskin and Efrat's Jewish-American community, the native Israeli settler movement, and the Palestinians. In many ways, ensuing clashes over Efrat set the first two parties on a collision course against the Palestinian camp. Yet unlikely alliances between Jewish-American immigrants and local Palestinian villages also formed in the wake of internal struggles within the Israeli settler movement. Land issues highlighted how the norms at Efrat, from its inception, were at odds with those of their supposed partners in Gush Emunim.

Riskin's changing views lie at the heart of this controversy, so it is necessary to understand his attitudes in historical perspective. Riskin deeply believed then, as he still does now, that the whole of the land of Israel belongs to the Jews. However, he also allegedly demanded that Moshkowitz and the Israeli government verify that the municipal boundaries of Efrat would not be drawn on parcels with pending Palestinian private ownership petitions, although he did not elaborate on how this was determined. In an interview he insisted, "It's very important to me, very very important" that the land be unclaimed. "I believe we have historic right, but they also have [it], we have biblical promise, but not everything that is promised in the Bible takes place immediately," he explained, affirming, "We have to make sure we're very proper, legally, ethically, morally. I don't want to take any land that wasn't, couldn't be mine."[107] Later in the interview he emphasized that Efrat was "completely empty" numerous times. "I didn't come like a thief at night," he protested, disputing allegations by his critics, "We first checked every inch, we made sure this was Jewish land, and I think we acted with full integrity."[108] However, others openly suggest that Riskin subscribed to the "fiction" of not disenfranchising Palestinians or expropriating their land in the founding of Efrat, a claim that still dogs the rabbi and his settlement today.[109]

Yet from the outset, Riskin also found himself at odds with the premier native Israeli settlement group Gush Emunim, which worked to establish communities across the West Bank regardless of the settlement's physical location or land ownership status. In an interview, Riskin related a vignette that powerfully illustrated this fundamental rift when he was summoned to an audience with Rabbi Tzvi Yehuda Kook, the spiritual leader of the Israeli settler movement.[110] "Rav Tzvi Yehuda Kook wanted to know why Efrat was not part of Gush Emunim. Why was it an independent project?" The Jewish-American rabbi responded, "We have every right to be in Yehuda and Shomron [Judea and Samaria], but there are two million Arabs. I don't want a state with Jews and Arabs together, I would have to give Arabs the vote, I would have to give them equality. It would be more Arab than Jewish. You couldn't give the Arabs less than we asked for ourselves when we were a minority people. And therefore, I'm very much in favor of the settlement blocs, and therefore Efrat, but I'm not necessarily in favor of the Greater Israel movement, which was Gush Emunim, and building settlements all over." Following this pronouncement, "Rav Tzvi Yehuda Kook took my hand and looked deeply into my eyes and said, 'You are worried about the Arabs here. Don't worry Rabbi Riskin, *hem yityahadu* [they will convert to Judaism].' "[111] Riskin allegedly retorted, "Honorable head of the yeshiva, when they become Jewish, I'm ready to become part of Gush Emunim. Until that point, we have to remain a separate group."[112] Despite ongoing ideological disagreements, Riskin preserved an uneasy tactical alliance with Gush Emunim and served as an American spokesperson for the Israeli settler movement in the United States.[113]

In truth, Riskin was more preoccupied with haggling with Israeli bureaucrats over building delays at Efrat than resolving the macro-conflict between Israelis and Palestinians in the early 1980s. After the groundbreaking ceremony, Victoria Riskin recalled, "We called Moshko every week for an update. Moshko sent pictures and we shared the excitement of the unfolding adventure."[114] As construction at Efrat finally got under way, the government discussed new plans for housing design and mortgage terms.[115] However, in response to pleas for more affordable housing (including an increased number of rental units),[116] Riskin apparently made the strategic decision to encourage the settlement of wealthier families, allegedly telling Marcus, "If I have a choice between a Cadillac community and a Ford community, I'll take [the Cadillac]."[117]

By the early 1980s Riskin found himself immersed in—and sometimes overwhelmed by—the all-consuming task of building a settlement. "The most important thing in my life for the last six years has been Efrat," he admitted, elaborating, "I think, to be very frank with you, if I had not announced so many times I was coming to Israel, I would have backed down." In retrospect, he acknowledged that "I came to Israel with a great deal of trepidation . . . nevertheless, in perspective, it's the best decision I ever made."[118] Others regretted his choice and the couple faced the resentment of congregants who did not want them to move to Israel. As Victoria Riskin later recollected, "Some members didn't get it; they didn't want to get it. We were in the middle of a cultural maelstrom—everything was changing at a rapid pace. There were power walks, power lunches, power everything. Lincoln Square was a refuge for all of us; no one wanted it to change."[119] By the early 1980s Riskin himself was eager to leave the rat race of rabbinical life in America behind, seeing Efrat not only as a religious Zionist endeavor but as an opportunity to escape the "pressures" of LSS for a more relaxed lifestyle in Israel.[120] This theme would motivate other immigrants to Efrat as well. Yet even his own family doubted at times that the project would succeed. Riskin's mother-in-law was said to have assured his own worried mother following a trip to Efrat in the summer of 1980 that

> I should pay the travel agent double. It was the most worthwhile trip I ever made in my life. The highlight was what they call "Efrat." . . . They took us to this empty mountaintop—at the end of the world, turn right— pretty enough in terms of scenic views, but with barely any vegetation and without a living soul. Your son and my daughter looked pleased as punch, as if they were showing off Switzerland, Paris, and New York all rolled into one. Then your son starts the tour. He points to one empty hill and he says, "there is the synagogue"; to another barren peak, and he says, "there is the school campus"; to another undeveloped flatland, "here are the first fifty cottages." Rose, we have nothing to worry about. Not only won't there be an Efrat for them to move into in our lifetime, there won't be an Efrat for them to move into in their lifetime, or their children's lifetime either. In the meantime, they're living in a Peter Pan, Alice in Wonderland dream world . . . believe me, if they're banking on Efrat, they're staying in Manhattan![121]

Closing the gap between enthusiasm and commitment was a major challenge for Garin Raishit Geula's organizers at the time. Outreach to families was the highest priority: Of the many members who enrolled with the group, most had never opened immigration files with the Israel Aliya Center.[122] Nonetheless, Riskin was optimistic, writing to the Jewish Agency in July 1982 to tout their success, judging, "The future of Raishit Geula looks especially bright . . . I do not know of any other Aliayat [sic] which has accomplished what we have in so short a time. You have believed in us until now; I am confident in your continued help to ensure the success of Aliyah."[123]

Yet, behind the scenes, Raishit Geula was confronting several vital challenges. First, they lost their group's designated immigration representation at the Israel Aliya Center in a Jewish Agency cost-cutting measure, which deprived the garin of critical staff and a U.S.-based government liaison as the membership prepared to immigrate and settle in Efrat in the summer of 1983.[124] More devastatingly, Raishit Geula was broke. Riskin described the garin as in "serious financial trouble" by 1981, desperately begging Israeli officials for financial assistance. "The matter is urgent . . . we simply cannot continue to operate . . . with such a huge debt, which is crippling the organization," he wrote, adding in a handwritten note in Hebrew, that "it would be a pity if the only organization which has succeeded in bringing hundreds of families to register aliya portfolios will have to close its office! Please help!"[125] Officials were ultimately persuaded to increase the garin's annual budget to help cover the debt but Raishit Geula continued to run at a loss.[126]

Despite these difficulties, the first group of twenty-three couples, one single, and fifty-one children,[127] including Rabbi Riskin, his wife Victoria, and their children, immigrated to Efrat in the summer of 1983. They were joined by another forty Jewish-American families already living in Israel and a large South African contingent in residence at the site. An additional 180 families had registered with the garin with plans to arrive in 1984–1985, although only 60 families from the original group ultimately settled at Efrat.[128] For these immigrants, their decade-long dream of living at Efrat had become a reality: in a final act signaling the denouement of their settlement endeavor, Garin Raishit Geula was officially dissolved in the fall of 1983.

"For a Jew, It's Home": Rabbi Shlomo Riskin and Efrat since 1983

According to documentation provided by Mayor Oded Revivi's office at Efrat, the settlement today is a municipality (soon to be formally approved as a city) of approximately 9,000 residents and 1,800 families,[129] 50 percent are English-speakers, colloquially called Anglo-Saxons, and their children.[130] Efrat occupies a land mass of 5,000 dunams (over twice the size of the parcel outlined in the 1974 plan) comprising seven hilltop neighborhoods named for the biblical species of land of Israel. Although there is variation across precincts, housing prices are considerably above the average for both the occupied territories and within the Green Line. An apartment in Efrat can easily cost in the range of 1.5 to 2 million NIS (approximately $500,000) and homes are valued at 4 million NIS (approximately $1 million) and upward. Even Efrat's rental housing exceeds national standards, with a one-bedroom apartment priced at approximately 4,000 NIS (approximately $1,000) per calendar month.[131]

With a generous annual operating budget of 51.8 million shekels (approximately $12.95 million), the municipality provides the panoply of services envisioned in the original Efrat plan. The settlement is anchored by a strong educational network that includes twenty-one kindergartens, three elementary and middle schools (one male, one female, one mixed gender), a religious high school for boys, two pre-university yeshivot that serve over 3,400 students, and several other religious schools and programs associated with Rabbi Riskin's Ohr Torah Stone Yeshiva, an independent framework. The city also offers afterschool children's programs, religious youth groups, and a clubhouse for teenagers at risk.

Spiritual life also remains at the heart of Efrat's community, a population that self-identifies as 90 percent national-religious and 10 percent secular.[132] Efrat is served by Chief Rabbi Shlomo Riskin, who presides over twenty-eight Orthodox synagogues (following Ashkenazic, Sephardic, North African, Yemenite, Carlebach-mystical, and other styles), four ritual baths (three for women, one for men), registration for weddings and other religious ceremonies, the settlement *eruv* (religious enclosure for Sabbath and festivals), and a burial society and cemetery. However, some subcommunities now hire their own rabbis and retain a kind of autonomous religious status.

Adult life is also an important part of daily life in Efrat. Most of its residents are white-collar professionals who commute to work in Jerusalem and Tel Aviv, although some entrepreneurs have home offices or own the settlement's small enterprises. The municipality also sponsors leisure-time activities such as a community center (including a fitness gymnasium and a swimming pool), a program for single parents, a senior citizens meeting room, and an umbrella charitable organization "Hand-in-Hand," which coordinates social action projects. The city has two major commercial complexes with full-service supermarkets and hosts other businesses, such as a dry cleaner, clothing boutique, optometry clinic, toy store, Judaica gift shop, post office, bagel bakery and café, pizzeria, and hamburger chain franchise. Efrat also hosts offices of all four national health plans and an emergency medical center, as well as regional branches of the Ministry of Interior and the National Insurance Service. The city is a gated community protected by a twenty-four-hour manned security center, a "smart camera defense system," and on-call emergency services.[133] Mayor Revivi recently campaigned for reelection on a platform to expand capacity to 30,000 residents, provide more social services, and strengthen Efrat's "Green City" environmental initiative. The standard of living at Efrat is considered to be among the highest in the occupied territories and comparable to that of major municipalities within the Green Line. It remains a preferred destination for Jewish-American immigrants moving to the occupied territories today.[134]

Efrat in its fourth decade can hardly compare to its rustic existence in its early years. Initially, there was great skepticism about the future of the settlement. "The time of my aliya was very romantic and very exciting—until I actually arrived in Efrat and reality set in," Riskin recalled, "The streets weren't paved, there were no private telephones—only one public telephone that generally didn't work—and during that first very rough winter we were often without heat, electricity, or without either of the two. Add to that the fact that within a few months I realized I had no clear means of earning a livelihood for my wife and four children . . . I would get up in the middle of the night in a cold sweat, thinking I had made a terrible mistake."[135] Efrat's religious affairs director Bob Lang of Nanuit, New York, who was living at the southern outpost of Karnei Tsur at the time, witnessed the slow progress on the ground, recounting, "When I came to Efrat in 1983, there was nothing here. I mean, I hiked in the hills here, it was empty still. On these hills, they will build, but they hadn't yet built anything."[136] (Again, the trope of emptiness was underscored to deemphasize Palestinian land claims.) By 1985–1986, construction had only commenced in three of seven planned neighborhoods in the Rimon (Pomegranate), Teena (Fig), and Gefen (Grape) hills. There were only single-family dwellings built by government contractors as the Baneh Beitekh homes had not yet been completed. In those years, there were few amenities: a small grocery store and one of four Israeli health funds. Residents regularly shopped in Bethlehem or took one of four daily buses to Jerusalem, a winding two-hour trip on public transportation before the construction of bypass roads built exclusively for Jewish-Israelis in the 1990s after the first intifada. In Efrat's early days, friction with neighboring Palestinian communities was low, quotidian interactions were common, and life in and around the settlement was mostly safe for its new residents. Riskin humorously reminisced about learning how to fire an Uzi machine gun before his first rollcall for male obligatory guard duty in the settlement, recalling how "My wife whispered to my older children, 'If Abba [Dad] is protecting us, maybe we should spend a night in Jerusalem!' "[137] Bob Lang noted that by 1986 "Efrat was considered the big town in the area," although it only housed approximately 150 young couples."[138]

Apart from quotidian difficulties, there was also great concern about an American-Israeli rabbi's ability to build a spiritual community in the city-settlement. Riskin railed against the Israeli religious establishment for rigging the process of rabbinical certification to become the rabbi of an Israeli city (a special status he needed to secure in addition to his Yeshiva University ordination), supposedly rejecting his pleas to offer him a qualification exam and then subjecting him to an abnormally difficult test.[139] He quickly proved his professional credentials but questions about his practical performance lingered in the first years of Efrat. "Can An American Rabbi Make It in Israel?" queried *Counterpoint,* the English-language periodical for Anglo-Saxon settlers in the occupied territories in January 1985, interviewing two other Jewish-American settler rabbis who cautioned their peer about the need to adapt U.S. spiritual leadership to the Israeli context.[140] Israeli settlers were also dubious about Riskin's prospects, entitling a 1986 interview with Efrat's rabbi "The Rabbi of a City or the City of a Rabbi?" in *Gushpanka,* the Hebrew-language newsletter of Gush Etzion.[141] Riskin openly acknowledged the need to reorient his approach, suggesting differences between the Jewish communities in the United States and Israel were so profound that "there almost isn't anything to compare. In the Diaspora, I was a rabbi that was engaged in education, in Israel—I am an educator that engages in rabbinics!"[142] Yet in his new surroundings, Riskin also saw the potential to realize a tripartite goal, declaring, "at Efrat, I saw the possibility to link the dream of building a city, immigrating to the land, and developing the subject of education which was close to my heart."[143]

By the mid-1980s, Riskin and his fellow Jewish-American immigrants were living their dream over the Green Line. The rabbi and other city residents elaborated on their early views of Efrat in a promotional film entitled *For a Jew, It's Home,* shot on location by the World Zionist Organization in 1985.[144] While the propaganda production was clearly intended as an advertisement for the new settlement, it also an important and fascinating source of archival footage that documents daily life in the community in its first decade.

The film opens with a rolling camera following a suit-clad Rabbi Shlomo Riskin bicycling with great exertion up the hill of a roughly paved street in Efrat, observing the construction of new houses and commenting on the historicity of the locale. A voice-over from the narrator intones, "We have chosen to tell the story of this religious town and its people because they illustrate the problems, possibilities, and promise of aliya . . . a story not only of continued Jewish survival, but of possible redemption." Clearly, from the beginning, the political controversy over Efrat was entirely elided in favor of a narrative focusing exclusively on Jewish experience. Riskin expounded upon these themes of messianism, pioneering, and building a new utopian suburbanized community at Efrat when he was later filmed sitting in his office at Yeshivat Ohr Torah Stone, the cornerstone of the educational network he founded, exhorting, "The destiny of the Jewish people is being written here. If you want to participate in that destiny, if you want to participate not only in Jewish survival, but in the possibility of Jewish redemption, that can only be done here in Israel." He didn't conceal the challenges inherent in realizing this vision, adding, "That doesn't mean there aren't problems here—religious and nonreligious, peace, war, important problems, [but] for the first time in 2,000 years, we have the opportunity and challenge to work them out and direct our own destiny." Looking out his office window at the city on a hilltop he helped establish, he prophesied, "I see here Judaism converging . . . in one direction, Hebron, the other direction is Jerusalem. Hebron symbolizes Jewish past and Jerusalem symbolizes Jewish future. Hopefully Efrat is the bridge between our origins and our dreams."

Certainly the film portrayed the community at Efrat as living the dream. "I wake up every morning with a thrill . . . I'm so happy living in Medinat Yisroel [The State of Israel]!" trumpeted one jubilant former resident of New York. Deborah Tobin, a modern Orthodox resident originally from Boston, highlighted the thrilling challenge of utopian pioneering and self-realization, suggesting, "If I had stayed in America, everything would have been predictable, absolutely predictable. I know the course our professional lives would have taken, we would have been upwardly mobile, bought a bigger house, it's all very predictable. Here it's very exciting—who knows what will be? The possibilities are before us. It's a little scary on the one hand, but it's also very exciting, there's such a feeling of empowerment that comes with that. We can make it be what we want it to be, the possibilities are incredible."

Despite perceptions of hardship associated with the settler lifestyle, Efrat had already grown into a community with a high standard of living by the mid-1980s. Riskin grinned as he related that in the early days when Efrat lacked basic amenities, his grandmother had exclaimed, "You went back to Lublin!" Another Jewish-American candidly noted the mundane difficulties immigrants had to persevere through in Efrat's first days, but embraced them as part of the challenge of building a new life in the settlement, as, "One day, when we face our maker, we aren't going to say we didn't come to Israel because we didn't like the toilet paper here." Yet by 1985, Riskin boasted that the American-style city had "all the amenities you might want, even a beauty parlor!" and observed, "The quality of life here, for me personally, is greater than it was in mid-Manhattan." It was plain to see in the film's promotional footage that tensions between a pioneering adventure and suburban living were almost entirely sublimated at Efrat. For Stanley Kirschenbaum of New York City, the new settlement curiously evoked a sense of familiarity, where, "From the moment of the landing of the plane, you feel like you're home. It's like walking in your own back-yard." Another American-Israeli touted the tight-knit fabric of Efrat's community, remarking, "It's a family." The film's narrator deemed the religious network "so intimate" that "Rabbi Riskin knows by name every schoolchild that comes to morning prayers in the synagogue!" Even if visitor Sheila Becker from San Diego was not convinced that she was prepared to move to Efrat in the near future, she embraced the contradictions of the city, observing, "It's the middle of nowhere. [But] it's also the middle of everywhere." Summing up his sentiments about living in the new settlement of Efrat, Rabbi Riskin proclaimed, "It's a pleasure living here day to day, and for a Jew, it's home."

The WZO film portrayed Efrat as "pioneering with a bit of luxury," and truth be told, many of the Efrat's Jewish-American homesteaders were happy not to have to rough it.[145] One Jewish-American journalist famously snickered at the opulence of "Occupied Scarsdale"; Riskin subverted the stereotype, dubbing his community "Central Park West Bank."[146] Sharon Katz from Woodmere, New York, described Efrat as a settlement where the Jewish-American immigrant could have it all—even a mansion with a twenty-minute commute to the future rebuilt third holy temple in Jerusalem! In her city on a hilltop, the holy coexisted with the mundane, rhapsodizing, "You just walk[ed] outside your house and look at these hills . . . this is where King David shepherded his sheep . . . Ruth and Naomi of the Megillah, this is where they lived. . . . This is where Abraham, Yitzhak, and Yaakov passed . . . We know Rachel died on the way to Efrat. . . . Suddenly you're like a regular person from Woodmere, and you're totally absorbed in Jewish history." At the same time, Efrat's familiar amenities served as recompense for the personal and political sacrifices made along the way, rationalizing, "You know what, nineteen years ago, I left my mother, and my sister, and my best friends in America. I left my beautiful house and the life that I knew. And I came to the big unknown. I gave up everything to come here. I think I gave up enough. So if I want to have a bagel once a week . . . or pizza on Thursday night, I think that's okay. I don't think a person has to give up everything to come here." (What Palestinians gave up went unremarked upon.) Yet with all the modern conveniences that the city now offers, Katz betrayed nostalgia for the olden days in the settlement, suggesting, "We definitely felt like pioneers coming here . . . when we first moved to Efrat nineteen years ago, you felt you were part of a whole mission . . . you can't help but feel like your life has a bigger purpose here. I still feel that way here. [But] I'm not sure if the people that move up to the Zayit [neighborhood], these beautiful new apartment houses and stuff, I don't know if they feel that way."[147]

If some Jewish-Americans at Efrat lamented a loss of pioneering spirit as time went on, the native Israeli settler population lambasted its residents for their apparent unwillingness to get their hands dirty in the interest of Jewish settlement. Fellow Israeli settlers joked of replacing the city's motto "quality of life" with their own moniker, "it's not cheap."[148] Yet largely their evaluation of Efrat was sober and antagonistic, roundly condemning the "luxury" of the Jewish-American community. "The first days of Efrat aren't a story of hard birth pangs and difficulties of creation," observed journalist Barbi Erlich of the leading Hebrew-language settler periodical *Nekuda* (The Point), "Efrat is different from everything we had known previously in YESHA . . . we were accustomed to settlers that lived for years in caravans or eshkubiot [prefabricated dwellings], the housing quarters were built slowly. With halting progress and not a few delays. Here the residents go straight to their private homes and the majority of the city ser-vices are already working." Implicitly characterizing Efrat's citizens as cos-setted and mollycoddled, she warned that the "settlements of the Gush didn't succeed against the enemy because we were suffering from a lack of willpower." Yet it wasn't just that the new settlement's Jewish-American immigrants were spoiled and self-indulgent; beyond the surface critique of creature comforts, their native peers' criticism was geostrategic: Efrat con-sciously billed itself as being "within the consensus" of settlement blocs in the occupied territories that would likely be absorbed into territorial Israel (in exchange for land swaps) in a final status agreement with the Palestin-ians. There was a bitter sense among Gush Emunim activists that Efrat's Jewish-American residents didn't have to fight for their political legiti-macy—and certainly didn't lend a hand to crusade on behalf of the larger enterprise. Though Riskin allegedly boasted as early as 1979 that "don't worry, Gush Etzion is in the national consensus. It will never be given back," one native Israeli settler rebutted, "I don't agree that someone would try to separate us [Gush Etzion] from Yehuda and Shomron and say that we're within the consensus. It's forbidden to differentiate between the set-tlements of Gush Etzion and the other settlements. I don't think this decla-ration adds anything to Efrat. The opposite is true."[149] The mainstream settler movement seemed to wish Efrat the best of luck but didn't truly be-lieve that the settlement had earned its success.

Further divisions between the native Israeli settler camp and Efrat's citizenry became apparent with the outbreak of the first intifada in 1987. Compared to other settlements in the West Bank (including nearby Tekoa, described in Chapter 4), Efrat had a relatively quiescent experience during the Palestinian national uprising. Only two major incidents marred the calm: an explosion near a bus stop in Efrat, which was blamed on local villagers (including a Palestinian youth who was tutoring Rabbi Riskin in Arabic, although he was later exonerated) and an effort by Efrat's settlers to erect a temporary blockade on the road between the settlement and the nearby Palestinian community of Wadi Nis.[150] There was also a sizable group of agitators on both sides, including followers of Meir Kahane's extremist party Kach at Efrat and Palestinian militants at the nearby De-heishe refugee camp, although the violent activist groups never seemed to come into direct conflict. Nevertheless, both populations were deeply affected by the cycles of fear and violence that swept across the occupied territories.

Riskin himself powerfully illustrated this psychological climate through a vignette he shared with two American journalists at the height of the intifada. He recounted that one morning, on his regular jog along the road near the stone quarries of Bayt-Fadjar, he spotted a lone Palestinian shepherd in adjoining fields. When the man reached for two stones to arm himself, the rabbi immediately feared for his life as an isolated settler stranded in a deserted stretch outside of the settlement's gates. He quickly realized, however, that the Palestinian had prepared to defend himself against an attack by the American-Israeli rabbi. "I started to cry," Riskin recalled, "we're afraid of each other. That's the tragedy of this kind of situation."[151]

The first intifada even divided Riskin's own family in Efrat. While Riskin pursued dialogue with some (but not all) neighboring *mukhtars* and invited them for meetings at his house, he and his wife had one the few fights in their married life when she "strenuously objected" to hosting the Palestinian leaders. "We were at war with the Arabs and I definitely did not want to have them in our home,"[152] Victoria argued, but Riskin opposed her viewpoint, asserting, "These are my neighbors. We let Jews in; we have to let Arabs in. And I want my children to see that too." His views notwithstanding, the intifada still managed to radicalize the members of his home— Riskin's son adopted Meir Kahane's racist platform, including his policies on population transfer, openly voicing these positions at the family dinner table—much to his father's deep chagrin.[153] Indeed, Riskin's home emerged as a microcosm of broader tensions between moderates and extremists in the settlement, as liberal values and settler realities came into sharp contrast. Alluding to the biblical parable of Moses and the rock (where the prophet violated God's instruction by hitting the rock rather than speaking to it to coax out its water supply and was punished by dying before reaching the land of Israel), Riskin professed his belief that dialogue was a divine commandment, stating: "All relationships begin and end with proper communication. I believe the message is very clear. God said to the Jewish people when they were up against a rock, 'You've got to speak to the rock. And if you speak to it and you learn to speak properly, then water can even come out of a rock. . . . You have to be willing to speak to those people who sometimes seem as hard-hearted to us as rocks. We've got to be willing to speak to anyone. Even to the rock. Even to people like Yasser Arafat or the Hizbollah. I would speak to anyone."[154] Moreover, no solution to the conflict should be off the table to quell the uprising—including plans for local autonomy or a Palestinian state. Seemingly speaking about both Palestinians and Israelis, Riskin opined in 1989, "I think that every nation requires independence—a sense of running its own affairs. It's the right of every nation-state to have its flag flying, to have a sense that it elects its own government heads. That's part of one's self image."[155] However, it is also important to recognize that by engaging in such diplomacy, Riskin himself was carefully cultivating the persona of religious liberal and political moderate. While his dialogue project and progressive doctrinal rulings helped him attain a kind of celebrity status within liberal modern Orthodox circles by the early 1990s, others critiqued the right-wing creep of his politics as the rabbi entered his second decade at Efrat.

Other Jewish-American settlers complained that the international community's perception contradicted their own self-image during the first intifada. Efrat resident Ephraim Zuroff, director of the Simon Wiesenthal Center in Jerusalem, an international human rights organization, was vexed by the "stereotypical image of 'the settler' with his bushy beard, his gun in his belt, his eternally pregnant wife. . . . [The word] settler has a become a pejorative term—it's as if we are a band of vigilantes." For a man who considered himself a moderate and a crusader for civil liberties, "the hatred and hostility of the left really hurts. It is as if anyone who crosses the Green Line immediately loses his moral sensibilities." Decrying the "dangerous extremism of Gush Emunim," Zuroff had been instrumental in hosting meetings between Efrat residents, Peace Now activists, and local Palestinian communities. Yet he struggled to reconcile his liberal values with new realities, musing, "This is no American melting pot . . . you've got to be blind not to realize that."[156] For those like Zuroff, the first intifada was an eye-opening political reckoning. Though they had already been living in the West Bank for several years, many of Efrat's contented suburbanites only confronted the consequences of living in the occupied territories for the first time during the uprising. Jewish-American journalist Tom Friedman wrote that it was initiation by fire, where "the street wars in Gaza and West Bank between Israelis and Palestinians are not some civil rights dispute or student protest. To put in American terms, these clashes are not the Israeli equivalent of Birmingham in 1960 or Berkeley in 1968; rather, they are the equivalent of Bull Run in 1861."[157]

The aftermath of the first intifada brought the institutionalization of civil war in the occupied territories. Its immediate consequence at Efrat was a reduction in interaction between the settlement and surrounding Palestinian villages. Before the uprising, Bob Lang suggested "no one thought twice about security" in the settlement and most settlers shopped in the Bethlehem market, bought petrol and had their cars repaired in local gas stations, engaged in charitable projects for Palestinian villages, and struck up acquaintanceships with Palestinian families. Neighbors helped each other near Efrat—with a twinkle in his eye, he reminisced about offering a ride to eight stranded Palestinian villagers in his tiny economy car when their own vehicle ran out of gas. These kinds of quotidian exchanges diminished or ceased entirely by the early 1990s.[158] When Sharon Katz immigrated to the occupied territories at the tail end of the first intifada in 1992, she envisioned Efrat as a model of everyday peace existing between the two parties on the ground. "Everybody got along fine, you want to talk coexistence?" she exclaimed, "That was coexistence. It was only when they decided they're going to have Oslo that we weren't allowed to talk to each other anymore. . . . The left is always talking about coexistence, but they don't mean coexistence, they mean separation. The right—and the majority of people who live Judea and Samaria are right wing—we are living in coexistence." However, as the Israel-Palestinian peace accords progressed she described the change that came over the area: "I'm a Long Island girl, I'm not going to move to some bad neighborhood—I'm not going to move to Harlem. . . . And when I moved to Efrat, it wasn't a scary place. It was an adventurous place, it was a pioneering place, it didn't have all the amenities I was used to at home . . . but I was never afraid. . . . Then the government made Oslo and suddenly when you drove through Bethlehem you had to be nervous. You weren't nervous the day before, but the day afterward you had to be nervous. . . . When it suddenly wasn't regular, it was scary. It was very, very scary."[159] Yet, with the uprising over and the Oslo process under way, Lang was optimistic, as "For the most part, living with the intifada has meant business as usual. At any rate, the intifada didn't scare people off."[160] The settlement was expanding at record speed, including increased building and infrastructure and new bypass roads subsidized by the Israeli government. If anything, there was nostalgia for a simpler time, with Riskin complaining that innovations like cable television would dis-tract from the "idealistic, Zionist, religious, spiritual élan" he hoped to create at Efrat.[161] Yet the happy days of a coexistence in the settlement's suburban paradise came to an end by the early 1990s.

Fault lines quickly emerged at Efrat over resistance to the Oslo process, which threatened the settlement's continued existence. One journalist observed, "Efrat's residents are not just arguing with the government, in-creasingly they are starting to argue among themselves. And the one thing that all Efrat's citizens—ideologues, pragmatists, and fence-sitters alike—seem to agree on is that the uncertainty is giving the suburb-settlement a serious case of angst."[162] At the center of the controversy was the clash be-tween liberal self-image and settler realities. Despite Efrat's suburban trap-pings, there was growing recognition within and outside of Israel that some of its settlers—and their famous rabbi—were gravitating to the right of the political spectrum. Early on, some of its Jewish-American settlers clung to the idea of Efrat as a bastion of moderation, but others began to express their skepticism about the settlement. Former LSS member David Kahan voiced his doubts about their city on a hilltop in a *Jerusalem Post* article pointedly titled "Borderline Schizophrenia," conceding, "It's pretty damn dif-ficult to be a light unto the nations when you're controlling a million and half hostile people . . . I don't think we can talk about inhabiting the land of Israel as the forerunner to the Jewish people's redemption when, by virtue of necessity, we have to subject another people to conditions that we wouldn't tolerate for ourselves."[163] While some residents prided Rabbi Riskin as a "passionate moderate" during the Oslo process, others con-fessed that they were "looking for more passion and less moderation" at Efrat and were even content to leave their liberal label behind to embrace violent activism.[164] Led (in part) by firebrand Los Angeles native Eve Harow, hardliners formed a citizens council known as the Efrat Action Committee.[165] One of its inaugural activities was stoning the car of dovish Housing Minister Binyamin Ben-Eliezer during a visit to the settlement while Riskin stood alongside. He later joined hundreds of residents in signing a public apology for the day's events.[166] Dutch-Israeli colleague Nadia Matar, who later co-founded the right-wing activist group Women in Green with her Jewish-American mother-in-law, Ruth Matar, and Harow, was unrepen-tant, however, commenting to a reporter that "we had to show that we will not receive a man like Fuad (Ben-Eliezer) pleasantly here, so he can go and say, 'Efrat is with us, they're the moderates,' " as she carried a sign reading "Efrat will not be the Theresienstadt of the settlements."[167] Harow affirmed that the mission of her council was to challenge the "implied message" that "I and other members of the Efrat Action Committee are portrayed as the 'fringe element of extremists' as opposed to the 'pragmatic Efrat residents who fear for their homes,'" seemingly admonishing Riskin directly that "my activism and those like me may be to the chagrin of some clergymen and citizens of Efrat . . . however our numbers are growing daily." She then vowed to continue her activities, refusing to acquiesce to "appeasement" or "national suicide."[168] Some residents pushed back on her views; one Jewish-American settler at Efrat penned an open op-ed charging, "By what right or mandate does she presume to present her views as that of the 'overwhelming majority'?"[169] Riskin himself, perhaps concerned not to be out-flanked, seized upon her outlook of self-defense, declaring, "I was always known as a liberal in the United States. I marched with Martin Luther King and feel very strongly about equal rights. But we're not fighting against an enemy who plays by the same rules as we do. . . . Horrible things happen here, and therefore one dare not be naïve. Given the cruelty and barbarism of the Arabs to their own people, our ethical imperative is not to commit suicide."[170]

The conflict between liberal values and settler realities was severely tested in the months before the assassination of Prime Minister Yitzhak Rabin. Efrat became the symbol of the larger struggle over the possible evacuation of the Etzion Bloc as part of a final status negotiation between Israel and the Palestinians. A dispute erupted in the winter of 1994, when Efrat residents engaged in unauthorized building on a hilltop called Givat Ha-Tamar (Date Hill) in protest over Oslo and Palestinian families from the village of al-Khader brought suit to the Israeli High Court for land theft.[171] A compromise was reached with the government that would divert new development to Givat Ha-Zayit (Olive Hill), an area within the municipal borders less proximate to its Palestinian neighbors, but resentment between the settlement's self-described pragmatic moderates and ideological activists simmered over the next several months. As Efrat Action Committee member Josh Adler, formerly of Brooklyn, New York, contended, "We are against any compromise on any part of Eretz Yisrael. We believe in the right to settle anytime, anywhere. This has set a dangerous precedent."[172] Riskin, as always, tried to straddle the middle ground both literally and metaphorically, judging, "[from] an Efrat perspective, the positive [parts of the agreement] outweigh the negative," yet, echoing Adler, he acknowledged, "there is a profound problem in the agreement. That the legal rights of Jews in the land of Israel have been pushed aside in favor of the forces of violence and terror is a humiliating defeat."[173]

Riskin's full radicalization was realized a few months later when the controversy over Efrat's expansion was reignited at a new location. In the summer of 1995, Sharon Katz gathered three of her close female friends, Nadia Matar, Eve Harow, and Marilyn Adler (Josh Adler's wife), to "try to think about what they could do to save our country." Embracing a strategy of "thinking globally, acting locally," the four women collectively decided that despite the government compromise in place, they would squat on another hilltop known as Givat Ha-Dagan (Corn Hill) in order to stake a claim to that territory. Concealing their true purpose, they proposed an overnight field trip to a few friends, instructing them to prepare food and a rucksack for the evening. The following afternoon a group of approximately twenty women led by Katz and her co-activists alighted to Givat Ha-Dagan. Within the hour, an army patrol arrived to investigate—when an IDF official questioned the leaders about their activities, they responded, "We are holding on to our land." "You're having a picnic," the soldiers laughed, cautioning the group to "have fun and make sure you are out of here before dark." Contradicting military orders, the women stayed but quickly realized they were wholly unprepared to weather the night. "We were very, very brave," reminisced Sharon Katz, but "suddenly when it turned dark, we were like, oh my gosh, we're in the middle of nowhere! We didn't have a gun, we didn't have anything, we had no lighting . . . we were right across the street from Arab houses. It was very scary." The next day the group was evacuated by the army.[174]

Unlike the short-lived squabble over Givat Ha-Tamar, the ritual of daily removal from Dagan Hill by the IDF became a communal outing over the course of the summer of 1995. "At first it was just the women," Katz recalled, "then we called our husbands to protect us, so they came, they were here with the guns, and then we were there for the duration of the summer, it was a whole family activity." When asked what inspired her political activism, Katz articulated a desire both to fulfill religious Zionist imperatives and participate in modern-day pioneering, explaining, "I was living on a hilltop because I told you that even though I'm from the Five

Towns, and I was a spoiled American, and maybe still am a spoiled American, when you get there and you realize where you are, you want to be part of history. We really felt that by being on the Dagan, we were saving Efrat. We were holding on to the land. And that's really why we went up."[175] Even fellow female native Israeli settler activists were impressed, noting that "these women live in homes three times bigger than ours and they still came here."[176]

Others traded more explicitly on their liberal values to justify their activism at Efrat. "I was brought up a liberal Democrat, supportive of civil rights," explained former New Jersey resident Barry Schlesinger, "With that background, there's no other way."[177] Yehudit Sidikman from Connecticut contended, "The rebellion on Givat Hadagan has shaken the government, for we are the liberals, the soft peace-loving 'Anglo-Saxons,' the civil rights supporters. We are the people who can't imagine hating someone because of their race, religion, creed, or color. We are the people whose goals are financial security and good education. We are the families with a white picket fence, a lawn, and a dog," that joined the protest because "the spirit is strong and the destruction of dreams isn't something to be taken lightly. Because the right of a Jew to live on his/her land and protect his/her family is indisputable. Because peace is something that comes from living it. It isn't something that governments can give or take away. It has to come from the people."[178] Despite their ambivalence about Efrat, native Israeli settlers were unsurprised that one of the largest and most successful acts of resistance against the Oslo process had taken place in the settlement, as Israeli lawyer and settler activist Elyakim Ha-Etzni elaborated: "Why Efrat? Because Efrat has a large number of Anglo-Saxons and precisely because of its moderation. Anglo-Saxons understand democracy. They understand civil disobedience. They understand that the citizen has certain rights that can't be trampled on . . . the fury of moderates who feel that they are betrayed is greater than those who saw the betrayal all along. People in Efrat thought they were part of the consensus. But when they saw that it was a bluff, they can't even go to a hill that is part of their master plan, then they fight back."[179] Former Kahanist and future YESHA Council foreign representative Yehiel Leiter from Scranton, Pennsylvania, confirmed this analysis, maintaining, "If a place like Efrat, which is condescendingly viewed as a yuppie village, is willing to wake up at midnight to place a trailer on a hill . . . it sends a message to other settlers who like to identify with Efrat's moderation. The feeling is that if things are taking place in Efrat, then the situation must indeed be serious."[180]

To further illustrate this point, Rabbi Riskin, who had initially been on the sidelines of the protest, purposefully joined the movement in July 1995. "This was not on the platform for election and is against the will of majority in every poll taken"[181] he contended of the Oslo process, drawing on principles of democratic decision making to deride the government as being a "small minority telling lies about giving up land that threatens the security of the people."[182] Considering that the State of Israel had broken the social contract to defend the settlers against violence, the rabbi declared, "This is the time for passive resistance."[183] Taking the analogy one step further, he even compared Efrat's conflict with the government over Givat Ha-Dagan with the civil rights struggle, attesting, "I marched in Selma with Martin Luther King. Now we, the settlers, have become the blacks of Martin Luther King." (This syllogism was tough to swallow for some of the rabbi's peers in the United States, one of whom wrote in to the *New York Times* to disavow that "the Israeli West Bank isn't another Selma.")[184] Then, echoing the discourse of hard-left activist groups like the Weather Underground, Riskin argued, "There are certain moments in time when acts of zealotry become necessary, especially when the leadership chooses to become silent. We have to do what we have to do in Israel." While he was clear to advocate for nonviolent resistance against the IDF, he pledged, "I will never leave Efrat on my two feet."[185]

To illustrate the point, Riskin was arrested at a sit-in later that summer protesting the evacuation of Efrat's illegal outpost while cloaked in a *talit* (ritual prayer shawl), holding a Torah scroll, and singing "We Shall Overcome" with a circle of Jewish-American activists as they locked arms in civil disobedience. As he was carried off by the IDF, the rabbi vowed to go to prison "a thousand times" to protect settlements in the West Bank from dismantlement.[186] In a jailhouse interview, Riskin framed himself a kind of political prisoner, lecturing a *Jerusalem Post* reporter that "the Prime Minister must understand that if we are prepared to put up a struggle for a desolate hill, imagine what will happen when they try to take us out of our homes. We haven't advocated taking Palestinians out of their homes, but we are against being taken out of our homes."[187] Elsewhere he underscored, "It is unthinkable that Israel might one day consider giving up this community, and we're not going to leave here."[188] Riskin also warned of emerging civil strife between government backers and Efrat's settlers, where "the government has made the split."[189] The rabbi's premonition came true: it was later revealed that Yigal Amir, who assassinated Prime Minister Yitzhak Rabin in November 1995, had taken part in protests at Givat Ha-Dagan that summer.[190]

Dagan Hill was later incorporated within the municipal boundaries of the settlement and the larger threat to the future of Efrat diminished with the downfall of the Oslo process, but the episode profoundly changed Efrat—and its American-Israeli spiritual leader.[191] In the aftermath of the protest, Riskin's famed reputation for moderation was severely compromised. If it had once been joked that Riskin was a proponent of land for peace "just so long as it's not his land," the Oslo process fundamentally altered the rabbi's political philosophy.[192] "We've worked hard to develop a reputation for fairness toward our Arab neighbors," Riskin boasted in an interview, but he had clearly had a change of heart about national sovereignty, as "this land is too small for a separate Palestinian state. It's a prescription for war, and I don't want to commit suicide—that's also an ethical value." He later added, "'Turn the other cheek' is not a Jewish ideal." He concluded that the settlers had right on their side, declaring, "To the victor belongs the spoils if the victor is moral, for the immoral loser, there can be no spoils."[193]

A bellicose Riskin emerged as the second intifada raged both within and outside Efrat following the final collapse of the Oslo process at Camp David II. "We are at war and we have to show them that they cannot beat us," he proclaimed, "only then can there be peace and we will be able to rehabilitate relations between Palestinians and Israelis."[194] In a debate with Palestinian activist and former Fatah official Salah Ta'ami, he opined, "You are wrong . . . dead wrong. You underestimate the Israeli and you underestimate the God of Israel. We have not just come to Israel. We have finally come home. And we will win. . . . We will win for our children's sake, we will win for our God's sake, and we will win for the free world's sake."[195] At the funeral of Jewish-American settler Sara Blaustein of Lawrence, New York, who was killed in a drive-by shooting only months after moving to the settlement, Riskin averred, "This is the continuation of our War of Independence."[196]

For all his bluster, Prime Minister Ariel Sharon called Riskin's bluff when his administration announced plans for a unilateral Israeli disengagement from the Gaza Strip. "I cannot deny the possibility that what happens in Gush Katif could just as easily happen in Efrat," Riskin acknowledged, recognizing that the final battle had come home to suburbia. Yet he publicly censured other rabbis who called for military personnel to disobey orders, admonishing would-be refuseniks that "Israel can withstand the evacuation of settlers from Gaza, it cannot withstand civil war." When asked in a 2007 interview after the Gaza disengagement what he would do if the government proceeded with further evacuations of the West Bank, including at Efrat, he asserted, "I do not believe in anarchy. If the government demanded it, I would reluctantly have to accept . . . [but] it will not happen again. It will not happen here."[197] More recently, Rabbi Riskin has expressed optimism about Efrat's status. "Look, I'm not a prophet," he prognosticated about the future of the settlement to which he had devoted his life efforts, "but I believe that Efrat will remain part of Israel."[198]

TODAY, AS EFRAT LOOKS to the historical horizon, her destiny remains unknown. Nonetheless, many of the settlement's Jewish-American residents have high hopes for its future. "I don't think Efrat will ever disappear," mused religious affairs director Bob Lang, while cautioning that "without any new building it's hard to see a real future for the community, the dynamics that happen anywhere in the world . . . [without] new people, new blood, that's not [a future]."[199] Mayor Oded Revivi, who coordinates closely with Lang, has recently been encouraging more secular families to move to Efrat. For him "part of the take-away of Gush Katif . . . was in the end we rotted in ghettos, that is to say, the communities were not sufficiently mixed." He also expressed the need to recruit native Israelis to move to Efrat to change the popular perception that the city was inhabited only by immigrants from New Jersey—he hoped by deliberately Israelizing the community, the general public would have deeper ties to its population and feel a visceral stake in the settlement. Yet, the mayor admitted these plans were a tough sell, as Revivi himself is unsure of the settlement's future. Weighing the discourse of the national consensus against the dictates of land for peace, he echoed the lyrics of the popular Bob Dylan song, where Efrat is a weatherman and "which way the wind will blow, it's hard to know."[200]

For some Jewish-American settlers like Sharon Katz, living under a Palestinian state could be an option they are willing to consider. To her mind, settling in Efrat not only was a messianic imperative but was part of her American liberal mindset, noting, "We were knowingly afraid . . . We wanted to do something to make it better. That's the John F. Kennedy in all of us . . . ask not what your country can do for you, but what you can do for your country." Yet as she ruefully acknowledged, "It doesn't work like it works in America—here's my road to peace—a road in Israel isn't like the ones you have on the New Jersey turnpike. And I think that's probably the problem." Over the years Katz has felt the need to leave behind her Americanness to some extent in order to confront the reality on the ground at Efrat, considering, "America is so movie oriented and wanting to have a happy ending and the right script; it's not like that in real life, especially life in Israel."[201]

When Rabbi Riskin was recently asked to sum up his involvement at Efrat, he too referenced a historical script, where "here [in Israel, as opposed to the Diaspora] the chapter headings are being written. If one has a chance at life as a Jew, I would want to be part of a chapter heading, rather than part of a footnote."[202] Clearly, he saw his own participation within the Israeli settler movement in grand historical terms, harboring the ambition of being a great man of Jewish history. Yet what conclusions can be drawn from the participation of Jewish-American immigrants in the Efrat project?

Riskin's fateful encounter with Moshe Moshkowitz on a West Bank tour offered the rabbi—and the Jewish-American settlers who would join in his endeavor—an opportunity to occupy an exalted position within the Zionist pantheon at Efrat. Their partnership to create this new city on a hilltop not only provided a new private-public model for settling in the occupied territories, but produced a unique historical narrative combining the mythology of pre-1948 Gush Etzion and messianic redemption alongside a distinctly American vision of pioneering (with a bit of luxury) beyond the Green Line. Efrat's mixed parentage is unique within the history of Jewish-American immigrants within the Israeli settler movement.

While Efrat may have symbolized the "bridge between our origins and our dreams," its pedigree often brought the settlement—and its quixotic chief rabbi—into conflict with the Israeli government, the native Israeli settler movement, and neighboring Palestinian communities. Though Efrat received unprecedented support for its establishment from the Israeli government in comparison to other Jewish-American settlements, its founders also faced down state forces during the Camp David and Oslo peace processes. Despite close ties to settler leaders, Moshkowitz successfully defeated early challenges from Ha-Kibbutz Ha-Dati and Riskin faced serious ideological strife with Gush Emunim, who condemned Efrat not only for its suburban comforts but for the luxury of its privileged status within the political consensus. Efrat has also had an unusual—and ambivalent—relationship with local Palestinian communities, engaging in quotidian interactions, dialogue projects, and charitable activities with some surrounding villages, while enduring a hostile and violent relationship with other townships. Most importantly, Riskin and his followers' progressive self-image has been challenged by charges that they expropriated Palestinian land to build Efrat and continue to obstruct Palestinian statehood. For many the clash between liberal values and settler realities has created profound cognitive dissonances and doubts about their city on a hilltop.

Rabbi Riskin has always attempted to occupy the middle ground in Efrat—even as the political landscape of his community has evolved over time. In our recent interview, Riskin denied his critics' indictments, asserting, "Nobody has ever accused me of sitting on the fence. I've never sat on the fence, sitting on the fence means you don't take a stand. I take a very, very strong stand." He then characterized his position as that of a "passionate moderate," contending: "I take a stand pro-settlement blocs. I take a strong stance against creating settlements in the middle of Arab territories, and illegal settlements. That's my position in Efrat as well . . . I am a passionate moderate. I do believe in peace. I do believe in democracy. I believe that democracy and Judaism are not antithetical, that without the foundations of democracy in this day, there will not be a Jewish state. I believe that they may not lift a hand against the IDF, but at the same time, we have the right to civil disobedience." Yet, in the end, he argued, "We have the right to be here, and I believe in Zionism with all my heart and soul."[203]

Despite Riskin's international reputation as a halakhic revolutionary,[204] a champion of Orthodox feminism,[205] and an innovator in modern Jewish life,[206] in the eyes of at least one progressive pundit, his attitudes about Efrat exemplify that "Riskin could no longer masquerade as the liberal orthodox rabbi" and that he truly is "a rightwing extremist in moderate's garb." At best, the rabbi's "yezer ha-tov [good inclination] had bowed to the realities of the yezer ha-ra' [evil inclination], eased by . . . moral rationalizations," and at worst, "through this life project, Riskin has caused more tragedy and pain to more Palestinians than any other rabbi of modern times, certainly more than Meir Kahane and his ilk."[207] The latter accusation might be an exaggeration, but the Efrat project has problematized conceptions of moderates and extremists—and the idea that religious and political progressivism go hand in hand—especially when personal beliefs and political realities have changed over time. As Riskin himself recognized, "I am being radicalized, but it is the conditions that are radicalizing me," quibbling over definitions of liberalism itself.[208] Today, Riskin remains a popular if quixotic figure as he energetically leads Efrat into the future four decades after his first encounter with his lifelong project on a West Bank hilltop. Certainly, another chapter heading of its unique story remains to be written.

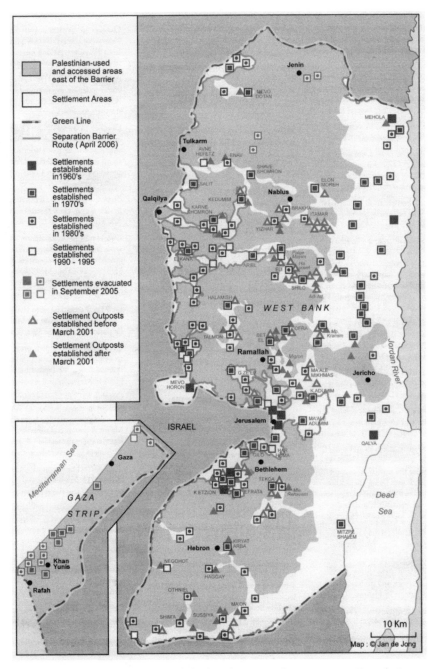

Map 1. Map of settlements established and evacuated, 1967–2008. Foundation
for Middle East Peace/Jan de Jong.

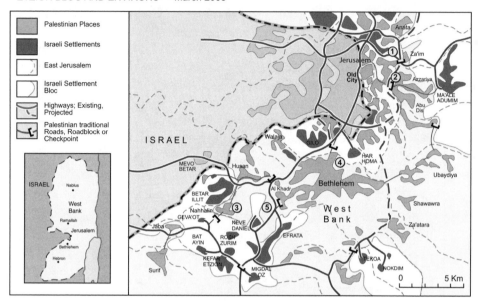

Map 2. Map of Gush Etzion region of the West Bank. Foundation for Middle East Peace/Jan de Jong.

Figure 1. American-Israeli settler Bob Smallman building the first houses at Yamit, January 1975. Moshe Milner/National Photo Collection/Government Press Office, Israel.

Figure 2. Gedaliah Mazal and his son Moshe on Israeli Independence Day at Yamit, ca.1980. Courtesy of Gedaliah Mazal.

Figure 3. Children in
Efrat, 1986. Herman
Chanania / National Photo
Collection / Government
Press Office, Israel.

Figure 4. Rabbi Shlomo Riskin dancing at a Torah dedication ceremony in
Efrat, 1997. Amos Ben Gershom / National Photo Collection / Government Press
Office, Israel.

Figure 5. Early housing at Tekoa against the backdrop of Mount Herodian, 1982. Herman Chanania/National Photo Collection/Government Press Office, Israel.

Figure 6. Tekoa, two decades after its founding, 1998. Saar Yaacov/National Photo Collection/Government Press Office, Israel.

Figure 7. Miriam Levinger *(back)* and Sara Nachshon taking charge of daily affairs in the new Jewish settlement of Hebron, summer 1968. Moshe Milner / National Photo Collection / Government Press Office, Israel.

Figure 8. Grave of Dr. Baruch Goldstein, Kiryat Arba. Hebrew Wikipedia Creative Commons, CC-BY-SA-4.0.

Figure 9. Jewish-American settlers, including Yisrael Medad *(far right)* and Shifra Blass, meet with Prime Minister Yitzhak Shamir at the Madrid Conference, 1991. Courtesy of Yisrael Medad.

CHAPTER FOUR

Turn Left at the End of the World

Garin Lev Zion and the Origins of Tekoa

G ARIN LEV ZION, a cooperative organization of Jewish-American immigrants who founded the West Bank settlement of Tekoa in 1979 considered themselves to be new pioneers staking a territorial claim with their seed colony at the "heart of Zion." These American-Israelis defiantly built a new community deep in the West Bank in the midst of the Camp David negotiations, seeing their destiny as guarantors of a Jewish presence in the occupied territories. From its first days, their "city on a hilltop" was a fountainhead for controversy over Israeli settlement policy and a point of friction with neighboring Palestinian communities.

Led by Robert (Bobby) and Linda Brown from the Upper West Side of Manhattan, a small coterie of Jewish-American Zionists believed that their bodies were on the East Coast of the United States but their hearts were in the West Bank. After several years of organizing in the United States and Israel, they followed in the footsteps of the Israel Defense Forces and a small Russian-Israeli civilian contingent to establish a permanent settlement at Tekoa. However, more than any other American-Israeli settlement founded in the occupied territories, their relationship with the Israeli government, the native Israeli settler movement, and surrounding Palestinian communities was fraught with tension and violence. While Tekoa was a key priority of the State of Israel after the Yom Kippur War, Garin Lev Zion was seen as an obstacle to peace during the Camp David process and the group ultimately decided to squat at the site in violation of IDF and official orders. Though the garin shared an ideological alliance with Gush Emunim, who helped them seize Tekoa in 1979, they often parted ways on tactics, and the controversial Israeli-Palestinian dialogue project established by Tekoa's rabbi Menachem Froman later caused a permanent rift between the two factions. Most importantly, despite the struggle for grassroots reconciliation spearheaded by the settlement's spiritual leader, Tekoa experienced the most hostile and bloody relationship with its Palestinian neighbors of the three American-Israeli settlements profiled in this book. Today Garin Lev Zion mostly seems to be a victim of its own success as the settlement thrives in its third decade, yet Tekoa's fate hangs in the balance of an Israeli-Palestinian final status agreement.

"Turn left at the end of the world" is how Tekoa's founder Bobby Brown once characterized the settlement's physical location, although this description also mapped the ideological landscape of left-wing 1960s Jewish-American activism in which Garin Lev Zion took root. For its residents, their settlement project paired ancient biblical promise and contemporary Jewish rights protection, making the Judean desert bloom and a modern-day pioneering, and Israeli ultra-nationalism and utopian pluralism. By bringing their American vision to the home of the prophet Amos, these Manhattanites saw historic opportunity in homesteading at the heart of Zion on the West Bank frontier.

Thirty years on, this narrative explores Tekoa's origins and legacy for the future.

"We Gained a Foothold": Early Settlement at Tekoa, 1973–1977

Much like the origins of Efrat (Chapter 3), permanent settlement at Tekoa was considered a key strategic objective of the State of Israel after the Yom Kippur War. On the very day in October 1974 that Moshe Moshkowitz first wrote Prime Minister Yitzhak Rabin about plans for an urban settlement at Efrat, the Ministry of Defense had already granted initial approval for a new township south of Bethlehem. The following spring, the site was declared a closed military zone to prepare the parcel for civilian settlement.[1] Tekoa received full-page billing in the World Zionist Organization's

1976 *Jerusalem District Regional Development Plan* as one of four new settlements to be built to ensure geographic and strategic continuity from Jerusalem eastward toward the new city-settlement of Maale Adumim (Red Hills) and the Dead Sea.[2] Tekoa, located along an eponymous stream south of Mount Herodian, would occupy the vital "axis of the road" between the Hebron Hills and the Jordan Valley.[3]

On the symbolic date of June 6, 1975, during the eighth anniversary of the Six Day War and the conquest of the occupied territories, members of the modern Orthodox Bnai Akiva (Sons of Akiva) youth movement attached to the IDF's Noar Halutzai Lohem (Fighting Pioneer Youth [NAHAL]) Brigade unit at nearby Kibbutz Kfar Etzion decamped for an outpost near the base of Mount Herodian.[4] Later that summer, the public caught its first glimpse of the new settlement at its inauguration ceremony, which was featured in the NAHAL Brigade newsletter under the headline "Takanu Yeted B-Tekoa" (lit. we gained a foothold at Tekoa, a Hebrew play on words). The event was sufficiently momentous to be presided over by the NAHAL's commanding officer himself alongside other prominent visiting dignitaries. In a long speech, General Yona Efrat quoted a passage from the Book of Amos about the Israelites planting vineyards at Tekoa— gesturing to both religio-historical claims and the Zionist idea of making the desert bloom. (If words couldn't suffice, an accompanying photo of a NAHAL couple chatting outside their spartan tent certainly brought fruitful multiplication to mind!) The ceremony closed by raising the Israeli flag over Tekoa.[5]

A visit by a Bnai Akiva reporter in the fall of 1975 returned to the theme of mastering nature at Tekoa, where "man can subdue the desert, can conquer, and overcome her."[6] The article framed the new settlement as part of the ancient patrimony of the tribe of Judah. Yet it also briefly noted a historic Palestinian presence, observing that the site was built on Arab ruins and that homes and villages were visible in the panorama.[7] Nonetheless, the landscape of Tekoa was viewed solely as a bridge between an ancient Jewish past and a thriving Israeli future.[8]

For the next two years, the NAHAL garin at Tekoa attempted to span that gap—the group was so industrious that they won the 1977 Jewish Agency prize for "outpost of the year"![9] Having fulfilled their mission, the Ministry of Defense transferred responsibility for Tekoa to civilian authorities in Gush Emunim on November 30, 1977.[10] Under its aegis, a handful of Russian immigrants primarily from the city of Beit Shemesh were recruited to settle at the site, although extreme isolation and harsh conditions saw steady attrition as the months went by. Without the influx of new settlers, Tekoa seemed fated to disappear off the map.

Heart of Zion: Bobby Brown and the Jewish-American Founders of Tekoa

Meanwhile, far away from the West Bank on the Upper West Side of Manhattan, a young and idealistic activist couple named Bobby and Linda Brown set out to form a new collective immigration association they called Garin Lev Zion (Seed Colony of the Heart of Zion) for settlement in the occupied territories in the late 1970s.

Born in 1952, Bobby Brown was raised by a family of German-Jewish immigrants in the Washington Heights neighborhood of Manhattan.[11] The Brown home was not strictly observant and was keen to integrate into American society. Their children were sent to public school, although they also received some Jewish education. Brown described himself as a lifelong Zionist, vowing at the age of twelve to immigrate to Israel in his teenage conviction that "after 2,000 years of praying for a Jewish state, we finally had one, and I thought to come here and be part of it."[12] Brown was studying at the elite Stuyvesant High School when the Six Day War broke out, a moment that inspired him to seek out Jewish activist movements in New York City.

Brown claimed to come to the Revisionist Zionist youth group BETAR without ideological convictions, "the usual way someone hears about any movement . . . because someone had a friend who went there purely because it was close to his house, or they had a ping-pong table, or the girls were a little better looking."[13] However, he was quickly attracted to its activist agenda. In his spare time he frequented a clubhouse where he studied Ze'ev Jabotinsky's philosophy of territorial maximalism, lionized the Zionist martyrs of Tel Hai, championed Revisionist Knesset opposition leader Menachem Begin, and sang "Shir Betar" (the BETAR anthem), vowing, "Lamut o Likbosh et Ha-Har [to die or conquer the hill]," pursuits that had a profound influence on his later activities at Tekoa. Comparing his experience in BETAR with a brief interest in *Bnai Akiva* where they "just talked, and talked and talked," he found "here was a group that talked but also acted" and "this interested me very much. The idea that a Jew could have some determination of his own history."[14] Eli Birnbaum, a co-founder of Tekoa and a friend of Brown's from their New York days, also noted how they bonded as a peer group of baby-boomers. "Knowing our parents' generation sat and watched and gave big excuses about why they shouldn't do anything during the Holocaust time, I think that also affected us." In contrast, their children "[were] saying . . . if we have an ideology, we're not going to sit back and let someone else do it." For both Brown and Birnbaum, "that idea, that if you believe in something, act on it, became my reason for making aliya."[15]

Convinced that "when you're eighteen years old, you have to be an extremist,"[16] Brown embraced the combative message of the BETAR youth movement, including the use of violence in the name of self-defense. (He even participated in Camp BETAR, a sleep-away camp in upstate New York that provided Zionist indoctrination alongside weapons training.) He made a mark for himself by taking part in group meetings and civil disobedience campaigns, rising in the ranks to BETAR's national leadership board by the late 1970s. He also met his wife, Linda, through his activism, remembering fondly, "In three years I went out with her fifty times. I don't think we ever saw a movie. Going out would be a Soviet Jewry demonstration. Or there would be a march on Washington,"[17] and together, the couple discovered a shared passion for Zionist activism and planned to immigrate to Israel.

The liberal social movements of 1960s and 1970s America also had an influence on Brown and his later compatriots at Tekoa. He recalling being "mildly against the Vietnam War" and aware of the SDS branch on his college campus at Long Island University ("which was of course run by Jews"[18]), though he was less inspired by their ideology than by the tactics of the New Left. For Eli Birnbaum, the civil rights struggle sparked a realization about his own political commitments, as "I started thinking, wait a minute, you are willing to demonstrate for the Eskimos, you are willing to demonstrate for civil rights, is there a reason why you won't demonstrate for something Jewish?"[19] By the mid-1970s both Birnbaum and Brown perceived a widening chasm between their Zionist allegiances and leftist activism where "the attention on questions of social justice and American imperialism were just nonissues for us." Further, Brown couldn't reconcile his positions on the Vietnam War and the State of Israel, suggesting, "To come out and fight the Pentagon and the military and in the next breath [to say] that Israel needs weapons and we should help Israel seemed to us to be counter-productive. We couldn't see any way of being morally right—we side-stepped the issue."[20] Domestically, Brown also sensed that Jewish-American activists were in a difficult position after 1967. To him, the New York City teacher's strike in 1968 was an indicator that "the civil rights movement was turning a little bad," and though "we felt we were naturally part of that generation, I do think that the nonviolence of Martin Luther King had turned into a very anti-whitey violent stream, obviously a small proportion, but that pitted often black militants against Jews, and we were clear where our stand would be."[21] While Brown praised black militancy for popularizing ethnic identification in the United States, crediting this trend with deepening his own connection to Judaism,[22] he cautioned against "other groups, especially Jewish groups . . . combining and working with what we conceived to be forces destructive to Israel" such as the Black Panthers. Instead BETAR initially attempted to forge common cause with other Jewish activist groups in the late 1960s, forming an alliance known as the Network, which quickly broke down over the question of Israel. Brown explained, "[At first] we reached an agreement that if you want to talk against capitalism, be my guest, you want to talk against Vietnam, right on man, you want to talk about civil rights, that's fine, but if you open your mouth about Israel, then we'll come down on you like a ton of bricks. And that worked for about a year and then they started talking about Zionism. And we just went into their office and tore them apart—destroyed their entire office and spray-painted 'Zionism=liberation' and stuff on it. We were activists of that nature. We were activists for Israel."[23] Yet as the gulf between Jewish activism and the New Left grew, Brown did not gravitate toward the budding neoconservative movement that appeared on the New York Jewish scene at the time. "Abortion issues, big government versus little government weren't our issue," he contended, "our portfolio and our agenda was a Jewish agenda. . . . We should do whatever helps the Jews the most. It wasn't ideologically right. It was very pro-Eretz Yisrael belongs to the Jewish People."[24]

Yet, for Brown and his future colleagues, it was not only being pushed out of the New Left but their own pull toward Israel after the catastrophic 1973 war that propelled them to the occupied territories a few years later: "Life in Israel was pretty idyllic between '67 and '73, and '73 was a rude awakening [as] we began withdrawals from the Sinai and all kinds of talks. . . . To me, we not only wanted to make aliya, but we wanted to make the highest contribution we could make to the State of Israel. And if people want to take away an area from the Jewish people, we felt we should keep that area, and that the borders of the Israel were determined by where people lived. So we decided we wanted to live somewhere in Judea and Samaria."[25] Moreover, Brown was increasingly aware of the painful distinction between rhetoric and reality in his own role in BETAR, ruefully recollecting, "I remember when I lived in America I used to talk about settlement in Judea and Samaria. And people used to say, you're a big talker, you're sitting here . . . and I said, I am going to go on aliyah and I am going to live in one of those places. I believe I will."[26]

Despite the fact that Linda Brown was the sitting national president of the Association of Americans and Canadians for Aliya (AACA) and had helped others organize cooperative immigration organizations both within and beyond the Green Line in the mid-1970s, the couple found it difficult to identify a project that would stir their own Zionist imaginations. The Bnai Akiva movement, a typical choice for modern Orthodox Jewish-Americans, had never held much appeal to Brown because "[it had] very little Zionism . . . any Zionism there was, was confused with being on a kibbutz" and he didn't feel it would fulfill his immigration aspirations, judging, "I understood the theme of kibbutz life and the importance of kibbutz life, but I never saw myself running after cows, or shuttling cow crap as the ultimate reason for being a Jew."[27] (He laughingly divulged, "We didn't know what the [Hebrew] word [for] tractor was" back when he was the president of BETAR in Manhattan, boasting, "They would be proud of me today, I bought one!"[28]) In contrast, the possibility of becoming part of a Gush Emunim project seemed promising to the Browns. Yet while Garin Lev Zion did eventually form an alliance with the native Israeli settlement enterprise, their path from the Upper West Side to the West Bank was far from predictable.

"Shape the Course of Jewish History instead of Staying Home and Watching the Rangers, the Knicks, and the Fonz": Garin Lev Zion and the Origins of Tekoa, 1977–1979

Garin Lev Zion was born at a meeting held at Bobby and Linda Brown's Manhattan apartment on Super Bowl Sunday in January 1977 when most Jewish New Yorkers opted to stay home and watch the football game rather than attend a Zionist settlement strategy session. One of the few attendees who showed up on the inauspicious date, a political scientist named Dr. Amiel Ungar, was "so shocked that any group would call a meeting on Super Bowl Sunday that he came 'dafka' [precisely] because of it and joined Garin Lev Zion" on the spot.[29] Initially, their meetings were nothing more than casual conversations about the possibility of organizing a cooperative immigration project in the occupied territories. Eli Birnbaum was reluctantly enlisted by his friend Brown that winter, recalling, "I mean I was a member, but I wasn't sold on the idea." In fact, he was far more interested in fulfilling his Zionist dreams as a psychologist in a development town within the Green Line after a recent extended stay in Israel, but he was won over to Garin Lev Zion's cause when "Bobby said, 'Well listen, I'm not going to argue with you. It's important, but Yeruham has problems that are going to be there thirty years from now. Do you believe in the ideology of Judea and Samaria, that Jews should be able to live everywhere? . . . Well, if you don't make the move, there won't be any Judea and Samaria.' " Other than the idea of settling in the occupied territories, the membership could agree on little more. Birnbaum recollected, "I attended all the meetings, where all the maniacs would be talking about what kind of ideology—would it be to live in Gush Etzion? No, no, we need to live in the middle of Arab Shechem [Nablus] on a hill, surrounded by Arabs, that's the only ideology." It was mostly idle but impassioned talk and "most of them are still in the States talking about aliya."[30]

After further discussion, Garin Lev Zion made its public debut in the Orthodox New York weekly, the *Jewish Press,* in an open letter that combined Zionist ideals with the contemporary American zeitgeist. "Somewhere, in a small apartment in upper Manhattan, an historic revolution has been taking place in the past few weeks," former Jewish Defense League member Dov Frisch revealed, "a revolution of Jewish spirit, Jewish determination, and Jewish pride . . . and it is a revolution worth the attention of all Jews everywhere. It is the revolution of 'Lev Zion,' the 'Heart of Zion.'" He quickly turned to the heart of the matter, describing a group of Jews who were situated on the East Coast of the United States but their souls were in the West Bank.[31] "Not only do they call their 'garin' by the name 'Lev Zion' because that is where they want to live," he attested, verily, "it is in such people as the Bobby and Linda Browns . . . that the heart of the People of Zion can be found beating most strongly."

Frisch argued that the decline of American civilization—especially what he perceived as the decadence of New York City in the 1970s—was a strong motive for immigration. "It is hard to make aliya," he conceded, "[but] the members of Garin Lev Zion are unconcerned by the excuses offered by their peers . . . they know what the Heart of Zion has to offer, and they know what the Heart of Manhattan has to offer." Rather that dwelling amid the debauchery of the Big Apple, he titillated recruits with the promise of adventure on the West Bank frontier, where they could "imagine the thrill and honor of helping build the first settlement ever to be established by American Jews on the soil of liberated Shomron—Samaria!" Further, he beguiled them with the prospect of making the desert bloom (while ignoring preexisting Palestinian presence), asking readers to "consider what it will mean to look on the barren land below your feet and to see the first flower growing; you will not be watching as a tree grows in Brooklyn but as a flower grows in Eretz Yisrael, the land of Israel. And you will have made the land come to life again—even as it will revitalize you."[32] His concluded with a seductive challenge for self-realization, evangelizing, "If you are interested in helping shape the course of Jewish history—rather than staying home and watching the Rangers, the Knicks, and the Fonz—then it is not too late for you to join this historic aliya effort."[33]

By May, twelve families and fourteen singles in the New York area had already registered with the group. They were mostly highly educated and upwardly mobile couples and singles who listed such diverse professions as psychologist, intensive care nurse, salesman, computer programmer, rabbi, hotel manager, accountant, potter, photographer, and political scientist on their intake forms.[34] After an aborted attempt to incorporate as a BETAR garin, they decided to officially affiliate with Ha-Noar Ha-Mizrachi (NOAM [the Mizrachi Youth]), which also sponsored the Bnai Akiva youth movement.[35] Their spring 1977 membership report seemed to hold potential, but Brown was also not above a little deliberate obfuscation to keep their NOAM representative interested in the project. He smiled as he recounted one humorous exchange with a staffer, who asked, "How many families do you have? I said twenty, so he believed ten, and we had two [the Browns and Ungar]."[36] Whether NOAM saw through this ruse remains unknown, but they granted the garin a small budget to promote their settlement plans.

For example, one advertisement summoned potential members to an open meeting at Mizrachi headquarters in New York in March 1977. "Join the dynamic Garin-Aliyah in the United States today!" and "Become members of the historic movement of the Young Religious Zionists to settle on a government-approved site in the liberated Shomron (Samaria)!" encouraged the flyer—the event itself would feature several guest speakers, including an army general, a right-wing scholar journalist, and a Talmudist (what insights they might have into the project was anyone's guess)—and if that failed to satisfy their curiosity, "refreshments will be served!" Reading between the lines of the promotional text, one notices several problematic misrepresentations: First and foremost, the West Bank is twice characterized as "liberated" territories and is referred to by biblical terminology alone, ignoring or denying Israel's occupation and disputed land claims. The advertisement also suggested that their new settlement had received official authorization, a blatant fabrication that would emerge as a critical issue for the future of the garin. Further, while only religious Zionists were recruited, Tekoa later became a mixed community of modern Orthodox and nonobservant settlers. These distortions had a deep impact on the garin's discourse from its earliest days.[37]

Garin Lev Zion held its first national convention at the Hotel Melbourne in the Catskills in May 1977, where it ratified a credo and constitution.[38] An interview with the *Jewish Week* that summer announced an ambitious program for restoring a historic patrimony while homesteading on the Tekoa hinterland in an article pointedly titled "Whose West Bank? 24 Pioneers Plan Aliya to Form Community." As Bobby Brown explained, the group hoped to establish their new city on a hilltop at Shilo between Ramallah and Nablus. He bolstered their project with a blend of biblical prophecy and civil liberties, as "this is the birthplace of the Jewish people. That's why we call our garin Lev Tzion, the heart of Zion. No Israeli govern-

ment has the right to take this land from the Jewish people and give it away."
Meanwhile, he downplayed Palestinian land claims, dismissing, "Anyway,
the territory is not the way people imagine it—teeming with refugee camps.
The fact is that the land is underutilized." "We want to pioneer a new
area . . . we are ready to do as Trumpeldor said—be [it] a pick, a shovel, or
a gun," Brown exclaimed, outlining his intent to trailblaze on the West
Bank frontier, although the journalist wryly observed that "none of them
look as if he or she has ever handled a tool other than a pencil or a type-
writer." Perhaps considering the pen mightier than the sword, the group
forswore taking up arms (or even legs) against the state to found an illegal
outpost as Gush Emunim had counseled Brown to do, averring, "We want
government approval. We don't want to come like thieves to take what
really belongs to us."[39]

Garin Lev Zion elaborated on its stance on legality in an open letter to
Israeli prime minister Menachem Begin in the *Jewish Press* in late September 1977, while, unbeknownst to the Jewish-American group, the State
of Israel had simultaneously initiated back-channel diplomacy with Egypt
that would culminate in the Camp David Accords. "Mr. Begin, we are
coming," declared Bobby Brown, introducing himself as the leader of a group
of twenty-five who hoped to "spearhead a new wave of American aliyah
that will inspire our fellow Jews in the Diaspora far and wide." At their
new city on a hilltop in the occupied territories, Garin Lev Zion would
soon be "creating the type of environment that will continue to set an
example, bolstering the identity of those we leave behind." Not only do "we
want to plough the land, enriching the holy soil," wrote Brown, he also
envisioned making the desert bloom in a uniquely American fashion, as
"we want to build and produce, to advance academic research, and infuse
the American style of professionalism into Israel's communication industry."
Above all, the group aspired "to do them in the Shomron, at Shiloah."

"You sent out a clarion call to return home, we will be amongst the first
to comply," Brown proclaimed to the prime minister, communicating his
message that "Mr. Begin, we are coming . . . [and] we need your help." The
garin president did made sure to pay lip service to his native Israeli allies in
passing tribute that "we respect and honor the pioneers of Gush Emunim,"
but he was also quick to distance Garin Lev Zion from their wildcat settlement activities, demurring, "We differ tactically from our colleagues . . . in

one respect. Call us naïve if you will, but we find it abhorrent the need for Jews to come like thieves in the night to settle land that is rightfully and legally ours to possess." Brown then beseeched the prime minister for official backing of Garin Lev Zion's efforts, writing, "We want your acknowledgment and endorsement not after we have camped out in Shiloah for three years, but now, before we arrive." He continued, "Let us be frank Mr. Begin. . . . We have been urged . . . to hold a press conference declaring our intentions at Lod, and proceed as a convoy to Shiloah to 'set up house,' let the bureaucracy be damned! Is this how you want us to come? Should it even be news when Jews return home to live in the heartland of Eretz Yisrael? Must our first step upon arriving involve a semi- or quasi-defiant step not in concert with the government we so admire: Can we not come proudly, publically, and legally to locate at Shiloah with full blessings? If not now, when?" Brown closed his petition with an ominous hint that other tactics might be necessary if the prime minister did not comply with their request for assistance (perhaps in light of previous settlement rows), emphasizing, "Even if forces beyond your control, God forbid, prevent you from doing. We want you to know one unalterable fact. We are coming, Mr. Begin."[40]

That month, the Israeli public also learned of Garin Lev Zion's plans to settle in the occupied territories in an article in the mainstream Hebrew language daily *Maariv*, which playfully explained how the group intended to immigrate from the mountains of the Catskills (where the garin's first convention had been held) to the hills of the northern West Bank. The journalist profiled several members of the organization, underscoring their dual identities as American "political activists" and observant Zionists. "As a religious person, as a Zionist, as a Beitar member, my heart is already in Israel, in the Shomron, in Shilo," explained Bobby Brown, citing "Jewish pride," "historical Zionist identity," and "spiritual life" in his decision to immigrate to the occupied territories. For recent recruit Hanoch Young, contemporary pioneering in the footsteps of the patriarchs drew him to the garin, reasoning, "'Lev Zion' for me is a return to the Shomron, where our forefathers lived. It is a challenge to build the land of Israel anew. Not the establishment of some kind of ghetto in Queens or Brooklyn. This fulfills the obligatory commandment of living in the land of Israel, of going home." Jewish Agency employee Shifra Stein agreed, stating, "I want to live in the Shomron. I like the atmosphere of the place and its history. At this stage,

the aspect of pioneering also appeals to me." Linda Brown too was "enchanted by the pioneering spirit," although she was the only one who emphasized the strategic element "to settle an area that isn't inhabited, where
there aren't enough people to settle it." But they would not come without
a proper mandate, reiterating their plea to Prime Minister Begin in insisting,
"We want official recognition to settle in the Shomron. A Jew must settle
all over the land in a law-abiding manner." While the reporter had her
doubts about Garin Lev Zion's resolve, noting that only a few members
had opened immigration portfolios, she urged the Israeli public to support
the endeavor if it ever came to fruition.[41]

Israel Aliya Center officials were cautiously optimistic about Garin Lev
Zion that fall, as candidacy files preserved in the Jewish Agency archives
reveal.[42] Bureaucrats evaluating Bobby and Linda Brown considered them
a "lovely couple" with a history of Zionist activism in the United States,
although they noted their poor Hebrew.[43] Amiel Ungar (age twenty-nine),
who had joined the group on its first meeting on Super Bowl Sunday, was
a bachelor born in Israel who held a PhD in political science and was found
to be "very appreciated by the other garin members and is one of the garin's 'guiding forces.' "[44] Hanoch Young (age twenty-two), a physical education teacher who had visited Israel on three separate occasions also met
with approval, as one official wrote in admiration, "I must say that I was
very impressed by Hanoch's personality and I strongly believe he will be a
positive force in the garin."[45] His fiancée Sharon Silver (age twenty), a college
student and ceramicist, also earned a favorable recommendation despite
the fact that "she does not have a strong Jewish background."[46] Accountant Jonathan Rosenberg (age twenty-seven) and his social worker wife,
Rebecca (age twenty-five), convinced authorities of their keen grasp of
future responsibilities with Garin Lev Zion, who deemed "they are both
ready to begin a new lifestyle in Israel."[47] (Officials were blunt in negative
appraisals as well, writing of secretary Shoshana Smithline [age twenty-
six] that "she did not make a definite impression on me regarding her
ability to fit into the framework of the moshav."[48]) For the most part, the
government found the group to be small, pluralistic, and highly motivated—
characteristics that later came to define their community at Tekoa.

Meanwhile Israeli authorities vacillated about where these Jewish-
American immigrants should live in the occupied territories. Despite the
group's expressed preference to settle at Shilo, the Jewish Agency considered

placing the group near other West Bank settlements like Ofra, Kiryat Arba, and Kochav Ha-Shachar (where, similar to Efrat, they ran up against the objections of native religious Zionist settlers[49]) and also discussed farther-flung locations like the Golan Heights and Gaza Strip.[50] Mostly, as was the policy with Garin Yamit, they encouraged these willing American Jews to immigrate first and worry about the site later.[51]

Frustrated that the Jewish Agency did not seem responsive to their needs, the garin wrote to the government in private correspondence that "the consensus of the membership is that the Shomron is the only area acceptable to them for a possible site. . . . This decision lies in the moral and ideological structure of the [garin's] constitution."[52] Bobby Brown also expounded on these prerogatives in a public interview in the NOAM movement magazine *Bechol Zot* (Nevertheless) in early 1978, expressing that Garin Lev Zion remained committed to a strategic immigration project for the Camp David era. Combining political exigencies with a back-to-the-land ethos, he professed that "keeping Shomron is an important part of our belief. The best way to deal with such a cause is by living on the land." Eschewing "the excuse Israeli officials give when asked how they can give up the land is, 'Well, you have no right to speak, you're only living in New York,'" Brown characterized Garin Lev Zion as "a wide classification of Jewish activists" whom he considered up to the challenge: "The people who go on aliyah to the liberated areas are a special kind of the best people. They're people who are not only willing to make a hard life for themselves, but almost the *hardest* in the appreciation of certain ideals . . . that living in Yehuda and Shomron is a mitzvah, living there will protect the land for future generations, [they] feel strongly enough about this that they're willing to tie their own futures with that of Shomron." While Brown candidly acknowledged the Carter administration's opposition to the construction of new Israeli settlements, he confirmed his group's plans, declaring, "One of the things that Jewish history teaches us is that to build on galut [diaspora] is like building on sand. The wind changes, the sand shifts, and things fall. So we would like to build something in the Shomron that we hope, in one thousand years, will still be there." Summarizing her impressions of Garin Lev Zion, the reporter concluded, "Essentially your motivation is idealism."[53]

However, the garin's dream was dashed when the Jewish Agency made clear that the group could not settle in the northern West Bank in July 1978. Instead, for the first time, officials vaguely alluded to placing Garin Lev

Zion in "the region of the Judean Desert, the area of Tekoa."[54] But a clear future for the garin remained elusive almost a year after they announced their expectations of the prime minister.

By mid-1978 the garin's aggressive recruitment drive succeeded in enrolling upward of fifty members (nineteen couples, twelve singles, and seventeen children), including the Browns, the Birnbaums, and Amiel Ungar already in Israel.[55] Perhaps it was inevitable that group cohesiveness waned as they remained in "frozen animation"[56] with the government. Even the Browns, who were living in temporary accommodations at the Gilo Absorption Center in Jerusalem, were exasperated. While they rejected a return to the United States, they recognized the need to evaluate their situation with fresh eyes and began to explore alternatives outside the *garin* framework. The couple agreed that "basically we knew we wanted to live in Judea and Samaria, we wanted to live near a major city [and] we preferred Jerusalem to all others, and we wanted a place where we could contribute and make a difference."[57] Eventually they contacted AMANA (Covenant), Gush Emunim's settlement arm, who arranged for the Browns and a few other members of the garin already in Israel to spend successive Sabbaths in settlements across the West Bank. These efforts were less than promising at first, as Eli Birnbaum conceded, "Each place was more problematic from our point of view." Their long-awaited first visit to Shilo, where the garin had originally aspired to settle, was a complete disaster and a profound letdown—he ruefully recalled how the five families on site were entirely unfriendly to outsiders and completely ignored the two Jewish-American couples who came for the weekend.[58] As their search dragged on, Brown later joked that AMANA officials started to suspect that "we're not sure these people want to settle there, they just want to go away for Shabbat!"[59]

One serendipitous Shabbat visit brought them to Tekoa in the summer of 1978. When Brown described the region at the time, he emphasized the emptiness of the land, expounding, "The whole Eastern Gush consisted of Tekoa. There was nothing else in the area. It was, as they say, 'go to the end of the world and turn left' and that's basically where Tekoa was."[60] A government official also told Birnbaum about the new settlement, paraphrasing, "You guys really want something? There is a place out down south, near Gush Etzion, there is no road, no water, no electricity, only a few crazy people down there, and we think you're perfect!" (He laughingly remembered, "Most people would get insulted when someone says that to you!"[61])

"Nonetheless, we came . . . and we fell in love with the idea behind Tekoa—a place for all people, for all Jews, religious and secular, Sephardi and Ashkenazi, old, young, not very identical type people—and it looked like a place that really needed us. We decided we'd like to give it a try here."[62] Their American ideals of pluralism and diversity—albeit a vision that excluded Palestinians from their city on a hilltop—would emerge as an important element in the history and discourse of Tekoa.

Garin Lev Zion faced both ideological and practical difficulties as it worked to reconstitute itself in the eastern corner of Gush Etzion. First, native Israeli settlers from Ha-Poel Ha-Dati (the Religious Workers' Party) registered their displeasure with the Jewish-Americans' ambiguous and fanciful settlement plans. Birnbaum admitted that these objections were not uncalled for, as "We talked out of our hats, we had no idea, we talked for idealistic reasons," and when they told a contact in the Ministry of Agriculture about their aspirations, he "was hysterically laughing."[63] However, like at Efrat, the intercession of the Jewish Agency converted the native Israeli settler movement from antagonist to ally.[64]

With its external opponents seemingly appeased, the garin confronted a more serious challenge from within. When eight families already in Israel convened at a caucus on Mount Gerizim near Nablus in mid-1978 to discuss the possibility of settling at Tekoa, the U.S.-based contingent of Garin Lev Zion, with little irony, viciously attacked their faction's idealism. "There were people in New York saying, 'They are selling out, they are going to Gush Etzion!'" Birnbaum guffawed, "They basically said, you have no right to make the decision for the garin, and we want to live in Shechem. And that was basically the end of the garin." Garin Lev Zion remained nominally intact so "we were able to tell anyone who we met with that we had a garin of 35 registered families,"[65] but Brown was seemingly unfazed by the collapse of the group, believing that "the truth is, if there is an Eastern Gush Etzion, and God-willing, it stays in Jewish hands, then I think those original pioneers who came here were really the ones who built it up from the ground."[66] Garin Lev Zion—or what was left of it—rapidly signaled its intent to settle at Tekoa.

Brown's cadre quickly found that Jewish Agency bureaucrats were as ignorant as they were about conditions on the ground.[67] The government also hesitated to provide material assistance and approvals in the early days of the Camp David accords, although authorization for new settlements in Gush Etzion persisted throughout peace negotiations. (See Chapter 3.) The group faced one delay after the next and began to lose faith in the state's promise to assist their settlement project. Although Garin Lev Zion had initially rebuffed Gush Emunim's proposal to illegally occupy the site, Brown and his colleagues reconsidered their suggestion as months went by without any progress on the ground.

In June 1979 Garin Lev Zion decided to take matters into its own hands and a contingent of ten families including the Browns, the Birnbaums, and Amiel Ungar began squatting intermittently at the site. That October, Gush Emunim initiated a series of wildcat land seizures at several sites across the West Bank. At Tekoa, activists broke through the old fence of the NAHAL outpost and secured the basecamp, subsequently setting up a series of small garrisons, including a shelter designated as a synagogue, and called upon the government to lay claim to the entire 950-dunam area. Defense Minister Ezer Weitzman seemed inclined to accede to their request, informing a reporter that he was in favor of further settlement but was dubious about Tekoa, suggesting, "I have a problem with the seizure of private lands, also [especially] when they are rocky terrain."[68] (It is unclear whether he was referring to preexisting Palestinian settlement, although this seems a likely explanation.) Two weeks later, the squatters at Tekoa came to a showdown with IDF soldiers. The comical eviction procedure was cheekily characterized as "'Hide Go Seek' Games in the Streets of Yehuda V-Shomron" by a *Yediot Ahronot* journalist who detailed the day's efforts, following settlers as they alighted to the hilltop, were chased down by soldiers, stopped to take a coffee break for a bit of respite, and then tried again. At Tekoa there had been pleasant weather for such a game, and the activists had succeeded in raising a flag and declaring a settlement, although "it was harder to find the settlement itself."[69] Participant Eli Birnbaum recalled, "The thing is, that [Tekoa] is so far in the middle of no-where's-ville that they didn't find us. They took down all the outposts in one day, but they didn't take us down. No one knew we existed. We actually had to call them and say, 'Hey, we're here.' And then they came to take us down!"[70] Despite early clashes with the IDF, Minister of Agriculture Ariel Sharon called for the construction of fifteen new settlements that fall, including the development of Tekoa.[71]

From the West Side to the West Bank:
Tekoa since 1979

Today, Tekoa is a thriving community that has grown from ten squatters to over 3,500 individuals (approximately 615 families) in the past thirty-seven years.[72] Yet, back in 1979, the isolated and rustic settlement truly seemed to be "turn left at the end of the world." In its first weeks and months, Tekoa was a crude makeshift camp of concrete *eshkubiot* (prefabricated caravans) hastily erected on a barren landscape without any public services, amenities, or décor. "Not even a tree," Birnbaum recalled of hot days squatting in the desert sun, though Tekoa's residents also considered the lack of natural resources as evidence that they could expropriate the land, as "There were no Arabs here. . . . No Arab trees. Not one Arab house. For that Tekoa was very lucky, there's no Arab land here."[73] While Tekoa wasn't much other than a few people on a hilltop, the settlement began to take on a rhythm of daily life. One major problem was producing a consistent flow of electricity in the otherwise pitch-dark nights on the hilltop—Birnbaum humorously related how nighttime entertainment often included gathering all ten families, which luckily included a Russian engineer, to swear at a rickety generator in multiple languages. All foodstuffs and services had to be procured from Jerusalem (a long drive in the days before the construction of the bypass road) or nearby Bethlehem, with transportation limited to the old jalopies that residents parked outside exposed to the elements. The four children at Tekoa, including Birnbaum's oldest son, learned together in a one-room kindergarten in a caravan. While the group weathered extremely harsh conditions in the first years at Tekoa, Eli Birnbaum felt strongly that these experiences encouraged the creation of a unique, tight-knit community that allowed them to endure both the challenges of the time and of the future: "There is something that builds you up when you live with these problems. We all shared. No matter what our background was, it forged us. We all, no matter whether we had money or we didn't have money, we all had blocks of fungus growing on our walls. We all had leaks from the walls and problems with electricity and sick kids that all got sick together. It went around. But that helped us. It formed a good little bond that got us through a lot of hard times [then and later on]. So that was our support system . . . [it] was as strong as family."[74]

Former New Yorker Gerry Bernstein Freund, who moved to Tekoa with her husband Gilad in the settlement's first year, reminisced, "Tekoa, in those days . . . it was a few families in little 'eshkubiot' . . . little concrete dwellings with dirt paths [she laughed]. But I had a certain feeling. It was . . . all *kinds* of people. They were from England and America and Israel and Russia and France and they were old and they were young and they were middle-aged and they were religious, and they were not religious. And considering it was such a small group of people, that was pretty amazing. . . . It was beautiful, it was absolutely beautiful."[75]

Despite Sharon's promises, the government was not attuned to Jewish-American settlers' needs in the early days of Tekoa. Brown, who later became a top official at the Jewish Agency and World Zionist Organization, chuckled at the idea that nepotism served the community's needs, laughing off the suggestion that "I might have used my high position in the Jewish Agency to force them to take us into this luxurious place." In fact, state agencies seemed entirely unequipped to address the needs of white-collar professionals turned homesteaders at their city on a hilltop. "I can remember, I had to sign all kinds of papers to live here. One was—how many chickens did you get? Zero. How many cows did you get? Zero. How many chicken coops did you get? Zero. They were using the same [agricultural] moshav forms. . . . I had three pages of zeros of all the stuff I didn't get," Brown bemoaned, although it is notable that Tekoa received high-level support even during the politically sensitive period of the Camp David peace negotiations.[76]

Despite the rough conditions, a reporter from the AACA who visited the Browns during their first summer in Tekoa in 1979 found their hearts finally content after their big transition from the Upper West Side to the Eastern West Bank. She met them standing outside of their simple concrete *eskubiah* (caravan), which Linda lovingly portrayed as "unexpectedly appealing and home-y." Bobby Brown expressed deep fulfillment with his (modest) lifestyle, also citing progress on planned construction of private homes and a town kindergarten, the integration of religious and secular populations, and an easy commute into Jerusalem. Apart from their quotidian successes, Jewish-American settlers were well aware of the larger political significance of their activities. Brown "would bristle at the phrase 'West Bank,'" the journalist remarked, as he would instead insist "to the

State Department and the New York Times, it's the 'West Bank,' but to God and the Jewish nation, it's the land of Yehuda." Even though the physical and ideological landscape where it took root in the Eastern West Bank was "turn left at the end of the world," Brown happily concluded that "Lev Tzion in Tekoa is winding up on the right side of history."[77]

By the time another American journalist journeyed to meet the Browns in Tekoa six months later, the population had grown 150 percent to a grand total of fifteen families, including seven couples from the United States whom she immortalized in the headline "New Yorkers Turned Colonists." Over a supper of peanut butter and jelly sandwiches under the stars, Bobby Brown defended his territorial claim, contending, "No one was living here—for miles. Yet, I'm sure someone is going to come here and say, 'This was arable land. You forced the native population off.' Or some Jesse Jackson is going to say, 'This is a greater threat than the Soviet troops in Cuba.'"[78] Citing the American legal tradition of property rights, he asserted, "Possession is nine-tenths of the law. We call occupying the land 'establishing facts.'"[79] He further drew on liberal discourses in his declaration that "we believe this is one of the unique places in the world, it is a democracy where all people have equal rights." While ignoring the fact that these liberties didn't apply to Palestinians under the occupation, he went on to call for a "law of settlement"[80] to allow Jews to settle across the occupied territories. "Tekoa is as important as Tel Aviv," Brown attested, decrying a policy where "this will become the only place on earth from which Jews are banned."[81] Responding to the reporter's concerns about the fate of West Bank Palestinians if Israel was to annex the area, he retorted, "That is an Arab problem . . . [and] when Arabs think they should have a second state on the West Bank, we disagree."[82] Linda Brown underscored her own concerns, noting the "sacrifices" and "dangers" at Tekoa that had upset her parents back in Yonkers.[83] She reiterated, "We who come here are idealists" and "Everyone knows pioneers sacrifice and struggle," although the reporter cast a skeptical eye upon her newly acquired TV, stereo, washing machine, stove, and car.[84] Summing up the group's sentiments about life on the West Bank frontier, Eli Birnbaum saw American-style grassroots democracy in action, speculating, "I guess if the meetings when the Constitution was adopted were like ours, the Founding Fathers must have been funny to watch. . . . Living here reminds me of what America was like two hundred years ago. Here you have the spirit of just starting, of being a pioneer."[85]

Brown later boasted, "Americans . . . we just ran life in Tekoa."[86] The new immigrants dominated Tekoa's local governance in its first years—Brown served as settlement secretary and Birnbaum chaired the absorption committee. As the settlement grew apart later, Birnbaum took great satisfaction in remembering how American-Israelis were "very hands-on" in the early years.[87] Brown pointed to innovations in the fields of ecology and sustainable development as notable American-Israeli achievements. In addition to town management, he and his colleagues were responsible for introducing new campaigns to improve waste water management, prevent illegal dumping, develop alternative energy sources, prohibit the use of pesticide spraying, and develop an organic crops business in the settlement.[88]

Concerns about environmental sustainability and resource management also thrust Tekoa into greater contact with the surrounding Palestinian population. For example, when a decision was taken to build a new water tower on the border of what Brown described as an "Arab village," the IDF and Tekoa's residents jointly resolved (while excluding the third major stakeholder) that the Palestinian community should be connected free of charge in the dual interest of securing a strategic asset and enhancing local ties. In a more patronizing way, Brown vaunted, "They learned about sheep vaccination from us, they gathered open-mouthed in front of our drip irrigation systems—and adopted them—we cleared a field of stones and sold them to an Arab contractor. That's the way peace will come, where their interests coincide with ours."[89]

Yet it was clear from the origins of Tekoa that its Jewish-American founders and Palestinian neighbors did not have coinciding interests when it came to the land. Tekoa's leaders did not—and do not—recognize Palestinian sovereignty in the West Bank, nor do they honor local territorial claims to their settlement or its surroundings. However, evoking their U.S. heritage, many American-Israelis in the settlements do envision a hierarchy of citizenship rights, especially if Israeli sovereignty is extended to the West Bank, a policy many of them support. Brown himself publicly endorsed this idea, asserting, "I feel strongly that [West Bank] Arabs must have personal rights—due process, even voting and representation if this comes along with duties like some form of [nonmilitary] national service."[90] Further, he recognized the legal and moral inequities of the occupation, remarking that "we grew up reading Thoreau, who wrote that an unjust law is not right. Obviously one man's unjust law is another man's just law." He also advocated for a more economically inclusive polity, insisting, "If he is a citizen and he wants things that are unconnected to security, he wants a job . . . he should be able to compete equally. If he qualifies, he qualifies, and if he qualifies he should get equal pay and equal conditions. Not only do I not have a problem with that, that's the kind of culture I believe in."[91] (In truth, however, Tekoa's residents would have preferred to adopt a policy of Avoda Ivrit [Jewish labor] but didn't have the manpower.) Further, Brown drew on the African-American experience to address broader issues of race and ethnicity, positing, "We don't need a race problem with Arabs, we don't need a race problem with Jews that are dark [Mizrahim and Ethiopian immigrants]." He ultimately concluded, "I think on the whole . . . there is a greater tolerance of civil rights, a greater ability to befriend our Arab neighbors amongst many American Jews who came here . . . we believe and we realize that we are going to be here forever and our Arab neighbors are going to be here forever, and we have to come to some kind of modus operandi with them."

Yet when the first years of extreme isolation at Tekoa gave way to violent clashes between its growing settler population and neighboring Palestinians, Bobby Brown found it increasingly difficult to reconcile his liberal ideas of rapprochement with the realities of the West Bank. He contended, "When I was sitting head of [Tekoa] we looked out with a certain amount of dignity and honor [at the Palestinians], but on all the issues that were clearly security, we felt we should come down hard." Put another way, "That doesn't mean we have to tolerate people who want to harm our children."[92] He even stressed the need for extralegal measures, observing, "This country was founded on activism . . . how many of our founding fathers didn't spend time in jail somewhere?" But Brown eschewed the kind of extremism "when you stop caring about anything but your issue. It's a very thin line, and it's important never to cross it."[93]

This line was fatally crossed at Tekoa with the murder of Jewish-American settler David Rosenfeld in 1982. Born in Philadelphia, the recent graduate of George Washington University and his wife Dorit immigrated to Israel only two days after their wedding and joined the fledgling settlement in its first days in the summer of 1979. While a reporter described Dorit Rosenfeld's initial view of Tekoa as "isolated, grim," her husband "saw in it every settler's vision, the reclamation of a biblical homeland." The couple soon settled in—Rosenfeld took a job at the nearby Mount

Herodian archeological site and two children quickly followed at Tekoa. However, tensions were also rapidly mounting between settlers and Palestinians in the Eastern Gush region. Rosenfeld seemingly even foreshadowed his own death in an unpublished letter to the editor of the *New York Times,* writing that he was "not surprised that other people, who have not shared in our historical experience, are unable to comprehend what Israelis—Jews—feel about violence. We abhor it; we have been victims of violence for centuries. We still are today."[94]

On what should have been a normal Friday morning at work on July 2, 1982, Rosenfeld was stabbed more than eighty times in the clerk's office of the Herodian National Parks Authority.[95] "I was coming back from work and I saw the police," Birnbaum related in chilling eyewitness testimony to the death of his close friend, ignoring his neighbor's warning that " 'you don't want to go there,' it didn't matter, I went, I saw what I saw." Since it was too late in the day to arrange a burial before the Sabbath, "I went there with paint scrapers and literally scraped what was left of David from the walls and the floor. I found pieces of him, fingers, this and that, and put them in a plastic bag. And I had to keep it until the funeral. I put it in my refrigerator. So not the easiest thing to keep parts of your friend in your refrigerator overnight."[96] Birnbaum is still deeply shaken by these events over thirty years later, although contemporaneous newspaper reports raised little public outcry.[97]

Within days Rosenfeld's killers were apprehended by the IDF and were allegedly tortured into full confessions. Teenage assailant Rajib Abu Mahamid avowed, "I wanted him to die, I wanted to do something to revenge what was happening to the Arab people [in Lebanon]." Both Mahamid and a co-defendant later claimed they were PLO assassins sent on a terrorist mission to kill Jews at Herodian.[98] With the terrorists in custody and their family home detonated in collective punishment, the case soon dropped out of the news.

Yet the story was just beginning to unfold for Tekoa and its American-Israeli residents.[99] It quickly became apparent after Rosenfeld's murder—which coincided with the death of native Israeli Eli Pressman, another one of the settlement's own, in the Lebanon war—that the attitude of the now thirty-five close-knit families had changed. Brown considered "the small community of Tekoa at that time was in shock."[100] Rosenfeld's neighbor Gerry Bernstein Freund recalled, "So my politics . . . my *world view* about where I was living—was very much defined by that. And you can have all of the discussions and arguments that you want, but that was the reality. That man was killed . . . by people he had showed kindness and hospitality to. I certainly didn't feel as if I was in a safe environment here."[101]

Although all of them felt newly fearful of local conditions, the small group of settlers at Tekoa were divided in their response to the crisis. Some residents called for revenge, Brown paraphrased "that we should go into the village where these guys came from and wreak havoc."[102] He urged the group to reject the use of physical violence, but it was clear that "for our self-respect we had to make some kind of response." He counseled that "the correct thing would be to give them: the Zionist answer . . . that was a non-violent answer, that was what we felt to be an effective answer." "That was our revenge," he confirmed, "the Arabs will see that when they killed a Jew, they got a Jewish town."[103] In fact, shortly following David Rosenfeld's funeral, a group of five families, including Linda Brown, was "escorted" by Israeli soldiers into the village of Ferdis, where they squatted in tents and "made it known that they were staying" at an illegal outpost they called El-David (combining the names Eli and David) in honor of their fallen friends. Settler terrorism operations followed: it was reported that Tekoa residents burned Ferdis's wheat fields and fired indiscriminately into houses adjoining the encampment. While Birnbaum denied these accounts, he accepted the necessity of violent measures, explaining, "They're all Bedouin and they understand revenge. They expected us to go in there and just wipe out the village. They really expected us to do that."[104]

Rather, the village of Ferdis was in uproar. A visiting American journalist in the fall of 1982 found resident Hashim Muhammed standing outside his house "clutching his grandfather's title" to the land, ready to assert his rights to land and civil liberties. "How can they expect me to live with them in peace when they take my land from me by force?" Muhammed mused, "They think by terrorizing us they will force us to leave. . . . But this land belonged to my father and his father, and it will belong to my sons. My land did not kill that man [David Rosenfeld]. I had nothing to do with it, and the Israelis will never force me to leave." Brown was unsympathetic to Muhammed's claims. "If he has a deed, let him take it to court," he contended, "the Israel Land Authority told us this was government-owned land. We hear this all the time—'my grandfather owned this' and 'I have a document' and 'it's in my father's name'—all these stories. If the courts say it's true, then we'll move." Muhammed later did take his case to the Israeli Supreme Court, although ultimately it did not go anywhere; neither did the residents of Tekoa or the squatters at the new outpost.

Further, Brown suggested without irony that both communities actually shared the same concerns. "If you could talk to the widow of David Rosenfeld you would hear the same thing. . . . Where there is no respect there is always fear," he confirmed, although he stressed that settler vigilantism should be "prosecuted to the fullest extent of the law."[105] His views notwithstanding, tension between Tekoa and Ferdis flamed up again a few years later when Dorit Rosenfeld announced that she would take an Uzi machine gun to "mete out the justice the Israeli government couldn't bring itself to apply" when the perpetrators of her husband's murder were released in a prisoner swap in 1985.[106] Today the Israeli settlement of El-David, later renamed Nokdim, has a growing population of approximately 1,200 residents[107] and is the current home of Israel's defense minister Avigdor Lieberman.[108]

Despite the trauma of Rosenfeld's death in 1982, most settlers at Tekoa considered the tragedy an isolated incident. "We had peace. Even more than that," Birnbaum expressed, recalling how he used to bring his children to visit regularly at a Palestinian neighbor's home where they would drink coffee and chat in Arabic.[109] Local Palestinian villagers would also shop at Tekoa's superrette and worked in settlement industries, including home construction. In spite of escalating tensions, the Jewish-American settlers at Tekoa intended to continue going about their business in what they considered a bedroom community to Jerusalem. As Bobby Brown maintained in the mid-1980s, "I don't believe you can fill Judaea and Samaria with [Jewish] ideologues, nor do I think it's a healthy thing."[110]

The highly selective image of a peaceful and pastoral existence at Tekoa was on display in the 1983 government propaganda film *Judea and Samaria—New Dimensions,* which was pitched to potential Jewish-American immigrants to the occupied territories. The movie opens with a panoramic sweep of the Judean desert that was intended to illustrate not only the beauty of the terrain but the absence of its indigenous population of Palestinians who never feature in the film's landscape. A voice-over accentuates the "brutal barrenness" of Tekoa with its "empty hills," citing "the compulsion of these settlers to restore life in this land that had been abandoned to the desert" and enliven "a new world that has to be created from scratch." Viewers first meet protagonist Larry Price visiting from Manhattan as he drives his rental car down an otherwise deserted West Bank two-lane highway.[111] Evoking biblical motifs, he stops for a "Jewish shepherd" guiding his flock across the road, observing that "there are no sheep in New York City!" However, he also quickly assures his audience that the commute to Tekoa was "not as far as I thought" and lauds the opportunity to live in close proximity to Jerusalem.

Upon his arrival in Tekoa, Larry meets a Jewish-American immigrant named Bruce who welcomes him into his home. This act of hospitality clearly makes an impression on the film's main character, who remarks on the friendliness and communal spirit of settlement life. His host relates some of the other virtues of homesteading at Tekoa, including opportunities for modern-day pioneering and social action. Here "[you] feel yourself a contributing part of . . . building something," he tells Larry, experiencing "the quality of life and spirit in the new frontier." Bruce then brags about Tekoa's safety (only a year after Rosenfeld's murder), an innovative educational curriculum in the school, the coexistence of religious and secular populations in the community, and new employment opportunities in agriculture, technology, and industry in the settlement. Larry even touts the possibility of creating a "Silicon Valley here in the middle of nowhere." The viewer is imbued with the notion that Tekoa is the ideal locale for a nonconformist inspired by both biblical imperatives and suburban aspirations, an unparalleled chance to succeed in "creating a lifestyle more fulfilling than anything they've ever experienced ever before." At the end of his visit, Larry is filmed making his own Zionist contribution to making the desert bloom by planting a tree at Tekoa, murmuring his heartfelt prayer that "the roots of our culture are deeply buried in this rocky soil and this soil seems to accept the presence of a new generation of pioneers."[112]

Yet the cycle of violence touched off by Rosenfeld's murder would challenge the rootedness and resolve of even the most committed of the approximately eighty families then living at Tekoa. When Israeli author Amos Oz visited Tekoa in his travelogue *In the Land of Israel* in 1983, he found its community deeply unsettled. Some, like an American named Harriet, were skeptical of peace, supporting policies to "enslave" the Palestinian population under Israeli sovereignty and even advocated starting a war with "the Arabs." To her mind, the bourgeois (if still somewhat bohemian) lifestyle Larry presented was turning settlers and Israeli society into

"sissies" who were "not willing to make sacrifices for the Redemption."
Amiel Ungar also expressed his concerns about the weakening of Israeli
resolve, drawing on U.S. history to harangue leftists in Peace Now: "They're
not idealists—they're just peaceniks. They want convenience, the easy life;
they want it to be like America here . . . so they won't have to fight for the
homeland. It's all an American import, from Vietnam, all this left-wing
stuff. . . . It's passé in America—pretty soon it'll be passé here too. It's all
an imitation, alien to the Jewish spirit." Bobby Brown looked inward, reiterating his intent "to fulfill, to realize . . . so the opportunity would not be
lost. I decided to go someplace where there was danger. Pioneering!" Yet
when Oz asked him about the future of his Palestinian neighbors, Brown
countered, "Who cares about the Arabs?"[113]

The luxury to ignore Arab civil liberties disappeared when the first intifada arrived on Tekoa's doorstep in 1987. Despite many years of tension,
Birnbaum related that the Palestinian uprising still took the settlement by
surprise, suggesting, "Until the intifada, we were living in, well, some people
might call it a fool's paradise."[114] Daily life in and around Tekoa was instantly transformed. "These were difficult days, days I call white-knuckle
driving," Brown described, detailing his crash course in defensive-motoring
to avoid roadblocks, burning tires, and beds of nails that were strewn on
the roadway to ambush travelers.[115] (In another "Zionist response," he recounted removing the nail clusters known as *ninjot* [ninjas] from his tires
and symbolically reusing the hardware to attach new *mezuzot* [symbolic
scrolls] to doorposts in the settlement.) Settler vehicles were also frequently
targeted with rocks, Molotov cocktails, and sniper fire. One journalist observed that these "flying telegrams" of stones were a summer seminar in
"the intifada's relevance to physics, demographics, political science, theology, and a number of other subjects on the curriculum of the West Bank
Open University which they share with the Palestinians."[116] Drawing from
their activist backgrounds, American-Israelis vigorously protested these acts
of violent resistance, despite some of their own participation in retaliatory
actions. As Bobby Brown opined in the *Jerusalem Post,* "Beit Sahur has
been practicing non-violent civil disobedience since the beginning of the
intifada—How wrong can you be! [Today] the No. 166 bus I rode home
on was once again hit by two 'non-violent' stones."[117]

Most settlers traveled armed and Brown and Birnbaum both told me
they had fired their weapons into the air in self-defense on at least one

occasion during the first intifada.[118] Yet when a *New York Times* reporter found Bobby Brown on patrol of the settlement with his loaded firearm in 1988, he tried to debunk the Western media's image of a violent settler fanatic, mocking the stereotype that "we're supposed to have a 20-foot high fence, prison lights, machine guns, and go around spouting about the Messiah."[119] Brown continued to shun physical violence, but other residents embraced settler terrorism. Birnbaum described his pursuits as merely "punitive actions," recounting how he and fellow settlers would "come with sticks and break the windows. A simple thing. Not overly violent. . . . We didn't go and beat anyone up . . . that was our way of telling the Arabs we are not going to sit and be quiet." Mostly, for him, the ends justified the means because "that started working after a while."[120]

Living under the seemingly unrelenting strain of attacks and reprisals in and around the settlement, Bobby Brown admitted that "many of the people, Americans and non-Americans, broke." Psychologist Eli Birnbaum treated settlers suffering from post-traumatic stress syndrome.[121] He recounted trying to support one of his neighbors after her car was stoned, when "she went into a panic . . . no one knew how to help her. She basically packed up the kids and left . . . said [to her husband] 'Eli, I love you very much, but it's either me or Tekoa. I'm outta here. I'm not going back.' She just broke. That's it. She couldn't handle it. I didn't blame her. I understood."[122] As the first intifada raged unabated, an overwhelming pessimism permeated the settlement. Local entrepreneurs lamented a significant loss of income when outside contractors refused to step foot in Tekoa or would venture out only under armed escort. As the American-Israeli owner of a now-empty youth hostel complained, "I guess I'm a little trapped: Takuah b'Tekoa."[123] A reporter from the *Jerusalem Post* who visited Tekoa in 1989 noted a palpable shift in attitude: "During a recent visit to the settlements, a change in mood could be detected . . . euphoric confidence . . . [has] given way to a sense of determination, sometimes grim determination. The residents of the ideological settlements . . . see themselves as clearly as ever leading the camp of Israel on its march towards its destiny, but . . . history is mitigated among many by an awareness that history can zig as well as zag."[124]

Some of Tekoa's residents also tried to frame their recent hardship in historical perspective. Another journalist who visited Brown that fall found him reaching for his Bible to compare prophetic trials with contemporary tribulations, where "living here gives me a sense of purpose and meaning. I am privileged to be born in a time when the Jewish people could return to the State of Israel, and I'm contributing to building something here." Former Capitol Hill aide Mark Amiel added that against all odds, he was living in the "natural heartland" of the Jewish people. Despite the dangers of the intifada, "you don't leave, because you'd never forgive yourself if you did. The pioneers of the 1930s had it so much worse, we're the pioneers deluxe." Later Brown likened himself to his own teenage hero, Joseph Trumpeldor, as "I said to myself, basically one thing: if you are scared and can't take it, leave. If you can put it out of your mind, this is one of the prices we are paying for Eretz Yisrael, then go forward. How much blood was shed by kibbutzim in the Galil [Galilee] when they started? We grew up around BETAR and BETAR was Tel-Hai. So we said there was a price to be paid, and we really hope it's not us."[125]

For many, the price they paid was the reappraisal of their own liberal American identities and their position toward their Palestinian neighbors. "It was peace, love, and happiness when I first moved here," maintained Murray Allon, formerly from Brooklyn, in 1991, invoking the hippie slogan of the 1960s, "I thought we're making peace with the Arabs by living with them. They work with me, I visit, they visit. I thought we were moving in the right direction, but the intifada threw me for a loop." "We didn't come here to provoke anyone,"[126] Amiel Ungar ventured to an American reporter in 1989, claiming that his wife Beverly's medical clinic never turned away "needy Palestinians" and that he and his four children were learning Arabic.[127] He was also painfully aware of the consequences of the first intifada, regretfully divulging that an elderly Palestinian villager whom he used to shuttle to Jerusalem "now turns his back on me and I understand it." The reporter observed that many of its settlers seemed to mourn a loss of relations with local Palestinians and that "Tekoa is considered something of a model of moderation amongst the settlements, which are often militant." However, their internal image contrasted sharply with the international media's perception that "Tekoa's settlers are a fringe group of Bible breathing, racist lunatics who inflame tensions with Palestinians and force Israeli soldiers to act aggressively to stem rioting . . . [and] to them, Bobby Brown is the kind of Israeli who Palestinians despise, many Jews criticize, and the Bush administration considers a major obstacle to a Middle East peace settlement."[128] Mostly, Brown himself was perturbed that his personal reality was a political abstraction to most Israelis, cautioning, "You can be as philosophical as you like in the cafes of Tel Aviv. But here is where the cutting edge of relationships are between Jews and Arabs. Here is where the kernels of peace must be protected."[129]

Yet as the Oslo peace process got under way, most residents of Tekoa saw negotiations only as a threat to their own existence. As accords were signed in Washington, violent clashes continued in and around their settlement, including the 1993 shooting death of Tekoa settler Mordechai Lipkin which was followed by civil disobedience protests and the creation of a new illegal outpost.[130] Most of Tekoa's residents bitterly concluded that the Rabin administration had turned a blind eye to their human rights in the interest of a peace deal.[131] The settlement breathed a sigh of relief with the collapse of Camp David II in 2000, as the possibility of their immediate dismantlement in a peace accord passed into the history books.

Nevertheless, the end of the Oslo process did not bring calm to Tekoa's neighborhood. Tragedy struck the settlement again during the second intifada in 2001 when a pair of fourteen-year-old teenagers, American-Israeli Kobi Mandell and his friend Yosef Ish-Ran, skipped school to go hiking in a desert ravine near Tekoa and were discovered gruesomely bludgeoned to death by Palestinian assailants.[132] Kobi's parents, Rabbi Seth and Sherri Mandell, had moved their children to the settlement three years earlier to raise their family in what they considered Tekoa's uniquely progressive community. Kobi's father explained, "We didn't come because of the politics, we came in spite of the politics,"[133] later adding, "I went for personal reasons, spiritual reasons. I ignored the political situation, to my ultimate tragic loss."[134] In the aftermath of their misfortune, the couple became unintentional public icons—Sherri Mandell later wrote a book and the family established a foundation to assist families of victims of terror, although it does not offer its services to bereaved Palestinians.[135]

The violence of the second intifada further radicalized the residents of Tekoa who strenuously defended their rights to live in the settlement. As Bobby Brown argued, "No agreement is going to work unless there's a certain amount of respect on two sides, and foremost is a respect for human life, which we haven't seen on the Palestinian side."[136] Amiel Ungar insisted on his own "right of return" to Israel/Palestine during the second intifada, pontificating, "I didn't come to Tekoa for myself but for the Jewish people. . . . We were too accommodating. Now there has to be a struggle over Tekoa."[137] Meanwhile, Tekoa's residents fought to protect their future at the expense of their neighbors, continuing to expropriate Palestinian land, demonstrate at protests, and participate in price-tag (settler terrorism) operations.[138] Tekoa's residents have also continued to be victims of Palestinian terror: the community recently mourned the death of twenty-six-year-old therapist Dalya Lamkus in a stabbing at the settlement's gates in the fall of 2014 and has been shaken by several subsequent nonlethal shooting and knife attacks.[139] For Eli Birnbaum, life at Tekoa remains a deadly zero-sum game where "basically, yeah, the idea was that we are not going to let you win. And we've been holding on to that."[140]

While some of its residents see a perpetual state of warfare, Tekoa has also been home to a new movement for religious peace-making. Since the first intifada, the settlement's spiritual leader Rabbi Menachem Froman (1945–2013) and his followers have emerged as a lightning-rod for controversy over their efforts at grassroots reconciliation.

Froman's early biography portrays both strong national-religious credentials and exposure to the secular world. Born on the religious *moshav* of Kfar Hasidim (Hasidim Village) in the Galilee in 1945, he attended an elite high school in Haifa and proudly served as a member of the paratrooper brigade that recaptured the Western Wall and the Old City of Jerusalem in 1967. Following military service, Froman studied at Yeshivat Mercaz Ha-Rav under Rabbi Tzvi Yehuda Kook and earned his rabbinical certification from IDF Chief Rabbi Shlomo Goren while also completing a degree in Israel studies at the Hebrew University. After a stint as the spiritual leader of Kibbutz Migdal Oz in Gush Etzion in the late 1970s, Froman, his wife Hadassah, and their ten children took a new pulpit in Tekoa.

Froman, a pious mystic who considered himself "a citizen of God's country," fully embraced Jewish claims to the whole of the land of Israel while also envisioning Jewish settlers and Palestinians living side by side.[141] Froman later confessed, "You have to believe me, we thought that the Arabs—the Palestinians—would be glad that we were coming." However, "the very concrete expression of Palestinian unhappiness was the first intifada." He acknowledged how the cycle of violence profoundly changed the course of his own life: "My first contact with the intifada was immediately after I had an interview published in a famous Palestinian newspaper. . . . On my way back to Tekoa where I live, I was in a car with a friend and was reading what I had said about peace and good intentions. While I was reading, I was hit by a stone, which wounded me. There was blood on the

page where I was talking about peace and hope for the future."[142] Undeterred, Froman founded a new social movement called Medina Enoshit
(Humane State), which, at the height of the first intifada in 1989, rejected
concepts of Western secular sovereignty and "national egoism" in favor of
a kind of binational state.[143]

During the Oslo era, Froman accelerated his dialogue efforts with Palestinians, believing that "if you want to make peace in Washington, or
Oslo, or on the moon, you can ignore the settlements, but not here."[144]
However, he emphasized, "I have a great deal of criticism of the Washington talks. We are drawing up a blueprint for the next war, not for peace.
Peace is not separation. Rabin's statements that he doesn't want the Arabs
crawling among us, or that he would be happy if Gaza just sank into the
ocean, won't lead to peace."[145] With these aims in mind, he met with Palestinian Authority head Yasser Arafat on numerous occasions—the PLO
leader is said to have dubbed Froman "al-Hakeem" (the wise)—and in his
most contentious move, Froman held a highly publicized meeting (following several secret talks) with Hamas spiritual leader Sheik Ahmed Yassin
in the Gaza Strip in 1997.[146] "Forty some-odd years from the Six Day War
already, many more, one hundred years from the first aliyot, we've been
trying to reach peace on a secular basis," he observed, quoting the Hamas
leader, "how did he once put it, Ahmed Yassin, yemah shemo v-zihro [that
his name and memory should be extinguished]? The Oslo Accords was
your heretics and our heretics making an agreement in order to subdue
religion."[147] To him, interreligious dialogue was a strategic imperative once
"it became clear that the religious sector is the root of the problem and
the root of the solution." "Why am I so supportive of a peace between religious [people]?" Froman ruminated, "Because that's realistic. It's possible
to sweep dust under the rug, but it's not possible to sweep a tiger under
the rug. Islam is a tiger."[148]

In his dialogue efforts, Froman took Islam seriously and on its own
terms while underscoring its commonalities with Judaism as a God-centric
faith motivated by ideals of peace and justice. He saw the basis for a new
religio-social order in the biblical parable of Isaac and Ishmael, recalling
the teaching, "You have to love your neighbors, says the Lord . . . [and] the
Palestines [sic] are my neighbors . . . so the love to the Palestines is the
essence of my religion."[149] While some snickered how "hugs and hummus"
resonated with the secular Israeli peace camp and the media, Froman

resoundedly rejected the notion that he was anything less than a religious fundamentalist, stipulating, "I don't have this kind of liberal idea of accepting the other. These ideals aren't mine. They are of the Kadosh Baruch Hu [The Holy One Blessed Be He]" and "It is forbidden to abandon the love of peace to leftists."[150] Ultimately, Froman saw democracy mostly as an ideal to be instrumentalized, as "peace is the ultimate value of the state," and he was merely "a citizen of the state of God . . . my president is God . . . it is not so important who is the man, who is the government."[151] In fact, he only viewed his peacemaking struggle as a practical, temporal solution until the supreme redemption at the end of days: "I also think that the day will come and the Messiah will be here, and things will be completely different. I, for example, believe that ultimately when the Messiah comes that the mosques on the Temple Mount will be replaced by a Temple. That ultimately I will realize my most maximalist dreams. This is what allows for flexibility in the meantime. The fact that a religious person can have an absolutist ideal that he can postpone. When I meet with leaders of other faiths, they always like it when I end by saying, 'I believe in God and you believe in God—we will let God do the job.'"[152] Froman receded somewhat from the public sphere in his last decade while battling terminal cancer, but he still found the energy to establish a new joint settler-Palestinian social movement called Eretz Shalom (Land of Peace). Until his last days, the rabbi demonstrated at public protests with Muslim leaders in condemning settler terrorism, campaigned for a ceasefire with Hamas, and helped broker the release of the kidnapped Israeli soldier Gilad Shalit. Celebrated by many, he died in 2013, although Eretz Shalom continues to outlive him.

Yet, for most of his life, there was little love lost between Froman and the mainstream Israeli settler community. For many years, to enter his home, visitors had to walk past a vandal's spray-painted sign reading "PLO–Tekoa Branch."[153] Most national-religious leaders viewed him "as a luftmench, a well-intentioned but hopelessly misguided dreamer"[154] or as "a good and naïve person who sometimes gets confused,"[155] allegations Froman vigorously refuted, noting, "I am no more naïve than the group of Hovevei Zion who sat in Galicia and dreamt of a Jewish state, or a small group at Mercaz Harav who dreamt of filling Judea and Samaria with 120,000 Jews."[156] Others judged him a mortal danger to their vision. In what one journalist dubbed "Froman's folly," spiritual leader Rabbi Benny

Elon gently rebuked that "sometimes he has too much originality,"[157] while
Gush Emunim founder Benny Katzover was far less charitable, characterizing Froman's views as those that "ranged between the stupid and the
idiotic." MK Geula Cohen of the ultra-nationalist Tehiya Party later ex-
horted, "You're entitled to your confused ideas, but you have no right to
confuse the people,"[158] vowing that she would personally see to it that the
rabbi was fired from his post in Tekoa, a charge later taken up by some of
its residents.

For the most part, American-Israelis in the settlement were sanguine
about their controversial spiritual leader. Amiel Ungar, the sitting head
of the town council, brokered an agreement allowing Froman to stay on as
Tekoa's spiritual leader on the condition that he offer a public apology to
his congregants.[159] When asked by a reporter about her settlement's rabbi,
former Brooklynite Gerry Bernstein Freund dodged the question, acknowledging it was "impossible to find one opinion here and he has a way of
connecting to human beings that is extraordinary."[160] Eli Birnbaum agreed,
adding, "I think he's a great person, as a human being, he has unbelievable
great feeling and empathy for people . . . I have great respect for his rabbinical acumen and love of his fellow person." Yet Birnbaum was also one
of Froman's harsher critics among the Jewish-American settler cohort, believing, "Unfortunately, I think he's made [bad decisions] and he's cost us a
lot of damage." He was candid in his view that negotiations with Hamas
"crossed a red line . . . all this bullshit about sitting with our enemies, I'm
sorry, they are not our enemies that want to make peace with us, they are
our enemies that want to kill us." Yet for the most part he saw Froman the
mystic as susceptible to the most human of frailties, considering, "I think
he did it because on the one hand he's very ideological, and on the other
hand, he loves the press, and that's his weakness . . . [it] get[s] in the way
of common sense, which he doesn't have a lot of . . . he never got it that
they were playing him for a fool. And that's sad because he's a good person."

Apart from his concerns about the rabbi himself, Birnbaum was also
chagrined that Froman's dialogue project had endeared Tekoa to the Israeli
left. He openly resented being labeled "good settlers" who were "unlike
those maniacs," scoffing, "We're good not because they want to give us a
compliment. . . . Don't use me because you want to hurt someone else. I've
got a problem with that."[161] Bobby Brown was more troubled that Froman's struggle had strained relations between Tekoa and the mainstream

settler movement. In one poignant vignette that illustrated these tensions, he recounted how he once tried to hitch a ride to Jerusalem with a resident of another settlement—upon realizing that Brown was a founder of Tekoa, the driver swerved to the side of the road and interrogated him on his views on Froman until he was satisfied to continue on the journey. In the end, Brown saw Froman's tenure as a testament to the free spirit of his community, suggesting, "Look, we have . . . a very special rabbi. He has warm relations with Hamas, with all kinds of people who I would say 99.9 percent of the community doesn't like. Some people like him less, some people like him more, certainly he is controversial in our eyes . . . yet he lives here."[162] Further, "Tekoa is a community based on tolerance. We don't believe a man's political belief is a reason to throw him out."[163] For Bobby Brown, Froman was a symbol of the ethos of "pluralism" and "openness" that he and his colleagues had nurtured from the settlement's earliest days, if this vision ends at Tekoa's security gate.[164]

Tekoa today is a community of approximately 615 families, a truly astonishing transformation from a camp of ten squatters in the summer of 1979. While Jewish-American immigrants comprised the majority of the population in its first decade, American-Israelis are now only about a quarter of the international mix of settlers hailing from Israel as well as "America, Russia, France, Britain, Argentina, Chile, South Africa, India, Burma, Mexico and elsewhere."[165] However, its community remains popular with American-Israelis as an Anglo-Saxon enclave close to Jerusalem and Nefesh B'Nefesh continues to consider Tekoa "a solid choice for English-speaking olim."[166]

Since 1979 the settlement has expanded into four separate subneighborhoods—Tekoa Alef, Bet, Gimmel, and Daled. Wards A and B host large single-family homes, many of them built to specification by the property owner, whereas precincts C and D are considered unrecognized outposts by the Israeli government, dotted with caravans. Modern houses in the developed areas sit on approximately 500 square meters (a quarter acre) and are priced starting at $250,000 for preexisting structures ($85,000 per plot). Tekoa was once considered a budget-friendly settlement that could be a bedroom community alternative to overpriced Jerusalem real estate, but increased demand for new properties (especially with government construction bans since 2010, although I witnessed continued construction at Tekoa during these so-called freezes), luxury renovations, and rising costs for infrastructure and utilities have boosted sales and rental values.[167] However, both government and local subsidies as well as tax incentives have helped reduce individual contributions.

Tekoa is administered under the umbrella of the Gush Etzion regional
council but also has its own institutions of self-governance. The municipality prides itself on its dedicated staff on payroll, including a chief of
operations, treasurer, security head, social chair, cultural affairs officer,
absorption coordinator, youth director, senior citizen programmer, librarian, and rabbi.[168] The settlement also provides an array of public
services catering to the community's needs, from rubbish pickup to twenty-
four-hour security and ambulance rescue. Tekoa expends the majority of
its financial resources on education. The main emphasis is on early childhood development—the settlement sponsors six playgrounds, a nursery
school, two kindergartens (community and Chabad-movement affiliated),
and an elementary school with an award-winning curriculum for religious pluralism in the classroom called "Ahdut Yisrael" (Unity of Israel)
led by Rebbetzin Hadassah Froman.[169] Teenage children are usually
bused to middle and high schools in nearby Alon Shvut and Efrat. A post-
secondary *yeshivat hesder* (part-time religious learning program for IDF
soldiers) under the supervision of the esteemed modern Orthodox scholar
Rabbi Adin Steinsaltz is available on site.[170] In nonschool hours, the settlement boasts a full range of afterschool courses including "basketball,
soccer league, arts and crafts, yoga, karate, chess, music lessons, choir,
ballet, hiking, and sewing," all supervised by professional instructors, as
well as a chapter of the Bnai Akiva religious youth movement. For adults,
Tekoa furnishes a variety of leisure activities and programming, including
a community house (with a full-sized auditorium/events space), a senior
center, a recreation and fitness room, library, two basketball courts, a
tennis pavilion, and independently owned riding stables. The jewel in the
crown of the settlement is the Tekoa Country Club with its two swimming pools, an independently financed complex dedicated to donors from
the United States.[171]

Another main focus of the settlement is on its spiritual life. Today, Tekoa
is estimated to be about 70 percent religious and 30 percent secular and it
trumpets that it is a tolerant community that does not compel its residents
to take on doctrinal observance unlike many other settlements. The municipality oversees several religious institutions including six synagogues

(Ashkenazi, Sephardi, Lubavitch, Carlebach-style, and others), a *mikvah* (ritual bath), and *hevra kadisha* (burial society).

Despite the availability of educational, recreational, and spiritual resources, the settlement has few commercial amenities and sustains only two small superettes and a wall of post office boxes. However, a new bypass road linking the settlement to south Jerusalem in a ten-minute drive has greatly facilitated access to shopping and services. Many residents have private cars or will offer a lift to hitchhikers (an obligation Tekoa unofficially mandates upon vehicle owners) and there is regular bus service from Tekoa for work and recreation.

Tekoa's population is an eclectic cohort of mostly white-collar professionals that the municipal website describes as "young and old, farmers, urban professionals, artists, craftspeople, doctors, lawyers, nurses . . . professors, musicians, businesspeople, teachers . . . students, lots of children, and retirees."[172] Most residents work in Jerusalem, although some 30 percent are now engaged in entrepreneurship in the settlement, including in its carpentry shop, graphic design studio, real estate agency, mushroom hothouse, goat and dairy farm, Volvo repair garage, Internet consultancy office, organic egg incubator, landscape architecture firm, and winery.[173] In recent years Tekoa has also become a popular choice for retirees, a subcommunity that now includes its Jewish-American founder Eli Birnbaum.

Most of all, Tekoa extols what it calls the "Tekoan social experiment": "Tekoa is blessed with people that who have chosen to live in a yishuv (community) based on social diversity and mutual respect . . . seeking to build a community of co-existence. Numerous studies have been conducted that document the fascinating success of the Tekoan social experiment that brings together religious and secular value systems. Openmindness is a key. . . . People who come to Tekoa tend to be thoughtful, seeking creative solutions, and drawn to be active community members. Our community reflects the diversity of Am Yisrael. . . . In Tekoa, your neighbors become your extended family."[174] Another motto from Tekoa's municipal website (which could be read as a pointed barb about Efrat) recommends, "Don't just live in suburbia! Find a home with some character!" Most of all, the settlement celebrates being a place where "the ancient land blooms" and one can "join the heroes, pioneering an ancient dream" while also having "rural life and urban access" and "a paradise for raising a family and for children." All in all, life in the settlement is summed up with the triptych slogan of "Tekoa. Israel. Home."[175]

In recent years Tekoa's main problems haven't been geostrategic concerns but mundane growing pains like lawsuits for faulty construction on new builds and concerns about group cohesion. For its American-Israeli founder Eli Birnbaum, "We've watched Tekoa change, that's really the big story." With a certain measure of sadness, he sees the settlement as a victim of its own success, sighing, "It's not a yishuv anymore." Birnbaum cited what he perceived as the erosion of community principles, pioneering spirit, and volunteer ethic as Tekoa reaches its population limits. "The bigger you get, the easier to say, 'Well, let him do it,' or say, 'I pay my taxes,'" he observed, noting that the new generation doesn't sufficiently esteem the settlement's early struggles and "they didn't pay their dues, so to speak, and get their cars rocked, and see friends die, and hold babies that were full of blood. Not to say it's a good thing, it's a bad thing . . . but it gives you a different appreciation for the area around you, and you feel it, you live it, and you breathe it." However, he recognized an imperative to continue to grow, as "having this many is a political necessity . . . the whole Gush Katif [thing]." Today Birnbaum is more concerned that Tekoa will be a casualty to communal dynamic than to a peace accord, acknowledging that over time "it's changed," but he betrayed a guarded optimism about the settlement that "I think we still have that spirit. And I don't think thirty years has changed that . . . I really believe it's still there."[176]

As TEKOA CONSIDERS its future today, it could reflect upon the words of Bobby Brown, the Jewish-American founder of Garin Lev Zion, on the settlement's second anniversary:

> I remember about half a year ago, we were putting up a fence around the area of Tekoa . . . after a whole day of putting up fences, barbed wire fences, your hands would get all bloody, your pants get ripped, and your coat gets ripped, and you're cold and you're dirty and everything. I got home and I felt pretty good . . . I was actually fencing in land that would belong to the Jewish people. It was a very scary feeling when we put the stick in the ground that one side might be Jewish land and on the other side might not be Jewish land. And after doing that a whole day I thought all the stuff I always thought was so important in America was not

important compared to what we were doing here . . . a very important thing . . . and the fact that I feel that we are doing something that is good for Israel, for me, is self-realization, self-satisfaction.[177]

As Eli Birnbaum echoed more than thirty years later about the community he helped establish, "our legacy will be that my children will carry this on and believe . . . if you have a problem, go and change it."[178] While Tekoa is likely to be dismantled under any future Israeli-Palestinian final status accord, its Jewish-American founders remain committed to the heartfelt Zionist convictions that took them from Manhattan's Upper West Side to the West Bank almost forty years ago.

CHAPTER FIVE

Scripture and Sound Bite

American-Israeli Settlers from Public Relations to Public Enemy

"To him and to those like him, we say: You are not part of the community of Israel. You are not part of the national democratic camp to which we in this house all belong, and many of the people despise you. You are not partners in the Zionist enterprise. *You are a foreign implant. You are an errant weed.* Sensible Judaism spits you out," thus declared Prime Minister Yitzhak Rabin before the Israeli Knesset, denouncing Dr. Baruch Goldstein three days after the Brooklyn-born Kiryat Arba settler terrorist gunned down 29 Palestinian worshippers and injured over 125 others at the Tomb of the Patriarchs/Ibrahimi Mosque in Hebron on February 25, 1994.[1] All of a sudden, a constituency that had mostly existed on the fringes of the Israeli settler community for over two decades was at the center of the conflict. Public opinion was unanimous: from the highest echelon of the Israeli political establishment to popular culture, the American-Israeli settler was presented as a pariah.[2] After the massacre, most saw Goldstein's attack as a microcosm of the misdeeds of his entire American-Israeli cohort in the occupied territories. Nearly thirty years after the 1967 war, their complex narrative was caricatured solely as crazed fanaticism.

If, to the international community, Jewish-American settlers appeared homogeneous and homicidal, the Hebron massacre magnified less-visible internal tensions among these immigrants over the use of physical violence, which had been a subject of intense debate since the early 1980s. Baruch Goldstein was only one of several American-Israeli assailants that have perpetrated acts of terror against Palestinians. This chapter will profile not only the Hebron Massacre, but other prominent American-Israeli cases of political violence, including Era Rapaport and the Jewish Underground, TNT and the Kahanist Network, and "Jewnabomber" Yaakov "Jack" Teitel.

Contrary to their public image, the vast majority of Jewish-American settlers rejected these men's vigilantism for both ideological and tactical reasons. Most were keen to separate themselves from terrorists and their ilk, judging that they seriously jeopardized domestic and international support for the Israeli settler enterprise. They preferred to cultivate a different image as moderate, law-abiding citizens part of a mainstream movement who wanted nothing to do with the murderers among them. Correspondingly, a group of savvy, cosmopolitan American-Israeli settlers sought to reinvent their role within the Israeli settler enterprise as media strategists rather than as scapegoats. Serving as English-language spokespeople, foreign "diplomats," lobbyists, journalists, tour guides, and campaign managers, they introduced a new discourse mixing prophecy and public relations (or scripture and a sound bite) to international news agencies, the corridors of Capitol Hill, European embassies, and the Israeli public. By deploying a liberal rights-based rhetoric that reconciled Western universalism with Jewish particularism, they revolutionized how the settler movement appeals to and mobilizes international audiences. This chapter will examine two major public relations projects spearheaded by Jewish-American immigrants in the 1990s: the American-Israeli settler delegation to the Madrid conference and the YESHA Council Foreign Desk/ICDF and the saga of Shmuel Sackett, Zo Artzeinu, and the Manhigut Yehudit movement.

Why did Jewish-American settlers choose such divergent paths of participation within the Israeli settler enterprise? It is beyond the scope of this study to plumb psychological motivations but scholars can consider the wider historical and ideological landscape in which these decisions were made. For some, the schism between "moderate" and "extremist" American-Israeli immigrants spoke to the stark contrast between their self-image and their settlement activities. Recognizing this cognitive dissonance after almost two decades in the settlements, they were confronted with a choice: to reify or to readjust ideology to realities on the ground. For those who committed acts of terror, it was often testimony to their changing attitudes, ambivalences, and even abandonment of liberalism over time. To them, the perceived incompatibility of American values with a "Middle Eastern" environment led them to perpetrate heinous acts they considered a historical imperative. In contrast, public relations activism often represented an attempt to reconcile liberal self-perception with local conditions, efforts that symbolized the entrenchment of their ideological identities. As the conflict becomes more bloody and bitter with each passing year, however, these distinctions may collapse under the weight of five decades of civil war in the occupied territories.

This chapter's focus on the contemporary period confers exceptional challenges upon the historian. Given the absence of archival material (due to Israel's thirty-year declassification law and the indefinite security hold on sensitive files) I could only draw upon the periodical press, media, Internet resources, and interviews to try to reconstruct these important events. It is my hope that future researchers will have access to a wider range of materials and the perspective of time to complete this narrative in the future.

Era Rapaport and the Jewish Underground
(1980–1987)

The decade of the 1980s was a turning point in the occupied territories. Friction between Israeli settlers and Palestinians in the West Bank quickly intensified and a cycle of violence traumatized both communities. In response, a loose coalition of vigilantes—later dubbed the Mahteret (Jewish Underground) by the media—carried out a series of terrorist attacks against Palestinian leaders and institutions between 1980 and 1983.

Era Rapaport, a Brooklyn-born Jewish-American settler living in the West Bank settlement of Shilo, played a prominent role in the Jewish Underground as one of the perpetrators of the June 2, 1980, car-bombing of Nablus mayor Bassam Shaaka, which maimed him for life. Rapaport's turn toward terrorism was part of a prolonged internal ideological dialogue over liberal values and tactics in Israel/Palestine. This intellectual journey was self-documented in his 1996 quasi-autobiography *Letters from Tel Mond Prison* (consciously modeled on Martin Luther King Jr.'s "Letter from a Birmingham Jail"), structured as a series of actual and reconstructed correspondence illuminating his transition from liberal to terrorist. In the words of his editor, Rapaport's story attempts to unravel the complex philosophical and psychological puzzle of "How does a nice Jewish boy from East Flatbush, Brooklyn, a gifted social worker, a marcher for civil rights, a loving husband and father, end up blowing off the legs of the PLO mayor of Nablus?"[3]

Era Rapaport was born in 1945 in the East Flatbush section of Brooklyn, one of three children raised in a religiously observant household. Their son was proud of his Zionist genealogy—they traced two generations of Jerusalemite lineage on his Israeli father's side (who spoke only Hebrew to his children) and his U.S.-born mother's family were active members of the American Zionist organization Hadassah.[4] Early in life, Rapaport became immersed in local Jewish and Zionist activism, participating in the Student Struggle for Soviet Jewry as well as Israeli Independence Day celebrations in New York. As a teenager, he also traveled in Jewish militant circles, joining a violent gang called the Hashmonaim (lit. Hasmaneans, a reference to the dynasty of the Maccabees that liberated the holy land from the Seleucids in the first century B.C.), which combatted anti-Semitism in his neighborhood in Brooklyn. While an undergraduate at Yeshiva University in the 1960s, he took part in generational debates on the Holocaust and Zionism and forged a lifelong friendship with the future prominent spiritual leader and political activist Rabbi Avi Weiss. During this period, Rapaport also became a passionate civil rights advocate and a visible proponent of African-American equality in New York City. His involvement in the social movements of his youth later informed his activism in Israel.

Rapaport's first sustained contact with his roots in Jerusalem came as a foreign-exchange student at Yeshivat Mercaz Ha-Rav in 1966–1967. He credited the course as a formative experience that "changed my entire life" and inspired his decision to move to Israel.[5] Following his academic studies, he remained in Jerusalem during the Six Day War, serving as a volunteer at Shaarei Tsedek Hospital in Jerusalem. By staying in the city, he professed to be taking part in "fighting a war of existence" and saw Israel's military victory as a defining moment of both personal and national destiny.[6]

In spite of his Zionist commitments, Rapaport returned to Yeshiva University's Wurzweiler School in the fall of 1967 to earn a master's degree in social work and also interned with juvenile delinquents and at-risk youth in the New York City area. After graduation, he immigrated to Israel in

1971. Back in the country, he promptly rekindled his connection with a coterie of activists from his days at Mercaz Ha-Rav and soon met his future wife, Orit Mintz, at a series of post–Yom Kippur War protests. Rapaport also quickly became acquainted with her prominent family of national-religious activists, including brother-in-law Yehuda Etzion, a pivotal figure in the coalescence of the premier settler group Gush Emunim in 1974. This network by marriage facilitated his entry as a Jewish-American immigrant into an inner circle of native Israeli activists and Rapaport took advantage of this otherwise unlikely opportunity to get "very much right into it."[7] He squatted alongside Etzion in Gush Emunim's first major settlement attempt at the old train station at Sebastia in the summer of 1975, recollecting of their violent clashes with police that "we left that evening with traumatic memories, but also with a determination and a knowledge. The determination to continue until we could succeed in settling the Land and the knowledge that we would succeed in doing so."[8]

In the winter of 1976, Rapaport, his wife, and his brother-in-law turned their attention to a new settlement project: the founding of Ofra, the first permanent community in the West Bank outside of the Etzion Bloc. He joined Gush Emunim activists—including American-Israeli colleague Jonathan Blass, who had been a fellow American student at Yeshivat Mercaz Ha-Rav—in a work camp at the abandoned Jordanian army base at Baal Ha-Tsor near Ramallah. The former students' cover story was that they would comprise a fence-building detail; in fact, they were preparing the structure for civilian settlement with the tacit permission of Defense Minister Shimon Peres. Shifra Blass, the first American-Israeli woman to live on site with her husband and infant son, recalled meeting Rapaport in the early days of Ofra—as she later attested, "He didn't seem to me American enough to my taste, because all the wacky Israeli ideas everyone had, he thought were pretty good!"[9] Despite his ties to an elite activist family, Rapaport too acknowledged the rift with native Israeli settlers that bonds of marriage could not surmount, recognizing, "With all that said, I am a Westerner. Western in my attitudes. I wasn't part of the army that most of them had gone through, I wasn't part of the culture, I was in a separate line."[10]

It became impossible to ignore this cultural divide once Rapaport became the mayor of a new settlement of mostly native Israeli Gush Emunim members at Shilo in 1978. He initially viewed his leadership as a kind of *mission civaltrix*, indicating, "[When] I first came to YOSH [Yehuda V'Shomron (Judea and Samaria)] and became the Mayor of Shilo, I said to myself, now is the opportunity to instill some of my Western values in the area." His views were put to the test early in his term following a series of vandalism and stoning incidents between Shilo and the Palestinian village of Sinjil. When the mayor chose mediation over militancy, his settler colleagues scoffed "You are trying to introduce Western values into an Oriental/Middle Eastern society. It won't work," and proposed violent reprisals against neighboring Palestinians. Instead, Rapaport met with the local *mukhtar,* heralding, "Here I was—the 'Westerner.' I would teach them all some democracy." After what he considered a successful meeting of the minds, he crowed to his wife and community, "See, I was right. A little Western methods. No need for retaliatory measures . . . a little American culture is so helpful."[11]

His exercise in dialogue with local village heads turned out to be less helpful than he had expected: as skirmishes between the settlement and surrounding villages escalated, his constituents engaged in increasingly open debates about the use of vigilante violence, though they framed the use of force as reactive self-defense against terrorism. Rapaport recalled being morally "unsure" in this approach. Despite recognizing its utility as a deterrent at Ofra, he wavered, "I had grown up with law and order. I remember 'walking the beat' with policemen in the East Flatbush section of Brooklyn where I was born. As a citizen of Israel, could I, we, willingly go against the law of the land?" Probing his own conscience and consulting both Israeli and Palestinian colleagues, Rapaport became convinced that "my Western ways expressed weakness" and that survival in the settlements "forces people into doing what I did."[12]

At first Rapaport claimed to take part only in preemptive acts of property damage and intimidation, favorably comparing his activities to the New York City police and FBI assault again the Weathermen, citing, "They didn't fire in the air first" and "Didn't the U.S. blow up at an entire block in Philadelphia to punish Black activists?" Yet he continued to express moral ambivalence about physical violence, racial profiling, and collective punishment during this stage in his ideological evolution. He relied on security imperatives to rationalize these positions, regretting, "Yes, there is a loss of life during preventive and responsive actions. Because we are fighting a war." Shrugging off the outrage of his American friends, he suggested,

"Once again, your Western culture will make it difficult for you to understand our situation." He grumbled, "You make me feel like an aggressor,
maybe even one who enjoys the situation. You are so far from understanding
the difficulties and intricacies of life here. Have you ever been to the West
Bank? No. It's so typical of the 'liberal' attitude. You can understand everybody, except of course, us."[13]

Rapaport came to see himself within a larger historical trajectory of
Jewish peoplehood and messianic redemption, harboring increasing doubts
about Israeli democracy. He also criticized the Israeli government for priv-
ileging Western universalism over Jewish particularist interests and correspondingly condoning territorial concessions.[14] He asked himself what the
significance of this worldview was when it came to taking action, wondering, "Do we 'turn our cheeks' and say that the geula [redemption] . . .
comes in stages, and right now we have to retreat? . . . Do we have a right
to sit back and not doing anything?"[15] Despite his rejection of liberal
ideology and his turn toward terrorism, rights-based rhetoric became a
prominent part of Rapaport's rationale to live in the whole of the land of
Israel. He also framed securing life, liberty, and property at Shilo in terms
of the social contract, considering violence against Israeli settlers, which
became a regular occurrence after 1980, as an abrogation of the Israeli
government's duty toward its citizens.[16] "It took a while for me to realize
that my government wasn't going to do anything about it," he admitted,
"That to me was very shocking and problematic. [And] then it became a
choice: whether you are going to become constantly being rock thrown at,
shot at . . . or were we going to do something about it."[17]

A circle of vigilante activists began to crystallize within the settler camp.
After many discussions about possible activities, Rapaport either agreed to
take part in, or, as he alternatively insinuates in his narrative, actually insti-
gated a campaign to car-bomb three Arab mayors affiliated with the PLO.
He would later characterize these acts as a "preventative action," especially
as they blamed these leaders for previous attacks against Israeli settlers,
including the brutal killing of six yeshiva students in Hebron in 1980. In
an unsent letter to Rabbi Avi Weiss in May 1980, he agonized, "I've never
been in such a dilemma throughout my entire life and I don't wish it on
anyone. Here I am thinking to myself, Era, where do you, Brooklyn born
and bred, who studied social work because you love working with kids—
where do you even come off thinking about attacking PLO mayors and

putting yourself in prison?" Ultimately Rapaport conceded that he had reached an ideological and emotional threshold and saw the attack as a way of restoring calm in a "situation of no law and order."[18] For Rapaport, this decision marked his absolute abandonment of liberal values: "It became a point . . . where my Western background had to be put aside . . . I'm not making a value opinion on which culture is better, if we can put it that way, just . . . I live within an Arab culture which is very different from Western culture. . . . It took me a long time to accept that . . . when I finally realized that I had to change my own thought-process and feelings . . . then the next step was to see what could be done . . . I came to realize that I was going to do something that would endanger the life of another person."[19]

In the early morning hours of June 2, 1980, after several weeks of stake-outs, a three-person terrorist squad surreptitiously entered the parking garage adjoining the home of Nablus mayor Bassam Shakaa and Rapaport planted a bomb beneath the chassis of his car. Meanwhile, two other vigilante teams were dispatched to Ramallah and Al-Bireh to target city leaders there. When the mayors turned the ignition switches in their cars the following morning, the devices detonated, grievously injuring Shakaa, who lost both of his legs, and maiming the mayor of Ramallah, amputating his foot. The IDF discovered the third bomb in Al-Bireh in time, but it blinded the Druze soldier who attempted to disarm it. Rapaport's cell remained undetected for months, even as other loosely affiliated groups within the Jewish Underground carried out further attacks against Arab targets, including a shooting at the Islamic college of Hebron, a bus ambush in Jerusalem, and a foiled plot to blow up the Temple Mount (spearheaded by Yehuda Etzion).[20] While the mainstream Israeli settler movement denounced the car-bombing—Rapaport's former colleague and YESHA Council spokeswoman Shifra Blass called the attack "an extreme deviation from morality and ethics"—other sectors of Israeli society considered the settler community and even the Israeli government complicit in supporting the criminals.[21] In late 1980, Rapaport was questioned by the Sherut Ha-Bitahon Ha-Klali (Shin Bet [General Security Service]) and released without charges, although native Israelis in his circle suggested that his American openness and eagerness to talk compromised the group.[22] In the meantime, Rapaport remained in his leadership role as the mayor of Shilo, averring to a visiting reporter that settlers sought cooperation with their Arab neighbors and flatly rejected allegations of vigilantism.[23]

In 1983 the Shin Bet finally began identifying perpetrators within the Jewish Underground. Rapaport promptly fled to the United States, living as a fugitive in New York City. For a time he worked undercover as an emissary for the Eretz Yisrael organization, the American branch of Gush Emunim, characterizing his success as an immigration representative as "saving lives" and "bring[ing] the land of Israel closer to the hearts of our brothers in New York."[24] In the spring of 1984, the Shin Bet made sweeping arrests of dozens of suspects in the occupied territories. Agents also contacted Rapaport in the United States as a warning, although they had no legal authority to extradite him to Israel.[25] Over the next thirteen months, twenty-seven Jewish Underground defendants stood trial, igniting major demonstrations across the country. Unfolding events galvanized Jewish-American settlers and also garnered major interest within the American Jewish community. Era Rapaport likely read the sympathetic coverage of the Mahteret in the right-wing New York periodical the *Jewish Press* while evading justice at his mother's home in East Brooklyn.[26]

In the spring of 1985 the *New York Times* broke the story that Era Rapaport was a fugitive in Flatbush.[27] A few months later, the newspaper also covered the conviction of fifteen of his co-defendants in the Jewish Underground—including participants in the car-bombing attacks—underscoring that Rapaport had fled from the law to the United States.[28] In spite of his shocking crimes, some friends reached out to assist Rapaport when his role in the Mahteret was revealed. Rabbi Avi Weiss, who coordinated his legal defense in the United States, told a reporter, "I pray my children grow up to be the kind of sensitive human being and Jew that Era is. It is absurd and outrageous that he has been identified as a terrorist."[29] Yet most of his American acquaintances were appalled, as Rapaport acknowledged in correspondence with his friend Aaron: "You wrote that you were surprised I was arrested for attacking Arabs. You would not have been surprised, you said, to learn that I had been arrested for demonstrating for their rights. . . . Era, what did Israel do to you? You, the freedom fighter. You who walked arm in arm with thousands of Blacks in D.C. . . . . Who got beaten up for defending the underprivileged. What happened to you? How could you? Are Arabs not people? What about them? My Judaism teaches 'Love thy neighbor.' Is the West Bank more important than that?"[30] Perhaps as a way of responding to this charge, Rapaport repatriated himself to Israel on his own accord in 1986, avowing "that for a Jew it is better to be in jail in the land of the Israel than to be free in America."[31] He was sentenced to thirty months in prison on charges of grievous bodily harm and membership in a terrorist organization, although he only served less than half his mandated sentence before returning to Shilo. He continues to live in the settlement and works as an Israeli tour guide.

Today, Rapaport is unrepentant. "You've asked me if I have any regrets about what I did to Bassam Shaaka," confessing, "I'd be a hypocrite if I told you I did because I really don't. At the time it was a necessity, 100%. Knowing that you're going to maim a person is not an easy action to take, but under the circumstances, non-action would have been harder."[32] He subsequently clarified this statement, stating it was appropriate only for its specific historical circumstance and suggested that the Israeli government had taken great strides to protect settlers in recent years. Yet Rapaport remains ambivalent about a Jewish and democratic state, declaring, "I don't think that democracy is holy. . . . It's a method. There are problems with this method. . . . The democracy of Israel is a method to get to a goal. For me, the goal is Torah Judaism."[33] In his final analysis, Rapaport has little compunction at being considered an extremist, expounding, "If being one who loves the land of Israel and believing that it is ours, fighting [so] it's ours, if that's called extreme, then I'm extreme. I don't believe that's extreme at all, but [if] people are going to box me that way, I'll accept it."[34]

The Kahanist Network—TNT and the Hebron Massacre

The Jewish Underground was particularly shocking to Israeli society because it emanated from the heart of the native Israeli Zionist elite. It also contradicted the narrative put forward by both the general public and Israeli settler activists that political violence was a foreign anomaly. In fact, for many years Gush Emunim had been locked in an ideological struggle with the Kach movement, an ideological front and political party led by Jewish-American immigrant Rabbi Meir Kahane, which they blamed for corruption and violence within their community.[35] During the early 1980s and 1990s, Kahane's followers carried out a series of infamous terrorists attacks that brought Jewish-Americans newfound notoriety and condemnation.

TNT—Terror K-Neged Terror

TNT—the acronym for explosive dynamite appropriated by the group Terror K-Neged Terror (Terror against Terror)—was a coterie of primarily young Jewish-American settlers living in Hebron who considered themselves acolytes of Rabbi Meir Kahane. Many members of this terrorist cell had been activists in the Jewish Defense League in New York and some had even immigrated to Israel to evade prosecution for violent crimes committed in the United States. Subsequently, this group served as a second generation of Kach directors in Israel.

TNT was led by Michael Guzofsky (also known as Yekutiel Ben Yaakov or Yekutiel Guzofsky), a teenager from Far Rockaway, Queens, who came to Israel in 1982. Raised in an Orthodox Zionist family, Guzofsky was roused by Rabbi Meir Kahane's call for radical activism in the late 1970s, relating in an interview that "Jews were fighting for every other cause, why shouldn't young Jews also fight for their own survival? Civil rights for blacks to live as they chose, what about the right to live for Jews . . . who were also being denied religious freedom and also physical freedom. And it spoke to me." At first, Guzofsky was a bit reluctant to take part in political violence, as "I was a yeshiva guy . . . you know, militancy, JDL, anything that doesn't exactly fit within the norms of this community, you gotta be like a freak to get involved." He was persuaded by "[what] Rabbi Kahane used to say, he wanted to have a Jewish fist connected to a Jewish head, you know a scholar-warrior, somebody who fights but understands the ideology and was prepared to take whatever risk necessary to be able to achieve the goal of saving fellow Jews."[36]

In the summer of 1983 the American-Israeli threesome of Guzofsky, Yehuda Richter (a member of the Kach suicide cell at Yamit), and Craig Leitner, later joined by Matthew Liebowitz and Levi Hazan, spent many late nights scheming about a violent response to the Egyptian-Israeli peace accords. That July they carried out a string of crimes, vandalizing Palestinian vehicles, torching cars, and setting the offices of the *al-Fajr* newspaper on fire.[37] As members of the Jewish Underground stood trial in the winter of 1984, the cell escalated their attacks, inflicting severe property damage to homes and businesses in both Hebron and Jerusalem, claiming responsibility to the press as the group TNT. The syndicate soon intensified its efforts, deciding to inflict human casualties in the interest of an "eye for an eye and a tooth for a tooth."[38] The conspirators began plotting the assault that would represent the culmination of their efforts: the ambush of a Palestinian bus in the West Bank.

On the night of March 13, 1984, the gang lay in wait by the village of Mazra'a e-Sharqiya, near Ramallah. When the bus approached, they opened fire with M16 rifles belonging to Guzofsky's father, injuring six Palestinians. The quintet quickly made their escape in a getaway vehicle, although the gang soon got lost in deep fog on the way back to Jerusalem. They decided to detour through the suburb of Ramot where they ditched disguises and telephoned the media to take responsibility for the terrorist attack. The Shin Bet, however, had been aware of TNT's plot all along. Tardy to reach the Palestinian village because of the weather, the security service failed to prevent the tragedy, but agents trailed the conspirators from the crime scene and arrested them on the spot.[39] According to Israeli police, once in custody the suspects confessed to the bus shooting and they were also interrogated for participation in previous incidents as the organization TNT.[40] Yet, authorities were at pains to assure both the Israeli and the American public that there was not a second *mahteret* in the making. "It's not a group, it's a number of men . . . whose views are Jewish-fanatical-religious. . . . No one was behind them. They are alone in their ideas and acts," a police spokesperson confirmed. The chief investigator added, "They don't have any characteristics of an underground movement."[41]

Two weeks later Guzofsky, Richter, Liebowitz, and Hazan were indicted in Jerusalem District Court. Leitner, who apparently agreed to testify against his co-conspirators, was released on bail and immediately returned to the United States.[42] The defendants cut ties with Leitner but they were eager to cultivate their other contacts in their country of origin. Incarcerated at Tel Mond Prison (where suspects in the Jewish Underground were also being held), the remaining foursome began an intensive letter-writing campaign to Brooklyn's *Jewish Press*, decrying a "McCarthy-style roundup" of Kach members and alleging the denial of their basic human, religious, and legal rights while being held in torture-like conditions.[43] Ultimately Hazan, Liebowitz, and Richter were convicted in the bus attack, while Guzofsky was acquitted for lack of evidence, likely because prosecutors could not introduce Leitner's testimony. Richter and Guzofsky continue to serve in

the leadership of Kahane Chai in Israel and both were arrested and imprisoned on subsequent occasions for violent activism during the Oslo peace
process and Gaza disengagement.

Baruch Goldstein and the Hebron Massacre

The Hebron massacre of 1994 was undoubtedly the most dramatic and
deadly terrorist act committed by a Jewish-American settler to date. Benjamin [Baruch] C. Goldstein was born in the Bensonhurst neighborhood of
Brooklyn in 1957. Benjy, as he was known, received a Zionist upbringing
in an Orthodox family of three sons that self-consciously traced its lineage
to victims of the 1929 massacre in Hebron.[44] As a teenager, he attended the
Orthodox Zionist Yeshiva of Flatbush; in the passionate essay he contributed to the school yearbook at the age of thirteen, citing biblical prohibi-
tions against murder, there were few hints that he would become a future
terrorist.[45] Like many other Orthodox Zionists of his generation, Goldstein attended Yeshiva University, where he graduated summa cum laude
and received commendations at his commencement ceremony for scholarship in Jewish studies and for "character, personality, and special services
to the class."[46] He then enrolled at the Einstein School of Medicine, earning
his medical degree in 1981 and later completing a residency at the Brook-
dale Hospital in Flatbush's emergency department. During his studies,
Goldstein became active in Rabbi Meir Kahane's Jewish Defense League
in Brooklyn, quickly earning the reputation as a radical—as one local
recalled, "he was always political, he was always an extremist."[47] In 1982,
Goldstein made his first public statement on the Arab-Israeli conflict in an
op-ed in the *New York Times,* where he called for the transfer of the
"Arab" population in the occupied territories and cautioned that "before
instinctively defending democracy as inviolate, Israelis should consider
whether the prospect of an Arab majority electing 61 Arab Knesset members is acceptable to them. Israelis will soon have to choose between a
Jewish state and democratic one."[48] It seemed clear where his own loyal-
ties lay.

   As one friend noted, "for him, Brooklyn was never home, for him Israel
was home" and Goldstein immigrated immediately after finishing his medical training at the age of twenty-six in 1983.[49] Upon completing active
duty in the IDF, Goldstein moved to the West Bank settlement of Kiryat

Arba, serving as its local general practitioner and emergency medicine physician. He also resumed his political activities, moonlighting as Rabbi Meir Kahane's campaign manager in his successful 1984 Knesset bid. Kahane officiated at Goldstein's wedding to his wife Miriam on the steps of the Temple Mount that year and the couple made their home in Kiryat Arba and went on to have several children there.

By accounts of both supporters and opponents, Goldstein was a highly talented and dedicated doctor who treated both Jewish and Palestinian patients in the distinct.[50] He apparently even received commendations of service from Kupat Holim (Israel's socialized medicine network) and the IDF. His position as the area's first responder during the violent years of the first intifada in Kiryat Arba and Hebron clearly made a profound impression on him. "My job isn't easy, and I think of it as a heavenly mission," he maintained, and he came to see the cycle of violence as a link in a historical chain of Jewish victimization since the 1929 riots carried out by an "enemy murdering Arab that aspires to annihilate all the Jews in the entire country in a second Holocaust, G-d forbid."[51] During the late 1980s Goldstein became increasingly politically active, serving as the local Kach representative on the Kiryat Arab citizens' council. He pushed a militant platform of combating terrorism through "the legal path" and frequently appeared in public with a yellow star (evoking the Holocaust-era Jewish badge) pinned to his chest to protest perceived neglect of Israeli settlers by the Israeli government and the IDF.[52] According to fellow Jewish-American settler Baruch Ben-Yaakov from Long Island, "he talked a lot about the Holocaust. He said Jews should never again be led like sheep to the slaughter" and likened the PLO to the Third Reich. Holocaust discourse was more than just a historical comparison, as "he always talked of revenge. He was a quiet man, but in his heart he was seething with anger." Others expressed that he was merely overcome by his passion for the Jewish people, recounting, "If the people he took care of died, we would see him crying. He loved Jews. He was a righteous man."[53] Goldstein was clearly partisan and lamented that he could never do enough to support his community but no one seemed to have predicted the events that followed.[54] As Lesly J. Lempert of the American Israeli Civil Liberties coalition recalled, "He was almost messianic in his strong commitment to the land. Did he strike me as someone that would go into the cave and do what he did? No. But he did strike me as a fanatic."[55]

On February 24, 1994, in his usual tradition, Goldstein attended the Scroll of Esther reading at the Tomb of the Patriarchs for the Jewish festival of Purim.[56] Unconfirmed chants of "Itbach al-Yahud" (Death to the Jews) were said to have echoed from the Muslim prayer hall during the Jewish service, which supposedly affected his frame of mind. Some American visitors allege that this call circulated in the mosque for weeks beforehand and other right-wing bloggers have promoted a completely unverified report that Palestinians had planned a premeditated attack on the Purim holiday. One account even contends that the IDF command had conveyed intelligence about these plans to the doctor in the interest of emergency preparedness. Goldstein supposedly responded, perhaps likening the situation in his own mind to the 1929 riots, "Will you allow this to happen? Why not take action to avoid this catastrophe?" His defenders suggest that the cumulative impact of these events precipitated a psychotic break that evening. While this version of events prior to the massacre has become an accepted mythology in certain right-wing circles and is commonly provided as context for his terrorist activities, I have found no evidence to support these claims and consider them to be conspiracy theories.[57] It is also impossible to evaluate Goldstein's psychological state based on available sources and there is no evidence of irrationality or temporary insanity.

What is known is that the following morning, Goldstein rose early before sunrise. He dressed in his IDF captain's uniform and carried his army-issued Galili rifle and at least four clips of bullets to the Tomb of the Patriarchs. Despite the fact that his wife Miriam later professed ignorance about his intentions, one report cited that the moment her husband left the house, she immediately made an emergency phone call to the IDF duty officer of Kiryat Arba, pleading, "Baruch is on his way to the Tomb, you have to stop him. I know he did not go to the tomb to pray."[58] Whether the message was received or acted upon remains unknown, but the doctor was not stopped by soldiers on guard at the checkpoint by the steps of the Tomb of the Patriarchs at around 5:30 a.m. that morning. Once inside the compound, he began running toward the mosque area. As Muslim worshippers knelt in prayer with their backs facing the door, Goldstein opened fire, shooting off more than one hundred rounds of ammunition in a two-minute spree, killing twenty-nine and wounding 125 Palestinians. When his rifle clip jammed in the midst of the chaos, remaining parishioners beat Goldstein to death with the mosque's fire extinguisher.

According to IDF officers on site, they "reacted immediately," although they were delayed in reaching the prayer hall by worshippers fleeing in panic in a scene later described as "complete pandemonium."[59] Kiryat Arba was immediately confined under military curfew but continued clashes led to the deaths of at least ten more Palestinians in the West Bank as well as a retaliatory fatal axe attack by a Palestinian terrorist that killed an innocent elderly Israeli man sitting on a park bench in Kfar Saba. The occupied territories seethed with unrest for months and Goldstein's act may have struck a fatal blow to the Oslo peace process.

In the aftermath of the massacre, Jewish-American settlers and the wider American-Israeli immigrant community withstood collective punishment from the Israeli government and public. Three days after the tragedy, Prime Minister Yitzhak Rabin addressed the Israeli Knesset with pointed remarks on Goldstein's foreign origins, railing: "This murderer . . . grew in a swamp whose murderous sources are found here, and across the sea; they are foreign to Judaism, they are not ours. To him and to those like him we say: You are not part of the community of Israel. You are not part of the national democratic camp to which we in this house all belong, and many of the people despise you. You are not partners in the Zionist enterprise. You are a foreign implant. You are an errant weed. Sensible Judaism spits you out. . . . You are a shame on Zionism and an embarrassment to Judaism."[60] Deeming the attack "the worst thing that has happened to us in the history of Zionism," Israeli president Ezer Weizman dubbed Goldstein and his supporters a "malignant growth in the body of the nation."[61] Former Israeli president Chaim Herzog collectively incriminated all American-Israeli settlers by characterizing the United States as "the breeding ground for Jewish extremists of varying backgrounds—religious, secular, and nationalist."[62] Foreign Minister Shimon Peres had cutting remarks for the settler community at Kiryat Arba, which he called "a breeding ground for murder," and he labeled Goldstein's allies "enemies of the people." He (ahistorically) contrasted Jewish-American settlers with native Israeli halutzim, pondering, "Did a murderer ever come out of the pioneering movement?"[63] One infuriated Knesset member derided all its immigrants with "American Jewry sends its 'dreck' [trash] . . . to Israel."[64] Minister of Absorption Yair Tsaban even proposed a migration ban on Jewish-Americans members of the JDL, Kach, and Kahane Chai, proclaiming, "I do not believe we have to permit the import of terror to Israel," and he pinpointed Brooklyn as the "the poisonous morass in which . . . the terrible massacre grew."[65] Under harsh criticism, Tsaban backpedaled on the bill, but the Israeli Shin Bet did conduct raids on Kahane sympathizers across the West Bank.[66]

Political condemnation led to calumny in the press and popular culture. Echoing the comments of parliamentarians, the Israeli Hebrew-language daily *Maariv* castigated Jewish-Americans who "send their lunatic children to Israel."[67] *Davar* reporter Teddy Preuss urged "operative steps against the Goldsteins of tomorrow," demanding that "any who possess American passports should be sent back."[68] The *New York Times* even launched an inquiry into local attitudes, noting that "in some Israeli circles, a new dirty word has popped up in the last few weeks: Brooklyn." The Hebron massacre was "enough to touch a certain anti-American streak just below the surface for many Israelis," and many natives had come to believe, as expressed by one Tel Aviv businessman, that "most American Jews are extremists and troublemakers too."[69] A construction worker in Efrat concurred, claiming, "The whole settlers' movement gets strength from the Americans . . . I think the country is going to hell, and America's got a hand in it. That's what hurts. That was the bosses' mistake. They didn't give us a chance to choose what we wanted from America. So we get American cars and American microwaves—and American settlers. Those people don't think the way we do."[70]

Jewish-American settlers themselves were at pains to convince the Israeli public—and even some parts of the native Israeli settler movement that would scapegoat them—that this was not the case. Efrat's religious director Bob Lang from Nanuit, New York, groused, "We're all tagged as 'settlers,' and with that word alone we're already put two pegs below everyone else. After the massacre, those of us who are Americans dropped down another peg. Now we're all seen as Baruch Goldsteins."[71] Joel Bloch, an alumnus of the Flatbush Yeshiva living in the settlement of Sha'arei Tikva, grumbled that he felt "under the gun," as "we feel the pressure from our fellow Jews in our daily lives, in our workplace, in business, in conversation. The tone I pick up when talking with other Israelis is that we are a bunch of wild-eyed fanatics who are screwing up the place." His wife Irene reckoned, "People have trouble closing the gap between the stereotype and the reality."[72] However, some moderate Jewish-American settlers like Jonathan Blass were adamant that fellow Israelis must distinguish between media caricatures and true character as the "only barrier against chaos." In a full-throated condemnation of Goldstein's act, he called for coexistence—if one that only recognized Israeli sovereignty—on behalf of his constituency:

> There can be no justification and no understanding for Goldstein's crime. Nor can responsibility for the bloodletting be shunted on the government that has sadly not succeeded or even tried seriously to deter Arab terror. No more convincing are explanations that the massacre was a direct result of the terrorist murders. . . . This undoubtedly would put a strain on anyone. But not every person who would buckle under the burden would allow himself to explode in a murderous frenzy against Arab civilians. At the root of the madness was an ideology of hatred built on a rejection of Jewish-Arab co-existence and a refusal to recognize the sovereign role of the State of Israel as the sole repository of Jewish military power.[73]

Others American-Israelis like Naftali Greenwood, who lived with Goldstein at Kiryat Arba, charged his own community with complicity in the terrorist attack in a column he titled "Confessions of a Co-Conspirator," confirming, "I am not washing my comrades' dirty linen in public, nor Israel's overseas. Together we have done this." "My message is therefore one of a challenge," he continued, citing the tradition of civil rights, where "for years we have affirmed that we as Jews dwell in these provinces not as occupiers or colonizers, nor as brutalizers or usurpers, but rather as the exercisers of a historical right to which the opposing side reacts with bloodshed. A revered member of our community had drenched this doctrine in the blood of innocents. Its recovery will depend on how well we restore our ethical equilibrium and demonstrate that it has been restored."[74]

Other Jewish-American settlers saw the massacre as a kind of complex moral calculus. David Wilder, a Jewish-American settler originally from Cleveland, Ohio, who served as the spokesperson for the Jewish settlement in Hebron for over twenty years and knew Goldstein personally, tried to balance security dictates with ethical duties. "First, to be clear, I do not agree with, or justify what Baruch Goldstein did," he declared, confirming, "I believe I can say, as I have stated many times before, that the Jewish community of Hebron also rejects such violence and bloodshed as a means to deal with the issues plaguing us." Yet, he also underscored that Goldstein's acts must be understood within the context of the Palestinian uprising, arguing:

> He made a tremendous, appalling error . . . which cost the lives of many people, which cost him his own life, and which left an indelible stain on Israel. That having been said, and realizing the horror of his act, it must be examined and remembered in the perspective of what was happening around us and to us. Had there not been an intifada, with some 160 Jews killed, with very few attempts to protect the Jewish victims, he never would have broken down and committed the acts that he did. And we cannot and must not forget that what he did, as ghastly as it was, was miniscule compared to the terror and death Israelis have faced at the hands of hundreds of Arab terrorists over the past decades.[75]

When I interviewed Wilder, he did not unequivocally condemn political violence. Rather, he framed these activities as self-defense and endorsed an efficacy test, suggesting: "I say look, the yishuv does now and always has rejected any and all illegitimate violence . . . [only] a person has to protect themselves, that's legitimate. . . . And I say, the proof of that is, that people don't do it. If people believed that what he did was the way to solve our problems, then people would do it. People are armed, we're all armed. Ok. They shot at us for 2.5 years [during the second intifada] and nobody took out their M16s and started plowing down Arabs—and we all could have done it. . . . I guess that means that people reject this way of doing things as a way to further a solution. . . . That's usually what I say to people about Baruch."[76]

A radical fringe of Jewish-American settlers was deeply inspired by Goldstein's heinous massacre of innocents, heralding violence as both an affective and effective means to combat terror and expand the settlement enterprise. Hebron resident Baruch Ben-Yaakov commented, "This act should not be condemned. If none of us condemn the act, it will make the Arabs afraid and prevent many attacks. This act, which sanctified God's name, shows the Arabs that we will not remain silent and watch them spill Jewish blood with impunity." Fellow New York native and Kiryat Arba resident Mattiyahu Alansky agreed, adding, "We are proud of what he did. He has given us pride as Jews. He is a hero. People may have died, but he has given life to the country. He has shown us that God is with us, that Jews will now fight back."[77] Former Kahanist David Axelrod (Ha'Ivri) espoused his hope to emulate Goldstein's act of terror, vaunting to reporters that he was capable of carrying out a violent attack, considering, "I'm a soldier in a war. We would be happy if the Israeli government pulls out of here entirely. Let them take their army and their police, and leave us alone. They're preventing us from fighting a just war."[78]

A generation since Goldstein's gun fell silent, the Hebron massacre continues to haunt both Israelis and Palestinians today.

The "Jewnabomber": American-Israeli Settler Terrorist Yaakov "Jack" Teitel

The most recent confirmed case of Jewish-American settler terrorism has implicated Yaakov "Jack" Teitel (alternately spelled Tytell). Born in Florida in 1972, Teitel experienced a tumultuous upbringing. Due to his father's reserve duty as a dentist in the U.S. military, the family of six moved frequently, living in four cities and two countries during his childhood. He was initially reared in a nonobservant Zionist home but his parents became *baalei teshuva* (returners to the faith) during his youth and later identified as ultra-Orthodox. Some have also alleged that there was domestic abuse within the family.[79] Teitel had violent fantasies of military combat, and by his high school years, classmates tagged Teitel as a troubled teen, confiding, "We were all afraid of him." Schoolteacher Ed Codish was aware of his young pupil's intentions, adducing that "Jack said when he grew up he wanted to go to Israel and kill Arabs."[80]

After graduating college in the early 1990s, Teitel made frequent trips to Israel and became involved in the hilltop youth movement in the south Hebron hills.[81] He was reportedly "enamored" with farming but was mostly unfamiliar to other settlers who noted that "he was somewhat active in the hilltop region, and people could recognize his face, but nothing beyond that."[82] While he was living in the West Bank in 1997, Teitel committed two terrorist murders against Palestinians, killing taxi driver Samir Balbisi of East Jerusalem and shepherd Isa Machmara of the village of Carmel in the Galilee. The Israeli Shin Bet suspected Teitel's involvement in the second attack and briefly arrested him. Upon his release from custody, he returned to the United States and the case was dropped due to lack of evidence.[83]

In 1999–2000 Teitel officially immigrated to Israel and moved to the West Bank settlement of Shvut Rachel, where he impressed the community's admissions committee as a "mensch with a love of the land of Israel who was looking to settle down and raise a family."[84] However, he had poor Hebrew language skills and could not hold a steady job. Teitel rarely socialized with neighbors or even left his home and was considered an "outcast" within the small community of one hundred families.[85] His only friend in Shvut Rachel seems to have been a middle-aged American-Israeli settler named Yosef Espinoza, who observed that the immigrant was obsessed with divine messages and "doomsday" scenarios, although he likely assisted him with arms training.[86] Teitel apparently also consorted with another Jewish-American in the community, twenty-two-year-old Kahanist Avraham Richland, who had likely been involved in terrorist activities himself.[87] In 2002 Teitel met and married British-Israeli Rivka Pepperman, seemingly settling down into a quiet life as a family man and father of five. He was visibly upset when his brother Moshe was non-fatally shot in a terrorist attack, although his sister-in-law alleged he was "very angry, but did not say revenge should be taken on the Arabs."[88]

When Teitel resumed his terrorist campaign in November 2006, he shifted to Jewish and Christian marks.[89] First, he planted a detonator at the police station in the nearby settlement of Eli to protest the annual gay pride parade in Jerusalem. In the spring of 2007, he bombed a church in the village of Bait Gemayal, wounding a Palestinian man and two Israeli police targets near Jerusalem. In March 2008 he hid an explosive in a traditional Purim gift-basket left on the doorstep of a Messianic Jewish family in the settlement of Ariel, maiming teenager Avi Ortiz. That fall he rigged a pipe bomb outside the residence of noted left-wing professor Ze'ev Sternhall, lightly injuring the academic. Teitel is also suspected of homophobic leafleting and confessed to bombing the gay cultural center in Tel Aviv in 2009, although intelligence officials claim that he did not actually carry out the attack.[90] The Shin Bet does suggest that Teitel could be responsible for at least five more murders of Palestinian victims that are currently under investigation.[91] It seemed apparent that Teitel was planning further attacks when authorities found a cache of guns and other incriminating materials at his home in Shvut Rachel.[92]

In November 2009 Teitel was arrested and questioned about a series of attacks that were carried out over the previous decade. An Israeli police spokesman surmised that he was "a serial killer" and a "Jewish terrorist" and the deputy commander of the Israeli police SWAT team described him as "a determined man with very deeply rooted ideology"—a particularly pithy pundit later dubbed him "the Jewnambomber." Ultimately Teitel was charged with fourteen crimes and held without bail in a mental facility to undergo psychiatric evaluation.[93] The case was brought to Jerusalem district court in 2011, although Teitel refused to recognize the trial's authority, exclaiming during proceedings that "the Lord is King" and that he was an "emissary of the Lord."[94] Based in part on his own confession, the court convicted him on multiple counts of murder and attempted murder, as well as numerous lesser charges including incitement to violence and terror.[95] At sentencing, Teitel flashed the "V" for victory sign as a verdict of two life terms plus thirty years was handed down, although he has subsequently appealed his conviction to the Israeli Supreme Court on the grounds of mental health concerns.[96] Meanwhile, Teitel's victims have filed a civil suit requesting 4 million shekels in damages.[97] While most of the Israeli public and its settler community condemned Teitel's crimes, the full extent of his terrorist activities may only be revealed in the years to come.

ACTS OF POLITICAL VIOLENCE in the 1980s and 1990s inspired some Jewish-American settler activists to turn instead toward public relations, civil disobedience, and other forms of nonviolent activism.

The Rise of Jewish-American Settler Public Relations in the Oslo Era: The Madrid Conference, YESHA Council Foreign Desk, and Israel Community Development Fund

The Israeli settler enterprise saw the first intifada as a shock to the system as well as a loss of both physical and metaphorical ground after twenty years of political struggle. Yet some Jewish-American immigrants saw these dark days of crisis not only as a chance to continue to contribute as settler leaders and cadres, but to reconceive of themselves and their role within the movement. Mobilizing their roots on two continents, this coterie of American-Israeli public relations experts sought to revolutionize the settlement project's message at a pivotal moment in its history by translating scripture into a sound bite. By serving as English-language spokespeople, foreign "diplomats," lobbyists, journalists, and fundraisers, they introduced a new liberal rights-based discourse about their activities to the international community. As media-savvy propagandists, Jewish-American immigrants changed the face of the movement while restoring their own tarnished image as settler terrorists.

In the late 1980s, Yisrael Medad, past national president of BETAR, Jewish-American settler at Shilo, and former Knesset aide to the ultra-nationalist MK Geula Cohen, called together some American-Israeli friends to discuss his brainchild: a public relations and foreign representation campaign on behalf of the settlement project. Medad himself was no stranger to this line of work, having previously served as a spokesperson for Gush Emunim and as a one-man informal embassy hosting Western diplomats at his home in the occupied territories. Medad soon had an ambitious plan in mind to organize an unofficial delegation of English-speaking settlers to attend the Madrid peace conference.

In the late fall of 1991, international, regional, and domestic conditions seemed ripe to convene the first mediated Israeli-Palestinian peace confab since the Camp David Accords. Medad recognized the danger of diplomatic engagement to the settlement project even before the conference was publicly announced, noting in an op-ed in the pages of the *Jerusalem Post*: "In the narrow theater of Israel vs. the Arab presence in Eretz Yisrael, the pressures on Israel . . . to divest itself of real security elements and portions of the nation's patrimony—the areas of Judea, Samaria, and Gaza—while at the same time ignoring the political/cultural impermanence of the opposing side, are as irrational as they are invidious. . . . If Messrs. Bush, Baker, Major, and Mitterrand seek peace, they must devote a period of time to be measured in decades and effort measured in many millions of dollars to turn the Arab peoples around."[98] Concerned that the views of Israeli settlers would not be represented at the conference, Medad decided to bring an entourage of eleven YESHA Council representatives, including veteran Gush Emunim leaders Yisrael Harel and Uri Elitzur as well as some American-Israeli colleagues like spokeswoman and translator Shifra Blass, international lawyer and Republicans in Israel head Marc Zell, and political activist and consultant Yechiel Leiter. "You see, we didn't trust Shamir," so the group set out to meet with the prime minister in Madrid and to communicate their point of view to other politicians and the international press attending the gathering.[99]

Little could they have known that the settlements issue would overshadow the opening of the conference. As talks got under way in Madrid, a bus heading from Shilo to a rally against territorial concessions in Jerusalem was shot at by Palestinian gunmen, killing the driver and a mother of seven and wounding five children. For Medad, the terrorist attack literally hit home and he felt moved to share his heartbreak with the international media, though he was not entirely unaware that this pulling of heartstrings might also have an emotional impact in favor of the settlement enterprise. Speaking to reporters on the first day of the conference, he excoriated European leaders that "physical violence" in Shilo had been substituted for "diplomatic violence" at Madrid and counseled Shamir to leave the conference immediately as "Israel is allowing itself to be maneuvered into positions that are not good for it."[100] Shifra Blass, one of the founding settlers at Ofra, not far from where the attack occurred, later recollected, "It struck me exactly where I lived, it hit me. . . . It was the mother of seven children who was pregnant (like the woman who died), that was exactly my situation and I was thinking about the family."[101] Transforming the personal into the political, she bluntly informed a reporter during the first day of proceedings in Madrid that "I'm afraid of Bush's amateurism here because it's turning quite deadly for us."[102]

The Israeli government recognized the need to respond to breaking news. Medad smiled as he told me in an interview that "finally . . . [the official delegation] turned around and said, idiots, we've got fifteen English-speaking honest-to-goodness Israeli settlers, okay—let's let them loose on the press." *Nekuda* editor Yisrael Harel snuck the group into the conference press center, stretching their journalism credentials with affiliations to local settlement newsletters like *Gushpanka* and *Counterpoint* (of which Medad was the editor). As word traveled through the building that the settlers had arrived, Medad later boasted that "everyone was pressing us for information . . . we were making the news . . . [we] finally began to make an indent on what was happening."[103]

At the close of the conference, some members of the group even had the opportunity to meet with Prime Minster Shamir. In Medad's telling, "he was political, he kept his distance until the last day, [when he chose] to receive us so that we could report to the press that the Jewish residents of Judea and Samaria [who] are here to make sure that Israel doesn't give away anything were received by the prime minister. . . . It was half photo-op and half serious." Either way, the event was orchestrated for maximal public relations benefit to the Shamir administration, especially as prior to the meeting, Medad's entourage was encouraged to organize a solidarity demonstration outside the hotel where they would be received. Medad later illustrated the scene with mixed emotion. "In the end, we stood outside the hotel . . . we walked, gritting our teeth because we didn't want to do this from our political point of view," he described, "but we did it . . . because in the end, it will serve our purposes, not only because it will help Israel in the short-run, but in the long-run, Shamir is beholden to us."[104]

This debt of gratitude was not necessarily recognized by the prime minister back in Jerusalem,[105] but the delegation capitalized on their momentum from Madrid upon their return to the settlements. Their first accomplishment was convincing the YESHA Council to set up a twenty-four-hour staffed command center of mostly American-Israeli English-speaking activists. They then sent a delegation on an outing to Rehalim—the new outpost named for Israeli settler Rachel Druck who was killed on the eve of the Madrid conference—as their first act of public diplomacy. Medad's version of this event poignantly depicted what public relations–savvy Americans had to offer to native Israeli settlers. Medad humorously recalled trying to escort Benny Katzover, a high-level Gush Emunim leader, to meet a U.S. diplomat at the event: "I walked over and said, 'Benny, do you see that guy over there in the suit? He's the American political officer from the consulate and I've been in touch with him, would you like to meet him?' He [Katzover] was like, 'What do I need him for?' I said, 'Benny, in America, even if you don't like someone, you smile, shake his hand, and say hello.' . . . He said 'okay.' . . . So I brought him over. . . . They chatted a few words, and that was it. So he of course goes home now and brags that he met the U.S. political representative!" While their brief conversation was not significant, it reflected Medad's assessment that "if an American wasn't there, a cultural-ideological divide could not have been bridged."[106]

With this vision of public relations in mind, the group launched the YESHA Council Foreign Desk, the International Relations Task Force (IRTF) in 1991. One of its initial efforts was to establish the YESHA Speaker's Bureau, an initiative billed as an opportunity for "diplomats, legislators, policy makers, academics, and community leaders all over the world . . . [who] can now meet and choose to hear advocacy of YESHA presented in a clear and lucid fashion by the very people who are involved in shaping the destiny of Israel and its heartland." A slick English brochure, featuring many Jewish-American settlers mentioned in this book, offered presenter headshots and biographies alongside contact information in the United States and Israel for arranging an interview or event with a spokesperson.[107] They also began publishing a monthly English-language bulletin entitled the *YESHA Report,* which its editors characterized in the debut edition as an instrument of public relations warfare. "Undeniably, the field of battle for continued Jewish civilian presence in those portions of the historic Jewish homeland not yet under Israeli sovereignty is as much on the television screens and newspaper pages as it is in the corridors of political power in Washington, London, and Jerusalem," they judged, hoping that their journalist venture would serve as "a vehicle to relay . . . the frontline of pioneering Zionism."[108] Under the leadership of Yechiel Leiter and Bob Lang during the Oslo process, the group founded an Information Task Force, which created the famous YESHA Zeh Kan (YESHA Is Here) campaign, organized press conferences, television, radio, and print broadcast appearances (so much so that Leiter was often mistaken for an employee of CNN), spearheaded a partnership with the Library of Congress to inform politicians on the Hill, and even inaugurated a presence in "cyberspace."[109] In addition to disseminating their own propaganda, they also served as media watchdogs of major news outlets and NGOs.[110] Further, the Foreign Desk orchestrated activities on the ground, creating a tourism authority, as well as organizing sightseeing trips, which they claimed brought more than 50,000 travelers on special English-language chartered bus tours to the occupied territories.[111] The Foreign Desk specialized in settlement tours for diplomats, political leaders, nongovernmental groups, and journalists. It also sponsored two "Leadership Mission to YESHA" trips in 1997, hosting a ten-day symposium for Diaspora Jewish officials that included aerial, Jeep, and bus sightseeing, visits across the West Bank with special meet-and-greet sessions with settlers, security briefings with military leaders, and a special address by Prime Minister Benjamin Netanyahu to "see Israel's heartland as you have never seen it before."[112] Following in the footsteps of Madrid, the Foreign Desk also continued to send delegations to United States and other world capitals to meet with Jewish groups and lawmakers.[113]

Reflecting on these successes, Leiter modestly suggested, "What I did was to put it all under one roof . . . get[ting] the Americans, who were all acting independently, into some single organized . . . effort."[114] He was perhaps

too humble—these Jewish-Americans helped make history in rehabili-
tating the Israel settler movement's strategy and tactics. "I'm old enough to
remember the civil rights movement, the campaign for Soviet Jewry, it
wasn't just demonstrations, it was calling your congressman, it was going
down to his office," Medad observed, and, "My friends think a lot like
that." However, despite their best efforts, he contended that "a basic conflict [remained] between Americans who had cut their teeth on Americans
for Democratic activism and tried to apply the same paradigms here and
basically were knocking their heads against the wall" and their native Israeli peers.[115] Leiter also advocated for a new kind of direct action inspired by his experiences in the United States "that would engage much
more of the Israeli population than these sit-ins at the Knesset gardens
which would end . . . with a Hassidic singer . . . and everyone danced for two
hours and it was over. I thought we needed to move more into the mode
of the civil rights movement, the antiwar movement, but my [Israeli]
colleagues didn't get it."[116]

Although they enhanced some of the settler enterprise's public engagement and outreach events, the core contribution of Jewish-American settlers involved with the Foreign Desk was revamping its communications
strategy. By introducing a new form of American-style "hasbara" (Zionist
propaganda) that hearkened back to their roots in the United States, they
revolutionized the rhetoric of the movement so it would resonate with the
international community. Leiter pointed to the parochial thinking of native Israelis, where "there is this attitude sometimes that it doesn't matter
what the *goyim* [gentiles] say, it's what the Jews do."[117] For Shifra Blass,
savvy public relations was not only good for interfaith relations, it could
actually bridge the gap between Western universalism and Jewish particularism. "That's right, very not postmodern, very not your narrative [my
narrative], and I know it's even less popular to say it," she admitted, but
argued that verily, "Jewish values are universal values . . . what is good for
the Jews is really good for everyone else." She understood the centrality of
this conflict between sectarian interest and social welfare, commenting,
"This is where we clash with people who don't want us to be doing what
we are doing, I think because we start with a different understanding of
what is a State of Israel and what does it mean to the world. As I say, I
think it means an opportunity—a place and time—where one can apply
the great ideals, goodness [and] justice . . . on a national level." To her mind,

"basically, Israel is an experiment for many people—can you take the great ideals and apply them and survive?" This broad conception of what Zionism represented was critical to Blass's public relations work, considering: "I think that hasbara is not just public relations . . . they share a wall, they go in and out of each other's offices all the time, but they aren't the same thing. Because hasbara is education—it's even one step further, it's saying the truth. It is releasing truth into the universe . . . I feel in a deep sense, a Jewish sense, that you should say the truth because it is good, because the world is built on truth, and truth is God's name—and you say it."[118]

For Blass and her fellow settler colleagues, American-style rights talk was the vehicle to relate their values and truths to international audiences. She vociferously objected to settlement bans in the occupied territories as policies that were "outrageous in terms of human rights. . . . Could they really say [you can't live here] because you're a Jew? It just seemed to us something that goes against everything we know about liberal values."[119] Her husband later added, "It seemed like a natural kind of thing to do [to settle]" and claimed, "We felt very much discriminated against."[120] Aliza Herbst, a Jewish-American settler at Ofra originally from Texas who worked for many years for Gush Emunim's settlement arm AMANA and the Foreign Desk, framed her rights struggle as a positive fight for equality, as "I find it very disheartening as a former left-wing person, [that] they're [i.e., the left is] passionate about destructing, about destroying things, they are passionate against things, against YESHA, but they're not passionate for things, you know? We, my generation in the States, we were passionate for things . . . we were passionate for women's rights, and we were passionate for gay rights, and we were passionate for helping people out of poverty . . . to do positive things, and I don't see that here."[121] Summing up these sentiments, Yisrael Medad concluded that settlement in the occupied territories is "the most important [political] campaign of all time."[122]

Leiter pushed the boundaries of this argument, suggesting that as an immigrant of choice who had left a comfortable life in America—as a "real Ziyoni [Zionist]"—he had "no less of a right" and perhaps more so than a native Israeli to pursue his destiny and defend the cause of settlement over the Green Line.[123] His writings from the period seamlessly combine U.S. history and Israeli hawkishness, liberal rhetoric with resistance to the peace process, civil disobedience with religious doctrine, and American political philosophy with settlement promotion.[124] For example, in leading the YESHA Council's campaign for nonviolent resistance against the Israeli-Palestinian peace process in 1994, he compared their goals to Martin Luther King Jr.'s leadership during the civil rights movement: "He made no apologies. 'It's their future that we are fighting for,' he argued. The Blacks' struggle for civil rights and human decency was not a partisan battle of a special-interest group. It was an all-encompassing struggle for justice and morality which in its scope spanned race, color, and age. Similarly, our struggle to realize the full historic bond of the Jewish people with the land of Israel."[125] Taking the city of Hebron as an example, he crusaded for "the most important matter at stake: ensuring Jewish civil rights." Evoking the African-American struggle for equality, he pronounced, "When the federal courts and government in the United States decided to protect the rights of blacks in the South to live in white neighborhoods and attend integrated schools, no cost was too great to defend that moral cause. . . . No one suggested that the cost and the pain were not worth the results. Rights do not have a price."[126] In the last years of Oslo, Leiter returned to this refrain, paraphrasing Abraham Lincoln's Gettysburg Address to illustrate that "independence and freedom have their price": "Lincoln . . . recount[ed] that four score and seven years prior the nation's fathers 'had brought forth a new nation conceived in liberty and dedicated to the proposition that all men are created equal.' . . . And what shall we say? . . . We shall say that: four millennia ago our forefathers brought forth on this land, a chosen nation, conceived by God, and dedicated to the proposition that all nations will one day cease to make war with one another, that death will vanish from the earth, and that all men will then be equal, at liberty to sit beneath their grapevine and fig tree, with no worry that such a government, under God, for the people, will perish from this earth."[127]

While rights may have a rich price, it was the financial cost of operating the YESHA Council Foreign Desk that truly took a toll and created a schism between Leiter and other Jewish-American settlers who were concerned that his politicized fundraising tactics were violating IRS tax laws. Ultimately, most of the Jewish-American settler media strategists abandoned the Foreign Desk to form a new organization called the Israel Communities Development Fund (ICDF).[128] Guided by the charitable philosophy of "money goes to money," ICDF was to serve as a sophisticated "supercollection agency" that would centralize fundraising and distribution efforts (avoiding the rampant duplication by local settlements and institutions) for strictly humanitarian projects in the occupied territories.[129] The group successfully raised funds for several years and even claimed to have obtained financing from a "mid-level" Jewish federation in the United States.[130] However, the project was eventually superseded by the YESHA Council's One Israel Fund, which continues to provide nongovernmental development assistance to settlements over the Green Line today.[131]

While the delegation to Madrid, the YESHA Council Foreign Desk, and ICDF were short-lived innovations of the 1990s, they inspired a new generation of Jewish-American public relations strategists. Until recently, former Kach activist David Ha-Ivri (Axelrod) directed the Shomron Liaison Office, which considers itself the unofficial diplomatic representation of settlers in the upper West Bank and devotes its energies to tourism promotion, media communication, and political outreach.[132] These activities are also taking place at the individual settlement level, including American-Israeli initiatives of the Ariel Development Fund, the Hebron Fund, and Friends of Ir David (East Jerusalem).[133] In an interesting development, Efrat's mayor Oded Ravivi announced the reestablishment of the YESHA Council Foreign Desk in July 2016.[134] Jewish-American settlers will likely continue to play a prominent role in the public relations of the Israel settler movement on the local, national, and global stage in the future.

Shmuel Sackett, Zo Artzeinu, and Manhigut Yehudit

Another important indication of the influence of Jewish-American discourses and tactics on the settlement project in recent years is the case of the contemporary Zo Artzeinu (This Is Our Land) and Manhigut Yehudit (Jewish Leadership) social movements led by Israeli ultra-nationalist Moshe Feiglin and American-Israeli settler Shmuel Sackett. Their importation of a civil disobedience campaign into the Israeli context illustrates the liminal nature of liberalism in the occupied territories.

Born in 1961 in Queens, New York, Sackett was reared in a modern Orthodox family and educated at the Zionist Yeshiva of Central Queens. Outside of school the restless teenager became active in the Struggle for Soviet Jewry and the Jewish Defense League, which, he later judged, "really completed my Judaism, because it wasn't just observing rituals in the synagogue and at home . . . but fighting for Israel . . . because without that, Judaism was too dry for me."[135] During a gap year in Israel in 1979, he became a deputy in Kach and demonstrated at right-wing rallies against the Camp David Accords. Sackett immigrated to Israel with his wife and four children in the final days of the first intifada in 1990.

"When I came on aliya, I wasn't looking to be the world's biggest activist," Sackett admitted, choosing to reside in the West Bank settlement of Karnei Shomron not only out of ideological convictions but for its affordable housing, proximity to relatives, and an easy commute to his marketing job in central Israel. Yet, if he did not move to the occupied territories looking for political opportunities, he quickly found them in the Neve Aliza neighborhood, a mainly American-Israeli enclave where "activism was contagious."[136] Sackett soon became acquainted with fellow resident Moshe Feiglin and his American-born wife, Tzippy, forming a friendship that rapidly became a political partnership.

As Feiglin put it, their alliance was "a rare union of two lunatics" worthy of "sociological research." Certainly, Feiglin's resume could not have read more differently than Sackett's: he was a native Israeli from a religious Zionist family that claimed its roots in the First Aliya, had a *sabra* upbringing in Haifa and Rehovot, served in an IDF combat unit during the first Lebanon War, and became a successful entrepreneur with a multimillion dollar Tel Aviv high-rise window-washing business. Despite a biography that shared little with his foreign-born neighbors, he deemed himself right at home in Neve Aliza, whose "American temperament and non-homogenous social fabric suited me to a tee."[137] Feiglin readily conceded that Jewish-American settlers made unlikely political collaborators, as "Actually, the residents of Neveh Aliza were the least suitable people of all those living in YESHA to undertake this initial push, since they were all new immigrants who could barely communicate in Hebrew and whose circle of acquaintances was quite limited. But these disadvantages were counter-balanced by their zeal and enthusiasm. The American mentality, which rejects all violation of basic civil rights and espouses the right to protest infractions, and if necessary, torment the makers of government policy—all of this was ingrained in their personality. . . . What they did not have was the acceptance of the authority of the establishment which was innate in the Israeli soul."[138] Feiglin credited his American immersion experience with new political horizons, yet he lacked any real exposure to direct action. To Sackett, their cultural divide could be summarized as "he's a big thinker, he's a wonderful person . . . he's very idealistic . . . [but] to the average Israeli, being idealistic was being a great soldier." Sackett considered Feiglin a kind of political naïf, noting "before he met me, [he] had never I think been to a rally before in his life . . . so we [together] were able to really focus and direct his tremendous energy into real activism."[139] A rough division of labor—Feiglin as visionary and Sackett as tactician—evolved in their partnership, and with these new roles in place, the duo soon intensified their political discussions.[140]

In 1993, Feiglin and Sackett began planning a protest action against the Oslo Accords. Feiglin's impressions as a platoon commander during the first intifada largely informed his subsequent thinking that "it seemed to me in such circumstances, the Left was indeed in the right. As long as we related to the Land as belonging to an enemy, as long as we refrain from internalizing our natural ownership of the Land and seeing ourselves as the proper, true claimant, we will merely be occupiers, and thus, by definition, immoral."[141] Both he and Sackett carefully portrayed themselves as outsiders and independent activists and condemned the right—especially a "pathetic" and "impotent" YESHA Council that "could do no more than pay lip-service to the struggle against government policies."[142]

Yet, initially, Feiglin and Sackett had tried to cooperate with the YESHA Council on their first initiative they called Mivza Mahpil (The Doubling Operation) to increase the number of new outposts and settlements in the occupied territories in the midst of the Oslo negotiations. As Sackett recalled, the two traveled at least thirty times to Jerusalem to meet with its representatives, later accusing them of sabotage. The duo then alleged that the YESHA Council was colluding with the Rabin government in a bid to demonstrate "We are respectable, it's only *they* that are trouble-makers."[143] This aborted collaboration built upon what Feiglin had already learned from his American neighbors. "By the end of the course, I understood that the world was divided, essentially, into the establishment—and whatever is not part of it," he explained, "The main thing I learned from Operation Double is to be completely independent of any institutions or political party."[144] In December 1993 Feiglin, Sackett, and their followers struck out on their own doubling operation across the West Bank (a place Feiglin often referred to as "the Wild West"), determined to break ground on over 130 new settlements.[145] To them, this mission would "say[ing] to the world that this is our land, that we will come and go wherever we want, whenever we want. The country belongs to us." A second stage was planned for the following month, when supporters across the country would come to demonstrate against Oslo from the new settlements for forty-eight hours, although Sackett forswore that "we will never raise a hand against Jewish soldiers."[146] Their ambitious plan was largely a failure and saddled the duo with financial debts. However, the pair learned an important lesson from this fiasco: the old incremental settlement model of "another dunam, another goat" was now defunct and the ultra-nationalist camp needed a comprehensive new strategy to deter the Oslo process.

The two activists then turned their attention to building a mass social movement that would mobilize opposition to the government and Oslo both within and outside the Green Line. The duo attended rallies against territorial withdrawals across the country throughout 1994, looking to recruit supporters. In June 1995, after a large demonstration that failed to attract much media coverage, public relations expert Sackett was fed up. "It's not that I don't believe in the cause, it's just that we're not marketing it right," assessed the American-Israeli settler, "I said, we have to hit page 1 [of the newspaper]—do you know how to get to page 1?' I asked Moshe. He says, 'Yes—if you remember, I was an explosives expert in the army, I can get to page 1.' And I said, 'Okay, is there any other way to get to page 1?'"[147] Eschewing violence, Sackett took to educating his colleague on the history of social protest in the United States. Feiglin was a quick study, recollecting, "Shmuel and I did not need long-winded debates in order to understand something that is obvious to every thinking person."[148]

With his new consciousness as a liberal, Feiglin formulated a vision of "Walden in the West Bank," citing everything from the Talmud to Thoreau to justify his theories of nonviolent civil disobedience.[149] "It is self-evident that there are limits to obedience [to government]" he observed, "The real question is where the line must be drawn."[150] For Feiglin and Sackett, the government had abrogated the social contract with the Oslo process and popular protest against the State was now a moral obligation. Moreover, the two believed that they served as the vanguard of an Israeli silent majority, professing, "We were prepared to go into the streets because we believed that we really represented the people."[151] Co-opting the model of the civil rights movement in the 1960s, Feiglin mused, "This is how it was with Martin Luther King in the USA . . . wasn't it?"[152]

In early 1995 Feiglin was so inspired by this political legacy that he "looked for ways to convert the theory of non-violent civil disobedience into reality . . . I thought of the march that Dr. Martin Luther King had led to Washington, D.C., I wanted to cook up something of that sort here in Israel."[153] The duo seized on a plan to organize nonviolent sit-ins at road and highway intersections across Israel and the West Bank to protest Oslo. They called their new social movement Zo Artzeinu (This Is Our Land), convinced of the logic that "whoever controls the roads, controls the areas."[154] In their first action on the eve of August 9, 1995, activists from both the settlements and territorial Israel took to the streets, blocking twenty-four major arteries by sitting down on the pavement and crossing their arms above their heads in a sign of passive resistance. Traffic across the country immediately came to a standstill at rush hour. Over 3,000 police forces were dispatched to eighty road junctions, which resulted in 130 arrests (including Feiglin and Sackett). As predicted, the protest made front-page news across the country—one traffic reporter even described the scene as "a catastrophe."[155] Activists empathized with waylaid travelers who were stranded for hours and they handed out broadsheets explaining their cause, reading, "We are sorry for the inconvenience, this is a struggle against a mad government that is giving our land to a foreign people, that is splitting our nation in two, making an alliance with a terrorist organization, bringing into the land an army of terrorists, and arming them with 20,000 automatic rifles."[156] While he acknowledged the outrage of average commuters, Sackett affirmed that civil disobedience action was a necessity, sensing, "We felt there was a conflict, but . . . we didn't worry about negativity. . . . While we won't resort to violence, we can't sit and be a good little boy anymore when Jews are being killed."[157]

Sackett and Feiglin escalated their activities across the country in the months preceding the Rabin assassination. In September 1995, Zo Artzeinu infamously organized an illegal rally at the Paris Square roundabout in Jerusalem where the two leaders and a crowd of activists with hands tied overhead chanted "This is our land [Zo Artzeinu]!" and "Police state!" as officers in riot gear used water cannons and other forms of crowd control and arrested twenty-two and injured thirty.[158] In another demonstration at Kikar Paris, protestors held posters reading "Gandhi. Martin Luther King. Moshe Feiglin."[159] A few weeks later, the group led a flock of sheep through the streets of Jerusalem as a symbol of how the government's efforts were leading Israelis like lambs to the slaughter. Before one of Prime Minister Rabin's last speeches, Sackett humorously recalled buying out the entire stock of handcuffs at a Tel Aviv sex shop so activists could chain themselves to their seats.[160] After countless arrests for leading illegal protests across the country, Feiglin and Sackett were charged with sedition against the State of Israel in the fall of 1995.

Feiglin's supporters were flabbergasted. "Here we are being Martin Luther King," maintained right-wing Knesset aide Uri Bank, "[and] instead of being treated like champions of democracy, we're getting kicked in the you-know-where."[161] Feiglin and Sackett saw their indictment as a show trial led by a politicized judiciary looking for a scapegoat in the aftermath of the Rabin assassination. They even contended that the prime minister's murder was the direct result of curbing their own civil disobedience campaign, echoing Martin Luther King's aphorism that "those that make peaceful revolution impossible will make violent revolution inevitable."[162] Yet the resourceful duo also recognized that media coverage of the case could pay dividends in terms of free publicity and support for their ideology.[163] Sure enough, the media circus outside the courthouse landed Zo Artzeinu back on the front pages of the newspaper. Supporters framed the duo's activities as prisoners of conscience, even bringing former refusnik Yosef Medelevitch to the hall of justice to bless the defendants with "From the prisoners of Zion of yesterday to the prisoners of Zion of today: Be brave and courageous."[164] As a former activist in the Soviet Jewry struggle, the blessing must have held cruel irony for Sackett. "Israelis think they live in a democracy, but they don't," he opined, "In the States we *really* did grow up in a democracy . . . I was involved in certain activities that *really* did have an effect on things . . . [we] were able to pierce the Iron Curtain, that was incredible."[165] "Israel equals demo-tatorship," he declared, later surmising, "Martin Luther King would have been found guilty of sedition here."[166] Feiglin also compared his plight to King's, citing his hero in his summation for the defense:[167] "Is the United States of Martin Luther King an unsavory regime? Is England, against which Gandhi struggled, an unsavory regime? Is the France of the students' revolts an unsavory regime? . . . Tiananmen

Square[?] . . . Israel is certainly not a dictatorship, but apparently, neither is it a true democracy. You, honorable judges, must decide where Israeli democracy is headed—toward 'Paris' or toward 'Tiananmen.' "[168] Judges determined that their brand of Israeli democracy was heading only to prison, convicting both Sackett and Feiglin of sedition and handing down twelve- and eighteen-month sentences (respectively), although both were allowed to complete their terms as community service.

Criminal records did not discourage the duo from continuing their activism. On the day of their release, Feiglin and Sackett reunited in the understanding that "a Jewish activist doesn't retire." However, Sackett had reached the conclusion "I'm out of the rally business . . . as long as the leftists control the media, and the courts, and the police, and the Knesset, you can hold a sign until you're blue in the face, nobody gives a damn . . . I was on page 1 . . . but our goal was ending the peace process and it was not affecting [it] at all." Moreover, he had come to realize that they needed to market a more positive message, maintaining, "There was our problem with Zo Artzeinu: all we did was scream 'no.' This is no good, that's no good, Rabin is no good, Peres is no good, Tzippi Livni is no good, Bibi is no good, Sharon . . . you can't keep doing this day after day—you have to come to people with an alternative."[169] Soon Feiglin and Sackett "had a dream" to lead the government of Israel where "we built the alternative, we designed the alternative."[170] The Manhigut Yehudit (Jewish Leadership) platform would resist a peace process, territorial concessions, and the creation of a Palestinian state, while embracing other causes such as Jewish settlement across the land of Israel and in East Jerusalem, prayer on the Temple Mount, and in a libertarian twist, the legalization of marijuana.[171] In the 2000s, Sackett and Feiglin maneuvered Manhigut Yehudit into the mainstream of Israeli politics. After several years of running in Likud party elections with Sackett serving as his campaign manager, Feiglin finally became of member of parliament in 2013.[172] After a poor showing in the primaries, he left the Likud in 2015 to form the new political party Zehut (Identity) on a right-wing platform with violent overtones. Sackett continues to serve as Feiglin's right-hand man, international spokesperson, and chief fundraiser, and travels frequently to the United States, where he raised over $5.2 million on behalf of Manhigut Yehudit in recent years.[173] Sackett feels "extremely optimistic" about the future and vows to "try to use the strength that God gave me to do good things for the Jewish people" with the goal of installing Moshe Feiglin as prime minister of the State of Israel in the next decade.[174]

TENSION BETWEEN MODERATES and extremists within the Jewish-American settler camp almost fifty years into their making of their city on a hilltop threatens to tear this constituency asunder. Some reject liberalism altogether and embrace political violence. Most recently, Jewish-American settlers have been implicated in a "price-tag" attack in the Palestinian village of Duma, where the Dawabsha family was burned alive in a horrific arson, killing both parents and an infant and leaving their other son a grievously injured orphan.[175] Others have consolidated their liberal identities and used the media to convey their views to the international community, such as Jewish-American settlers Jeremy Gimpel and Ari Abramowitz, who host the *Tuesday Night Live* television show (based on New York City's network comedy *Saturday Night Live*), which draws a large fan-base from the occupied territories and projects its message on worldwide cable television. In the fall of 2016, American-Israeli supporters of then GOP presidential nominee Donald Trump, with the assistance of Republicans Overseas Israel director Marc Zell, even opened an office in the West Bank settlement of Karnei Shomron as a public relations and voter recruitment outpost of the official campaign.[176] At the time this book went to print, president-elect Trump had just announced his nomination of Attorney David Friedman, the sitting chair of the American Friends of Beit El and a major settlement proponent, as his new U.S. ambassador to Israel. President Trump even hosted a delegation of settlers, including American-Israelis Zell and MK Yehuda Glick, as well as Efrat mayor and the relaunched YESHA Council Foreign Desk chair Oded Revivi, at his inauguration in Washington in January.[177] Stranded in the middle of this debate are the majority of Jewish-American settlers—mobilized as scapegoats for some and suffragettes by others—though many would prefer that ideological debates not interfere with their suburban modality. As the debate over the occupied territories enters its fifth decade, it remains to be seen whether these factions will become more polarized or these distinctions will collapse in the face of further conflict.

Conclusion

A S THE ARMORED bus lumbered along the two-lane highway from Hebron to Jerusalem, my thoughts lingered on the story of the Chaiken family and their saga from my hometown area of Springfield to settlement. My conversation with Malka, which was the last interview I conducted for this book, seemed like a fitting culmination of a nearly decade-long research project. Yet after discussions with dozens of Jewish-American immigrants in the occupied territories, I still struggled to understand how they saw themselves and their role within the Israeli settler enterprise. What does it mean for both American Jewry and for Israel that a disproportionate number of American-Israeli migrants have dedicated their lives and careers to participating within the settler movement?

During the ride back, I reflected upon Malka Chaiken's memories of her own bus trip to Jerusalem to take part in a Young Judea youth movement reunion on Israeli Independence Day in 1985. "We have our nice day [together] . . . and I'm sitting in the back schmoozing with people," a relaxed interlude that went irrevocably awry once she informed her year-course colleagues that she had recently settled in Hebron with her husband and children. Suddenly, "They all lunge at me like a bunch of rabid dogs and they're screaming at me like, 'You're a fascist, you're a racist!' " She was shaken by the confrontation, "I was just totally flipped out . . . it was pretty unbelievable and it gave me food for thought."

The harsh judgments of her peers were a painful realization for Malka, who credited Young Judea with the religious and Zionist awakening of her teenage years that changed her life. She was chagrined that her colleagues disapproved of her life choices and considered her activities deluded and dangerous. "It was pretty amazing for me to discover that so many people [had these views]," about her—and by extension—the settler enterprise, bemoaning, "It was a big shock for me." Since that day she has tried to divine whether this outlook had been "something subtle under the surface" that she had been oblivious to, perhaps even her own kind of Zionist blindness. "I didn't miss it!" she insisted in our interview, "I also picked up on that sorta liberal '60s, '70s message. The question is: what do you do with it? When you start seeing reality . . . you can either adapt your ideology to reality, or you can ignore the reality and try to go with your ideology."

"How did you respond to your critics?" I asked her in the comfort of her living room in Hebron that hot day in August more than three decades later. "It was thirty years ago. . . . Did I know a lot?" Malka replied, mentally returning to her days as a young migrant newly arrived in the settlement. Trying to reconstruct her riposte to an academic on the bus who was particularly antagonistic toward her, she ruminated, "Was I really prepared to answer him? Am I prepared today to answer him?" In the years since, she inferred that the ideology of her youth was perhaps inherently flawed. For a Jewish-American settler who saw her life's work as defending Jewish human and civil rights in the occupied territories, the critique of her Young Judea classmates who called her a racist and a fascist confounded her into concluding, "If that's the ultimate result of liberalism, you begin to wonder what people are really all about." As a mature woman who has now spent most of her adult life in the settlement in Hebron, she remains ambivalent about how others have construed her activities. "I've never really resolved that question," Malka admitted three decades later—and perhaps she never will.

As we look back through the rearview mirror at the participation of Jewish-American immigrants within the Israeli settler movement in the occupied territories, the objects in the looking glass are nearer than they appear, especially for the generations of American Jews whom they left behind in the United States. (Many readers of this book will have a relative, friend, or colleague who moved to the occupied territories, an interesting and important development within American Jewry over the past five decades.) For some, these activities and discourses often seem too close for comfort.

This book is a snapshot—if often a distorted view—of how Americans and Israelis see each other and themselves. For the approximately 60,000 American-Israeli settlers in the occupied territories, it is a narrative of backward glances across the ocean to the United States of the 1960s and 1970s, tracing the mobilization of a group of young American Jewish activists from the "1967 moment" to their later decision to migrate to Israel and join the settler movement beyond the Green Line. Yet it has also been a forward-looking vision of shaping the settlements, and even the entirety of the Zionist enterprise, in a version of their own image. In their cities on a hilltop, they encountered how the Israeli government cast a cynical gaze on eager immigrants who they would galvanize for manpower and capital for a state agenda in the occupied territories, but often had little compunction about dealing with them indirectly and derisively. In contrast, American-Israeli activists did forge strong tactical alliances with native Israeli settlers, but were often discomfited by differences in their worldview and lifestyle, which departed so dramatically from their own. Meanwhile, despite some charitable and social ties, Jewish-American settlers also recognized the increasingly suspicious and hostile glare of their Palestinian neighbors, who saw this group from the United States as usurpers of their land and rights. As the settlement enterprise has evolved over five decades, personal considerations about the compatibility of liberal values with settler realities have helped determine the divergent paths of Jewish-American settlers from public relations to public enemy.

Like the parable of Lot's wife, if we peek over our shoulders at the settlements only as a Sodom of stereotypes, we stare at our own peril—we cannot allow our vision of the settlements to remain a chiseled caricature after nearly five decades of dramatic change. In the Israeli context, this book has pushed the boundaries of scholarship on Israeli settlers in 2016, making clear the multiplicity of ideologies, constituencies, and discourses within this movement today.[1] While Jewish-American immigrants are only one of several factions within this heterogeneous and dynamic enterprise who are largely overlooked by both academia and the media, they represent the changing face of the settlement project in the occupied territories. As the influence of early generations of Gush Emunim activists and their messianic outlook wanes in influence, it is imperative to understand the roles of other ethnic, class, gender, religious, and ideological enclaves within the settlements today.

While this book promotes a more nuanced and complex picture of the settlement project fifty years on, I have not sought to circumscribe the 1967 border as the perimeter of concern about the future of Zionism and Palestinian self-determination. There is little doubt that the occupation has drawn tensions between liberalism and nationalism into stark relief. To some, the activities and discourses of Jewish-American settlers over the past five decades may seem like cynical deflection, cognitive dissonance, or even conscious discordance to their own sensibilities. Yet the settler movement does not bear sole culpability for the crisis of liberal Zionism. Post-1967 settlers beyond the Green Line, like earlier generations in territorial Israel, evince a kind of aspirational astigmatism about the Zionist project. This is not to absolve the State of Israel for political or moral responsibility for how Jewish settlement has disenfranchised the indigenous population from pre-State Palestine to the present, but it does mean that resolving the settlements question alone will not harmonize the Herzlian dream. At the same time, Israel shares a settler-colonial past with many other modern Western nations, including the United States, Canada, and Australia, but only the Zionist state is held particularly accountable and even denied the right to exist by segments of the international community. Possibly this is because the State of Israel came of age in the time of the twenty-four-hour news cycle (which Jewish-American settlers are keenly aware of and try to influence), whereas the troubled pasts of older liberal democracies were more easily hidden from the public centuries ago. However, there are some contemporary historical parallels to Israel/Palestine—the most notable being India/Pakistan in 1947–1948—that are not portrayed in the same way in scholarly or popular debate. Without being an apologist for Israel's occupation, it is possible to acknowledge that the particular animus directed at the only state of the Jews suggests anti-Semitism, or at least a deep-seated antipathy toward Jewish sovereignty and power.

All those who desire peace in the region must comprehend the complexity of the contemporary Israeli settler project in order to craft appropriate policy programs. It is far too simple to blame the settlements for the seemingly intractable Israel/Palestine conflict. Certainly the future of Israel as a Jewish and democratic state is in profound crisis and a full disengagement from the occupied territories could mitigate some of these tensions internally for Israeli Jews within the Green Line and the liberal Diaspora Jewish community abroad. An end to the occupation might also alleviate

Palestinian hardship by removing the daily presence of IDF soldiers and checkpoints, reducing human rights violations, and restoring lost territory, while accelerating preparation for self-government and statehood. Yet this policy would be no guarantee that Palestinians will accept a two-state solution as it is currently configured (on 95 percent of the West Bank with settlement blocs and land swaps) or safeguard Israel's borders and security when the occupation ends; the lessons learned from two devastating wars after the 2006 withdrawal from the Gaza Strip. The locus of today's debate is no longer about the occupation after 1967, but about the legacies of 1948—the dual narrative of Jewish nationhood and Palestinian Naqba. While I deeply believe that the two-state solution is the best (if perhaps not the only) alternative for Israelis and Palestinians, I would be remiss not to offer the scholarly opinion that a tacit agreement to partition the land was a historical anomaly of the Oslo era and that it is unclear whether it will be possible or preferable for both parties to accept it in the future. Further, settlements are only one of several outstanding final status issues, which include borders, security, resource management, the status of Jerusalem, and the right of return of Palestinian refugees, that are equally—if not more—difficult to solve. Although the Oslo I accord promised a resolution to the conflict within five years, it must be recognized that this has yielded mostly process without peace and that policies that were acceptable to majorities of Israelis and Palestinian populations in the mid-1990s may no longer be applicable today.[2] Further, while technical plans have addressed many aspects of final status topics, including settlements, there can be no full and durable resolution of the conflict that does not acknowledge underlying ideological and historical tensions, perhaps through the mechanism of a truth and reconciliation commission. The international community and its many well-intentioned peacemakers must acknowledge that they cannot impose a solution that Israelis and Palestinians cannot or will not accept today. Suffice to say, the settlements are a subject of much controversy but settling the debate over this issue alone is not a panacea for the Israel/Palestine conflict.

THIS BOOK IS NOT only about the boundaries of scholarship in Israel/Palestine, but about the limits of liberalism within American Jewish life and the role Israel has played in demarcating its borders since World War II.

As I have argued, the disproportionate participation of Jewish-American immigrants within the Israeli settler movement is a product of their lived experience in the United States as much as in the Middle East. For many, moving to the occupied territories was their attempt to reconcile tensions between Zionism and liberalism after the 1967 war. In a sense, Malka Chaiken, Chaim Feifel, Shifra Blass, Bobby Brown, Shlomo Riskin, and the many other Jewish-American settlers encountered in this story found an expedient solution to the dilemma of American Jewry after the Six Day War. For the majority who stayed behind in the United States, the answer to the question "Given who I am, where do I belong?" was not about aliya or international migration, rather about the ability to be accommodated within the American Jewish community and electoral politics.

While the crisis of American Jewish liberalism in the contemporary period is a complex phenomenon that many other scholars have studied, I point to post-1967 U.S. Zionism as pivotal to this shift. The united front of the Six Day War was forever fractured in its aftermath,[3] yet centrifugal forces within the community have remained strong. Further, as Israel and its leadership have become less liberal since 1967, organized American Jewry has had less flexibility about how to express their fealty to Israel without contradicting their own progressive values.

The function and status of mainstream Zionist Jewish organizations and the so-called Israel Lobby have changed over the past five decades as American Jewry increasingly distances itself from communal life and Israel.[4] It is an open secret that the old guard are often out of touch with the current generation.[5] Contemporary U.S. Zionists are still largely presented with the same binary choices as their parents: American Israel Public Affairs Committee (AIPAC) or apathy, the Jewish Federation or feeling left out, Hadassah or "self-hatred," entrenchment in Jewish and Zionist particularism or an exit from establishment communal life. Although what scholar Theodore Sasson has dubbed "the new American Zionism" has produced important alternatives since 1967, including new advocacy groups such as JStreet and Open Hillel, these organizations have been aggressively marginalized by the mainstream American Jewish establishment and might not even represent self-identified young liberal Zionists. For millennials especially, Diasporic liberal Zionism is adrift and heated debates on campus are less likely to inspire activism than to evoke the old 1960s slogan of "tune in, turn on, drop out."[6] Shifra Blass, Eli Birnbaum, and Yisrael Medad may have been mobilized by campus politics to move to the occupied territories, but the future of Israel hardly occupies the mind of today's generation.[7]

Zionism was always a polarizing force within the American Jewish polity. However, the Israeli-Palestinian conflict has more recently become a wedge issue in U.S. electoral politics.[8] While Milton Himmelfarb's quip that "Jews earn like Episcopalians and vote like Puerto Ricans" was sanctioned as a kind of shorthand for the legendary liberalism of American Jewry, and most American Jews still vote overwhelmingly for the Democratic Party and support many progressive social causes, there are big changes taking place behind the curtain at the voting booth.[9] The "Israel issue" has propelled some—especially baby-boomer Zionists and the modern Orthodox—toward the Republican Party, whose platform largely has been more sympathetic to Israeli government Policy and Zionist ideals since the 1980s.[10] As a consequence, these supporters must also embrace a conservative social, economic, and political agenda. Concurrently, the ranks of the Democratic Party now boast the largest percentage of self-identified liberals in history, bolstered by the influx of left-leaning millennials. Postcolonial discourses, which dovetail with the Palestinian cause, have also become increasingly popular in the party. From this perspective, some of the newly conservative (especially those that switched parties under the tenure of President Barack Obama) consider that the Democratic Party has pushed them out—as the Jewish philanthropist Sheldon Adelson famously opined before the 2012 election, "I didn't leave the Democrats. They left me."[11] Echoing Irving Krystol's maxim that the neoconservative is "a liberal mugged by reality," some right-leaning intellectuals managed to recast their "retreat" from American Jewish liberalism and the Democratic Party not as a betrayal of cherished ideals, but as a "beneficial returning" to Jewish interests that had been forsaken.[12] Although Israel remains near the bottom of the list of voter priorities for most American Jews (only 4 percent cited it as their top issue in the 2012 elections), those who do rank it highly may have to barter liberal policy preferences for perceived Zionist benefits.[13] At the time this book went to press, a full profile of Jewish-American voting behavior in the recent presidential election was not yet published, but the Israel issue may have played an even more important role than in previous contests. Early exit polls estimated that 24 percent of American Jews voted for the Republican candidate Donald Trump and that the Democratic nominee Hillary Clinton actually garnered less Jewish support than

Al Gore, John Kerry, or Barack Obama (in 2008).[14] Although denominational data was unavailable, small polls conducted in the months prior to the election suggested strong support from Orthodox Jews for Donald Trump[15] and a preliminary analysis of religious voters of all faiths found that over 50 percent of those who attended worship services at least once a week (which would likely include the Jewish Orthodox) cast ballots for him.[16] As Trump embraced hard-line views on the Israel/Palestine conflict[17] and even opened a campaign office in the West Bank staffed by Jewish-American settlers to sway the American-Israeli vote (see Chapter 5), it is likely that many Jews who voted for the Republican candidate chose him as the more pro-Israel candidate, despite Clinton's own strong Zionist credentials.[18] While a comprehensive analysis of the Jewish-American vote in the 2016 elections is highly anticipated, today Milton Himmelfarb might say that Jews earn like Episcopalians but don't vote like Puerto Ricans—of all ethnic groups in the United States, popular sympathy and political support for Israel is the lowest among Catholic Hispanics.[19]

The role of American-Israelis within the settler movement raises important questions not only about the conduct of self-described Jewish-American liberals abroad but about the roots of their attitudes at home. Although the Gordian knot of universalism and particularism is particularly evoked beyond the Green Line, I have looked beyond the traditional left–right paradigm in these chapters to demonstrate how complicated this grand narrative is for both domestic and foreign policy. This book calls into question some basic convictions (and caricatures) of American Jewish political behavior, both in the United States and in Israel, as the political spectrum has shifted rightward across both continents over time.

RETURNING TO MY CHARACTERIZATION (borrowed from Kevin Avruch) that this is a study that is "half about 'Jewishness' in contemporary America, and half about 'Americanness' in contemporary Israel," I have sought to recast the American-Jewish relationship with Israel within a transnational paradigm.[20] Rather than reifying Jewish-American settlers and their rights rhetoric, couldn't they be classified within a larger category of "Americans abroad"? If so, what would their participation within the Israeli settlement enterprise say about U.S. foreign policy and human rights history in the post-Vietnam era?

The focus of this book has been on the frontiers of Jewish-American thinking and action, both at home and overseas.[21] Frederick Jackson Turner's 1893 thesis on U.S. expansionism envisioned America's "Wild West" not only as empty land—one that failed to countenance its indigenous population—but also as crucible for the formation and expression of individualism and democracy with a "distinctly American character."[22] The pioneers of manifest destiny believed that they brought progress imbued with divine providence.[23] So too, did the subjects of this study see the West Bank and the Sinai Peninsula as their own terra incognita, a site where they would tame both the land and themselves, if by way of suburbia as much as the sword or scripture. For those who missed out on the original pioneering experience on two continents, the occupied territories offered the opportunity not only of a lifetime, but perhaps also of messianic time, after the frontier had mostly closed in the United States and Israel. Yet, as revisionist scholars point out, at "discrete turning points . . . co-existence turned borderlands into bordered land" and created hierarchies of citizenship between the colonial and the indigenous—a historical parallel that could also be found in Israel/Palestine.[24]

Moreover, in building their "city on a hilltop," Jewish-American settlers were often confronted with the boundary between ideology and reality. Like many generations of American pioneers before them—including the Puritans and the Halutzim of pre-state Palestine—they were not the first to discover the difficulty in reconciling theory and praxis, lofty ideals and the local situation *b-shetakh* (on the ground).[25] For some, this cultural clash and cognitive dissonance manifested in the abandonment of the outlook and lifestyle they brought from the Old Country. Others chose a retreat inward and a reinforcement of cherished values, even when to outsiders their self-characterization hardly corresponded to objective conditions in the occupied territories.

Covenantal communities have often made unholy alliances with political violence.[26] The vast majority of Jewish-American settlers have found the pen mightier than the sword, but some of those who have turned to terrorism have perversely seen their activities as being within the tradition of sacred bloodshed. Further, like their forefathers in both the United States and Israel, generations of liberal democrats on both continents have defended their ideals down the barrel of the gun.

The United States and Israel are cousins linked by their settler-colonial legacy. Yet the history of American-Israelis in the settlements is not simply one of parallels between the two nations' pasts and liberal pretensions at home. Jewish-American settlers should be considered among a larger cohort (and historiography) of American actors abroad who have actively engaged in a long tradition of liberal empire.[27]

The field of American studies has recently embraced a new kind of diplomatic history that has moved beyond traditional studies of "businessmen, academics, diplomats, spies, and soldiers . . . [of] the foreign policy elite" and I consider Jewish-American settlers as another example of these American private citizens, organizations, and ideas at work overseas.[28] This book also speaks to the "religious turn" in the discipline.[29] Further, Jewish-American settlers join other faith-based actors in American foreign policy (including left-leaning Jewish humanitarians) who have been prominent voices in promoting a human rights agenda since the post-Vietnam period.[30] This study follows a larger scholarship on U.S. foreign policy that is skeptical about the so-called "human rights revolution" with its liberalism at home and illiberalism abroad.[31] This book also connects to a legal and historical canon that stresses the susceptibility of rights discourses to cynically servicing many less-than-liberal causes.[32] Putting many of these arguments in perspective, Michael Ignatieff has pointed to an enigma, arguing, "What is exceptional here is not that the United States is inconsistent, hypocritical, or arrogant. Many other nations, including leading democracies, could be accused of similar things. What is exceptional, and what is worth explaining, is why America has both been guilty of these failings and also been a driving force behind the promotion and enforcement of global human rights. What needs explaining is the paradox of being simultaneously a leader and an outlier."[33]

Perhaps my study can occupy a new space in these debates, if at first blush this book on Jewish-American settlers appear to be an outlier. The participation of American-Israelis in the settlement project, which has strengthened the connection of citizens to the state (at the expense of equal treatment for Palestinians under the occupation), seemingly reverses recent trends that have seen rights protection moving from the national to international sphere.[34] Further, while scholarship on U.S. ethnic lobbies has emphasized their role as net exporters of liberal ideology and as stabilizing influences both at home and abroad,[35] American-Israeli immigrants within the settlement movement have contributed to making Israel less democratic while increasing conflict in the United States. Rather than joining the new "grand narrative" of transnational history, Jewish-American settlers are neither postcolonial nor postsecular, a relic of a different kind of past.[36]

Yet perhaps this group presents an important case of the "mediators and go-betweens" of the new global intellectual history and can help illuminate the instrumentalization of rights discourses in international perspective.[37] As Richard Primus has observed, "At the crudest level, Americans often claim the satisfaction of any needs or interests they consider important as deserving of special protection as 'rights,'"[38] but, he continues, "it does not follow . . . that the language of rights . . . should be able to settle substantive questions by reference to rights alone."[39] Perhaps this study is symbolic of our historical overreliance on rights to produce a just and durable resolution to the Israeli-Palestinian conflict. However, if rights are also a "social practice" that can adapt to conditions on the ground, there perhaps is still hope for a future where both Israeli and Palestinian self-determination can be reconciled within a space of political reconfiguration.[40]

WHILE THIS HISTORY continues to unfold today, as Rabbi Riskin once underscored in describing his own life's work, it is clear that Jewish-American settlers in the occupied territories will be part of a chapter-heading rather than a footnote of the future in this region.[41]

In these chapters I have unsettled some paradigms about the Israeli settlement enterprise. Those who have read this book will surely come away with different ideas, but my intention has never been to settle these debates. History can only approximate lived experience, but I hope this book has offered one vision of this city on a hilltop.

Appendix

It is a serious challenge for a historian to obtain an accurate and objective head-count of Jewish-American settlers in the occupied territories. I am neither a professional statistician nor a demographer and independent researchers do not have the means or ability to carry out their own census surveys. In order to ascertain a reliable estimate of the number of American-Israelis beyond the Green Line without classified sources, I collected and reconciled four discrete sets of available data on this population.

The earliest published evidence is Chaim I. Waxman's 1984 study of American-Israeli settlers, which found that this cohort accounted for approximately 5,250 of 35,000 individuals living in the occupied territories at the time—which was 15 percent of the total Israeli settler population.[1] A decade later, the *New York Times* cited unattributed sources that considered the Jewish-American settler concentration to be 15 percent (19,500 individuals) of the 130,000 settlers in 1994.[2] Even though this percentage had remained constant over the course of two decades, to simply extrapolate this data to the current settler population nearly twenty years later seemed insufficient. In an attempt to address these concerns, I gathered three more sets of data in the course of my research which constitute the best available figures for Jewish-American immigrants beyond the Green Line.

The first source of statistics came from the State of Israel's Central Bureau of Statistics (CBS), which produces its annual *Statistical Abstract of Israel* series. In 2007 the United States was added as a discrete category in immigration tables that chart the selected country of last residence and first district and subdistrict of residence in Israel (which includes "Judea and Samaria"), thus making it possible to determine where Jewish-Americans settled after their immigration.[3] Data from 2007–2015 reveals that an average of 12 percent (with a high of 13.6 percent in 2007 and low of 9.7 percent in 2011) of Jewish-American immigrants immediately relocated to the occupied territories. However, there are no directly correlated figures until 2007—unfortunately, that means that there is little that can be determined for the entire period of peak Jewish-American migration to Israel between 1967 and 1977. Moreover, recent volumes of the *Statistical Abstract of Israel* quantify only the first district of settlement, so it is impossible to know how many Jewish-American immigrants may have temporarily resided elsewhere in Israel but moved to the occupied territories months or years after their arrival. A researcher may also speculate that the State of Israel might interfere in the publication of politically sensitive information.[4]

My second set of data was provided by the YESHA Council, the nongovernmental settlement lobby. In the summer of 2009, their American-Israeli representative, Aliza Herbst, officially estimated that American-Israelis constituted approximately 15 percent of West Bank settlers—although she conceded that this statistic was more of an educated guess than a scientific accounting, as the YESHA Council purports not to calculate the population of immigrant-settler constituencies.[5] Another former spokesperson for the YESHA Council also stressed that the figure of 15 percent is not standard for individual settlements and is instead an average across all settlements in the West Bank, with high concentrations of Jewish-American immigrants in the Gush Etzion Bloc, Kiryat Arba / Hebron, and parts of the Ariel region, but small populations in outlying communities, secular suburban metropolises, and settlement outposts.[6] However, since this data was obtained, there is some new evidence to suggest that there are increasing populations of Jewish-American settlers in large city settlements like Ariel and Maale Adumim, as well as hilltop encampments that were once almost exclusively inhabited by native Israelis.[7] However, the YESHA Council has cause to overestimate the figure of Jewish-American settlers in the interest of encouraging further Western immigration, bolstering its fundraising initiatives in the United States, and fostering state interest in the settlement project as a site of immigrant absorption. When contacted for updated statistics in 2016, the YESHA Council refused to cooperate with me, so I could not collect any more current information.

These three sets of data were (initially) seemingly contradicted by secret statistics from the U.S. Consulate, Jerusalem, which records all passport-holding dual citizens born or living in the West Bank and East Jerusalem. In spring 2009, Political Officer I identified 96,600 registered Jewish-American and Palestinian-American citizens in the consular district.[8] It should be noted that the geographical borders encompassed in this estimate of citizenry in the West Bank contravenes the public stance of the U.S. government, which generally considers the occupied territories to include all settlements over the Green Line, including areas that the State of Israel formally annexed to the municipality of Jerusalem in 1967. This larger geography would also include sizable populations of Jewish-American immigrants who live in suburbs of Jerusalem like Ramot and Gilo that are not accounted for in this figure—or in this study as a whole. In fall 2009, I received additional confidential data from Political Officer II, who inexplicably revised the consular district U.S. citizen population estimate downward, providing an aggregated figure of 30,000 individuals, of which 18,000 to 20,000 are Palestinian-Americans and 10,000 to 12,000 are Jewish-Americans. These new statistics would put the Jewish-American settler presence at 4 percent of the population of the West Bank beyond the municipality of Jerusalem. However, I challenged the validity of these new lower statistics with this official, given the discrepancy with data provided only a few months earlier. I also noted that the U.S. Consulate requires its citizens in the consular district to take the initiative to self-register, but that American-Israeli settlers have mounted a vigorous and successful campaign against enrollment over recently reconfirmed U.S. government policy not to recognize the occupied territories as part of the State of Israel or Jerusalem as its capital on birth certificates, passports, and other official documents. The official admitted both the inconsistency with Political Officer I's assessment as well as the impact of the antiregistration initiative, suspecting the inaccuracy of her data. Political Officer II then partially retracted these findings, acknowledging that the Jewish-American settler concentration in the consular district is likely significantly larger—even tallying 10 to 12 percent of the total settler population, figures that largely align with previous data sets.[9] Last but not least, the U.S. government may also have political reasons to provide inaccurate data to researchers—especially as they learned more about my work.

In sum, I find that all available data supports that finding that 15 percent of settlers in the occupied territories (60,000 individuals) are American-Israeli citizens and there may be many more unregistered Jewish-American immigrants and their children in the occupied territories today. It is my hope that an independent and objective professional survey of this population will be conducted in the near future.

Abbreviations

AACA	Association of Americans and Canadians for Aliya
AACI	Association of Americans and Canadians in Israel
ADL	Anti-Defamation League
AIPAC	American Israel Public Affairs Committee
CBS	Central Bureau of Statistics
HAMAS	Harakat al-Muqawama al-Islamiya (Islamic Resistance Movement)
ICDF	Israel Communities Development Fund
IDF	Israeli Defense Forces
ISA	Israel State Archives
IZL	Irgun Tsavi Leumi (National Military Organization)
JAFI	Jewish Agency for Israel
JDL	Jewish Defense League
JTA	Jewish Telegraphic Agency
KKL	Keren Kayemet L-Yisrael
LEHI	Lohamai Herut Yisrael (Fighters for the Freedom of Israel)
LSS	Lincoln Square Synagogue
MFA	Ministry of Foreign Affairs
MHRS	Movement to Halt the Retreat in the Sinai
NAHAL	Noar Halutzai Lohem (Fighting Pioneer Youth)
NIS	New Israel Shekel
NOAM	Ha-Noar Ha-Mizrachi (Mizrachi Youth)
PLO	Palestine Liberation Organization
SNCC	Student Nonviolent Coordinating Committee

SSSJ   Student Struggle for Soviet Jewry
TNT   Terror K-Neged Terror (Terror Against Terror)
UJA   United Jewish Appeal
WUJS   World Union of Jewish Students
WZO   World Zionist Organization
YESHA   Yehuda, Shomron V-Aza (Judea, Samaria, and Gaza)
YOSH   Yehuda V-Shomron (Judea and Samaria)

Notes

Introduction

1. Robert I. Friedman, "In the Realm of Perfect Faith," *Village Voice,* 12 November 1985, reprinted under the title "Inside the Jewish Terrorist Underground," *Journal of Palestine Studies* 15, no. 2 (Winter 1986): 190–201.

2. Marilyn (Malka) Chaiken, interview with the author, 6 August 2014.

3. Ibid.

4. In addition to having endured playground slurs and violence, Chaiken would later sue the Springfield public school system for discrimination when he was dismissed from a position as a substitute teacher for wearing a beret to cover his head in accordance with his religious beliefs. See "Mass. Man Ruled Victim of Bias over Hat," *Lewiston Daily Sun,* 10 March 1979, 5.

5. *Classical High School Blue and White Yearbook,* 1968, 78–79.

6. Gary Stein, "Ex-Bostonian Calls Life in Hebron Rare Chance to Make Jewish History," *Florida Sun-Sentinel,* 24 February 1988.

7. David Grady, "Friends, Family Call Chaikin Man of Strong Faith, Courage," *Boston Globe,* 25 June 1988, 4.

8. Mary Curtius, "West Bank Settler from Boston Is Stabbed," *Boston Globe,* 25 June 1988, 1.

9. Marilyn (Malka) Chaiken, interview with the author, 6 August 2014.

10. Ibid. Note, Chaiken uses the terminology of Arabs as she does not recognize a distinct Palestinian peoplehood.

11. Ibid.

12. Ibid.

13. Ibid.

14. Ibid.

15. Shtruck was one of the founders of Hebron and has had a long career in settlement activism. She was recently reelected as a parliamentarian in the 20th Knesset elections as a member of the Bayit Ha-Yehudi (Jewish Home) party, where

she leads its radical right-wing Tekuma (Resurrection) faction. See https://knesset
.gov.il/mk/eng/mk_eng.asp?mk_individual_id_t=884.

16. Marilyn (Malka) Chaiken, interview with the author, 6 August 2014.

17. Stein, "Ex-Bostonian Calls Life in Hebron Rare Chance to Make Jewish
History."

18. Ibid.

19. Marilyn (Malka) Chaiken, interview with the author, 6 August 2014.

20. Robert I. Friedman, *Zealots for Zion: Inside Israel's West Bank Settlement
Movement* (New York: Random House, 1992).

21. Friedman, "Inside the Jewish Terrorist Underground," 190–191.

22. See *John Chaiken and Marilyn Chaiken v. VV Publishing Corp d/b/a The
Village Voice, Robert Friedman, Modiin Publishing House d/b/a Maariv and Ron
Dagoni,* 119 F3d 1018 U.S. Court of Appeals, 2nd Circuit, No. 292, Docket
95-9301, 21 July 1997, http://openjurist.org/119/f3d/1018.

23. Stein, "Ex-Bostonian Calls Life in Hebron Rare Chance to Make Jewish
History."

24. Marilyn (Malka) Chaiken, interview with the author, 6 August 2014.

25. I have not been able to verify or view a copy of the tape.

26. "Israeli Civilians Avenge Attacks with Gunfire," *Deseret News,* 25
June 1988.

27. Marilyn (Malka) Chaiken, interview with the author, 6 August 2014.

28. Curtius, "West Bank Settler from Boston Is Stabbed."

29. Marilyn (Malka) Chaiken, interview with the author, 6 August 2014.

30. Ibid.

31. Ibid.

32. Although the subject of Western liberalism—and particularly American
Jewish liberalism—will be extensively problematized in this work, I rely upon the
Dictionary of Social Sciences standard definition, which considers "modern
liberalism . . . organized around a number of not-always-harmoniously related
principles: the priority of individual rights and freedoms, including broad enfran-
chisement; the belief that any use of authority must be justified; the conviction that
ethical choices or ideas of the good life should be left to individuals; the separation
of private from public life and the belief that the former should be protected; the
belief in the rule of law and the impartiality of the state; and, somewhat more
contentiously, faith in human rationality and progress." See "Liberalism," in Craig
Calhoun, ed., *Dictionary of the Social Sciences,* http://www.oxfordreference.com
/view/10.1093/acref/9780195123715.001.0001/acref-9780195123715-e-962.
There is an immense canon on classical liberalism, which traces its roots back to
the Enlightenment and the revolutionary thought of Montesquieu, Locke, Voltaire,
Jefferson, and Paine. See Eamonn Butler, *Classical Liberalism: A Primer* (London:
Institute of Economic Affairs, 2015) and George H. Smith, *The System of Liberty:
Themes in the History of Classical Liberalism* (Cambridge: Cambridge University
Press, 2013). Economic liberalism was developed by thinkers like Smith, Bentham,
Mill, and later, Keynes, see Razeen Sally, *Classical Liberalism and International
Economic Order: Studies in Theory and Intellectual History* (London: Routledge,
2002). Twentieth-century U.S. political and social liberalism, especially of the

Roosevelt era, was particularly influential upon American Jews, see Michael E. Staub, *Torn at the Roots: The Crisis of Jewish Liberalism in Postwar America* (New York: Columbia University Press, 2002) and Marc Dollinger, *Quest for Inclusion: Jews and Liberalism in Modern America* (Princeton, NJ: Princeton University Press, 2000). For debates about the compatibility of liberalism with the traditions of the Arab and Muslim world after the French Revolution, see Albert Hourani, *Arabic Thought in the Liberal Age: 1798–1939* (Cambridge: Cambridge University Press, 1983). Further, debates about Wilsonianism have rocked the Middle East since the First World War; see Erez Manela, *The Wilsonian Moment: Self-Determination and the International Origins of Anticolonial Nationalism* (Oxford: Oxford University Press, 2007). Recently, liberalism in international institutions and transnational thought has been the focus of many scholars including Glenda Sluga, *Internationalism in the Age of Nationalism* (Philadelphia: University of Pennsylvania Press, 2013), Mark Mazower, *No Enchanted Palace: The End of Empire and the Ideological Origins of the United Nations* (Princeton, NJ: Princeton University Press, 2009), and Samuel Moyn, *The Last Utopia: Human Rights in History* (Cambridge, MA: Harvard University Press, 2010). My work relies upon these and other readings in the field, but I make every effort to underscore how the subjects of my study themselves defined and deployed liberal values and rhetoric rather than imposing external understandings upon them.

33. Marilyn (Malka) Chaiken, interview with the author, 6 August 2014.

34. Concepts of historical empathy have infused the historiographical canon; see R. G. Collingwood, *The Idea of History* (Oxford: Oxford University Press, 1993). I define its usage in this study as the space where contextualization, perspective taking, and affective understanding meet in an unfolding process, borrowing from Jason Endacott and Sarah Brooks, "An Updated Theoretical Model for Promoting Historical Empathy," *Social Science Research and Practice* 8, no. 1 (Spring 2013): 43–44, and Bruce A. VanSledright, "From Empathetic Self-Regard to Self-Understanding: Im/Positionality, Empathy, and Historical Contextualization," in *Historical Empathy and Perspective Taking in the Social Sciences,* ed. O. L. Davis, Elizabeth Anne Yeager, and Stuart J. Foster (Lanham, MD: Rowman and Littlefield, 2001), 55. I radically distinguish between historical empathy and sympathy; see Peter Lee and Rosalyn Ashby, "Empathy, Perspective Taking, and Rational Understanding," in Davis, Yeager, and Foster, *Historical Empathy and Perspective Taking in the Social Sciences,* 24. Like other contemporary scholars, I consider it a mandate for historians, especially those working on the contentious histories of conflict zones; see James Dawes, *Bad Men* (Cambridge, MA: Harvard University Press, 2013) and Gabrielle Rifkind and Giandomenico Picco, *The Fog of Peace: The Human Face of Conflict Resolution* (London: I. B. Tauris, 2014), 3.

35. American settler stereotypes will be fully discussed in Chapter 5. However, these portrayals have been discussed extensively in the media. See, for example, "Stereotype of American Olim Questioned," *Counterpoint,* August 1984, 2; Stuart Schoffman, "My Fellow Lunatics," *Jerusalem Report,* 21 April 1994, 50; Clyde Haberman, "Massacre at Hebron Exposes Anti-American Mood in Israel," *New*

York Times, 20 March 1994, 1, 14; Teddy Preuss, "An Easy Excuse for Murder," *Jerusalem Post,* 28 February 1994, 6; and Herb Keinon, "Walking a Thin Line over the Green Line," *Jerusalem Post,* 18 March 1994, 3B.

36. See, for example, Zahava Englard, *Settling for More: From Jersey to Judea* (New York: Devora, 2010).

37. See Chaim I. Waxman, *American Aliya: Portrait of an Innovative Migration Movement* (Detroit: Wayne State University Press, 1989); Chaim Waxman, "Political and Social Attitudes of Americans among the Settlers in the Territories," in *The Impact of Gush Emunim: Politics and Settlement in the West Bank,* ed. David Newman (New York: St. Martin's Press, 1985); Avi Kay, *Making Themselves Heard: The Impact of North American Olim on Israeli Protest Politics* (New York: American Jewish Committee, 1995); Uzi Rebhun and Chaim I. Waxman, "The 'Americanization' of Israel: A Demographic, Cultural, and Political Evaluation," *Israel Studies* 5, no. 1 (Spring 2000): 65–91; Kevin Avruch, *American Immigrants in Israel: Social Identities and Change* (Chicago: University of Chicago Press, 1981); Zvi Gitelman, *Becoming Israelis: Political Resocialization of Soviet and American Immigrants* (New York: Praeger, 1982); Calvin Goldscheider, "American Aliya: Sociological and Demographic Perspectives," in *The Jew in American Society,* ed. Marshall Sklare (New York: Behrman House, 1974); Jay Shapiro, *From Both Sides Now: An American-Israeli Odyssey* (Tel Aviv: Dvir Katzman, 1983); S. Ilan Troen, "Frontier Myths and Their Application in America and Israel: A Transnational Perspective," *Journal of American History* 86, no. 2 (December 1999): 1209–1230; S. Ilan Troen, *Imaging Zion: Dreams, Designs, and Realities in a Century of Jewish Settlement* (New Haven, CT: Yale University Press, 2003); S.Ilan Troen, "Spearheads of the Zionist Frontier: Historical Perspectives on Post-1967 Settlement Planning in Judea and Samaria," *Planning Perspectives* 7, no. 1 (January 1992): 81–100; Gershon Shafir, "Challenging Nationalism and Israel's 'Open Frontier' on the West Bank," *Theory and Society* 13 (1984): 803–827; Ian Lustick, *Unsettled States, Disputed Lands: Britain and Ireland, France and Algeria, Israel and the West Bank–Gaza* (Ithaca, NY: Cornell University Press, 1993); Baruch Kimmerling, *Zionism and Territory: The Socio-Territorial Dimensions of Zionist Politics* (Berkeley: University of California Press, 1983); Aharon Kellerman, *Society and Settlement: Jewish Land of Israel in the Twentieth Century* (Albany: SUNY Press, 1993); and Etan Diamond, *And I Will Dwell in Their Midst: Orthodox Jews in Suburbia* (Chapel Hill: University of North Carolina Press, 2000).

38. See Tom Segev, *1967: Israel, the War, and the Year That Transformed the Middle East,* trans. Jessica Cohen (New York: Metropolitan Books, 2007); Gershom Gorenberg, *The Accidental Empire: Israel and the Birth of the Settlements, 1967–1977* (New York: Times Books, 2006); Idith Zertal and Akiva Eldar, *Lords of the Land: The War over Israel's Settlements in the Occupied Territories, 1967–2007,* trans. Vivian Eden (New York: Nation Books, 2007); Ian S. Lustick, *For the Land and the Lord: Jewish Fundamentalism in Israel* (New York: Council on Foreign Relations, 1988); Newman, *The Impact of Gush Emunim;* Michael Feige, *Shetai Mapot L-Gedah: Gush Emunim, Shalom Ahshav, V-Eizuv Ha-Merhav B-Yisrael* (Jerusalem: Magnes, 2002); Michael Feige, *Settling in the Hearts: Jewish*

Fundamentalism in the Occupied Territories (Detroit: Wayne State University Press, 2009); Gadi Taub, *Ha-Mitnahalim V-Ha-Maavak Al Mashmauta Shel Ha-Tziyonut* (Tel Aviv: Yediot Ahronot, 2007); Aviezer Ravitzsky, *Messianism, Zionism, and Jewish Religious Radicalism* (Chicago: University of Chicago Press, 1996); Gideon Aran, *Kukism: Shorashei Gush Emunim, Tarbut Ha-Mitnahalim, Teologia Ziyonit, Meshihut B'Zemanenu* (Jerusalem: Karmel, 2013); Nadav Shelef, *Evolving Nationalism: Homeland, Identity, and Religion in Israel, 1925–2005* (Ithaca, NY: Cornell University Press, 2010); Meron Benvenisti, *The West Bank Data Project: A Survey of Israel's Policies* (Washington, DC: American Enterprise Institute, 1984); and Israel Shahak and Norton Mezvinsky, *Jewish Fundamentalism in Israel* (London: Pluto Press, 2004).

39. See Gershon Shafat, *Gush Emunim: Ha-Sipur M-Ahorei Ha-Klaim* (Beit El: Sifriyat Beit El, 1995); Meir Harnoi, *Ha-Mitnahalim* (Or Yehuda: Maariv, 1994); and Haggai Segal, *Dear Brothers: The West Bank Jewish Underground* (Woodmere, NY: Beit Shamai Publications, 1988). This work also draws heavily on periodical press and other media produced by and for settlers in the occupied territories.

40. See, for example, "Introduction: The Fundamentalism Project: A User's Guide," in *Fundamentalisms Observed,* ed. Martin E. Marty and R. Scott Appleby (Chicago: University of Chicago Press, 1991), vii–xiii.

41. One important exception that distinguishes among the various camps within the Israeli right is Jonathan Rynhold, "Re-conceptualizing Israeli Approaches to 'Land for Peace,' and the Palestinian Question since 1967," *Israel Studies* 6, no. 2 (Summer 2001): 33–52.

42. Charles S. Liebman, "Jewish Ultra-Nationalism in Israel: Converging Strands," in *Survey of Jewish Affairs,* ed. William Frankel (Rutherford, NJ: Farleigh-Dickinson University Press, 1985), 28–50.

43. Ehud Sprinzak, *The Ascendance of Israel's Radical Right* (Oxford: Oxford University Press, 1991); Ehud Sprinzak, *Brother against Brother: Violence and Extremism in Israeli Politics from the Altalena to the Rabin Assassination* (New York: Free Press, 1999); Sprinzak, "The Iceberg Model of Political Extremism," in Newman, *The Impact of Gush Emunim,* 27–45; and Ehud Sprinzak, *Ish Ha-Yashar B-Enav: Ilegalism B-Hevrah Ha-Yisraelit* (Tel Aviv: Sifriat Poalim, 1986), 21.

44. See, for example, Emmanuel Sivan, "The Enclave Culture," in Marty and Appleby, *Fundamentalisms Comprehended,* 11–68; and Karen Amit and Ilan Riss, "The Role of Social Networks in the Immigration Decision-Making Process: The Case of North American Immigration to Israel," *Immigrant Minorities* (2007): 290–313.

45. The 2015 edition of the *Statistical Abstract of Israel* lists approximately 370,000 settlers in the West Bank, although some data on individual settlements and outposts is incomplete or missing, see http://www1.cbs.gov.il/reader/shnaton /templ_shnaton_e.html?num_tab=sto2_13&CYear=2015. However, Israeli ministers (including the Interior Ministry) regularly cite figures of 400,000 settlers, which is the standard widely adopted by the international media and scholars; see http://www.reuters.com/article/2014/05/16/us-palestinian-israel -idUSBREA4FoAD20140516. Further, more than 150,000 additional settlers live

in neighborhoods over the Green Line that have been annexed to the municipality of Jerusalem, which are also home to large numbers of Jewish-American immigrants.

46. The Central Bureau of Statistics officially counts about 100,000 migrants from the United States; see http://www1.cbs.gov.il/reader/shnaton/templ_shnaton _e.html?num_tab=st04_04&CYear=2015. However, it is thought that considerably more Americans are living in the country as noncitizens, unregistered children of American-born parents, students, tourists, and workers.

47. For a full discussion of this statistical analysis and demographic profile, see Chapter 1.

48. Avruch, *American Immigrants in Israel,* 5.

49. For a classic model, see William Petersen, "A General Typology of Migration," *American Sociological Review* 23, no. 3 (June 1958): 256–266.

50. The preeminent scholar of Jewish-American immigration to Israel largely subscribes to this paradigm: see Waxman, *American Aliya.*

51. See Takeyuki Tsuda, ed., *Diasporic Homecomings: Ethnic Return Migration in Comparative Perspective* (Stanford, CA: Stanford University Press, 2009). Although I have mentioned it here by way of reference to the existing literature, I especially eschew the ideologically loaded Zionist terminology of *aliya* (lit. ascent), which has been utilized by a previous generation of scholars of immigration to Israel.

52. Matthew Frye Jacobson, *Roots Two: White Ethnic Revival in Post–Civil Rights America* (Cambridge, MA: Harvard University Press, 2006), 222–223.

53. Avruch, *American Immigrants in Israel,* 93.

54. Harold R. Isaacs, *American Jews in Israel* (New York: John Day, 1967), 89.

55. Other scholars, like Matthew Silver, have considered the kulturkamph between Jewish-American immigrants and native Israelis as intrinsic to the Diaspora–Zionist relationship. While I find his history overdetermined, it does evoke similar struggles that self-identifying "pioneers" among Jewish-American settlers confronted after 1967. See Matthew Silver, *First Contact: Origins of the American-Israeli Connection—Haluzim from America during the Palestine Mandate* (West Hartford, CT: Graduate Group, 2006).

56. See Linda Renée Bloch, "Communicating as an American in Israel: The Freier Phenomenon and the Pursuit of an Alternative Value System," *Research on Language and Social Interaction* 31, no. 2 (Winter 1998): 177–208.

57. See Gitelman, *Becoming Israelis;* Pearl Katz, "Acculturation and Social Networks of American Immigrants in Israel" (PhD diss., SUNY at Buffalo, 1974); and Avruch, *American Immigrants in Israel,* 173.

58. Gitelman, *Becoming Israelis,* 239.

59. The phrase "City on a Hill" first appeared in Jesus's Sermon on the Mount as a directive to Christians to spread the gospel. This idea was later adopted by the first governor of the Massachusetts Bay Colony, John Winthrop, in his speech "A Model of Christian Charity" (1630), as the mission of the city of Boston to serve as a beacon to the fledgling colonies. I have adapted this idiom as a kind of ideological shorthand for the progressive vision Jewish-American settlers believed they brought to the occupied territories.

60. I have been deeply influenced by the idea of the cultural encounter and alternatives to traditional diplomatic history theorized in Melani McAlister, *Epic Encounters: Culture, Media, and U.S. Interests in the Middle East since 1945* (Berkeley: University of California Press, 2005).

1. From Moment to Movement

1. Jay Shapiro, interview with the author, 17 May 2009.

2. Of this group, scholars estimate that one-third returned to the United States permanently, with a smaller, undefined percentage making subsequent attempts at immigration or traveling back and forth on a regular basis. See Chaim I. Waxman and Michael Appel, *To Israel and Back: American Aliyah and Return Migration* (New York: American Jewish Committee, 1986), 10.

3. See Pew Research Center, *A Portrait of Jewish Americans: Findings from a Pew Research Center Survey of U.S. Jews,* 2013, http://www.pewforum.org/files /2013/10/jewish-american-full-report-for-web.pdf.

4. Goldscheider, "American Aliya," 348.

5. Chaim I. Waxman, "In the End Is It Ideology? Religio-Cultural and Structural Factors in American Aliya," *Contemporary Jewry* 16 (1995): 50–67. This data appears somewhat less dramatic when the decision of the Israel Central Bureau of Statistics to add the designation "temporary residents" to the total number of immigrants, thus artificially inflating migration figures, is taken into account. Yet many temporary residents—including those described in this chapter who came as tourists, volunteers, and students—did later officially convert their status to immigrant. The May 1967 U.S. Supreme Court ruling allowing for dual American-Israeli citizenship encouraged this process.

6. Goldscheider, "American Aliya," 355.

7. Israel Central Bureau of Statistics, *Statistical Abstract of Israel,* 2015, table 4.4.

8. Obtaining an accurate and objective headcount of Jewish-American settlers in the occupied territories poses serious challenges for the researcher. See the Appendix for a full discussion of these statistics.

9. Gerald Berman, "Why North Americans Migrate to Israel," *Jewish Journal of Sociology* 21, no. 2 (1979): 135–144.

10. I base my work for this period on Goldscheider, "American Aliya," with one major change to his methodology: he compared Jewish-American immigrants to the *National Jewish Population Survey* of 1957 (as later statistics were not yet available), whereas I utilize the contemporaneous *National Jewish Population Survey* of 1971. See Fred Massarik, Bernard Lazerwitz, and Morris Axelrod, *National Jewish Population Survey, 1971,* ed. Fred Massarik and the Council of Jewish Federations and Welfare Funds (New York: Council of Jewish Federations, 1972).

11. Yocheved Miriam Russo, "Personal Encounters: The Meatman of Yamit," *Jerusalem Post,* 18 April 2007.

12. See Goldscheider, "American Aliya," 358–359, and Fred Massarik and Alvin Chenkin, "The Jewish Population of the United States in 1970: A New Estimate," in *National Jewish Population Survey 1971,* table 1, p. 2.

13. See Diamond, "And I Will Dwell in Their Midst."

14. Sharon Katz, interview with the author, 17 August 2011.

15. Shmuel Sackett, interview with the author, summer 2009.

16. Bobby Brown, interview with the author, 25 March 2009.

17. See, for example, Waxman, "In the End Is It Ideology?"

18. Only 5 percent of Waxman's subjects offered economics-driven assessments to their immigration decisions and not a single Jewish-American settler I interviewed offered fiscal-minded decision making as an explanation for their migration to the occupied territories. See Waxman, *American Aliya.*

19. Goldscheider, "American Aliya," 364.

20. Ibid. This cohort was set apart from the mean American Jewish population, which was more than thirty years old at the time; see Alvin Chenkin, "Demographic Highlights: Facts for Planning," in *National Jewish Population Survey 1971*, table A, p. 2.

21. Goldscheider, "American Aliya," 364–366.

22. Deloitte Consulting Group, "The Economic Impact of Nefesh B'Nefesh Aliya on the State of Israel," unpublished working paper, October 2009, 7–8.

23. See OECD, "Society at a Glance 2014—Highlights: Israel," http://www .oecd.org/israel/OECD-SocietyAtaGlance2014-Highlights-Israel.pdf.

24. For educational and occupational qualifications compared to those of their American peers, see Goldscheider, "American Aliya," 368–371, and Chenkin, "Demographic Highlights," tables 5c and 6, pp. 20, 22. The data is especially striking when seen in contrast to the contemporaneous native Israeli population; see Goldscheider, "American Aliya," 368–371.

25. On the falling years of schooling and professional qualifications of more recent migrants, see *Statistical Abstract of Israel* 2015, table 12.5, although note that this conflates European and American immigration statistics, which is highly problematic. This survey touts their credentials; see Deloitte Consulting Group, "Economic Impact of Nefesh B'Nefesh Aliya on the State of Israel," 9–10.

26. Ibid. Note: this takes together the unemployed, those not seeking employment, students, and retirees.

27. Waxman, *American Aliya,* 151–152.

28. Aaron Antonovsky and Abraham David Katz, *From the Golden to the Promised Land* (Darby, PA: Norwood Editions, 1979), 51.

29. Goldscheider, "American Aliya," 380–381.

30. Antonovsky and Katz, *From the Golden to the Promised Land,* 38–39.

31. Fred Massarik, "Highlights: Jewish Identity," in *National Jewish Population Survey 1971*, table 1, p. 2.

32. Ibid., tables 3 and 9, pp. 4, 11.

33. Ibid., 152. This correlates with a report in the Israeli journal *Barkai*, which noted that of 1,900 Jewish-American immigrants in 1986, 1,200 (63 percent) were Orthodox Jews and the remainder considered themselves at least "somewhat religiously observant." Waxman also points to the influence of modern Orthodox-aimed Diaspora immigration organizations like Tehila and Nefesh B'Nefesh for the notable increases among these populations. Both movements specifically assist Jewish-American immigrants to settle in the occupied

territories. See Waxman, "In the End Is It Ideology?," 60–64, and "OU Announces Aliyah Fund Drive," *Arutz Sheva,* 3 July 2003, http://www.israelnational news.com/News/News.aspx/40113.

34. Waxman, *American Aliya,* 154.

35. Ibid., 153.

36. Ibid., 158–159.

37. Antonovsky and Katz, *From the Golden to the Promised Land,* 44–45.

38. Waxman, *American Aliya,* 154. Interestingly, only 3 percent of Waxman's sample had participated in BETAR, a group I found overrepresented in my own study.

39. Arnold Dashefsky and Bernard Lazerwitz, "The Role of Religious Identification in North American Migration to Israel," *Journal for the Scientific Study of Religion* 22, no. 3 (September 1983): 263–275.

40. Gitelman, *Becoming Israelis,* 209.

41. Waxman, *American Aliya,* 159.

42. Ibid., 155.

43. Ibid., 157.

44. Ibid.

45. Ira Chernus, "Legacy of the Six Day War Still Shapes Jewish Life," *Common Dreams,* 7 June 2002, http://spot.colorado.edu/~chernus/Newspaper colums/Israel/LegacyOfSixDayWar.htm; Ben Harris, "War Galvanized American Jews," *Jewish Telegraphic Agency,* 30 May 2007, http://jta.org/news/article-print /2007/05/30/102116/AmericanJews; Marc Gellman, "Israel's Six Day War Offered American Jews a Refuge from the Social Traumas of the 1960s," *Newsweek,* 6 May 2007.

46. Abraham H. Foxman, "The Six-Day War: 40 Years Later," *New Jersey Jewish Standard,* 25 May 2007.

47. See Melvin I. Urofsky, *American Zionism from Herzl to Holocaust* (Garden City, NY: Anchor Press, 1975); Jeffrey S. Gurock, ed., *American Zionism: Mission and Politics* (New York: Routledge, 1998); Mark A. Raider, *The Emergence of American Zionism* (New York: NYU Press, 1998); Naomi W. Cohen, *The Americanization of Zionism* (Hanover, NH: University Press of New England, 2003). Dues-paying members of Zionist movements comprised only 10 percent, at most, of the American Jewish population by 1945, as cited in Joe Stork and Sharon Rose, "Zionism and American Jewry," *Journal of Palestine Studies* 3, no. 3 (Spring 1974): 39–57.

48. These luminaries included Reform movement spiritual leaders such as Rabbis Stephen Wise and Abba Hillel Silver, U.S. Supreme Court justice Louis Brandeis, and Revisionist movement agitator Peter Bergson. See Stephen Wise, *Challenging Years: The Autobiography of Stephen Wise* (New York: Putnam's Sons, 1949); Melvin I. Urofsky, *A Voice That Spoke for Justice: The Life and Times of Stephen S. Wise* (Albany: SUNY Press, 1982); Mark A. Raider, Jonathan D. Sarna, and Ronald W. Zweig, *Abba Hillel Silver and American Zionism* (London: Frank Cass, 1997); Jeffrey Rosen, *Louis D. Brandeis: American Prophet* (New Haven, CT: Yale University Press, 2016); Melvin I. Urofsky, *Louis D. Brandeis: A Life* (New York: Pantheon, 2009); Ben Halpern, *A Clash of Heroes:*

Brandeis, Weizmann, and American Zionism (New York: Oxford University Press, 1987); Judith Baumel-Schwartz, *The "Bergson Boys" and the Origins of Contemporary Zionist Militancy* (Syracuse, NY: Syracuse University Press, 2005); and Rafael Medoff, *Militant Zionism in America: The Rise and Impact of the Jabotinsky Movement in the United States, 1926–1948* (Tuscaloosa: University of Alabama Press, 2002).

49. See John B. Judis, *Genesis: Truman, American Jews, and Origins of the Arab/Israeli Conflict* (New York: Farrar, Straus and Giroux, 2014); Michael T. Benson, *Harry S. Truman and the Founding of Israel* (Westport, CT: Praeger, 1997); and Zvi Ganin, *Truman, American Jewry, and Israel, 1945–1948* (New York: Holmes and Meier, 1979).

50. Norman Podhoretz, "Now, Instant Zionism," *New York Times Magazine*, 3 February 1974. For sources on Jewish-American anti-Zionism, see Thomas A. Kolsky, *Jews against Zionism: The American Council for Judaism, 1942–1948* (Philadelphia: Temple University Press, 1990); Jack Ross, *Rabbi Outcast: Elmer Berger and American Jewish Anti-Zionism* (Washington, DC: Potomac Books, 2011); and Adam Shatz, *Prophets Outcast: A Century of Dissident Jewish Writing about Israel and Zionism* (New York: Thunder's Mouth Press, 2003).

51. The fledgling state of Israel was also not keen to foster stronger ties as it aggressively pursued its independent-minded Mamlahtiut (stateship) agenda; see Mordechai Bar-On, *Etgar Ha-Ribonut: Yetsirah V-Hagut B-Asor Ha-Rishon L-Medinah* (Jerusalem: Yad Yitzhak Ben-Tzvi, 1999).

52. As quoted in Daniel Navon, "'We Are a People, One People': How 1967 Transformed Holocaust Memory and Jewish Identity in Israel and the US," *Journal of Historical Sociology* (2014), 5.

53. See "The State of Jewish Belief: A Symposium," *Commentary*, 1 August 1966, 71–160.

54. Podhoretz, "Now, Instant Zionism."

55. Morris Kertzer, *Today's American Jews* (New York: McGraw-Hill, 1967), 295.

56. Leonard Fein, "Failing God: American Jews and the Six-Day War," in *The Impact of the Six Day War: A Twenty Year Assessment*, ed. Stephen J. Roth (Houndmills, UK: Macmillan, 1988), 278.

57. As quoted in Charles E. Silberman, *A Certain People: American Jews and Their Lives Today* (New York: Summit Books, 1985), 185.

58. Marshall Sklare, "Lakeville and Israel: The Six-Day War and Its Aftermath," *Midstream* 14, no. 8 (October 1968): 6.

59. Melvin I. Urofsky, *We Are One!: American Jewry and Israel* (Garden City, NY: Anchor Press, 1978), 358–359. Italics appear in the original text.

60. Arthur Hertzberg, "Israel and American Jewry," *Commentary*, 1 August 1967, 69.

61. See Edward S. Shapiro, *A Time for Healing: American Jewry since World War II* (Baltimore: Johns Hopkins University Press, 1992), 206, and Lucy Dawidowicz, "American Public Opinion," *American Jewish Yearbook 1968*, vol. 69 (New York: American Jewish Committee, 1968), 206.

62. Sklare, "Lakeville and Israel," 10.

63. "Jewish Communal Services: Programs and Finances," *American Jewish Yearbook 1968*, vol. 69 (New York: American Jewish Committee, 1968), 294.

64. Menachem Kaufman, "From Philanthropy to Commitment: The Six Day War and the United Jewish Appeal," *Journal of Israeli History* 15, no. 2 (1994): 175–176.

65. Dawidowicz, "American Public Opinion," 207–208.

66. Sklare, "Lakeville and Israel," 9.

67. Urofsky, *We Are One!*, 356.

68. Dawidowicz, "American Public Opinion," 208.

69. Urofsky, *We Are One!*, 356

70. Hertzberg, "Israel and American Jewry," 71.

71. Urofsky, *We Are One!*, 354.

72. Herzberg, "Israel and American Jewry," 70.

73. Dawidowicz, "American Public Opinion," 202.

74. Arthur Hertzberg, "Jewish Identification after the Six-Day War," *Jewish Social Studies* 31, no. 3 (July 1969): 268.

75. On the New York Jewish leadership meeting, see Hertzberg, "Israel and American Jewry," 72. Others described these sentiments as well. See Silberman, *A Certain People,* 201. This is not to say that rabbinic leaders did not attempt to explore this phenomenon; see Henry Siegman, ed., *The Religious Dimensions of Israel: The Challenge of the Six-Day War* (New York: Synagogue Council of America, 1968); Commission on Social Action of Reform Judaism, *Israel and American Jewry—1967 and Beyond: A Study-Guide for Program and Action* (New York: Union of American Hebrew Congregations, 1967); and Jonathan S. Woocher, *Sacred Survival: The Civil Religion of American Jews* (Bloomington: Indiana University Press, 1986).

76. Milton Himmelfarb, "In the Light of Israel's Victory," *Commentary,* 1 October 1967, 59.

77. Kaufman, "From Philanthropy to Commitment," 163. The war prompted intense theological debates, especially within American modern Orthodoxy, about the significance of the Six Day War in the process of messianic redemption. It also saw the introduction of rituals such as the inclusion of the Sabbath prayer for the State of Israel and the liturgy of Hallel on Israel Independence Day, as well as the celebration of Yom Yerushalayim (Jerusalem Day). Some points of departure include Shear Yashuv Cohen, Norman Lamm, Pinchas Peli, Michael Wyschogrod, and Walter S. Wurtzburger, "The Religious Meaning of the Six Day War: A Symposium," *Tradition* 10, no. 1 (Summer 1968): 5–20 and Michael L. Morgan, *Beyond Auschwitz: Post-Holocaust Thought in America* (Oxford: Oxford University Press, 2001).

78. Elie Wiesel, as quoted in American Histadrut Cultural Exchange Institute, *The Impact of Israel on American Jewry: A Symposium Sponsored by the American Histadrut Cultural Exchange Institute* (New York: American Histadrut Cultural Exchange Institute, 1969), 71–76.

79. As quoted in Urofsky, *We Are One!*, 353.

80. Nancy Weber, "The Truth of Tears," *Village Voice,* 15 June 1967.

81. Hertzberg, "Israel and American Jewry," 72.

82. See Sklare, "Lakeville and Israel," which argued for the measured and transient impact of the Six Day War on the community he studied in the Midwest. Waxman also holds a minority position in asserting the "limited impact" on the baby-boomer generation; see Chaim I. Waxman, "The Limited Impact of the Six-Day War on America's Jews," in *The Six Day War and World Jewry*, ed. Eli Lederhendler (Bethesda: University Press of Maryland, 2000), 99–115.

83. This work joins other studies of the "Jewish 1960s" that highlight the synergy between Jewish participation in social movements and American studies. See, for example, the excellent unpublished dissertation by Amaryah Orenstein, "Let My People Go! The Student Struggle for Soviet Jewry and the Rise of American Jewish Identity Politics" (PhD diss., Brandeis University, 2014).

84. On the Holocaust in Jewish-American discourse prior to 1967, see, for example, Hasia R. Diner, *We Remember with Reverence and Love: American Jews and the Myth of Silence after the Holocaust, 1945–1962* (New York: NYU Press, 2009). Public discussion also accelerated following the publication of Elie Wiesel's harrowing Holocaust autobiography (which had been repeatedly rejected by publishers in the 1950s); see Elie Wiesel, *Night* (New York: Bantam Books, 1960). The kidnapping and trial of Adolph Eichmann by the State of Israel in 1960 and its discussion among intellectuals was also a subject of significant controversy; see Hannah Arendt, *Eichmann in Jerusalem: A Report on the Banality of Evil* (London: Penguin, 2006). For extensive analysis of comparisons between the Holocaust and 1967, see Peter Novick, *The Holocaust in American Life* (Boston: Houghton Mifflin, 1999).

85. *The Impact of Israel on American Jewry*, 71–72.

86. Hertzberg, "Israel and American Jewry," 72.

87. See Dawidowicz, "American Public Opinion," 206.

88. Jay Shapiro, interview with the author, 17 May 2009.

89. Novick, *The Holocaust in American Life*, 148–151.

90. Jacobson, *Roots Two*, inset.

91. Silberman, *A Certain People*, 201.

92. Lucy Dawidowicz, "American Public Opinion," 206. Images of "tough Jews" permeated American Jewish popular culture of the period, including the smash-hit film "Exodus," tales of Jewish gangsters, and the so-called Rambowitz novels, which challenged the image of the weak, neurotic intellectuals of Woody Allen and Philip Roth. See Paul Breines, *Tough Jews: Political Fantasies and the Moral Dilemma of American Jewry* (New York: Basic Books, 1990); Leon Uris, *Exodus* (New York: Bantam Books, 1959) (which was subsequently made into a film directed by Otto Preminger in 1960); Matthew Silver, *Our Exodus: Leon Uris and the Americanization of Israel's Founding Story* (Detroit: Wayne State University Press, 2010); Rich Cohen, *Tough Jews: Fathers, Sons, and Gangster Dreams* (New York: Vintage Books, 1999); and Thomas Harris, *Black Sunday* (New York: G. P. Putnam and Sons, 1975). Encapsulating the moment, one famous poster from the post-1967 era depicted an ultra-Orthodox man in a phone booth shedding his traditional black costume to reveal a Superman suit; see Shapiro, *A Time for Healing*, 210.

93. Shapiro, *A Time for Healing*, 211.

94. Bobby Brown, interview with the author, 25 March 2009.

95. As quoted in Jacobson, *Roots Two*, 220.

96. Eli Birnbaum, interview with the author, 25 August 2011.

97. On post-1967 American Jewish liberalism, see, for example, Dollinger, *Quest for Inclusion;* Staub, *Torn at the Roots;* Norman Podhoretz, *Why Are Jews Liberals?* (New York: Doubleday, 2009); Ruth R. Wisse, *If I Am Not for Myself: The Liberal Betrayal of the Jews* (New York: Free Press, 1992); and Michael Shapiro, *Divisions between Traditionalism and Liberalism in the American Jewish Community* (Lewiston, ME: Edwin Mellon, 1991). Both Dollinger and Staub question the mythology of American Jewry's adherence to liberal values, seeing the postwar period as a time of ideological retreat. Further, some scholars of the 1960s argue that the New Left was an explicitly radical movement that rejected liberalism entirely and that the emergent clash between Jews and the New Left was part of this larger process; see Allen J. Matusow, *The Unraveling of America: A History of Liberalism in the 1960s* (New York: Harper and Row, 1984). Adherents of the prophetic tradition within American Judaism who became spiritual leaders to the civil rights movement included Rabbi Abraham Joshua Heschel and Rabbi Arnold Wolf; see Edward K. Kaplan, *Spiritual Radical: Abraham Joshua Heschel in America,1940–1972* (New Haven, CT: Yale University Press, 2007) and Arnold Wolf and Jonathan S. Wolf, *The Unfinished Rabbi: Selected Writings of Arnold Jacob Wolf* (Chicago: Ivan R. Dee, 1998). For Cherrie Moraga's view, see Jacobson, *Roots Two,* 375. See also Eric L. Goldstein, *The Price of Whiteness: Jews, Race, and American Identity* (Princeton, NJ: Princeton University Press, 2006) and Karen Brodkin, *How Jews Became White Folks and What That Says about Race in America* (New Brunswick, NJ: Rutgers University Press, 1998).

98. Both Staub and Dollinger emphasize that the Six Day War only vastly accelerated trends already under way. See also Rebecca E. Klatch, *A Generation Divided: The New Left, the New Right, and the 1960s* (Berkeley: University of California Press, 1999).

99. See G. Calvin MacKenzie and Robert Weisbrot, *The Liberal Hour: Washington and the Politics of Change of the 1960s* (New York: Penguin Press, 2008) and Allen J. Matusow, *The Unraveling of America.*

100. For further detail on the passing of the SNCC resolution, see Claybourne Carson, *In Struggle: The SNCC and the Black Awakening of the 1960s* (Cambridge, MA: Harvard University Press, 1995). For more on Jewish reactions, see also Martin Peretz, "The American Left and Israel," *Commentary,* November 1967, 27–34; Leonard Fein, "Israel and the Universalist Ideal," *Midstream* 17, no. 1 (January 1971): 38–46; and Nathan Glazer, "Jewish Interests and the New Left," *Midstream* 17, no. 1 (January 1971): 32–37. One major figure in this debate who remained in solidarity with the New Left was activist I. F. Stone, who wrote an important salvo immediately after 1967: see Stone, "Holy War," *New York Review of Books,* 3 August 1967. The New York teachers' strike in 1968, which pitted Jewish and black activists against one another, also deepened the deterioration of the civil rights alliance; see an account by the Jewish-American activist Charles S. Isaacs, *Inside Ocean-Hill Brownsville: A Teacher's Education* (Albany:

SUNY Press, 2014), and the wider historical treatment in Jack Salzman and Cornell West, *Struggles in the Promised Land: Towards a History of Black-Jewish Relations in the United States* (New York: Oxford University Press, 1997) and Cheryl Lynn Greenberg, *Troubling the Waters: Black-Jewish Relations in the American Century* (Princeton, NJ: Princeton University Press, 2006).

101. Norman Podhoretz, "Neoconservativism: A Eulogy," in *The Norman Podhoretz Reader,* ed. Thomas L. Jeffers (New York: Free Press, 2004), 269–284.

102. See Gal Beckerman, *When They Come for Us, We'll Be Gone: The Epic Struggle to Save Soviet Jewry* (Boston: Houghton Mifflin Harcourt, 2010) and Shaul Kelner, "Ritualized Protest and Redemptive Politics: Cultural Consequences of the American Mobilization to Free Soviet Jewry," *Jewish Social Studies* 14, no. 3 (Spring/Summer 2008): 1–37. Also see Orenstein, "Let My People Go!"

103. See Janet L. Dolgin, *Jewish Identity and the JDL* (Princeton, NJ: Princeton University Press, 1977); Meir Kahane, *The Story of the Jewish Defense League* (Radnor, PA: Chilton Books, 1975); Hyman Lumer, *The "Jewish Defense League": A New Face for Reaction* (New York: Outlook, 1971); and Sara Yael Hirschhorn, "Constructing Kahane: Zionism, Judaism, and Democracy in the Religio-Political Discourse of Rabbi Meir Kahane" (MA thesis, University of Chicago, 2005).

104. Jacobson, *Roots Two,* 221.

105. See James A. Sleeper and Alan L. Mintz, eds., *The New Jews* (New York: Vintage Books, 1971).

106. An excellent source for understanding these movements through the voice of founders and participants is Michael E. Staub, ed., *The Jewish 1960s: An American Sourcebook* (Waltham, MA: Brandeis University Press, 2004).

107. See RZA founding manifesto, 1970, in ibid. See also Staub, *Torn at the Roots,* chap. 6.

108. One fascinating account of a Jewish-American Zionist activist's disillusionment with the New Left that led to his eventual decision to move to Israel can be found in Joshua Siskin, "From Berkeley to Beit Shean: Portrait of a Jew as a Young Man" (Jerusalem, 1974), an unpublished manuscript catalogued at the National Library of Israel.

109. For an introduction to this debate, see Staub, *Torn at the Roots,* chap. 4; Albert Vorspan, "Vietnam and the Jewish Conscience," *American Judaism* 15 (1966); Michael Wyschogrod, "The Jewish Interest in Vietnam," *Tradition* 8 (Winter 1966); Charles S. Liebman, "Judaism and Vietnam: A Reply to Dr. Wyschogrod," *Tradition* 9 (Spring–Summer 1967); Emil L. Fackenheim, *God's Presence in History* (New York: Harper, 1970); and Meir Kahane, Joseph Churba, and Martin King, *The Jewish Stake in Vietnam* (New York: Crossroads, 1967). Note: Martin King was likely a fictional alias used by Kahane.

110. See Staub, *Torn at the Roots.*

111. See Eric Lee, *Saigon to Jerusalem: Conversations with U.S. Veterans of the Vietnam War Who Emigrated to Israel* (Jefferson: McFarland, 1992).

112. Ibid., 182.

113. Ibid., 108–109.

114. Ibid., 100.

115. Ibid., 153.

116. Sharon (Shifra) Blass, interview with the author, 29 March 2009.

117. Avruch, *American Immigrants in Israel,* 104–105.

118. Some 93 percent of American Jews claimed to pay "special attention" to news items on Israel and 56 percent considered themselves "very well informed" on the subject in 1968. See Silberman, *A Certain People,* 200. An interesting overview of the books available to Jewish-American readers on Israel in the aftermath of the Six Day War is presented in Daniel Elazar, "The Rediscovered Polity: Selections from the Literature of Jewish Public Affairs, 1967–1968," in *American Jewish Yearbook 69.* For more on the Jerusalem "industry" of books, memorabilia, consumer goods, and tours available to Jewish-Americans after 1967, see Sara Yael Hirschhorn, "From Goldineh Medinah to Jerusalem of Gold: American Jews and the Image of Jerusalem in 1967," unpublished conference paper, Association for Israel Studies, 2016.

119. Only a month and a half following the end of military operations, famed Jewish-American entertainer Danny Kaye was invited to Israel at the behest of the director-general of the Ministry of Tourism, Moshe Kol, to film an hour-long travel promotion television spot; see "Danny Kaye to Film for Israel," *Israel Digest,* August 1967, 6.

120. "Travel Agents on Study-Tour in Israel," *Israel Digest,* 15 December 1967, 7.

121. Sergio Della Pergola, Uzi Rebhun, and Rosa Perla Raicher, "The Six Day War and Israel-Diaspora Relations: An Analysis of Quantitative Indicators," in *The Six Day War and World Jewry,* ed. Eli Lederhendler (Bethesda: University of Maryland Press, 2000), fig. 7, 31.

122. "1968 Tourism to Israel Tops Predictions," *Israel Digest,* 27 December 1968, 7.

123. See advertisement by the Histradrut Summer Camps, "Teenagers Invited to Israel," *Midstream* 14, no. 4 (April 1968), backmatter. See also Erik H. Cohen, *Youth Tourism to Israel: Educational Experiences of the Diaspora* (Clevedon, UK: Channel View, 2008). American Jews were particularly enthralled with the account of one summer trip to a kibbutz in the Golan Heights; see Hugh Nissenson, *Notes from the Frontier* (New York: Dial Press, 1968).

124. "U.J.A. Fact-Finding Mission," *Israel Digest,* November 1968, 6.

125. For some participants, these trips to Israel and the occupied territories became virtually "sacramental acts," see Morgan, *Beyond Auschwitz,* 80. By 1983, 94 percent of UJA board members had been to Israel at least once, 78 percent twice or more; see Silberman, *A Certain People,* 200.

126. For new young adult programs, see advertisements such as American Zionist Youth Foundation, "Israel Now: Summer 1973: College Age (18–25)," *Midstream* 19, no. 1 (January 1973): backmatter; El-Al Airlines, "Spend Passover with 2 ¾ Million Relatives," *Midstream* 19, no. 4 (April 1973): backmatter; and Israel Seminars Foundation, "Israel Now!," *Midstream* 20, no. 1 (January 1974): backmatter. Similar advertisements appeared in many other American Zionist periodicals, such as *Hadassah.* Religious denominations also inaugurated new projects; for example, the Reform Movement's Central Council for American Rabbis (CCAR) held their annual conference in Jerusalem for the first time in 1970; see Morgan, *Beyond Auschwitz,* 80.

127. "Paterson, N.J. adopts 'El Al'," *Israel Digest,* 7 March 1969, 5.
128. "Senior Branch," *AACI Jerusalem Voice* 8, no. 1 (September 1973): 1–2.
129. Ibid., 2.
130. Shifra (Sharon) Blass, interview with the author, 29 March 2009.
131. Della Pergola, Rebhun, and Raicher, "The Six Day War and Israel-Diaspora Relations," 32. Despite great enthusiasm and turn-away lines at Israeli consulates and Hillel houses during the week of battle, fewer than 500 Jewish-Americans actually made it overseas during the war itself, due to a U.S. State Department travel ban. The scholarship lacks a full demographic profile of these volunteers, but a small sample from one New York City office revealed that 80 percent had received at least some kind of Jewish education, which may have motivated their activism; see Dawidowicz, "American Public Opinion," 213. Rabbi Arthur Hertzberg also studied this sample, adding that more than half currently had no Jewish affiliation on their college campuses, attributing home life and high rates of Jewish schooling, rather than ties to the community, as the inspiration for their activities. Further, those who did arrive in Israel during wartime were primarily drawn from Zionist youth movements. See Hertzberg, "Jewish Identification after the Six-Day War," 267–268.
132. For a demographic sociological treatment of kibbutz volunteerism, see David Mittelberg, *Strangers in Paradise: The Israeli Kibbutz Experience* (New Brunswick: Transaction Books, 1988).
133. Segev, *1967,* 558.
134. Ibid.
135. See Michael Zimmerman, "Volunteers, Six Days Plus," *Midstream* 49, no. 4 (May–June 2003): 23. For another account, see Marc I. Pinsky, "613 Words: The Summer of '67," *American Jewish Life Magazine,* May / June 2007, http://www.ajlmagazine.com/content/062007/613words.html.
136. Many foreign-exchange students were lured by advertisements in Jewish periodicals, promotional presentations at Hillel Houses on campus, or published guides to study abroad; see "Get Involved in Israel this Summer!" *Midstream* 17, no. 1 (January 1971): backmatter; "Live-Work-Study with Israeli Teenagers in the American Israeli Secondary School Program," *Midstream* 19, no. 1 (January 1973): backmatter; and State of Israel Ministry of Immigrant Absorption and Jewish Agency Department for Aliya and Absorption, *Higher Education in Israel: A Guide for Overseas Students* (Tel Aviv: Yarom Press, 1970). Candid accounts of the realities of foreign-exchange programs also appeared in Jewish-American periodicals at the time; see Helen Epstein, "Overseas Students: Problems and Possibilities," *Midstream* 16, no. 2 (February 1970): 3–16, and Charles S. Liebman, "American Students in Israel and Israel-Diaspora Relations," *Diaspora and Unity* 12 (1968).
137. For example, Hebrew Union College initiated its "First Year Israel" program in 1970; see Morgan, *Beyond Auschwitz,* 80.
138. Silberman, *A Certain People,* 200.
139. Simon N. Herman, *American Students in Israel* (Ithaca, NY: Cornell University Press, 1970). See also Herman, *Jewish Identity: A Social Psychological Perspective* (New Brunswick, NJ: Transaction, 1989).

140. Urofsky, *We Are One!*, 352.

141. Yisrael Medad, interview with the author (II), 20 July 2009.

142. Yisrael Medad, correspondence with the author, 10 January 2010.

143. On the early history of Kibbutz Kfar Etzion, see Segev, *1967*, 577–578; Gorenberg, *The Accidental Empire*, 102–120; and Amia Leiblich, *Yalde Kfar Etzion* (Haifa: Universitat Haifa, 2007). A full discussion of Jewish settlement in the region appears in Chapter 3.

144. "Sons of Etzion Return to Build Homes," *Israel Digest*, 20 October 1967, 1.

145. "Etzion Settlements Draw American Immigrants," *Israel Digest*, 18 September 1970, 7.

146. "Americans in the Border Settlements," *AACI Bulletin* 12, no. 2 (November 1969): 19.

147. Judy Simons (interviewer), "Gush Etzion: Tragedy and Rebirth," Arutz 7 Radio broadcast, 21 April 2010, http://www.israelnationalnews.com/Radio/News .aspx/2135#.VVZKtpOvbSY. Note: Sandy Amichai declined to participate in an interview with me so I have relied on other sources.

148. Yossi Klein Halevi, *Like Dreamers: The Story of the Israeli Paratroopers Who Reunited Jerusalem and Divided a Nation* (New York: HarperCollins, 2013), 148.

149. Ibid., 150–151.

150. Judy Simons (interviewer), "Gush Etzion: Tragedy and Rebirth."

151. "Americans in the Border Settlements," 19.

152. Byron Appleyard, "Israel's 50th Anniversary," *Sunday Times*, 14 May 1998, http://bryanappleyard.com/israels-50th-anniversary/.

153. Judy Simons (interviewer), "Gush Etzion: Tragedy and Rebirth."

154. See Aryeh Routtenberg and Sandy Amichai, eds., *The Etzion Bloc in the Hills of Judea* (Kfar Etzion: Kfar Etzion Field School, 2005).

155. For various scholarly treatments of Hebron, reflecting different historical and political attitudes, see Jerold S. Auerbach, *Hebron Jews: Memory and Conflict in the Land of Israel* (Lanham, MD: Rowman and Littlefield, 2009); Michael Feige, *Settling in the Hearts*, chap. 7; and Menachem Klein, *Lives in Common: Arabs and Jews in Jerusalem, Jaffa, and Hebron* (Cambridge: Cambridge University Press, 2014).

156. John Wallach and Janet Wallach, *Still Small Voices* (New York: Citadel Press, 1989), 35.

157. Ibid., 35.

158. Friedman, *Zealots for Zion*, 13.

159. Ibid., 5–6.

160. Wallach and Wallach, *Still Small Voices*, 23.

161. One key proponent of Hebron's resettlement was American-Israeli MK Yehuda Ben-Meir of the National Religious Party. See Yehuda Ben-Meir, interview with the author, 19 May 2009.

162. Friedman, *Zealots for Zion*, 6.

163. Auerbach, *Hebron Jews*, 90.

164. Miriam Levinger, interview with Judy Lev, 1. A 23-page transcript (Record no. 247[1], 1999—Women in the Settlements after the Six Day War

Project) is available through the Oral History Division, Abraham Hartman Institute of Contemporary Jewry, Hebrew University. (NB: Miriam Levinger declined to participate in an interview with me.)

165. Greenberg, *The Accidental Empire*, 148.

166. Auerbach, *Hebron's Jews*, 91.

167. Shifra (Sharon) Blass, interview with the author, 29 March 2009.

168. Peter Gross, "After 42 Years, Jews are Part of Hebron," *New York Times*, 24 July 1971, 3.

169. Miriam Levinger, interview with Judy Lev, 10.

170. Gross, "After 42 Years, Jews are Part of Hebron."

171. Miriam Levinger, interview with Judy Lev, 10. A recently revealed document demonstrates how the Israeli government concealed the construction of Kiryat Arba for a civilian population, misleading the Mayor of Hebron and others that it would be used for military purposes. See Yotam Berger, "Secret 1970 Document Confirms First West Bank Settlements Built on a Lie," *Haaretz*, 28 July 2016, http://www.haaretz.com/israel-news/.premium-1.733746.

172. For maternalist and feminist dimensions of the resettlement of Hebron, see Tamara Neuman, "Reinstating the Religious Nation: A Study of National Religious Persuasion, Settlement, and Violence in Hebron" (PhD diss., University of Chicago, 2000).

173. Wallach and Wallach, *Still Small Voices*, 29.

174. Ibid., 30.

175. William E. Farrell, "Jews Settle on a 'Volcano' in the Center of Hebron," *New York Times*, 10 November 1982, A12.

176. See Friedman, *Zealots for Zion*.

177. Herb Keinon and ITIM News Service, "Levinger Sentenced for Attacking Policemen," *Jerusalem Post*, 19 December 1995, 2. She received an additional ten-day contempt of court charge for shouting slogans like "Onward, Bolsheviks!" "Onward, Stalin!" "Onward, McCarthy!" "Onward, Murderers of Jews!" at the judge during her trial; see "Miriam Levinger Gets 10 Days for Contempt of Court," *Jerusalem Post*, 21 November 1995, 2.

178. Joel Greenberg, "Settlers Rejoice, Arabs Are Uneasy," *New York Times*, 1 June 1996, 7.

179. Yegar to Yafeh, 8 November 1967, Israel State Archives (ISA), 6433/12-ל. Note: All archival material cited in this book was written in Hebrew and translated into English by the author, unless specifically indicated otherwise in the footnotes.

180. In fact, the Association of Americans and Canadians in Israel (AACI) had already called for the creation of a Peace Corps at their 16th annual conference in Jerusalem in the spring of 1968. See " 'Peace Corps for Israel' Proposed for U.S. Jewry," *Israel Digest*, April 1968, 6.

181. Yegar to Mashal, 8 November 1968, ISA, 6433/12-ל.

182. Yegar to Yafeh, 8 November 1968, ISA, 6433/12-ל.

183. The Samson family had deep roots in pre-state Palestine in the village of Karkur-Pardes Hanna; see Gloria Deutsch, "Streetwise: A Name Unshorn," *Jerusalem Post*, 24 April 2008, http://www.jpost.com/Magazine/Streetwise-A-name-unshorn.

184. See Samson to Eshkol [cover letter], 17 January 1968, ISA, 6433/12-ג [English]; and "A Prospectus of an American City in Israel—By Norman Samson," December 1967, ISA, 6433/12-ג [English]. All further quotes describing Shalom City are contained in the latter document.

185. "Re: Samson Proposal for the Establishment of an American City in Israel," Rosen to Pincus, 20 February 1968, ISA, 6433/12-ג [English]. All quotes follow from this document.

186. See Barbara M. Kelly, *Expanding the American Dream: Building and Rebuilding Levittown* (Albany: SUNY Press, 1993); David Kushner, *Levittown: Two Families, One Tycoon, and the Fight for Civil Rights in America's Legendary Suburb* (New York: Walker, 2009); and Dianne Harris, ed., *Second Suburb: Levittown, Pennsylvania* (Pittsburgh: University of Pittsburgh Press, 2010).

187. Winer to Yafeh, 7 March 1968, ISA, 6433/12-ג.

2. City of the Sea

1. Dan Yahav, *Mifal Ha-Hityashvut B-"Hevel Yamit"—Halom Sh-Negoz: Esrim Shana L-Hakama, Asor Le Pinui (1971–1992)* (Tel Aviv: Y. Golan, 1992), 18–19.

2. Ibid.

3. Ibid., 224–228.

4. Ibid., 227. See also William Wilson Harris, *Taking Root: Israeli Settlement in the West Bank, the Golan and Gaza-Sinai, 1967–1980* (Chichester: Research Studies Press, 1980), 55.

5. See Nurit Kliot and Shmuel Albeck, *Sinai: Anatomia Shel Prida* (Tel Aviv: Misrad Ha-Bitahon, 1996), 40.

6. Jewish Agency Settlement Division, *Hevel Eskhol* (Jerusalem: Jewish Agency, 1972).

7. Gorenberg, *The Accidental Empire*, 248.

8. Chaim and Sarah Feifel, interview with the author, 12 August 2014. What Feifel did not mention was that Cincinnati at the time was largely dominated by the Reform movement and he had difficulty holding a conservative pulpit. Perhaps it had become clear that a rewarding and remunerative future in that city was unlikely, increasing their desire to leave. The Feifels' mobility and ability to reinvent themselves was important in the last days of Yamit.

9. Ibid.

10. Feifel to Narkiss, 10 January 1973, Jewish Agency Internal File Code 222586. Emphasis in the original text.

11. Yakir to Amitai, 10 February 1974, and Shadur to Bar-Giora, 22 March 1973, Jewish Agency Internal File Code 222586.

12. Chaim and Sarah Feifel, interview with the author, 12 August 2014.

13. "Westchester-Rockland County Chug Aliya—Special Meeting," 6 September 1973, Jewish Agency Internal File Code 222586 [English].

14. Sarah and Chaim Feifel, "Garin Yamit," *Aliyon* (October 1973): 5–6.

15. Eli Eyal, "Yamit after the Compromise," *Aliyon* (October 1973): 6–9.

16. "Yamit: Chalutz Aliyah of the Mid. '70s," *Aliyon* (October 1973): 4–5.

17. Chaim Feifel, "Yamit," *Aliyon* (November 1973): 8. The article appears to have been written before the outbreak of the October war.

18. Feifel to Narkiss, 21 September 1973, Jewish Agency Internal File Code 222586 [English].

19. Rozeman to Feifel, 19 October 1973, ISA, 8396/6-גל.

20. Chaim and Sarah Feifel, interview with the author, 12 August 2014.

21. He noted the transfer of authority for the Yamit project to the Ministry of Housing, discussed earlier, although this correspondence did not imply direct support for the Jewish-American group. See Chaim Feifel, "Dear Friends of Yamit," *Aliyon* (December 1973): 10–11.

22. Chaim Feifel, "Yamit News," *Aliyon* (February 1974): 16.

23. Feifel to Avni, 5 December 1973, Jewish Agency Internal File Code 222586 [English].

24. See Feifel to Harel, 1 January 1974, [English] and Harel to Feifel, 27 January 1974, Jewish Agency Internal File Code 222586.

25. Feifel to Dayan and Feifel to Meir, 5 February 1974, ISA, 8396/6-גל [English]. The Feifels had learned through trial and error to carbon-copy every member of the government and the press they could think of to garner attention, as evidenced here. Chaim and Sarah Feifel, interview with the author, 12 August 2014.

26. Rozeman to Yakir, 28 February 1974, ISA, 8396/6-גל.

27. Narkiss to Feifel, 28 May 1974, Jewish Agency Internal File Code 222586 [English].

28. Feifel to Narkiss, 10 June 1974, Jewish Agency Internal File Code 222586 [English].

29. See "Report of Garin Yamit Conference," *Aliyon* (May 1974): 4, 10.

30. Gedaliah Mazal, interview with the author, 23 March 2009.

31. Carole Rosenblatt, interview with the author, 28 July 2014.

32. Applications for Membership, undated (1974–1975) and "List Submitted to Housing Ministry for Housing," 9 April 1975, ISA, 8396/6-גל [English].

33. Russo, "Personal Encounters: The Meatman of Yamit."

34. Elsewhere, eleven families and eight singles were reported. See Feifel to Gazit, 8 April 1974, ISA 8396/6-גל. On candidate files, see Feifel to Narkiss, 30 January 1974, Jewish Agency Internal File Code 222586 [English].

35. Feifel to Avni, 23 March 1974, ISA, 8396/6-גל [English].

36. Feifel to Bar-Giora, 27 March 1974, Jewish Agency Internal File Code 222586 [English].

37. See Feifel to Narkiss, 3 April 1974, ISA, 8396/6-גל [English]; Yakir to Rozeman, 21 January 1974, Jewish Agency Internal File Code 222586; Avni to Feifel, 7 March 1974, ISA, 8396/6-גל; and Yakir to Shadur and Dar, 9 May 1974, ISA, 8396/6-גל.

38. Gedaliah Mazal, interview with the author, 23 March 2009.

39. Smallman to Avni, 22 May 1974, ISA, 8396/6-גל [English] and handwritten memo in file from Yakir, 6 June 1974, Jewish Agency Internal File Code 222586.

40. See Pushkin to Avni, 17 April 1974, ISA, 8396/6-גל and Feifel to Yakir, 19 May 1974, Jewish Agency Internal File Code 222586 [English].

41. See Yakir to Dar and Shadur, 9 June 1974, Jewish Agency Internal File Code 222586.

42. Russo, "Personal Encounters: The Meatman of Yamit." His description is also evocative of Avraham Soskin's famous "before and after" snapshot entitled "Before Tel Aviv," which has a storied history in the imagining of Zionist settlement; see Maoz Azaryahu, *Tel Aviv: Mythography of a City* (Syracuse, NY: Syracuse University Press, 2006), 54–55.

43. Gedaliah Mazal, interview with the author, 23 March 2009.

44. "Press Release: The First Families of the American Garin That Will Settle in Yamit Have Arrived," World Zionist Organization, Public Relations and Press Office, 30 July 1974, Jewish Agency Internal File Code 222586 [English].

45. Russo, "Veterans: Carole Rosenblatt." See also "Garin Yamit Newsletter," *Aliyon* (September 1974): 5, 15.

46. Carole Rosenblatt, interview with the author, 28 July 2014.

47. "Garin Yamit Newsletter," *Aliyon* (September 1974): 15.

48. Sybil Kaufman, "Pioneering—1975: Come to Yamit!," *Israel Digest*, 22 November 1974, 2.

49. Carole Rosenblatt, interview with the author, 28 July 2014. Emphasis in original speech.

50. "Expenses for Garin Yamit—American," 2 September 1974, Jewish Agency Internal File Code 222586.

51. Feifel to Narkiss, 5 September 1974, Jewish Agency Internal File Code 222586 [English].

52. See Feifel to Yedlin,13 October 1974, Jewish Agency Internal File Code 222586 [English]; Sarah Feifel to Minister of Housing, 18 January 1974, ISA, 8396/6-גל [English] (emphasis in the original text); and Sarah Feifel to President, Prime Minister, and Ministers of the Israeli Government, 17 December 1974, ISA, 8396/6-גל [English].

53. Feifel and Arenstein to Sapir, 18 October 1974, Jewish Agency Internal File Code 222586 [English].

54. "Garin Yamit Newsletter."

55. In fact, between 1973 and 1979, no less than fifteen segments aired on the U.S. evening news broadcasts of the three major television networks; see listings at the Vanderbilt Television News Archive, http://tvnews.vanderbilt.edu/tvn-displayindex.pl?SID=2011123016815185&pagenumber=1&code=tvn&.

56. "Letter of Obligation," 15 December 1974, Jewish Agency Internal File Code 222586 [English].

57. See Y. Vardimon to Sarah Feifel, 12 January 1975, ISA, 8396/6-גל; "Association of the Pioneers of Yamit Association for Settlement of Western Immigrants at Yamit: Articles of Association," 2 February 1975, ISA, 8396/7-גל [English]; and Sarah Feifel to Yedlin, 14 January 1975, Jewish Agency Internal File Code 222586 [English].

58. Chaim and Sarah Feifel, interview with the author, 12 August 2014.

59. Chalutzei Yamit Membership Form, winter 1975, Jewish Agency Internal File Code 222586 [English].

60. Menachem Talmi, "Ha-Amerikanim Miztarfim L-Rusim B-Yamit," *Maariv* (Sof Shavua), Spring 1975 [exact date unknown], 3–5. Personal collection of Gedaliah Mazal.

61. "Chalutzei Yamit Newsletter—Spring 1975," ISA, גל-8396/7 [English].

62. Summary of meeting, 9 April 1975, ISA, גל-8396/6.

63. "Housing List—Chalutzei Yamit," 15 May 1975, ISA, גל-8396/6.

64. Sarah Feifel and Members of Chalutzei Yamit to Ministry of Housing, 5 May 1975, ISA, גל-8396/6. Emphasis appeared in the original text. [English].

65. Sarah Feifel to Sherman, 21 May 1975, Jewish Agency Internal File Code 222586 [English].

66. Chaim and Sarah Feifel, interview with the author, 12 August 2014.

67. Aharon Dolav, "The Minister of Housing Is Destroying the Seed Colonies for Settlement," *Maariv*, 20 July 1975, 18 [Hebrew].

68. Chaim and Sarah Feifel, interview with the author, 12 August 2014.

69. Carole Rosenblatt, interview with the author, 28 July 2014.

70. Chaim and Sarah Feifel, interview with the author, 12 August 2014.

71. Gedaliah Mazal, interview with the author, 23 March 2009.

72. Steve Schiffman, "Pioneer Who Followed a Dream," *Israel Digest,* 12 August 1977, 9.

73. Chaim and Sarah Feifel, interview with the author, 12 August 2014.

74. See Maoz Azaryahu and S. Ilan Troen, *Tel Aviv, the First Century: Visions, Designs, Actualities* (Bloomington: Indiana University Press, 2012) and Azaryahu, *Tel Aviv.*

75. Russo, "Veterans: Carole Rosenblatt."

76. Gedaliah Mazal, interview with the author, 23 March 2009.

77. Russo, "Personal Encounters: The Meatman of Yamit."

78. Chaim and Sarah Feifel, interview with the author, 12 August 2014.

79. Gedaliah Mazal, interview with the author, 23 March 2009.

80. Carole Rosenblatt, interview with the author, 28 July 2014.

81. Print advertisements in early issues were often written in Hebrew, English, and Russian, exemplifying the multinational, multilingual community in the new settlement. See, for example, Ar-Mex Ltd. advertisement, *Yamiton,* 23 January 1976, 5.

82. "Attention Americans & Canadians," *Yamiton,* 6 February 1976, 8–9; "English News," *Yamiton,* 27 February 1976, 6–7; "English News," *Yamiton,* 12 March 1976, 6.

83. "Greetings from Yamit," *Aliyon* (April 1976): 8–9.

84. "Kol Bo Chaim," Undated, ISA, גל-8396/7.

85. According to the *Jerusalem Post,* Yamit residents complained that fifteen families were unemployed and up to 25 percent of potential members had canceled their plans to move into the city due to the unemployment crisis in its first year alone.

86. For a list of businesses, see Rosenblatt to Ben-David, 1 February 1976, ISA, גל-8396/7 [English]. Rosenblatt vigorously protested this policy on behalf of

the group; see Rosenblatt to Ben-David, 22 February 1976, ISA, 8396/7-גל [English].

87. Rosenblatt tirelessly advocated for job creation for her group within these enterprises; see Rosenblatt to Yishai, 8 March 1976, ISA, 8396/7-גל [English].

88. "Yamit Residents Blame Government 'Ineptness,' for Slow Development," January 1976, Jewish Agency Internal File Code 222586.

89. Yakir to Leket, 19 January 1976, Jewish Agency Internal File Code 222586.

90. Ben-Dor to Narkiss, 12 April 1976, Jewish Agency Internal File Code 222586; Yishai to Nudel, 28 April 1976, ISA, 8396/7-גל.

91. See Asher to Avni, 6 June 1976, and Narkiss to Avni, 7 September 1976, Jewish Agency Internal File Code 222586.

92. Yakir to Leket, 13 May 1976, Jewish Agency Internal File Code 222586.

93. See Rosenblatt to Dr. and Mrs. S. Lazarus, 12 January 1976 and Rosenblatt to Leshem, 3 March 1976, ISA, 8396/7-גל [English].

94. Dorit Nudel to Avni, 13 September 1976, ISA, 8396/7-גל.

95. Jerry Nudel to Avni, 7 July 1975, ISA, 8396/7-גל.

96. Russo, "Veterans: Carole Rosenblatt."

97. Carole Rosenblatt, interview with the author, 28 July 2014.

98. Chaim and Sarah Feifel, interview with the author, 12 August 2014.

99. Gedaliah Mazal, interview with the author, 23 March 2009.

100. Yakir to Leket, 13 May 1976, Jewish Agency Internal File Code 222586.

101. "A Survey of Immigrant Absorption at Yamit for the Period of July 1976–March 1977," undated, Jewish Agency Internal File Code 222586.

102. Chaim and Sarah Feifel, interview with the author, 12 August 2014.

103. Carole Rosenblatt, "English News," *Yamiton,* 28 May 1976, 10.

104. Rafi Leshem, "L-Maan Shituf Peula," *Yamiton,* 28 May 1976, 6.

105. Herman to Narkiss, 8 July 1976, Jewish Agency Internal File Code 222586.

106. Avni to Leket, 15 December 1976, Jewish Agency Internal File Code 222586.

107. Jane Mendelsohn, "Yamit: Hard Work and Determined Efforts Are Building a City," *Israel Digest,* 12 August 1977, 8.

108. Carol Rosenblatt, "Amerika, Amerika," *Yamiton,* 14 October 1976, 13 [Hebrew].

109. Gedaliah Mazal, interview with the author, 23 March 2009.

110. See Sprinzak, *The Ascendance of Israel's Radical Right,* 101.

111. "Moshav Naot Sinai Is Inaugurated," *Haaretz,* 30 September 1977, 1 [Hebrew].

112. Benny Morris, *Righteous Victims: A History of the Zionist–Arab Conflict, 1881–2001* (New York: Vintage Books, 2001), 447.

113. Zvi Arenstein, "Shifting Sands at Yamit," *Jerusalem Post Magazine,* 6 January 1978, 4. Gedaliah Mazal's copy of this article included notations where he circled his home on the cover photo of an aerial view of Yamit. Personal collection of Gedaliah Mazal.

114. "Dayan, Sharon Face Angry Sinai Settlers," *New York Times,* 2 January 1978, 3.

115. Arenstein, "Shifting Sands at Yamit," 4.

116. William E. Farrell, "Israelis Who Farm the Sinai Fear Uncertain Future," *New York Times,* 16 February 1978, A3.

117. Robert Slater, "Angry Settlers at 'Little Sea,'" *Time,* 30 January 1978.

118. Gedaliah Mazal, "A Letter from Yamit," *Jewish Press,* 10 February 1978, 52.

119. Carole Rosenblatt, "'Sister City,' Yamit Adopted by PB [Palm Beach]," *Jewish Floridian of Palm Beach Country,* 16 December 1977, 10.

120. See http://www.mfa.gov.il/MFA/PeaceProcess/GuidetothePeaceProcess /CampDavidAccords.

121. See http://www.mfa.gov.il/MFA/PeaceProcess/GuidetothePeaceProcess /Israel-EgyptPeaceTreaty.

122. Don Canaan, "Paradise Regained, Paradise Lost," *Israel Faxx,* 24 April 1995, http://blog.worldvillage.com/society/paradise_regained_paradise_lost .html.

123. Sprinzak, *The Ascendance of Israel's Radical Right,* 101.

124. Jonathan Kandell, "Jews in Sinai Jeer, Then Applaud Begin," *New York Times,* 6 April 1979, A1.

125. Begin to Feifel, 29 November 1978, Personal Archive of Chaim Feifel.

126. Aharon Grunbitz, "Yishlakh L-Kaiz Yamit," *Yom Ha-Shishi,* 27 March 2002 [Hebrew].

127. Kandell, "Jews in Sinai Jeer."

128. David K. Shipler, "Israeli Cabinet Approves Payment to the Displaced Settlers in Sinai," *New York Times,* 8 January 1982, A3. Despite the State of Israel's thirty-year declassification law, access to archival files pertaining to the individual compensation of Yamit's settlers remains barred indefinitely due to a state-mandated security and privacy hold at the Israel State Archives.

129. However, these allegations are seemingly contradicted by available evidence, which suggest that property ownership had been calculated into individual compensation plans and that the average small businessperson in Yamit was expected to receive approximately $228,000 in restitution. It's likely that Rosenblatt's claims were rejected because she did not hold an official business contract. See David K. Shipler, "Settlers Protest Sinai Compensation Plan," *New York Times,* 12 January 1982, A3.

130. Carole Rosenblatt, interview with the author, 28 July 2014. Emphasis in original speech.

131. Russo, "Veterans: Carole Rosenblatt."

132. Carole Rosenblatt, interview with the author, 28 July 2014.

133. Harry Wall, "The Road from Yamit," *Jerusalem Post International Edition,* 16–22 December, 1979, 16.

134. Carole Rosenblatt, interview with the author, 28 July 2014.

135. Chaim and Sarah Feifel, interview with the author, 12 August 2014. Emphasis in original speech.

136. Grunbitz, "Yishlakh L-Kaiz Yamit."

137. Russo, "Personal Encounter: The Meatman of Yamit."

138. Notably, most of the secular residents of Yamit eschewed the Holocaust discourse of "survivors" and "refugees" adopted by Gazan settlers in the aftermath of the withdrawal in 2006, see Feige, "The Trauma That Never Was," 196–211.

139. Chaim and Sarah Feifel, interview with the author, 12 August 2014.

140. See Gadi Wolfsfeld, "Collective Political Action and Media Strategy: The Case of Yamit," *Journal of Conflict Resolution* 28, no. 3 (September 1984): 363–381. See also Sprinzak, *The Ascendance of Israel's Radical Right,* 102–105.

141. Chaim and Sarah Feifel, interview with the author, 12 August 2014.

142. Carole Rosenblatt claimed to mobilize American audiences back home by giving interviews to television programming like *60 Minutes* and network nightly news, and even to have been included in a *Doonesbury* comic strip! Carole Rosenblatt, interview with the author, 28 July 2014. The American Jewish community rallied to their cause—the New England Jewish rock band *Safam* even recorded a poignant song about the destruction of Yamit, a song I remember from my childhood. See "Yamit," track 5, *Bittersweet* album, 1983. Lyrics can be found at http://www.safam.com/safamlyrics.shtml#bittersweetyamit.

143. For further commentary on the final days and remembrance of Yamit by its residents, see Feige, "The Trauma That Never Was."

144. Russo, "Personal Encounter: The Meatman of Yamit."

145. Gedaliah Mazal, interview with the author, 23 March 2009.

146. Russo, "Personal Encounter: The Meatman of Yamit."

147. Gedaliah Mazal, interview with the author, 23 March 2009.

148. For treatment of theological debates regarding resistance against the State of Israel in the Camp David era, see Motti Inbari, "Gush Emunim and the Israeli-Egyptian Peace Agreement," in *Messianic Religious Zionism Confronts Israeli Territorial Compromises* (Cambridge: Cambridge University Press, 2012), 37–58. On protest tactics, see David K. Shipler, "Militants Try to Reach Sinai by Boat," *New York Times,* 2 April 1982, A3, and Henry Kamm, "In Chaos, Israel's Soldiers Pry Resisters Out of Sinai," *New York Times,* 22 April 1982, A1.

149. As nineteen-year-old Jewish-American immigrant activist Yehuda Richter told reporters; see "Israel," *Deseret News,* 21 April 1982, 2. Richter was later imprisoned for his role in the Kahanist terrorist group TNT and continues to participate in violent activism, including during the 2006 Gaza disengagement.

150. Henry Kamm, "Militants Wait for Authorities to Move," *New York Times,* 20 April 1982, A3.

151. Henry Kamm, "Israelis Bury a Settlement in Sinai Sand," *New York Times,* 24 April 1982, 1.

152. Azi Feifel, "The Muddy Waters of Yamit," *Sh'ma: A Journal of Jewish Responsibility,* http://shma.com/may04/Azi.htm.

153. Chaim and Sarah Feifel, interview with the author, 12 August 2014.

154. Carole Rosenblatt, interview with the author, 28 July 2014.

155. Grunbitz, "Yishlakh L-Kaiz Yamit."

156. Russo, "Personal Encounter: The Meatman of Yamit."

157. Carole Rosenblatt, interview with the author, 28 July 2014.

158. Chaim and Sarah Feifel, interview with the author, 12 August 2014. Emphasis in original speech.

3. Redemption in Occupied Suburbia?

1. Freddi Gruber, director, *For a Jew, It's Home*, World Zionist Organization—Dept. of Immigration and Absorption, 1985. This film is available through the Steven Spielberg Film Archive at the Hebrew University of Jerusalem and has recently been released on YouTube; see http://www.youtube.com/watch?v=hUg3U1w7l1k.

2. See http://www.efrata.muni.il/?CategoryID=94.

3. Shlomo Riskin, *Listening to God: A Gift for My Grandchildren* (London: Toby Press, 2010), 303. Riskin has repeated versions of this story on numerous occasions, see also, Rabbi Shlomo Riskin, interview with the author, 27 July 2009; "Rav Shel Ir O Ir Shel Rav?," *Gushpanka* 1, no. 21 (November 1986): 4; and Shlomo Riskin, "Retorika Shel Manhig V-Hakamat Ha-Yishuv Efrat," http://clickit3.ort.org.il/Apps/WW/page.aspx?ws=b81b2747-764d-421d-b994-7e1bc1ff4c82&page=7bbe8ecd-b325-4cd3-a177-22foea69584b&fol=1da52f9a-f1a7-4d83-b4do-ccac1ee572fa&box=ec806471-f9fa-4204-8coa-9002a06b17bd&_pstate=item&_item=fa666239-a5aa-4c34-b917-f4979ad5e3ff.

4. Azaryahu and Troen, *Tel Aviv*, 39.

5. See a short official biography at http://www.moskowitzprize.com/win_2008/moshko.com. Another source cites his year of birth as 1929. See David Morrison, *The Gush: Center of Modern Religious Zionism* (Jerusalem: Gefen, 2004), 2.

6. Ibid.

7. Gorenberg, *The Accidental Empire*, 19.

8. See David Amit, "Tmorot B-Nofei Gush Etzion," in *Gush Etzion M-Raishito Ad TS"H*, ed. Mordechai Naor (Jerusalem: Yad Yitzhak Ben-Tzvi, 1986), 3–18.

9. See Yohanan Ben-Yaakov, "Migdal Edar: Sipuro Shel Ha-Yishuv Ha-Yehudi Ha-Rishon Bein Hevron V-Yerushalayim," in Naor, *Gush Etzion M-Raishito Ad TS"H*, 23–40.

10. See Yossi Katz, *Ha-Hityashvut Ha-Yehudit B-Harei Hevron V-Gush Etzion, 1940–1947* (Ramat Gan: Universitat Bar-Ilan, 1992), appendix 2. See also Zeev Ener, "Holtzman: Ha-Ish Sh-Natan Et Shemo L-Gush Etzion," and Tzvi Ilan, "Ha-Shotafim Shel Holtzman," both in Naor, *Gush Etzion M-Raishito Ad TS"H*, 53–62, 63–74.

11. Feige, *Settling in the Hearts*, 171.

12. On Ha-Shomer Ha-Tsair, see Aviva Halamish, *Meir Ya'ari: Biografia Kibbutzit* (Tel Aviv: Am Oved, 2009); Zeev Tsahor, *Hazan: Tenuat Hayim—Ha-Shomer Ha-Tsair, Ha-Kibbutz Ha-Arzi, Mapam* (Jerusalem: Yad Yitzhak Ben-Zvi, 1997); and David Zait, *Ziyonut B-Darkhei Ha-Shalom: Darkho Ha-Rayonit Politit Shel Ha-Shomer Ha-Tsair, 1927–1947* (Givat Haviva: Mercaz Tiud Shel

Ha-Shomer Ha-Tsair, 1985). On the history of the settlement of Revadim, see *Gush Etzion and the Hebron Hills* (Jerusalem: Jewish Agency, 1974), 10–11.

13. See *Jewish Defense in the Hebron Hills* (Gush Etzion: Gush Etzion Field School, 1970), 3. There is reason to suspect that these population estimates might be inflated for political purposes.

14. Most famous among the battles of the siege of Etzion was the full-scale assault by thirty-five Jewish settlers under the leadership of Commander Danny Masa in January 1948, where all were killed. The Lamed-Heh, a numerological expression equaling 35, were extensively memorialized and became an important part of the historical mythology of Gush Etzion and the 1948 war. See Morrison, *The Gush*, 7, and Anda Finkerfeld, *Lamed-Heh* (Jerusalem: Rubin Mass, 1998). See also Haim Gouri's poem commemorating the event, "Hineh Mutlot Gufotainu" (Here Lie Our Bodies), the text with analysis is reproduced at http://www.haaretz .co.il/hasite/spages/1227313.html.

15. Morrison, *The Gush*, 20.

16. See Dov Knohl, *Siege in the Hills of Hebron: The Battle of the Etzion Bloc* (New York: Thomas Yoseloff, 1958). This theme of the 1948 war was subsequently challenged by the Israeli revisionist school of the New Historians; see Simha Flapan, *The Birth of Israel: Myths and Realities* (New York: Pantheon Books, 1987).

17. See Benny Morris, *The Birth of the Palestinian Refugee Problem, 1947–1949* (Cambridge: Cambridge University Press, 1987), 113–115. Morris has also suggested that the massacre at Gush Etzion may have been used as a pretext for retaliation against the nearby Palestinian village of al-Dawayima (where seventy to eighty were killed) and as a larger justification for the transfer of Palestinian refugees during and after the 1948 war.

18. Gorenberg, *The Accidental Empire*, 20.

19. Ibid., 20.

20. See Feige, *Settling in the Hearts*, 172.

21. Gorenberg, *The Accidental Empire*, 21.

22. Feige, *Settling in the Hearts*, 170.

23. Morrison, *The Gush*, 10.

24. Adi Grasiel, "Ha-Rishon L-Etzion," *Arutz Sheva*, 6 April 2003, http://www.inn.co.il/Besheva/Article.aspx/1622.

25. A mimeograph is reproduced in Morrison, *The Gush*, 10–11.

26. Later, Weitz would raise some early objections to the Efrat project, citing broader planning priorities. See Weitz to Galili, 19 March 1975, ISA, 7457/4-ל.

27. Morrison, *The Gush*, 10–11.

28. See Chapter 1 on the role of Jewish-American immigrants in the resettlement of Kibbutz Kfar Etzion and Hebron.

29. Moshkowitz has suggested he included a subtle addition to the original document that also paved the way for a new settlement at nearby Alon Shvut, in addition to the yeshiva. See Morrison, *The Gush*, 13.

30. Ibid.

31. Ibid., ix.

32. At this time neither a specific location nor a name for the new settlement had been designated.

33. Moshkowitz to Rabin, 9 October 1974, ISA, 7457/4-ג. The memo was also sent to other administration officials sympathetic to the settler agenda, including Foreign Minister Yigal Allon, Minister Without Portfolio Yisrael Galili, Defense Minister Shimon Peres, and MK Michael Chazani, a leader of the National Religious Party.

34. Morrison, *The Gush*, 47.

35. Admoni to Galili, 18 October 1974, ISA, 7457/4-ג.

36. "Yishuv Ironi—Efrat," 13 December 1974, ISA, 7457/4-ג.

37. He even suggested that the settlement might boast a population of 3,000 families/12,500 individuals within a decade and would double to 6,000 families/25,000 individuals by 1990.

38. Ibid., 2.

39. Ibid., 8.

40. Ibid.

41. Jeremiah Haber, "Shlomo Riskin: Bad Moral Luck?," 10 April 2008, http://www.jeremiahhaber.com/2008/04/shlomo-riskin-bad-moral-luck.html.

42. Morrison, *The Gush*, 11.

43. Vinshal to Galili, 24 December 1974, ISA, 7457/4-ג.

44. Azriyahu to Moshkowitz, 8 January 1975, ISA, 7457/4-ג.

45. Moshkowitz to Rabin, 19 February, 1975, ISA and Admoni to Galili, 10 March 1975, ISA, 7457/4-ג.

46. "Efrat—Proposal by the Judean Mountain Development Co., Ltd.," 13 December 1975, Jewish Agency Internal File Code 222568. It should be noted that two versions appear in the archival file, one dated 13 December 1974 and another 13 December 1975, with the year changed or corrected in black ink. The earlier pamphlet seems to be either a draft or an excerpt from the 1975 document. I will be discussing the more comprehensive 1975 version here.

47. Ibid., 2. Later, in a claim that seems patently false to readers of the Hebrew edition of the booklet, the founders promised that "a homogeneous community of new immigrants will be integrated into the Israeli society which has the same interests as proposed in this plan."

48. Ibid., 3–4.

49. See Aryei Fishman, *Judaism and Collective Life: Self and Community in the Religious Kibbutz* (London: Routledge, 2002); Aryei Fishman, ed., *The Religious Kibbutz Movement: The Revival of the Jewish Religious Community* (Jerusalem: Jewish Agency, 1957); and Yossi Katz, *Torah V-Avoda B-Binyan Haaretz: Ha-Kibbutz Ha-Dati B-Tekufat Ha-Mandat* (Ramat Gan: Universitat Bar-Ilan, 1996).

50. See, for example, Daniel Gavron, *The Kibbutz: Awakening from Utopia* (Lanham: Rowman and Littlefield), 2000.

51. This lack of secrecy reveals two important dynamics of the Israeli settler enterprise: First, settlement plans were often well known on the ground even when politicians, especially those outside Israel, were caught unaware. Second, it is likely that these discussions were leaked (even in a staged leak), underscoring the regular

coordination between settler leaders and the government, even in cases when Labor administrations claimed to oppose development activity.

52. The tract of Etzion Daled would later become the settlement of Kibbutz Migdal Oz, although there is no evidence that this parcel had been definitively selected for Efrat at that time.

53. Kochba to Galili, 13 March 1975, ISA, 7457/4-ג.

54. Secretariat of Rosh Tsurim to Galili, 21 March 1975, ISA, 7457/4-ג. Emphasis in the original text.

55. See Moshkowitz to Galili, 21 March 1975, ISA, 7457/4-ג.

56. See Kochba to Azriyahu, 10 April 1975; Kochba to Galili, 12 May 1975; and Azriyahu to Kochba, 1 June 1975.

57. Kochba to Galili, 25 July 1975, ISA, 7457/4-ג. Moshkowitz joyfully confirmed the news to Galili by sending him a newspaper clipping from Ha-Kibbutz Ha-Dati's newsletter *Amudim* (Pages) that confirmed the arrangement to its organization's members. See Moshkowitz to Galili, 18 August 1975, ISA, 7457/4-ג. See also "Yediot," *Amudim* 358, 23, no. 12 (Elul 1975): 438.

58. Menachem Roei, "Ha-Im Takum Ir Hadash Bein Gush Etzion L-Yerushalayim?," *Yediot Ahronot*, 3 June 1975, 20.

59. See Moshkowitz to Galili, 12 September 1975, ISA, 7457/4-ג.

60. Galili to Minster of Housing and Minister of Agriculture, 14 August 1975 and Ofer to Galili, 1 September 1975, ISA, 7457/4-ג.

61. See Moshkowitz to Galili, 30 December 1975 and 11 January 1976, ISA, 7457/4-ג.

62. Edward Abramson, *A Circle in the Square: Rabbi Shlomo Riskin Reinvents the Synagogue* (Jerusalem: Urim, 2008), 55.

63. Ibid., 58.

64. See, for example, Jeffrey S. Gurock, *The Men and Women of Yeshiva* (New York: Columbia University Press, 1988) and Menachem Butler and Zev Nagel, eds., *My Yeshiva College: 75 Years of Memories* (New York: Yashar Books, 2006).

65. Abramson, *A Circle in the Square*, 101.

66. Ibid.

67. Riskin, *Listening to God*, 102.

68. Rabbi Shlomo Riskin, interview with the author, 27 July 2009. At the time, Riskin expressed no special commitment to living in what he called "Judea and Samaria," which was typical of most religious Zionists in the early 1960s. He also had no personal contact with the occupied territories, although he expressed great nostalgia about an aborted visit to the Western Wall with a Christian missionary he met at Hebrew University. Ibid., 105–106.

69. Jonathan Sarna, *American Judaism: A History* (New Haven, CT: Yale University Press, 2004), 276.

70. Riskin, *Listening to God*, 137.

71. See David Kaufman, *Shul with a Pool: The Synagogue-Center in American Jewish History* (Hanover, NH: University Press of New England, 1999).

72. This spirit at LSS, and later Efrat, is especially important as it resonates with how some scholars of American religious history characterize 1960s counterculture, arguing that it was not necessarily liberal in ideology or practice

and took shape in ways that were more aesthetic than political; see Mark Oppen-heimer, *Knocking on Heaven's Door: American Religion in the Age of Countercul-ture* (New Haven, CT: Yale University Press, 2003).

73. Abramson, *A Circle in the Square,* 147n3.

74. Rabbi Shlomo Riskin, interview with the author, 27 July 2009. See also "Religion: The Sound of the Shofar," *Time,* 4 October 1971, http://www.time.com/time/magazine/article/0,9171,905446-1,00.html.

75. Riskin, *Listening to God,* 298.

76. According to one source, the two were introduced serendipitously when the rabbi, a frequent hitchhiker, hailed a ride in his car to Jerusalem.

77. Rabbi Shlomo Riskin, interview with the author, 27 July 2009.

78. See Grasiel, "Ha-Rishon L-Etzion."

79. Ibid.

80. A separate group of South African Jews organized independently to settle at the site, although both Riskin and Moshkowitz were in frequent contact and traveled regularly to Johannesburg to coordinate activities. An in-depth history of their movement is of scholarly interest, but it is beyond the scope of this book.

81. By the 1980s many of the themes explicitly related to the occupied territories. One example is a joint presentation with Gush Emunim leader Rabbi Chaim Druckman titled "The People of Israel and the Land of Israel, Including Judea and Samaria," Religious Services listings, *New York Times,* 27 February 1981, classified ad 286, D15.

82. Morrison, *The Gush,* 59.

83. Abramson, *A Circle in the Square,* 205.

84. Dr. Ralph Marcus, interview with the author, 28 December 2011. Marcus was inspired by the opening line of the prayer for the State of Israel, which reads "Avinu She-Ba-Shamaim, Tsur Yisrael V-Goalo, Barech Et Medinat Yisrael, Raishit Tsmihat Geulatainu" (Our father in heaven, Rock and Redeemer of Israel, Bless the State of Israel, the first flower of the promised redemption of thy People). The prayer was instituted by the Israeli Chief Rabbinate in September 1948 and widely adopted in the United States, including at Lincoln Square Synagogue. See Dr. Ralph Marcus, Correspondence with the author, 9 January 2012. See also *The Koren Sacks Siddur: A Hebrew-English Prayerbook* (Jerusalem: Koren Pub-lishers, 2009), 523. For a historical analysis, see Joel Rappel, "The Convergence of Politics and Prayer: Jewish Prayers for the Government and State of Israel" (PhD diss., Boston University, 2008).

85. Dr. Ralph Marcus, interview with the author, 28 December 2011.

86. "Raishit Geula: A New Religious Aliya Movement," undated 1977, Jewish Agency Internal File Code 222568 [English]. Emphasis in the original text.

87. Menachem Marcus, "Raishit Geula: The Untold Story Behind the Establishment of Efrat." Unpublished. Emphasis in the original text.

88. Moshkowitz to Narkiss, 18 October 1977, Jewish Agency Internal File Code 222568. However, no official documentation could be found in the archival file.

89. President Carter and the Role of Intelligence in the Camp David Accords (Collection), National Intelligence Cable, "Israel: Pressure for Settlements,"

20 December 1978, Doc. No. ESDN 527b88eb993294098d5177bf, http://www
.foia.cia.gov/sites/default/files/document_conversions/1821105/1978-12-20.pdf.

90. "Israel Said to Urge More Settlements: Security Plan Reported to Involve
a Major West Bank Influx," *New York Times*, 2 September 1977, 1, A4.

91. Yakir to Friedman, 1 March 1979, Jewish Agency Internal File Code
222568.

92. See "Colony for U.S. Jews Is Approved by Israel," *New York Times*,
8 February 1979, A14, and David K. Shipler, "Israelis to Expand Seven Settlements
in the West Bank—But Cabinet, in a Unanimous Vote, Decides Not to Seize Private
Arab-Held Land for Them," *New York Times*, 15 October 1979, A1.

93. See Klater to Kirschenbloom, 22 November 1977; Frank to Goldberg
and Tadmor (Telex), 12 December 1977; Moshkowitz to Narkiss, 18 October
1977; and Yakir, 29 October 1978; all Jewish Agency Internal File Code
222568.

94. David Landau, "New Town Planned for Gush Etzion," *JTA*, 8 February
1979.

95. Riskin to Kotlowitz, 21 June 1979, Jewish Agency Internal File Code
222568 [English]. Elsewhere Riskin claimed that 195 families each put down a
$1,500 deposit—a substantial amount at the time—toward a home in Efrat. See
Riskin, *Listening to God*, 305.

96. A subsequent press release touted the conference's success and noted that
a pilot trip and seminar program were in development. See "First National
Convention of Religious Aliya Movement," undated 1979, Jewish Agency
Internal File Code 222568 [English].

97. Friedman to All Representatives, 1 February 1979, Jewish Agency
Internal File Code 222568.

98. Marcus, "Raishit Geula."

99. On houses and mortgages, see Amit to Moshkowitz, 9 July 1979; on
government apartments, see Dominitz to Viner, 28 February 1979; both Jewish
Agency Internal File Code 222568. According to Marcus, the government later
reneged on its commitments and doubled housing prices between 1980 and 1981,
although this is not substantiated in the documentary record.

100. Marcus, "Raishit Geula."

101. Invitation to Cornerstone Laying Ceremony, undated (1980), Jewish
Agency Internal File Code 222568.

102. On the airport meeting, see Morrison, *The Gush*, 60. On Moshkowitz's
advice, see Riskin, *Listening to God*, 312.

103. Morrison, *The Gush*, 60.

104. Ibid.

105. Riskin, *Listening to God*, 313–314.

106. "Land Close to Bethlehem Is Seized," *New York Times*, 17 March 1980, A3.

107. Rabbi Shlomo Riskin, interview with the author, 27 July 2009.

108. Ibid.

109. Haber, "Shlomo Riskin, Bad Moral Luck?"

110. While the American-Israeli rabbi did not consider himself a follower of
the Mercaz Ha-Rav leader, he was "very impressed with his charisma and his

charm" and greatly admired his father, Rabbi Abraham Yitzhak Ha-Cohen Kook, whom he considered alongside Rabbi Soloveitchik as one of his two "intellectual influences." Photographs of both figures are prominently displayed on the walls of his office. Rabbi Shlomo Riskin, interview with the author, 27 July 2009.

111. According to Riskin, Kook was referencing a passage from the Scroll of Esther that described the conversion of the Persians to Judaism.

112. Rabbi Shlomo Riskin, interview with the author, 27 July 2009.

113. See, for example, Jill Smolowe, "Americans Talk of Plan for Life on West Bank," *New York Times*, 23 March 1980, 11.

114. Morrison, *The Gush*, 67.

115. See Yakir to Moyel, 9 May 1980 and Yakir to Cohen, 7 December 1980; both Jewish Agency Internal File Code 222568. Garin Raishit Geula began making concrete demands for a "lump sum" of $20,000 from each family toward mortgage down-payments.

116. See Freedman to Kotlowitz, 10 March 1981, Jewish Agency Internal File Code 222568.

117. Dr. Ralph Marcus, interview with the author, 28 December 2011.

118. Rachel Shadar, "Bridge from Manhattan," *Israel Scene* (December 1982): 26.

119. Morrison, *The Gush*, 67.

120. Abramson, *A Circle in the Square*, 186.

121. Riskin, *Listening to God*, 442.

122. See "Din V-Heshbon Mifgashim Im Havrei R"G V-Shlihai Mahleket Ha-Aliya," Rokach to Friedman, 25 February 1981, Jewish Agency Internal File Code 225404.

123. Riskin to Kotlowitz, 6 July 1982, Jewish Agency Internal File Code 225404 [English].

124. See "Sikum Pegisha Sh-Hukam B-Misrado Shel Rosh Ha-Mahlaka," 20 July 1982, Jewish Agency Internal File Code 225404.

125. Riskin to Dulczin, 11 June 1981, Jewish Agency Internal File Code 225404 [English].

126. On budget increases, see Riskin to Kotlowitz, 4 December 1981 [English]; for annual accounting, see "Raishit Geula, Ltd.—Statement of Operations, Year Ended August 31, 1983," undated 1983 [English]; both Jewish Agency Internal File Code 225404.

127. See untitled list in Raishit Geula file, undated 1983, Jewish Agency Internal File Code 225404.

128. See Moshe Einhorn and Elaine Jacobs to Dominitz, 2 March 1984, Jewish Agency Internal File Code 225404 [English].

129. The latest official survey from the Israel Central Bureau of Statistics on 31 December 2014 lists a population of 8,100 individuals. See *Statistical Abstract of Israel 2015*, table 2.24, "Population and Density Per Square Kilometer in Localities Numbering 5,000 Residents or More," http://www.cbs.gov.il/reader/shnaton/templ_shnaton_e.html?num_tab=sto2_24&CYear=2015. In contrast, the Efrat municipality provided an estimate of 8,945 individuals (1,832 families) in the summer of 2011, a figure likely inflated to serve a political agenda. See "Profile of

the Yishuv: Efrat Municipality," internal document, Mayor's Office, Municipality of Efrat, summer 2011 [Hebrew]. Further, in interviews conducted on the same day during the summer of 2011, Efrat's mayor, Oded Revivi, provided a figure of 9,050 individuals and Religious Council Director Bob Lang estimated that 9,025 individuals were currently residing in Efrat. See Mayor Oded Revivi, interview with the author, 17 August 2011; Bob Lang, interview with the author, 17 August 2011.

130. Mayor Oded Revivi, interview with the author, 17 August 2011.

131. Ibid.

132. Ibid.

133. "Profile of the Yishuv: Efrat Municipality."

134. See Nefesh B'Nefesh Community Profiles, http://www.nbn.org.il/component /content/article/1597-efrat.html.

135. Riskin, *Listening to God*, 319.

136. Bob Lang, interview with the author, 17 August 2011.

137. Riskin, *Listening to God*, 319.

138. Bob Lang, interview with the author, 17 August 2011.

139. Morrison, *The Gush*, 61.

140. Rachel Katsman, "Can an American Rabbi Make It in Israel?," *Counterpoint*, January 1985, 2.

141. "Rav Shel Ir, O Ir Shel Rav?"

142. Ibid.

143. Ibid.

144. Gruber, *For a Jew, It's Home*. All quotations here are from the film.

145. Ibid.

146. See David Makovsky, "Breaking Ranks in 'Occupied Scarsdale,'" *U.S. News and World Report*, 119, no. 7, 14 August 1995, 31, and Wallach and Wallach, *Still Small Voices*, 192.

147. Sharon Katz, interview with the author, 17 August 2011.

148. Barbie Erlich, "Yamim Rishonim B-Efrat," *Nekuda* 62, 13 August 1983, 26–27.

149. On Riskin and the national consensus, see Haber, "Shlomo Riskin Bad Moral Luck?" For the native Israeli settler critique, see Erlich, "Yamim Rishonim B-Efrat."

150. Wallach and Wallach, *Still Small Voices*, 203–204. Ultimately the group upheld the desire of the original garin and did not build a fence around the settlement.

151. Ibid., 204–205.

152. Riskin, *Listening to God*, 409.

153. Wallach and Wallach, *Still Small Voices*, 216–219.

154. Ibid., 208.

155. Ibid., 207.

156. David Horovitz, "If We Give Back Hebron, They'll Cry in Borough Park," *Jerusalem Post*, 7 December 1989.

157. Thomas L. Friedman, "How Long Can Israel Deny Its Civil War?," *New York Times*, 27 December 1987, E3.

158. Bob Lang, interview with the author, 17 April 2011.

159. Sharon Katz, interview with the author, 17 August 2011. Katz self-identified in this and other statements as "right-wing."

160. "Behind the Headlines: After 5 Years of the Intifada, Israelis Have Learned to Adjust," *JTA*, 9 December 1992.

161. See Liat Collins, "Efrat Being Connected to Cable TV," *Jerusalem Post*, 18 May 1994, 3.

162. Warren Bass, "Borderline Schizophrenia," *Jerusalem Post*, 28 January 1994, 16.

163. Ibid.

164. Ibid.

165. See Eve Harow, interview with the author, 21 July 2014.

166. See Haim Shapiro, "Ben-Eliezer Says Settlers 'Almost Blew Up' His Car," *Jerusalem Post*, 5 October 1993, 4; Eve Harow, "Distorted Portrayal," *Jerusalem Post*, 18 February 1994, 2; Bass, "Borderline Schizophrenia."

167. Bass, "Borderline Schizophrenia."

168. Harow, "Distorted Portrayal."

169. Professor Joshua Schwartz, "Modicum of Validity," *Jerusalem Post*, 11 February 1994, 2.

170. Bass, "Borderline Schizophrenia."

171. The municipality contended that the parcel had been purchased by the government from a private buyer in the early 1980s, but Palestinian families from the village of Al-Khader claimed it as a tract they called Baaten al-Massen and brought suit to the Israeli High Court in protest. See Jon Immanuel, "Both Sides Dig In over Disputed Hill," *Jerusalem Post*, 29 December 1994, 2, and David Makovsky, Evelyn Gordon, and Herb Keinon, "Government Likely to Stop Efrat Construction," *Jerusalem Post*, 2 January 1995, 1.

172. Herb Keinon, "Unlikely Place for a Battle," *Jerusalem Post*, 6 January 1995, 7.

173. David Makovsky and Herb Keinon, "Entire Cabinet to Review Settlement Expansion Plans," *Jerusalem Post*, 4 January 1995, 1. In a show of protest against the Rabin administration that week, Riskin called upon American Jews to cease contributions to the United Jewish Appeal due to its affiliation with the government, although he was reprimanded by communal leaders and forced to withdraw his comments. See "Efrat Chief Rabbi Apologizes for Remarks about Giving to UJA," *JTA*, 10 January 1995.

174. Sharon Katz, interview with the author, 17 August 2011.

175. Ibid.

176. Steve Rodan, "Efrat Women Execute Secret Mission for the Land of Israel," *Jerusalem Post*, 4 August 1995, 8.

177. Ibid.

178. Yehudit Sidikman, "Efrat, City of Dreams," *Jerusalem Post*, 15 August 1995, 6.

179. Herb Keinon, "Settlers Choose Civil Disobedience as Their Best Shot," *Jerusalem Post*, 4 August 1995, 7.

180. Herb Keinon, "The Army Faces Off against a Rabbinical Battalion," *Jerusalem Post*, 14 July 1995, 9.

181. "Riskin, on U.S. Visit, Defends Civil Disobedience by Settlers," *JTA*, 18 July 1995.

182. "Rabin Raps Israeli Settlers as Protesters Continue Campaign," *JTA*, 2 August 1995.

183. "Riskin, on U.S. Visit, Defends Civil Disobedience."

184. Serge Schmemann, "Rabbi Takes U.S.-Style Protest to Israel," *New York Times*, 7 August 1995, A5. While the reporter observed that "like many other American immigrants, the Rabbi insisted that there was no contradiction between their current activities and their past as American liberals," one of Riskin's friends wrote to the newspaper to dispute this view, noting, "I too was in Selma . . . Jews in Judea and Samaria had been the favored child of the Israeli Governments for almost 16 years . . . Blacks in Selma were an oppressed minority, subject to discrimination over centuries, asking for elemental justice in the land of segregation and racism. Once Rabbi Riskin calms down, he too will be shocked by what he said. He may be right politically (though I do not believe so), but he is on false ground intellectually and historically. And that is of grave concern to those who revere this wonderful man." See Michael Berenbaum, "Letter to the Editor: Israeli West Bank Isn't Another Selma," *New York Times*, 12 August 1995, 20.

185. "Riskin, on U.S. Visit, Defends Civil Disobedience."

186. See Greer Fay Cashman, "Efrat Protestors Vow to Struggle On," *Jerusalem Post*, 4 August 1995, 2, and Uriel Masad, "Settlers and Soldiers Face Off as Efrat Becomes Flashpoint," *JWeekly*, 4 August 1995, http://www.jweekly.com/article/full/1373/settlers-and-soldiers-face-off-as-efrat-becomes-flashpoint.

187. Cashman, "Efrat Protestors Vow to Struggle On."

188. Ira Rifkin, "Liberals Turn Right: U.S.-Born Settlers Fight for Turf as Peace Looms," *JWeekly*, 28 July 1995, http://www.jweekly.com/article/full/1335/liberals-turn-right-u-s-born-settlers-fight-for-turf-as-peace-looms.

189. Cashman, "Efrat Protestors Vow to Struggle On."

190. "Behind the Headlines: Ignored as an Average Israeli, Confessed Assassin Fits Profile," *JTA*, 6 November 1995.

191. Dagan Hill is still considered an outpost by the Israeli government.

192. Bass, "Borderline Schizophrenia."

193. Rifkin, "Liberals Turn Right."

194. Margot Dudkevitch, "Man Killed in Drive-By Shooting," *Jerusalem Post*, 24 February 2002, 1.

195. Riskin, *Listening to God*, 417.

196. Margot Dudkevitch, "We Are Diamonds in the Ring Protecting Jerusalem," *Jerusalem Post*, 31 May 2001, 3. Her death was one of several casualties at Efrat during the second intifada.

197. David E. Kaplan, "The View from Over There," *Jerusalem Post*, 20 July 2007, 10.

198. Rabbi Shlomo Riskin, interview with the author, 27 July 2009.

199. Bob Lang, interview with the author, 17 August 2011.

200. Mayor Oded Revivi, interview with the author, 17 August 2011.

201. Sharon Katz, interview with the author, 17 August 2011. She has suggested, however, that she would prefer a policy of Arab transfer, with economic compensation.

202. Rabbi Shlomo Riskin, interview with the author, 27 July 2009.

203. Ibid.

204. See, for example, his recent groundbreaking essays on dilemmas in Jewish law, Shlomo Riskin, *The Living Tree: Studies in Modern Orthodoxy* (Jerusalem: Maggid Books, 2014).

205. Riskin has been outspoken on issues related to prayer, divorce, and gender roles in modern Orthodoxy. Most recently, Riskin stimulated new debate over his controversial appointment of Dr. Jennie Rosenfeld as a *yoetzet halakha* (halakhic advisor) in Efrat, the first initiative of its kind in Israel, although some similar roles have been created in the Diaspora. See Jeremy Sharon, "Orthodox Woman Appointed to Serve as Communal Spiritual Leader in Efrat," *Jerusalem Post,* 18 January 2015, http://www.jpost.com/Israel-News/Orthodox-woman-appointed -to-serve-as-communal-spiritual-leader-in-Efrat-388145.

206. In his last stand prior to forced retirement at age eighty, Riskin has taken on the Chief Rabbinate in Israel, especially in regards to policies on marriage, conversion, and interdenominational and interfaith dialogue; see Yair Ettinger, "The Torah Doesn't Belong to Any One Denomination," *Haaretz,* 15 September 2015, http://www.haaretz.com/jewish/news/premium-1.675905.

207. Haber, "Shlomo Riskin Bad Moral Luck?"

208. Eric Silver, "The Radicalization of Rabbi Riskin," *Jerusalem Report,* 23 March 1995, 16.

4. Turn Left at the End of the World

1. Yair Doar, *Lanu Ha-Magel Hu Herev* [Kerah Bet] (Tel Aviv: Yad Tabenkin, 1997), 309.

2. World Zionist Organization Settlement Division, "Hevel Yerushalayim— Tohnit Pituah Eizorit," March 1976, ISA, 7152/6-ג, 1-2.

3. Ibid., 2א. See also Jewish Agency for Israel Settlement Division, "Suggested Settlements for Establishment in 1975 and 1976," 16 March 1976 and memo from S. Kahane, 28 June 1976, ISA, 7438/5-ג [Hebrew].

4. See "History of Bnai Akiva," http://www.bneiakiva.net/about/?catID=89 &id=21, and Mordechai Bar Levi, Yedidya Cohn, and Shlomo Rozner, eds., *B-Meshokh Ha-Yovel: Hamishim Shanot Tenuat Bnai Akiva B-Yisrael* (Tel Aviv: Tenuat Bnai Akiva B-Yisrael, 1987). The NAHAL Brigade served as the settlement wing of the Israel Defense Forces responsible for the initial development of new communities both within and outside the Green Line; see Yair Doar, *Sefer Garinei Ha-NAHAL-40 Shana:1987–1948* (Tel Aviv: Yad Tabenkin,1989); David Koren, *Ha-NAHAL: Tsava Im Erekh Mosaf* (Tel Aviv: Yad Tabenkin, 1997); and Joshua Nathan Peters, "The Origins and Development of the NAHAL Brigade of the Israeli Defense Forces, 1949–1999" (MA thesis, University of New Brunswick,

2008). For more of the decampment to Tekoa, see "Tekoa," *Zeraim* 9 (Sivan 1975): 16; "Ha-NAHAL M-Alef Ad Taf," *B-Mahane Ha-NAHAL*, no. 2–1 [309–310] (October 1977): 27; and "Ma Hadash: Meahaz Tekoa," *Zeraim*, no. 11 (Av, 1975): 16.

    5. "Takanu Yeted B-Tekoa," *Zeraim*, no. 11 (Av 1975): 3, 5.

    6. See "We Went Out to Tour in Tekoa," *Zeraim* 12 (Elul 1975): 2–3 [Hebrew]. Another journalist was not so lucky, complaining that pouring rain spoiled his visit; see "Siyur Sh-Kazeh," *B-Mahaneh Ha-NAHAL* 3 [287] (December 1975): 21 [Hebrew].

    7. Excavation experts from Wheaton College in the United States publicly noted a Palestinian presence of upward of 15,000 as early as 1964 when they began work at the Herodian site under Jordanian rule. See Martin H. Heicksen, "Tekoa: Excavations in 1968," *Grace Journal* 10, no. 2 (Winter 1969): 3–10, http://www.biblicalstudies.org.uk/pdf/grace-journal/10-2_03.pdf.

    8. "We Went Out for a Tour."

    9. For details of the NAHAL group's work at Tekoa in 1976, see a site visit description in the bulletin of the Kibbutz Ha-Dati: Yossi Nach, "B-Hiahazut Tekoa," *Amudim* 374, no. 25 (Kerah G') Kislev 1977, 106 [Hebrew]. On the prize, see "Makom Rishon L-Harubit, Tekoa: Rishon Bein Ha-Mehazim," *B-Mahaneh Ha-NAHAL* 5 [301] (February 1977): 1 [Hebrew].

    10. Doar, *Lanu Ha-Magel Hu Herev*, 310.

    11. See Steven M. Lowenstein, *Frankfurt on the Hudson: The German-Jewish Community of Washington Heights, 1933–1983, Its Structure and Culture* (Detroit: Wayne State University Press, 1989).

    12. Bobby Brown, interview with the author, 25 March 2009.

    13. The U.S. branch of the revisionist Zionist organization was founded in New York City in 1929. By the 1960s, BETAR was approximately 300 members strong, with regional branches across North America that promoted Zionist education and activism and required its leaders to pledge to ultimately immigrate to Israel. In the United States, the movement became known for its militancy, including both prominent civil disobedience protests and violent actions. On joining the movement, see Bobby Brown, interview with Zvi Frazer, 18 February 1981, 2.

    14. Ibid., 3–4.

    15. Eli Birnbaum, interview with the author, 25 August 2011.

    16. Bobby Brown, interview with Zvi Frazer, 18 February 1981, 27.

    17. Ibid., 12.

    18. Bobby Brown, interview with the author, 25 March 2009.

    19. Eli Birnbaum, interview with the author, 25 August 2011.

    20. Bobby Brown, interview with Zvi Frazer, 18 February 1981, 18.

    21. Bobby Brown, interview with the author, 25 March 2009.

    22. Bobby Brown, interview with Zvi Frazer, 18 February 1981, 18–19.

    23. Bobby Brown, interview with the author, 25 March 2009.

    24. Ibid.

    25. Ibid. Brown suggested that these ideas were also in ascendancy in BETAR in the late 1970s, as "the issue of Judea and Samaria became much more central."

And also the Sinai. . . . In other words, *shtei gadot ha-Yarden* [two banks of the Jordan] which was a very hazy, historical type concept, became much more clarified and important," see Bobby Brown, interview with Zvi Frazer, 18 February 1981, 23.

26. Bobby Brown, interview with Zvi Frazer, 18 February 1981, 33.

27. Ibid., 5.

28. Ibid., 24.

29. Bobby Brown, interview with the author, 25 March 2009.

30. Eli Birnbaum, interview with the author, 25 August 2011.

31. Spanish-Jewish medieval philosopher Yehuda Ha-Levi's poem "My Heart Is in the East, but I Am in the West" was popularized by the contemporaneous Student Struggle for Soviet Jewry (SSSJ) campaign and surely resonated for activists like Brown who had participated in the movement.

32. Referencing the title of a coming-of-age novel about Irish-American immigrants in Williamsburg, Brooklyn; see Betty Smith, *A Tree Grows in Brooklyn* (New York: Harper and Brothers, 1943).

33. Dov Frisch, "The Heart of Zion," *Jewish Press,* 11 March 1977.

34. Marmor to Weininger, 1 May 1977, Jewish Agency Internal File Code 127646 [English].

35. According to Brown, when he attempted to organize under BETAR, ideological battles surfaced where "BETAR immediately got into a fight over whether the pool should be open on Shabbat or not . . . it was a bit premature," leading Brown to the realization that his group was unprepared to sponsor the project. Bobby Brown, interview with the author, 25 March 2009.

36. Ibid.

37. "Join the Dynamic Garin-Aliyah in the United States Today!," March 1977, Jewish Agency Internal File Code 127646 [English].

38. "Credo—Garin Lev Tzion," May 1977 and "Garin Lev Tzion Constitution," Sivan 5737 [May 1977]; both Jewish Agency Internal File Code 127646 [English].

39. Gush Emunim did sponsor a media event in the U.S. on behalf of the group, seemingly without their permission, in August 1977; see "U.S. Group Formed to Create Settlement in the West Bank," *JTA News Bulletin,* 8 August 1977, 1.

40. Bobby Brown, "Mr. Begin, We Are Coming . . . ," *Jewish Press,* 16–22 September, 1977.

41. Livia Lisky, "'Lev Zion' Oleh M-Harei Catskills L-Hityashev B-Shomron," *Maariv,* 18 September 1977, 1.

42. Weininger to Ben-Naeh, Abotubul, and Gissin, 3 November 1977 and Meeting with Joseph Marmour, 9 October 1977; both Jewish Agency Internal File Code 127646.

43. Moti Friedman to Joe Romanelli, "Linda and Robert Brown NY-28,672" 6 January 1978, Jewish Agency Internal File Code 127646 [English].

44. Moti Friedman to Eldad Gissin, "Ungar, Amiel NY-28, 694," 18 January 1978, Jewish Agency Internal File Code 127646 [English].

45. Moti Friedman to Eldad Gissin, "Young, Hanoch NY-28, 605," 25 January 1978, Jewish Agency Internal File Code 127646 [English].

46. Moti Friedman to Eldad Gissin, "Silver, Sharon NY-28, 604," 31 January 1978, Jewish Agency Internal File Code 127646 [English].

47. Moti Friedman to Joe Romanelli, "Rosenberg, Rebecca and Jonathan NY-28,627," 24 March 1978, Jewish Agency Internal File Code 127636 [English].

48. Moti Friedman to Eldad Gissin, "Smithline, Shoshana NYQ7300," 23 January 1978 Jewish Agency Internal File Code 127646 [English].

49. This proposition came up against the stiff objections of would-be settler allies in the *moshav* union of *Ha-Histadrut Ha-Poel Ha-Mizrachi* [the Mizrachi Worker's Organization], who made it clear that "under no circumstances would we agree to the establishment of a new moshav shitufi, especially when the existing moshavim were experiencing manpower problems," suggesting the new settlement be developed as far away from them as possible, as distant as Gush Katif! See Weininger to Friedman, 29 December 1977, Jewish Agency Internal File Code 127646.

50. See Weininger to Ben-Naeh, Abotubul, and Gissin, 3 November 1977; Marmor to Weininger, 12 December 1977; and "Summary of Points from Meeting with Yossi Marmor, Representative of Garin Lev Zion," 29 December 1977; all Jewish Agency Internal File Code 127646.

51. Meeting with Joseph Marmour, 9 October 1977, Jewish Agency Internal File Code 127646 [English].

52. Marmor to Weininger, 16 January 1978, Jewish Agency Internal File Code 127646 [English].

53. Sari Walker, "Lev Tzion—A Stronghold on Sand: An Interview with Bobby Brown," *Bechol Zot* 2, no. 1 (1978).

54. Ravid to Garin Lev Zion, 23 July 1978, Jewish Agency Internal File Code 127646.

55. See "Garin Lev Zion" list (Eichenholz to Ravid), undated 1978, Jewish Agency Internal File Code 127646.

56. Bobby Brown, interview with the author, 25 March 2009.

57. "Psst . . . Wanna Join a Garin?," *Aliyon* (March 1978): 14–16.

58. Eli Birnbaum, interview with the author, 25 August 2011.

59. Bobby Brown, interview with the author, 25 March 2009.

60. Ibid.

61. Eli Birnbaum, interview with the author, 25 August 2011.

62. Bobby Brown, interview with the author, 25 March 2009.

63. Eli Birnbaum, interview with the author, 25 August 2011.

64. See "Lev Zion" (Untitled Questions), undated 1978; and Ben-Zeev to Friedman, 3 August 1978; both Jewish Agency Internal File Code 127646.

65. Eli Birnbaum, interview with the author, 25 August 2011.

66. Bobby Brown, interview with the author, 25 March 2009.

67. Friedman to Weininger, 8 June 1979, Jewish Agency Internal File Code 127646.

68. Chaim Shivi, "B-Ofra Huhzara Ha-Puga, U B-Tekoa Hehala Prizat Ha-Geder L-Har Haba," *Yediot Ahronot*, 5 October 1979, 2. See also Gil Sedan, "Gush Demands Appear to Have Split the NRP Leadership," *Jewish Telegraphic Agency*, 9 October 1979.

69. Chaim Shivi, "Yom Shalem Nihalu Hayalai TZHAL V-Ha-Mitnahalim Mishakai 'Tofeset V-Mehaboim' B-Rehavai Yehuda V-Shomron," *Yediot Ahronot,* 16 October 1979, 3.

70. Eli Birnbaum, interview with the author, 25 August 2011.

71. Chaim Shivi, "Tokhnit Sharon Kolelet Hakamat Gush Yishuvim M-Daron L-Hevron," *Yediot Ahronot,* 4 November 1979, 4.

72. See Israel Central Bureau of Statistics Internal Findings (2008), http://www.cbs.gov.il/www/mifkad/mifkad_2008/profiles/rep_h_3563000000000.pdf.

73. Eli Birnbaum, interview with the author, 25 August 2011.

74. Ibid.

75. "I Decided I Could Live Here," Oral History with Israeli and Palestinian Women—Interview with Geri Bernstein Freund, 18 June 2011, http://womens-voices .net/2011/07/04/"i-decided-i-could-live-here.

76. Bobby Brown, interview with the author, 25 March 2009. He agreed with my characterization of a "cover-up" to prevent public disclosure of these funding diversions by the Israeli government during the Camp David period.

77. "Garin Lev Tzion from the West Side to the West Bank," *Aliyon* (July–August 1979).

78. Grace Halsell, "New Yorkers Turned Colonists" *Boca Raton News,* 21 January 1980, 3.

79. Grace Halsell, "'Pioneering' on the West Bank," 1 December 1980, *Worldview Magazine,* http://worldview.carnegiecouncil.org/archive/worldview /1980/12/3485.html/_res/id=sa_File1/v23_io12_a 04.pdf.

80. Halsell, "New Yorkers Turned Colonists."

81. Halsell, "'Pioneering' on the West Bank."

82. Ibid. Presumably the first state was the Kingdom of Jordan, which did not renounce its territorial claims to the West Bank until 1985.

83. Halsell, "New Yorkers Turned Colonists."

84. Halsell, "'Pioneering' on the West Bank."

85. Ibid.

86. Bobby Brown, interview with the author, 25 March 2009.

87. Eli Birnbaum, interview with the author, 25 March 2009.

88. Today the organic mushroom farm at Tekoa, which was started by American-Israeli Oren Kessler, is one of the settlement's largest industries and supplies grocery stores across Israel. See http://tekoafarms.co.il/index.php/en/?lang =he. Former New Yorker Gilad Freud's goat cheese business used to distribute as widely as Manhattan's gourmet food emporium Zabar's, although I could not locate their products on a recent visit.

89. David Horovitz, "In Tekoa, Looking Beyond the Intifada," *Jerusalem Post,* 10 December 1989, 2.

90. Ned Temko, "West Bank's Changing Face: New Settlers Less Politicized, Arab Youths More So than Their West Bank Predecessors," *Christian Science Monitor,* 18 October 1985.

91. On Avoda Ivrit [Jewish Labor], see Gershom Shafir, *Land, Labor, and the Origins of the Israeli-Palestinian Conflict, 1882–1914* (Cambridge: Cambridge

University Press, 1989) and Anita Shapira, *Ha-Mavak Ha-Nikhzav: Avoda Ivrit, 1929–1939* (Tel Aviv: Tel Aviv University, 1977). Leadership soon gave up due to a lack of skilled workers, including in the construction of homes in the settlement, which are almost exclusively built by Palestinians. In a somewhat patronizing aside, Brown mentioned to me on a drive to Tekoa's illegal outposts that he considered economic development in the settlement as mutually beneficial, citing his relationship with an acquaintance, a construction boss named Muhammed, who we met in passing on the road in Brown's car, where "you witnessed my relationship . . . it's a good relationship," jokingly suggesting, "the only problem I have is that he's making so much money now, he forgot about us!" Bobby Brown, interview with the author, 25 March 2009.

92. Bobby Brown, interview with the author, 25 March 2009.

93. Carl Schrag, "Flower Power," *Jerusalem Post*, 14 February 1992.

94. "Remembering David Rosenfeld," undated (1982) at http://tekoa.org.il /david.htm.

95. "Manager of the Herodian Site in the Judean Desert Murdered," *Haaretz*, 4 July 1982, 8 [Hebrew].

96. Eli Birnbaum, interview with the author, 25 August 2011.

97. The Israeli government did publicly acknowledge the incident with two paid death notices; see obituary column, *Haaretz*, 5 July 1982, 5. A moment of silence was also held that weekend at a World Zionist Organization meeting led by Tekoa patron Rafael Kotlowitz; see "Zionist Organization Unites In Memory of David Rosenfeld," *Haaretz*, 6 June 1982, 5 [Hebrew].

98. James R. Gaines, "The Birth of a Settlement," *People*, 15 November 1982. Both Brown and Birnbaum reflected the common wisdom among Tekoa's settlers that the murder was an initiation ritual of the Fatah paramilitary wing; see Bobby Brown, interview with the author, 25 March 2009, and Eli Birnbaum, interview with the author, 25 August 2011.

99. See "Suspects Detained in the Murder of Herodian Manager," *Haaretz*, 5 July 1982, 6 [Hebrew], and "House of David Rosenfeld's Murderer Explodes," *Haaretz*, 6 July 1982, 8 [Hebrew].

100. Bobby Brown, interview with the author, 25 March 2009.

101. "I Decided I Could Live here." Emphasis in the original text.

102. Bobby Brown, interview with the author, 25 March 2009.

103. Gaines, "Birth of a Settlement." I quote Brown's assertion of nonviolence, but I do not accept his description.

104. Ibid.

105. Ibid.

106. Bruce Brill, "Justice Never Done," *Jerusalem Post*, 1 July 1994, 5A. The local mukhtar interceded to quell the violence by banishing the assailants to Jordan.

107. See Central Bureau of Statistics Internal Record, Nokdim, http://www .cbs.gov.il/www/mifkad/mifkad_2008/profiles/rep_h_372600000000.pdf.

108. At time of writing in 2016.

109. Eli Birnbaum, interview with the author, 25 August 2011.

110. Temko, "West Bank's Changing Face."

111. Today Price lives in the Jerusalem neighborhood of Ramot Bet (which is considered a settlement by the U.S. government) and continues to work as a film producer.

112. Moshe Golan, Stan Moss, and Larry Price, *Judea and Samaria: New Dimensions,* Ministry of Absorption, 1983. This film is available through the Steven Spielberg Film Archive at the Hebrew University, Mount Scopus, Jerusalem.

113. Amos Oz, *In the Land of Israel,* trans. Maurie Goldberg-Bartura (London: Fontana, 1983), 59–70.

114. Eli Birnbaum, interview with the author, 25 August 2011.

115. Bobby Brown, interview with the author, 25 March 2009.

116. Abraham Rabinovich, "Between a Rock and a Hard Place," *Jerusalem Post,* 7 July 1989.

117. Bobby Brown, "Beit Sahur," *Jerusalem Post,* 6 May 1991. Other American-Israelis also attacked the evocation of civil rights discourse during the intifada at Tekoa; see Dr. J. Reuben Freeman, Dr. Amiel Ungar, Dr. Yosef Templeman, Dr. Eduardo Recanati, and Rabbi Avraham Walfish, "The Situation in Beit Sahur," *Jerusalem Post,* 13 October 1989. In 1991 a Russian-Israeli settler from Tekoa was accused of killing a teenager in Beit Sahur when he began firing indiscriminately at a roadblock; see Jon Immanuel, "Tekoa Man Held in Death of Boy in Beit Sahur," *Jerusalem Post,* 22 February 1991. It appears Moscowitz was also found guilty in a second incident of the shooting death of a Palestinian youth in the village during the second intifada; see "Tekoa Resident Loses Appeal in Self-Defense Shooting Case," *Israel National News,* 3 March 2002, http://www.israelnationalnews.com/News/Flash.aspx /19386#.VRWg4eFv7SY.

118. See Bobby Brown, interview with the author, 25 March 2009; Eli Birnbaum, interview with the author, 25 August 2011.

119. Francis X. Clines, "Where Ram's Horns Blew, New Fears," *New York Times,* 3 February 1988, A8.

120. Eli Birnbaum, interview with the author, 25 August 2011.

121. He later authored an online reference guide based on his experiences; see Eli Birnbaum, "Crisis or Challenge? A Guide to Bereavement, Stress, and Modern Day Terror," 2009, available at http://crisis.org.il/.

122. Eli Birnbaum, interview with the author, 25 August 2011.

123. "The Intifada Is Souring Business Ventures in Judea: Trapped in Tekoa," *Jerusalem Post,* 12 September 1989, 9. Note the same play on words as the hopeful first article about the NAHAL at Tekoa.

124. Rabinovich, "Between a Rock and Hard Place."

125. Bobby Brown, interview with the author, 25 March 2009.

126. Clines, "Where Ram's Horns Blew."

127. Rabinovich, "Between a Rock and Hard Place."

128. Brown even led a delegation of Tekoa's settlers requesting to meet with U.S. Secretary of State James Baker during his late 1989 shuttle diplomacy to the region in order to "correct the 'many misconceptions' outsiders have about Israel's 150 Jewish settlements"; see ibid.

129. Clines, "Where Ram's Horns Blew."

130. Greer Fay Cashman, "Newsline with Bobby Brown," *Jerusalem Post,* 12 July 1993.

131. See Beverly Anne Ungar, "Outraged," *Jerusalem Post,* 25 April 1994, 6.

132. Matthew Kalman, "Two Israeli Teenagers Stoned to Death," *USA Today,* 20 June 2001.

133. Jake Wallis Simons, "Meet The Settlers: Chapter Four—The Murder of Kobi Mandell," *The Telegraph,* http://www.telegraph.co.uk/meetthesettlers /chapter4.html.

134. Mary Rourke, "In Pursuit of Non-Violence," *Jerusalem Post,* 11 January 2002, 19.

135. For the book, see Sherri Mandell, *The Blessing of a Broken Heart* (New Milford, CT: Toby Press, 2003). On the foundation, see http://www.kobymandell .org.

136. "Passover and Easter in the Holy Land," *Religion & Ethics Newsweekly,* 18 April 2003, http://www.pbs.org/wnet/religionandethics/2003/04/18/april-18 -2003-passover-and-easter-in-the-holy land/15595.

137. Yossi Klein Halevi, "Culture War," *New Republic,* 20 June 2003.

138. Peace Now estimates that 10 percent of the settlement is built on private Palestinian holdings; see "Contesting History: A Tale of Two Tekoas," *Ma'an News Agency,* 17 August 2012. See also State of Palestine Negotiations Affairs Department, "Media Brief: Israel's Colonization in Western Bethlehem and Its Policy of Destroying the Prospects for Peace," September 2014, http://www.nad -plo.org/userfiles/file/media%20brief/MB_SETTLEMENTS_BETHLEHEM.pdf. Residents actively protested political developments; see Hillel Fendel, "Gush Etzion Residents Protest 'Obama Intifada,' " *Israel National News,* 21 March 2010, http://www.israelnationalnews.com/News/News.aspx/136624. Unexpectedly, recent demonstrations over the separation wall in the West Bank have actually united Tekoa's settlers and surrounding Palestinian villages, with both groups opposing the routing of the fence; see Raffi Berg, "Settlers 'Cut Off' by West Bank Barrier," BBC News, 29 November 2005. However, those like former Brooklynite Gilad Freud have been reluctant to see this temporary alliance as a promising indicator for the future—drawing on his American background, he told U.S. public broadcasting that "once segregation ended, it was not overnight that things change, and there's still a lot of problems today." See "Israeli Settlers and Palestinians," *Religion & Ethics Newsweekly,* 17 September 2010.

139. Tova Lazaroff, "Gush Etzion Terror Attack Victim Dalya Lamkus Laid to Rest in Tekoa," *Jerusalem Post,* 11 November 2014.

140. Eli Birnbaum, interview with the author, 25 August 2011.

141. Daniella Cheslow, "As Mideast Talks Begin, Palestinians Find Unlikely Support from Jewish Settlers," *Christian Science Monitor,* 1 September 2010, http://www.csmonitor.com/World/Middle-East/2010/0901/As-Mideast-talks-begin -Palestinians-find-unlikely-support-from-Jewish-settlers.

142. "The Settler Who Spoke with Arafat: Rabbi Menachem Froman" in *Peacemakers in Action: Profiles of Religion in Conflict Resolution,* ed. David Little (Cambridge: Cambridge University Press, 2007), 341–345.

143. See Haim Shapiro, "Tell It on the Mountain," *Jerusalem Post,* 7 May 1999, 14; Daniel Gavron, "A Plea for Utopia," *Jerusalem Post,* 13 October 1989.

144. "The Settler Who Spoke with Arafat," 346.

145. Herb Keinon and Miriam Feldman, "A Perpetual Optimist," *Jerusalem Post,* 21 May 1993.

146. "The Settler Who Spoke with Arafat," 349. However, he remonstrated Hamas leaders for a perversion of their faith, repudiating the sheik with "You will go to hell because you are taking Islam, a religion that has connotations of peace, and turning it into a religion of terror." At another point, he declared, "I pray that Gaza [under Hamas] will burn under the night sky! That there will be vengeance!" See Isabel Kershner, "From an Israeli Settlement, a Rabbi's Unorthodox Plan for Peace," *New York Times,* 5 December 2008.

147. Based on their shared religious worldview, the sheik had once assured him in Arabic that they could conclude a peace agreement "b-hamsa dakika [in five minutes]"; see Nachum Avniel, "Ha-Seter Ha-Adom: Raayon Im Ha-Rav Menachem Fruman," *Makor Rishon,* 1 April 2011.

148. Ibid.

149. Harvey Stein, "The Peace-Seeking Settler Rabbi," *Tablet Magazine,* 12 March 2013; see video at http://tabletmag.com/jewish-news-and-politics/126661/the-peace-seeking-settler-rabbi.

150. Avniel, "Ha-Seter Ha-Adom."

151. Stein, "Peace-Seeking Settler Rabbi."

152. Aaron Lerner, "Interview: Rabbi Menachem Fruman—Permanent Peace Not Possible." *IMRA,* 17 May 2001.

153. Shapiro, "Tell It on the Mountain."

154. See Larry Derfner, "Always Look on the Bright Side," *Jerusalem Post Magazine,* 2 February 2006.

155. See Joshua Brilliant, "Tekoa Rabbi's Talks with Husseini Draws Anger, Ridicule," *Jerusalem Post,* 24 September 1989, 2.

156. Keinon and Feldman, "A Perpetual Optimist."

157. Ibid.

158. Joshua Brilliant, "Tekoa Rabbi Rapped over Bi-National State Idea," *Jerusalem Post,* 7 January 1990, 2.

159. Sara Rivka Ernstroff, "Troubled Times for Tekoa," *Jerusalem Post,* 30 November 2001, 3.

160. Ibid.

161. Eli Birnbaum, interview with the author, 25 August 2011.

162. Bobby Brown, interview with the author 25 March 2009.

163. Keinon and Feldman, "A Perpetual Optimist."

164. Ibid.

165. See the English-language website for the settlement of Tekoa at http://tekoa.org.il. Note: This website has not been updated recently.

166. See Nefesh B'Nefesh A-Z Community Guide, "Tekoa," http://www.nbn.org.il/aliyahpedia/community-a-housing/index.php?option=com_content&view=article&Itemid=1230&id=1816%3Atekoa.

167. See the English-language page for Tekoa on the Gush Etzion Regional Council website at http://www.tekoa.co.il.

168. See http://www.gush-etzion.co.il/tekoa.asp.

169. Ibid. See also Aryeh Dean Cohen, "Pupils Who Write Their Own Ten Commandments," *Jerusalem Post,* 30 September 1997, 9.

170. See http://www.yeshivatekoa.org/English/about.asp. There is a special track for American overseas students.

171. Ibid.

172. See http://www.tekoa.org.il.

173. Ibid.

174. See http://www.gush-etzion.co.il/tekoa.asp.

175. See http://www.tekoa.org.il. As Bobby Brown suggested, Tekoa represented an escape from the rigid norms and aesthetic dictates of suburban America, where "I didn't want someone to tell me how high the grass [on my lawn] should grow." Bobby Brown, interview with the author, 25 March 2009.

176. Eli Birnbaum, interview with the author, 25 August 2011.

177. Bobby Brown, interview with Zvi Frazer, 18 February 1981, 34–35.

178. Eli Birnbaum, interview with the author, 25 August 2011.

5. Scripture and Sound Bite

1. 168th Statement in the Knesset by Prime Minister Yitzhak Rabin on the Hebron Murders, 28 February 1994, Israel Ministry of Foreign Affairs, *Israel's Foreign Relations—Selected Documents,* vols. 13–14, 1992–1994, http://www .mfa.gov.il/MFA/ForeignPolicy/MFADocuments/Yearbook9/Pages/168%20 Statement%20in%20the%20Knesset%20by%20Prime%20Minister%20Rab.aspx. Emphasis is my own.

2. For further analysis of Goldstein and ethnic subcultures within the Israeli settler movement, see Michael Feige, "Jewish Ideological Killers: Religious Fundamentalism or Ethnic Marginality?," in *Contemporary Israel: New Insights and Scholarship,* ed. Bruce E. Greenspahn and Arieh Bruce Saposnik (New York: New York University Press, 2016).

3. Era Rapaport, *Letters from Tel Mond Prison: An Israeli Settler Defends His Act of Terror,* ed. William B. Helmreich (New York: Free Press, 1996). The book was modeled on Martin Luther King Jr., "Letter from a Birmingham Jail," 16 April 1963, http://www.africa.upenn.edu/Articles_Gen/Letter_Birmingham.html.

4. Rapaport, *Letters from Tel Mond Prison,* 44–45.

5. Era Rapaport, interview with the author, 24 July 2009.

6. Rapaport, *Letters from Tel Mond Prison,* 49–50.

7. Era Rapaport, interview with the author, 24 July 2009.

8. Rapaport, *Letters from Tel Mond Prison,* 71.

9. Shifra (Sharon) Blass, interview with the author, 29 March 2009.

10. Era Rapaport, interview with the author, 24 July 2009.

11. Ibid., 24–26.

12. Ibid., 30–34.

13. Ibid., 38–40.

14. Ibid., 99.

15. Ibid., 118.

16. For statistics on terrorist attacks committed against Israeli settlers in the 1980s, see David Weisburd, *Jewish Settler Violence: Deviance as Social Reaction* (University Park, PA: Pennsylvania State University Press, 1989).

17. Era Rapaport, interview with the author, 24 July 2009.

18. Ibid., 149–150.

19. Era Rapaport, interview with the author, 24 July 2009.

20. For further details of the Dome of the Rock attack and Yehuda Etzion's role in its theological and tactical planning, see Gershom Gorenberg, *The End of Days: Fundamentalism and the Struggle for the Temple Mount* (Oxford: Oxford University Press, 2000) and Inbari, *Jewish Fundamentalism and the Temple Mount.*

21. See, for example, "Ha-Pisasa Ha-Revia," *Nekuda,* 27 June 1980. For wider treatment of the reaction in both settler and mainstream media, see Gerald Cromer, "'The Roots of Lawlessness': The Coverage of the Jewish Underground in the Israeli Press," *Terrorism* 11 (1988): 43–51. Shifra Blass's statement is quoted in Rafael Medoff, "Gush Emunim and the Question of Jewish Counterterror," *Middle East Review* (Summer 1986): 19.

22. Haggai Segal, *Dear Brothers: The West Bank Jewish Underground* (Woodmere, NY: Beit Shamai Publications, 1988).

23. "Special Interview: Mayor of Shiloh Believes West Bank Is No Longer an Issue for International Negotiation," *JTA,* 11 March 1983.

24. "Nekuda L-Inyan Im: Era Rapaport, Shaliah 'Gush Emunim' B-New York— Shalihai Ha-Mitsvah," *Nekuda* 72, 16 April 1984, 8–9.

25. Rapaport, *Letters from Tel Mond Prison,* 198.

26. *Counterpoint,* the English-language version of *Nekuda* produced by and for English-speaking settlers in the occupied territories, which was edited by Rapaport's neighbor in Shilo Yisrael Medad, devoted extensive coverage to the issue; see *The Underground: Jewish Settlers Fight Back,* special supplement, *Counterpoint,* August 1984, and Yisrael Medad, "Of Terrorists, Undergrounds, and Demonstrations: Special Report," *Counterpoint,* July 1985, 6. There was regular coverage in New York's *Jewish Press* as well. The broadsheet initially condemned the violence, but the editorial line of the newspaper quickly turned in favor of the perpetrators; see "Editorial: There Are No Jewish Terrorists, Only Defenders of Israel," *Jewish Press,* 25 May 1984, 5. The newspaper also organized a major fundraising campaign on behalf of the Jewish Underground's legal defense; see advertisement and list of signatories and contributors for Special Family and Legal Defense Fund, *Jewish Press,* 8 June 1984, 41. (This promotion ran in several subsequent issues throughout 1984–1985.) For further treatment of the role of the *Jewish Press,* see Medoff, "Gush Emunim and the Question of Jewish Counterterror," 21. It is unclear whether the newspaper was aware that Rapaport was a member of the Jewish Underground or was hiding in New York City, as his photo and profile was glaringly absent in a montage of perpetrators; see Ken Fishman and Rachel Katsman, "The Suspects," *Jewish Press,* 29 June 1984, 51. Others have

suggested that Rapaport knew the editors well and even hand-delivered a religious justification for his acts of terror to their offices; see Tzvi Fishman, "My Incredible First Day in Israel," *Jewish Press,* 14 May 2012.

27. David Margolick, "Man Sought by Israel Is in New York," *New York Times,* 24 May 1985.

28. Thomas L. Friedman, "Jewish Settlers Are Convicted in Terror Cases," *New York Times,* 11 July 1985, A1.

29. See Margolick, "Man Sought by Israelis Is in New York." See also synopsis of Orthodox Union coverage of a panel titled "Jewish Extremism in Israel," *Jewish Action* 45, no. 3 (Spring 1985): 21.

30. Rapaport, *Letters from Tel Mond Prison,* 21–22.

31. Ibid.,15.

32. Ibid., 273.

33. Rapaport, interview with the author, 24 July 2009. Although he did not cite him directly, the formulation "Torah Judaism" is reminiscent of the writing of Rabbi Meir Kahane; see, for example, Meir Kahane, *Uncomfortable Questions for Comfortable Jews* (Secaucus, NJ: Lyle Stuart, 1987).

34. Ibid.

35. For an analysis of the ideology of Rabbi Meir Kahane, see Sara Yael Hirschhorn, "Constructing Kahane: Zionism, Judaism, and Democracy in the Religio-Political Philosophy of Rabbi Meir Kahane" (MA thesis, University of Chicago, 2005).

36. Michael Guzofsky, interview with the author, 23 July 2009.

37. Ami Pedahzur and Arie Perlinger, *Jewish Terrorism in Israel* (New York: Columbia University Press, 2009), 89.

38. Ibid.

39. Ibid., 90.

40. David K. Shipler, "Israel Calls Jewish Terrorists Isolated," *New York Times,* 9 March 1984, A3.

41. David K. Shipler, "Israel Accuses 4 Jews of a Dozen Grenade Attacks," *New York Times,* 10 April 1984, A4; Shipler, "Israel Calls Jewish Terrorists Isolated," A3.

42. "Four U.S. Olim Indicted," *JTA,* 28 March, 1984; Jesus Rangel, "Man Sought in Israel for Attacks on Arabs Is Seized," *New York Times,* 16 January 1986.

43. See Yekutiel Ben Yaakov, "Letters to the Editor: Shocking Report," *Jewish Press,* 1 June 1984, 5; Ben Yaakov, "Jewish Underground Suspect Replies to Rabbi Bernstein: Challenges Abuse of Religious Rights in Israeli Prisons," *Jewish Press,* 21 September 1984, 56B; Yekutiel Guzofsky, "'Al Fajr' and Israel's Double Standard," *Jewish Press,* 5 October 1984, 41; letter written by Michael Guzofsky's father, Yaakov Guzofsky, "Letters to the Editor: Open Letter from the Father of an Imprisoned Settler," *Jewish Press,* 8 June 1984, 40; op-ed by co-defendant Meir Leibowitz, "Letter to the Editor," *New York Times,* 2 September 1984, SM46; and an interview with Yehuda Richter's mother conducted by Kahane supporter Shifra Hoffman, "Mother of 'Underground' Suspect Pleads for His Release," *Jewish Press,* 8–14 June 1984, backmatter.

44. Jerold S. Auerbach, *Hebron Jews: Memory and Conflict in the Land of Israel* (Lanham, MD: Rowman and Littlefield, 2009), 124. For a history of the 1929 riots, see Hillel Cohen, *Tarpat: Shnat Ha-Efes B-Siksukh Ha-Yehudi-Aravi* (Jerusalem: Keter, 2013).

45. The yeshiva later came under attack following the massacre; see exchange of letters, Rabbi Shlomo Sternberg, "From Orthodox Jewish Education to Hebron," *New York Times*, 9 March 1994, A14, and Rabbi David Eliach and Joel B. Wolowelsky, "Orthodox Jewish Education Doesn't Teach Killing of Innocents," *New York Times*, 18 March 1994, A28. On the yearbook entry, see Aaron D. Maslow, " 'Do Not Murder,' " *New York Times*, 9 March 1994, A15.

46. Alison Mitchell, "A Killer's Path of Militancy," *New York Times*, 26 February 1994, 7.

47. Ibid. Goldstein's activities first came to the attention of police in 1980 when he was given a summons for disturbing a rally for Israeli prime minister Menachem Begin at Hunter College in New York City.

48. Baruch Goldstein, "A History of Anti-Arab Feeling," *New York Times*, 30 June 1981, 7.

49. Mitchell, "A Killer's Path to Militancy," 7.

50. It appears that on occasion Goldstein refused to treat Palestinian patients; he admitted as much in an interview, affirming, "I declined in some cases but I don't want to get into it." This statement was viewed positively by the editor of a hagiography published following the massacre, which is an important, if highly polemical, source for researchers. See "Baruch: Rofeh Holim," reprinted in Mikhael Ben-Horin, ed., *Baruch Ha-Gever: Sefer Zikharon L-Kadosh Dr. Baruch Goldstein HY"D* (Jerusalem: Golan, 1995), 340.

51. Ayelet Lerman, "Baruch's Answers—In His Handwriting," in Ben-Horin, *Baruch Ha-Gever*, 332–333.

52. For his views on terrorism, see broadsheet circulated in advance of elections, "Shelot V'Teshuvot Im Dr. Baruch Goldstein," in Ben-Horin, *Baruch Ha-Gever*, 347. On the yellow star, see Robert Paine, "Beyond the Hebron Massacre, 1994," *Anthropology Today* 11, no. 1 (February 1995): 12.

53. See Chris Hedges and Joel Greenberg, "Before Killing, Final Prayers and Final Taunt," *New York Times*, 28 February 1994, A1; Mitchell, "A Killer's Path to Militancy," 7.

54. "Baruch: Rofeh Holim," reprinted in Ben-Horin, *Baruch Ha-Gever*, 337.

55. Mitchell, "A Killer's Path to Militancy," 7.

56. Some scholars have argued that this holiday is associated with a general trend of Jewish violence; see Elliot Horowitz, *Reckless Rites: Purim and the Legacy of Jewish Violence* (Princeton, NJ: Princeton University Press, 1996). The festival has also taken on profound significance in contemporary Hebron; for two perspectives on this issue, see Michael Feige, *Settling in the Hearts*, chap. 7, and Auerbach, *Hebron Jews*, chap. 7.

57. Hedges and Greenberg, "Before Killing, Final Prayers and Final Taunt," A1. On chants in the mosque, see Carl Bishop, "A Visitor to Israel Tells of the Horrors of Visiting Cave of Machpella," *Jewish Press*, 11–17 March 1994. On

planned attacks, see, for example, Dr. Chaim Sim, "Op-Ed: Baruch Goldstein and Hebron Ten Years Later," *Israel National News,* 2 March 2004, http://www .israelnationalnews.com/Articles/Article.aspx/3408; Barry Chamish, "Was Baruch Goldstein Completely Innocent?," http://vaam.tripod.com/Aug2198.html; and Manfred R. Lehmann, "One Year Later . . . Purim Hebron Remembered," http://www.manfredlehmann.com/sieg440.html. On warnings, see Auerbach, *Hebron Jews,* 125.

58. "Warning Reported before Hebron Massacre," *New York Times,* 13 March 1994, 19. This news was first reported in the Israeli weekly *Shishi;* the authenticity and reaction to the message remain unknown.

59. Clyde Haberman, "New Clashes Likely: Massacre Sets Off Riots Causing More Deaths in the Territories," *New York Times,* 26 February 1994, 1.

60. 168th Statement in the Knesset by Prime Minister Yitzhak Rabin.

61. See Batsheva Tsur, "Weizman: Worst Thing in Zionism," *Jerusalem Post,* 27 February 1994, 3.

62. Chaim Herzog, "A Dagger in Democracy's Back," *Jerusalem Post,* 18 March 1994, 4A.

63. Dan Izenberg, "Peres Outraged at Supporters of Goldstein," *Jerusalem Post,* 1 March 1994, 2.

64. Schoffman, "My Fellow Lunatics."

65. Batsheva Tsur, "Tsaban: US Extremists Should Be Forbidden to Immigrate," *Jerusalem Post,* 1 March 1994, 2.

66. The bill was quickly condemned by leading human rights groups in Israel as well as Jewish Agency aliya department director Uri Gordon, who proclaimed, "I would rather see one million Gush Emunim supporters making aliya than one million socialists remaining in the Diaspora . . . this government may be able to prevent extreme right-wingers from coming and another government would do that to the extreme left. Where will our democracy be?" See Batsheva Tsur, "Gordon: Rejecting Immigrants for Their Political Views Is Not Acceptable," *Jerusalem Post,* 16 March 1994, 2.

67. Haberman, "Massacre at Hebron."

68. Teddy Preuss, "An Easy Excuse for Murder," *Jerusalem Post,* 28 February 1994, 6.

69. Haberman, "Massacre at Hebron."

70. Clyde Haberman, "Some Expect Violence; Others See Pressure for Peace Talks," *New York Times,* 27 February 1994, 1.

71. Haberman, "Massacre at Hebron."

72. Keinon, "Walking a Thin Line."

73. Jonathan Blass, "Only Barrier against Chaos," *Jerusalem Post,* 3 March 1994, 6.

74. Naftali Greenwood, "Confessions of a Co-Conspirator," *Jerusalem Post,* 4 March 1994, 5A.

75. David Wilder, "I Was Baruch Goldstein's Friend," *Jewish Press,* 28 February 2014.

76. David Wilder, interview with the author, 7 July 2009.

77. Hedges and Greenberg, "Before Killing, Final Prayers and Final Taunt."

78. Clyde Haberman, "Israeli Curbs on Far-Right Settlers Provoke Only Scorn from Targets," *New York Times* 4 March 1994, A10.

79. Elli Fisher, "Portrait of an Accused Jewish Terrorist as a Young Man," *Jewish Week,* 12 February 2009, http://www.thejewishweek.com/features/portrait _accused_jewish_terrorist_young_man.

80. Will Yakowicz, "'V' is for Victory—The Odyssey of Jack Teitel: An Intimate Look at the Accused Jewish Killer," *Tablet Magazine,* 14 July 2010, http://tabletmag.com/jewish-news-and-politics/32679/tytell.

81. In fact, there is growing evidence of the pivotal role of Jewish-American immigrants in this new branch of the Israeli settler movement; see Matt McAllester, "American Teens Are Fighting Back in Israel," *Details,* July 2009, http://www.details.com/culture-trends/news-and-politics/200907/american-teens -are-fighting-back-in-Israel.

82. Chaim Levinson, "Who Is Suspected Jewish Terrorist Yaakov Teitel?," *Haaretz,* 1 November 2009.

83. Ibid. See also the public Shin Bet report on Jack Teitel, "Sherut Bitahon Klali: Hakirat Yaakov (Jack) Teitel—Pianuah Sharsheret Piguim," n.d., http://www .shabak.gov.il/SiteCollectionImages/Hebrew/TerrorInfo/docs/shotef111109.pdf.

84. Settlement officials claimed to know nothing about, and to be unsupportive of, his violent activities, although Teitel turned out not to be the only terrorist in their midst; in 2006, native Israeli Shvut Rachel resident Asher Weisgan was convicted of committing a quintuple homicide against Palestinian co-workers. See Joshua Mitnick, "The Two Faces of Accused Terrorist Jack Teitel," *Jewish Week,* 4 November 2009, http://www.thejewishweek.com/features/two_faces _accused_terrorist_jack_teitel.

85. Levinson, "Who Is Suspected Jewish Terrorist Yaakov Teitel?"

86. Yakowicz, "'V' is for Victory."

87. Levinson, "Who Is Suspected Jewish Terrorist Yaakov Teitel?"

88. Chaim Levinson, "Psychiatrist Rules Accused Jewish Terrorist Jack Teitel Psychotic, Unfit to Stand Trial," *Haaretz,* 5 May 2010.

89. Some have suggested that a change of targets led to his later arrest, as state authorities may have been more aggressive in pursuing justice for Jewish victims than Palestinians. See Gershom Gorenberg, "Yaakov Teitel and the Allure of Lawlessness," *American Prospect,* 5 November 2009, http://prospect.org/article /yaakov-teitel-and-allure-lawlessness-0.

90. See "Sherut Bitahon Klali: Hakirat Yaakov (Jack) Teitel."

91. Yoni Gabbai, "Ha-Shabak Hoshed: Teitel Rasah Od Hamisha Palestinim," *Kikar Ha-Shabbat,* 3 November 2009, http://www.kikarhashabat.co.il/.

92. See photos of the weaponry in "Sherut Bitahon Klali: Hakirat Yaakov (Jack) Teitel," appendix.

93. See "Israeli Settler Yaakov Teitel Goes on Trial for Murder," BBC, 9 December 2009. Teitel was originally declared mentally incompetent (Levinson, "Accused Jewish Terrorist Jack Teitel Pscyhotic"). However, this position was reversed in 2011; see Joanna Paraszczuk, "Court Rules Yaakov 'Jack' Teitel Fit to Stand Trial," *Jerusalem Post,* 12 July 2011.

94. "Israeli Settler Yaakov Teitel Goes on Trial for Murder."

95. Aviel Magnezi, "'Jewish Terrorist' Jack Teitel Convicted," *Yediot Ahronot,* 16 January 2013.

96. "Jack Teitel, 'Jewish Terrorist,' Appeals Verdict to Supreme Court," *Yediot Ahronot,* 21 May 2013.

97. Nurit Rot, "Korbanotav Shel Yaakov Teitel Tovaim Pizui B-Sah 4 Milion Shekel," *The Marker,* 12 November 2009, http://www.themarker.com/law/1.549332.

98. Yisrael Medad, "Waging a War for Democracy," *Jerusalem Post,* 15 October 1991, 6.

99. Yisrael Medad, "I Wasn't Invited," *My Right Word* (blog), 11 January 2007, http://myrightword.blogspot.co.uk/2007/01/i-wasnt-invited.html. Medad also posted a photo of his group meeting with Prime Minster Shamir. See photo insert, figure 9.

100. See Allison Kaplan, "Violence Clouds Shamir's Arrival," *Jerusalem Post,* 30 October 1991, 2, and Robert Ruby, "To Extremist Arabs and Israelis, Peace Effort Call for Increase in Violence—To Hardliners, Talks Threaten Basic Belief in Right to Territory," *Baltimore Sun,* 30 October 1991.

101. Shifra (Sharon) Blass, interview with the author, 29 March 2009.

102. "Crossroads: Israelis of Differing Viewpoints Gather in Madrid for Historic Peace Conference," *Harrisonberg Daily News Record,* 30 October 1991, 31.

103. Yisrael Medad, interview with the author (I), 3 March 2009.

104. Ibid.

105. In contrast, Benjamin Netanyahu has been keen to utilize the talents of Jewish-American settlers during his administrations, appointing Yechiel Leiter as his chief of staff at the Ministry of Finance and helping him run as a contender in the 2008 Likud primary, setting up an advocacy group called Likud Anglos with a large American-Israeli settler membership (see http://www.likudanglos.org.il/), and most recently appointing Jewish-American settler Ari Harow (son of Efrat settler Eve Harow, see Chapter 2) as his chief of staff; see http://www.timesofisrael.com/pm-to-appoint-us-born-harow-as-chief-of-staff/. Harow has since left his position under a fraud probe, although at the time of writing was exonerated.

106. Yisrael Medad, interview with the author (I), 3 March 2009.

107. *YESHA Speaker's Bureau: Sponsored by the Jewish Communities in Judea, Samaria, and Gaza* (Jerusalem: Moetzet Ha-Yishuvim Ha-Yehudiyim B-Yehuda, Shomron, V-Hevel Aza, 1992).

108. "Bottom Bar," *YESHA Report* 1 (April 1992): 1.

109. On the YESHA Zeh Kan promotion, see "Yesha Information Campaign Launched," *YESHA Report* 19 (February–March 1994): 5. On media appearances, see Yechiel Leiter, interview with the author, 23 June 2009. On the Library of Congress campaign see "Yesha and Washington Share Resources," *YESHA Report* (February 1995): 6. For the Internet initiative, see "Yesha in Cyberspace," *YESHA Report* (July–August 1996): 11.

110. See, for example, Jason Elbaum, *Peace Now: Playing with the Facts* (Jerusalem: Foreign Desk, YESHA Council of Jewish Communities in Judea, Samaria, and Gaza, 1993). See also Yedidya Atlas, Mike Altmann, and Eliyahu Tal, eds., *Israel in Medialand: A Study of the International Media's Coverage of the*

Uprising (Intifada) in Judea, Samaria, and the Gaza Strip—December 1987 to August 1988 (Tel Aviv: Jerusalem Post/Tal Communications, 1988); Yisrael Medad and Eli Pollack, *Israel's Electronic Broadcasting: Reporting or Managing the News?* (Tel Aviv: Ariel Center for Policy Research, 1988); and Yisrael Medad, *"But I Saw It . . . I Read It . . . I Heard It . . .": The Activist's Guide to Monitoring Media Bias toward Israel* (Jerusalem: Israel's Media Watch, 2003). Medad also formed Israel Media Watch (http://www.imw.org.il/english/) and Efrat resident David Bedein established two linked organizations of the Israel Resource News Agency and Center for Near East Policy Research (http://israelbehindthenews.com /about-cfnepr-irna/#CFNEPR) to serve as media watchdogs. See David Bedein, interview with the author, 8 July 2014.

111. See Yehudit Tayar, "Yesha Council Unveils Ambitious Tourism Campaign," *YESHA Report* (August 1997): 5; Yehudit Tayar, "Yesha Launches Tourism Campaign," *YESHA Report* (November 1997): 5; and "Yesha News—The Yesha Tourist Authority," *YESHA Report* (March–April 2000): 12.

112. See "Save the Dates" (special advertising section), *YESHA Report* (June 1997) and an account by participant Alan H. Rauzin, "The Yesha Mission's Journey," *YESHA Report* (September–October 1997): 12.

113. See, for example, "YESHA Attends the CJF General Assembly," *YESHA Report* (November–December 1994): 4, and "Yesha's Leaders on the North American Campaign Trail," *YESHA Report* 26 (January 1995): 1.

114. Yechiel Leiter, interview with the author, 23 June 2009.

115. Yisrael Medad, interview with the author (I), 3 March 2009.

116. Yechiel Leiter, interview with the author, 23 June 2009.

117. Ibid.

118. Shifra (Sharon) Blass, interview with the author, 29 March 2009.

119. Ibid.

120. Rabbi Jonathan Blass, interview with the author, 15 June 2009.

121. Aliza Herbst, interview with the author, 26 June 2009.

122. Yisrael Medad, interview with the author (II), 20 July 2009.

123. Yechiel Leiter, interview with the author, 23 June 2009.

124. During this period Leiter wrote three treatises published by the YESHA Council Foreign Desk and other affiliates that help elaborate his political philosophy. See Yechiel M. Leiter, *A Peace to Resist: Why the Rabin-Arafat Deal Must Be Stopped and How It Can Be Done* (Jerusalem: YESHA Council Foreign Desk, 1993); Leiter, *Crisis in Israel* (New York: S.P.I. Books, 1994); and Leiter, *Israel at the Crossroads: The View from the Hills of Judea and Samaria* (New York: One Israel Fund/YESHA Heartland Campaign, 1999).

125. Yechiel Leiter, "Children of the Opposition," *YESHA Report* (undated 1994).

126. Yechiel M. Leiter, "Hebron: A Microcosm of the Middle East," *YESHA Report* (April–May 1994): 4.

127. Yechiel Leiter, transcript of Arutz Sheva radio show *At the Crossroads,* reprinted as "Their Unfinished Work," *YESHA Report* (February 1997): 5.

128. Bobby Brown, interview with the author, 25 March 2009.

129. Yisrael Medad, interview with the author (I), 3 March 2009. From Leiter's perspective, this kind of consolidation was an antidemocratic disadvantage

and decision making should be the charge of the "representative body" of the YESHA Council rather than "a few individuals." Yechiel Leiter, interview with the author, 23 June 2009.

130. Bobby Brown, interview with the author, 25 March 2009.

131. See http://www.oneisraelfund.org/.

132. See http://www.goshomron.com. Mr. Ha-Ivri declined my request for an interview on a number of occasions.

133. On Ariel, see Avi Zimmerman, interview with the author, 31 July 2014.

134. See Oded Ravivi, "Beyond the Lines," *Times of Israel,* 28 July 2016.

135. Shmuel Sackett, interview with the author, summer 2009.

136. Ibid.

137. Moshe Feiglin, *Where There Are No Men: Zo Artzeienu's Struggle against the Post-Zionism Collapse,* trans. Menachem Block, Jay Shapiro, and Yitzhak Sapir (Jerusalem: Jewish Leadership Institute, 1999), 24. Note the translation work of Jewish-American settler activist and Karnei Shomrom resident Jay Shapiro.

138. Ibid., 63.

139. Shmuel Sackett, interview with the author, summer 2009.

140. Feiglin, *Where There Are No Men,* 62.

141. Ibid., 10.

142. Ibid., 42–43.

143. See Shmuel Sackett, interview with the author, summer 2009; Feiglin, *Where There Are No Men,* 84, italics in the original text.

144. Feiglin, *Where There Are No Men,* 76; Herb Keinon, "Feiglin & Co. Hit the Big Time," *Jerusalem Post,* 15 September 1995, 9.

145. Feiglin, *Where There Are No Men,* 21.

146. Herb Keinon, "Group Plans Groundbreaking for 130 'New Settlements' Tomorrow," *Jerusalem Post,* 23 December 1993, 2. Feiglin and Sackett assured the reporter that land was chosen following "a careful check of ownership of the land, and no private Arab land will be used," without detailing any efforts or methodology in doing so.

147. Shmuel Sackett, interview with the author, summer 2009.

148. Feiglin, *Where There Are No Men,* 105.

149. Feiglin later admitted that the Jewish foundation for civil disobedience was weak and might violate Jewish ethics; see Michael Arnold, "Taking It to the Streets," *Jerusalem Post,* 19 December 1997, 19.

150. Feiglin, *Where There Are No Men,* 105.

151. Ibid., 111–112.

152. Ibid., 154.

153. Ibid., 140.

154. Ibid. The original iteration of the plan sounded more like vigilante action than nonviolent resistance, as Sackett added, "We will stop suspicious Arab cars and check for weapons . . . we are ready for gunfights with the Palestinians if it will come to that," although he added that they would utilize only passive resistance (without defining this term) against IDF forces. See also Herb Keinon, "Revived Settler Group Plans Roads Takeover," *Jerusalem Post,* 28 July 1995, 2.

155. See five full pages of coverage and photographs in "Medina Stuma," *Yediot Ahronot,* 9 August 1995, 1–4. Israel Radio's traffic reporter surveyed the scene from a helicopter, as reported in Herb Keinon and Jacob Dallal, "Protestors Snarl Traffic All Over the Country," *Jerusalem Post,* 9 August 1995, 1.

156. Keinon and Dallal, "Protestors Snarl Traffic All Over the Country."

157. Shmuel Sackett, interview with the author, summer 2009.

158. Herb Keinon and Bill Hutman, "Police Break Up Anti-Gov't Protest in Capital. 22 Arrested, 30 Injured; Shahal: We Showed Restraint," *Jerusalem Post,* 14 September 1995. Police activity resulted in an investigation by the Ministry of Justice.

159. Arnold, "Taking It to the Streets."

160. Shmuel Sackett, interview with the author, summer 2009.

161. Arnold, "Taking It to the Streets."

162. Ibid. See also, Feiglin, *Where There Are No Men,* 205–206.

163. Feiglin, *Where There Are No Men,* 221.

164. Herb Keinon, "Protestors Back Zo Artzenu Leaders Going on Trial Today," *Jerusalem Post,* 17 January 1996, 2.

165. Shmuel Sackett, interview with the author, summer 2009. Emphasis was his. On Sackett's comparison to Soviet Jewry, see also Feiglin, *Where There Are No Men,* 234.

166. See Keinon, "Protestors Back Zo Artzenu Leaders" and Herb Keinon, "Zo Artzenu Leaders Guilty of Sedition," *Jerusalem Post,* 3 September 1997, 3.

167. See Feiglin, *Where There Are No Men,* 231–232. Feiglin also called Yisrael Medad as a witness on his behalf to describe 1960s civil disobedience, including the civil rights movement, to the court. See Feiglin, *Where There Are No Men,* 237.

168. Ibid., 166.

169. Shmuel Sackett, interview with the author, summer 2009.

170. Ibid. For the platform of Manhigut Yehudit, see http://www.jewishisrael .org/. For a scholarly analysis of the movement, see Inbari, *Messianic Zionism Confronts Israeli Territorial Compromises* (Cambridge: Cambridge University Press, 2012), chap. 5.

171. See Moshe Feiglin, "God Owns Cannabis Patent," *Yediot Ahronot,* 20 September 2012, http://www.ynetnews.com/articles/0,7340,L-4284110,00.html.

172. Both activists have repeatedly criticized Netanyahu from the right flank. Feiglin indicted him as part of the "the Zionist establishment [which] had been submerged by post-Zionism"; see Feiglin, *Where There Are No Men,* 255. Similarly, Sackett considered that "Netanyahu has lived down all my expectations" and alleged that "our new Prime Minster . . . doesn't have the mandate he thinks he has." See Shmuel Sackett, "Disappointed? Not Me," *Jerusalem Post,* 11 September 1996, 6. Sackett also attempted to run for political office in 2008 in the designated immigrant spot on the Likud list; see Shelly Paz, "New York-Born Likud Contender Promises to Promote Aliya and Fight a Two-State Solution," *Jerusalem Post,* 7 December 2008, 2. He and other Anglo candidates ultimately lost to Russian and Ethiopian immigrants, but American-Israeli contenders like Yechiel Leiter and Yossi Fuchs alleged intimidation by "the Feiglin machine" for their electoral failure; see Gil Hoffman, "Anglo Likud Candidates Shut Out of the Knesset," *Jerusalem Post,* 10 December 2008, 3. This charge was repeated by

Jewish-American settler Jeremy Gimpel in the 2012 elections; see Gil Hoffman, "Aiming High," *Jerusalem Post,* 10 August 2012, 8.

173. Jim Rutenberg, Mike McIntire, and Ethan Bronner, "Tax-Exempt Funds Aiding Settlements in the West Bank," *New York Times,* 6 July 2010, A1. Sackett has self-consciously modeled his fundraising strategy on U.S. president Barack Obama's small-donations campaign, telling a reporter that "our campaign is a grassroots effort, it's important to enable as many people as possible to feel like they are a part of it." See Gil Hoffman, "Feiglin Adopts Obama's Fund-Raising Strategy," *Jerusalem Post,* 22 January 2012, 4.

174. Shmuel Sackett, interview with the author, summer 2009.

175. See Sara Yael Hirschhorn, "Israeli Terrorists, Born in the U.S.A.," *New York Times,* 4 September 2015, http://www.nytimes.com/2015/09/06/opinion/sunday /israeli-terrorists-born-in-the-usa.html?_r=0.

176. "Israeli Trump Supporters Open Campaign Office in West Bank," *Reuters,* 5 September 2016, http://www.reuters.com/article/us-election-westbank -idUSKCN11B1XP.

177. Josef Federman, "Invites in Hand, Settlers See Trump Inauguration as Sign They've Arrived," *Times of Israel,* 20 January 2017, http://www.timesofisrael.com /invites-in-hand-settlers-see-trump-inauguration-as-sign-theyve-arrived/.

Conclusion

1. In June 2014, I took part in the Tel Aviv University Minerva Center conference "The Settlements in the West Bank (1967–2014): New Perspectives," which brought together the first generation of scholars on settlements with a new group of early-career researchers addressing new developments and lacunae in the canon. See https://settlementsworkshop.wordpress.com/programme/. It is my hope that the fruits of this research agenda will be an important contribution to a second generation of literature on the Israeli settler movement.

2. Provocative commentary on the failure of the two-state solution can be found in Ian S. Lustick, "The Two-State Delusion," *New York Times,* 14 September 2013, http://www.nytimes.com/2013/09/15/opinion/sunday/two-state-illusion .html; and Padraig O'Malley, *The Two-State Delusion: Israel and Palestine—A Tale of Two Narratives* (New York: Viking, 2015).

3. Much scholarship and punditry has been devoted to this issue; see two recent commentaries: Dov Waxman, *Trouble in the Tribe: The American Jewish Conflict over Israel* (Princeton, NJ: Princeton University Press, 2016); and Michael Barnett, *The Star and the Stripes: A History of the Foreign Policies of American Jews* (Princeton, NJ: Princeton University Press, 2016).

4. See Mosaic Magazine, "If American Jews and Israel Are Drifting Apart, What Is the Reason?," roundtable, April 2016, http://mosaicmagazine.com/essay /2016/04/if-american-jews-and-israel-are-drifting-apart-whats-the-reason/, although it should be noted that many of the leaders who penned these essays have presided over these failures for the past five decades.

5. One interesting trend to watch will be the changing of the guard at many Jewish organizations run by an aging leadership that has been in office for

decades, such as the recent appointment of a new CEO of the Anti-Defamation League to replace veteran Abe Foxman; see Nathan Guttman and Noah Smith, "Anti-Defamation League Signals New Path as Jonathan Greenblatt Takes Helm," *Jewish Daily Forward,* 13 November 2014.

6. See the recent in-depth investigative report; see Judy Maltz, "From the BDS Frontlines: How the On-Campus Brawl Is Turning Young Jews Off Israel," *Haaretz,* 9 May 2016, http://www.haaretz.com/jewish/features/1.717781.

7. See Pew Research Center, *A Portrait of Jewish Americans: Findings from a Pew Research Center Survey of U.S. Jews* (Washington: Pew Research Center, 2013). Peter Beinart has also pointed specifically to the impact of the Israeli occupation on millennials; see Peter Beinart, *The Crisis of Zionism* (New York: Times Books, 2012). However, I disagree with his analysis and contend that millennials' disengagement from Israeli and Zionism has more to do with Jewish identity (or lack thereof) than with specific developments or policies in Israel/Palestine.

8. See, for example, Richard North Patterson, "Israel Is the GOP's New Wedge Issue," *Boston Globe,* 28 July 2015, https://www.bostonglobe.com /opinion/2015/07/28/israel-gop-new-wedge-issue/xorLiSr5vfFnuM4zXSTBDO /story.html, and Jason Horowitz and Maggie Haberman, "A Split over Israel Threatens the Democrats' Hope for Unity," *New York Times,* 25 May 2016, http://www.nytimes.com/2016/05/26/us/politics/bernie-sanders-israel-democratic -convention.html.

9. A somewhat less concise version of his oft-repeated quote originally appeared in Milton Himmelfarb, "The Jewish Vote—Again," *Commentary* 55, no. 6 (June 1973): 81. On larger trends, see recent data from the 2013 Pew Survey, *A Portrait of Jewish Americans,* 96–101. See also discussions in Staub, *Torn at the Roots;* Dollinger, *Quest for Inclusion;* and Steven M. Cohen, *The Dimensions of American Jewish Liberalism* (New York: American Jewish Committee, 1989).

10. See Pew Research Center, *A Portrait of Jewish Americans* and Jonathan Rynhold, *The Arab-Israeli Conflict in American Political Culture* (Cambridge: Cambridge University Press, 2015).

11. This may be seen as the culmination of a decades-long demographic and ideological shift within the Democratic Party; see Rynhold, *Arab-Israeli Conflict.* On Adelson, see Sheldon G. Adelson, "I Didn't Leave the Democrats, They Left Me," *Wall Street Journal,* 4 November 2012, http://www.wsj.com/articles/SB10001 424052970204712904578092670469140316.

12. See Norman Podhoretz, *Why Are Jews Liberals?* (New York: Doubleday, 2009) and Ruth R. Wisse, *If I Am Not for Myself: The Liberal Betrayal of the Jews* (New York: Free Press, 1992).

13. On voter priorities, see Robert P. Jones and Daniel Cox, *Chosen for What? Jewish Values in 2012* (Washington, DC: Public Religion Research Institute, 2012), http://publicreligion.org/site/wp-content/uploads/2012/04/Jewish-Values -Report.pdf.

14. Jon Huang, Samuel Jacoby, Michael Strickland, and K.K. Rebecca Lai, "Election 2016: Exit Polls," *New York Times,* 8 November 2016 and Gregory A.

Smith and Jessica Martinez, "How the Faithful Voted: A Preliminary 2016 Analysis," Pew Research Center, 9 November 2016, http://www.pewresearch.org /fact-tank/2016/11/09/how-the-faithful-voted-a-preliminary-2016-analysis/.

15. Armin Rosen, "The Orthodox Vote for Trump," *Tablet Magazine,* 27 September 2016, http://www.tabletmag.com/scroll/214696/the-orthodox-vote-for -trump.

16. Smith and Martinez, "How the Faithful Voted."

17. See, for example, "Joint Statement from Jason Dov Greenblatt and David Friedman, Co-Chairmen of the Israel Advisory Committee to Donald Trump," *Medium,* 2 November 2016, https://medium.com/@jgreenblatt/joint-statement -from-jason-dov-greenblatt-and-david-friedman-co-chairmen-of-the-israel-advisory -edc1ec50b7a8#.ojpj2u2zb.

18. See, for example, "Factsheet—Hillary Clinton and Israel: A 30-Year Record of Friendship, Leadership, and Strength," https://www.hillaryclinton.com /briefing/factsheets/2015/09/08/israel-friendship-leadership-strength/.

19. Rynhold, *Arab-Israeli Conflict,* 85.

20. This perspective has been adopted more widely in the field of American Jewish history of late; see Ava Fran Kahn and Adam Mendelsohn, eds., *Transnational Traditions: New Perspectives on American Jewish History* (Detroit: Wayne State University Press, 2014).

21. One scholar who has examined these comparative frontiers and deeply inspired my own line of inquiry is S. Ilan Troen; see his "Frontier Myths and their Applications in America and Israel." See also Silver, *First Contact;* and Henry Near, *Frontiersmen and Halutzim: The Image of Pioneer in North America and Pre-state Jewish Palestine—Discussion Paper* (Haifa: University of Haifa, 1997).

22. See Frederick Jackson Turner, *The Significance of the Frontier in American History* (London: Penguin, 2008). For a more contemporary analysis of his ideas, see John Whitehead, "How Have American Historians Viewed the Frontier?," meeting of Frontiers Conference, Library of Congress (summary), 21 September 2010, https://www.loc.gov/rr/european/mofc/whitehead.html.

23. For a revisionist history of manifest destiny, see Anders Stephanson, *Manifest Destiny: American Expansion and the Empire of Right* (New York: Hill and Wang, 1995).

24. See Jeremy Adelman and Stephen Aron, "From Borderlands to Borders: Empires, Nation-States, and the People in between in North American History," *American Historical Review* 104, no. 3 (June 1999): 816. For a critique of this article beyond American borderlands, see Evan Haefeli, "A Note on the Use of North American Borderlands," *American Historical Review* 104, no. 4 (October 1999): 1222–1225. See also Patricia Nelson Limerick, *The Legacy of Conquest: The Unbroken Past of the American West* (New York: Norton, 1987); Howard Roberts Lamar and Leonard Monteath Thompson, *The Frontier in History: North America and South Africa Compared* (New Haven, CT: Yale University Press, 1981); and Gregory H. Nobles, *American Frontiers: Cultural Encounters and Continental Conquest* (New York: Hill and Wang, 1997).

25. For some introductory texts on the Puritans, see Michael Parker, *John Winthrop: Founding the City upon a Hill* (New York: Routledge, 2014); Loren

Baritz, *City on a Hill: A History of Ideas and Myths in America* (New York: Wiley, 1964); Francis J. Bremer, *First Founders: American Puritans and Puritanism in an Atlantic World* (Durham: University of New Hampshire Press, 2012); and David D. Hall, *Puritans in the New World: A Critical Anthology* (Princeton, NJ: Princeton University Press, 2004). See also a lay treatment of the revisionist history of the Salem witch trials, Stacy Schiff, "The Witches of Salem," *New Yorker,* 7 September 2015. On the Halutzim, see, for example, Boaz Neumann, *Land and Desire in Early Zionism,* trans. Haim Watzman (Waltham, MA: Brandeis University Press, 2011).

26. See, for example, Jonathan Sacks, *Not in God's Name: Confronting Religious Violence* (London: Hodder and Stoughton, 2015); Mark Juergensmeyer, *Terror in the Mind of God: The Global Rise of Religious Violence* (Berkeley: University of California Press, 2000); and Richard Brian Miller, *Terror, Religion and Liberal Thought* (New York: Columbia University Press, 2010).

27. One important recent study is Mazower, *No Enchanted Palace.*

28. See Elliot Abrams, *The Influence of Faith: Religious Groups and U.S. Foreign Policy* (Lanham: Rowman and Littlefield, 2001), x. Other contributions to the scholarship include Stephen R. Rock, *Faith and Foreign Policy: The Views and Influence of U.S. Christians and Christian Organizations* (New York: Continuum International, 2011); Robert W. Merry, *Sands of Empire: Missionary Zeal, American Foreign Policy, and the Hazards of Global Ambition* (New York: Simon and Schuster, 2005); Robert Wuthnow and John Hyde Evans, eds., *The Quiet Hand of God: Faith-Based Activism and the Public Role of Mainline Protestantism* (Berkeley: University of California Press, 2002); Michael N. Barnett and Janice Gross Stein, *Sacred Aid: Faith and Humanitarianism* (New York: Oxford University Press, 2012); and R. Marie Griffith and Melani McAlister, *Religion and Politics in the Contemporary United States* (Baltimore: Johns Hopkins University Press, 2008).

29. There is an increasingly robust canon utilizing this approach. See, for example, Andrew Preston, *Sword of the Spirit, Shield of Faith: Religion in American War and Diplomacy* (New York: Knopf, 2012); Andrew Preston, Bruce J. Schulman, and Julian E. Zelitzer, eds., *Faithful Republic: Religion and Politics in Modern America* (Philadelphia: University of Pennsylvania Press, 2015); Nan Goodman and Michael P. Kramer, eds., *The Turn around Religion in America: Literature, Culture, and the Work of Sacvan Bercovitch* (Burlington, VT: Ashgate, 2011); Jonathan Chaplin and Robert Joustra, eds., *God and Global Order: The Power of Religion in American Foreign Policy* (Waco, TX: Baylor University Press, 2010); William Inboden, *Religion and American Foreign Policy, 1945–1960: The Soul of Containment* (Cambridge: Cambridge University Press, 2008); Dianne Kirby, ed., *Religion and the Cold War* (New York: Palgrave, 2003); Jonathan P. Herzog, *The Spiritual-Industrial Complex: America's Religious Battle against Communism in the Early Cold War* (New York: Oxford University Press, 2011); William Steding, *Presidential Faith and Foreign Policy: Jimmy Carter the Disciple and Ronald Reagan the Alchemist* (New York: Palgrave Macmillan, 2014); Malcolm D. Magee, *What the World Should Be: Woodrow Wilson and the Crafting of a Faith-Based Foreign Policy* (Waco, TX: Baylor University Press, 2008); and Seth Jacobs, *America's Miracle Man in Vietnam: Ngo Dinh Diem,*

Religion, Race, and U.S. Intervention in Southeast Asia, 1950–1957 (Durham, NC: Duke University Press, 2004).

30. Barbara J. Keys, *Reclaiming American Virtue: The Human Rights Revolution of the 1970s* (Cambridge: Harvard University Press, 2014), 11–12.

31. From a historical perspective, one excellent study is Manela, *The Wilsonian Moment*. See also the classic critique, William Appelman Williams, *The Tragedy of American Diplomacy* (New York: W. W. Norton, 1972); as well as Frank Ninkovich, *The United States and Imperialism* (Malden, MA: Blackwell, 2001); Tony Smith, *America's Mission: The United States and the Worldwide Struggle for Democracy in the Twentieth Century* (Princeton, NJ: Princeton University Press, 1994); Michael H. Hunt, *Ideology and U.S. Foreign Policy* (New Haven, CT: Yale University Press, 1997); and Niall Ferguson, *Colossus: The Rise and Fall of the American Empire* (London: Penguin, 2005).

32. See, for example, Richard A. Primus, *The American Language of Rights* (Cambridge: Cambridge University Press, 1999); Mary Ann Glendon, *Rights Talk: The Impoverishment of Political Discourse* (New York: Free Press, 1991); and Lynn Hunt, *Inventing Human Rights: A History* (New York: W. W. Norton, 2007).

33. Michael Ignatieff, *American Exceptionalism and Human Rights* (Princeton, NJ: Princeton University Press, 2005), 2.

34. See Moyn, *The Last Utopia*.

35. See Yossi Shain, *Marketing the American Creed Abroad: Diasporas in the U.S. and Their Homelands* (Cambridge: Cambridge University Press, 1999).

36. See C. A. Bayly, Sven Beckert, Matthew Connelley, Isabel Hofmeyr, Wendy Kozol, and Patricia See, "AHR Conversation: On Transnational History," *American Historical Review* 111, no. 5 (December 2006): 1441–1464. See also Ian Tyrrell, *Transnational Nation: United States History in Global Perspective since 1789* (New York: Palgrave Macmillan, 2015). They may more closely resemble other religious internationals; see Abigail Green and Vincent Viaene, eds., *Religious Internationals in the Modern World: Globalization and Faith Communities since 1750* (Basingstoke, UK: Palgrave-Macmillan, 2012).

37. See Samuel Moyn and Andrew Santori, eds., *Global Intellectual History* (New York: Columbia University Press, 2013), 9.

38. Primus, *American Language of Rights*, 6.

39. Ibid., 3.

40. Ibid., 28

41. Rabbi Shlomo Riskin, interview with the author, 27 July 2009.

Appendix

1. See Waxman, *American Aliya*, 230n7.

2. See Haberman, "Massacre at Hebron."

3. Prior to the 2007 volume, the CBS alternatingly aggregated immigrants from the United States with Canada, Europe, and Oceania in a single category.

4. See *Statistical Abstract of Israel*, table 4.9 (Jerusalem: Central Bureau of Statistics, 2007–2014).

5. See Aliza Herbst, interview with the author, summer 2009.

6. See Yisrael Medad, Correspondence with the author, fall 2009.

7. On city settlements, see Avi Zimmerman, interview with the author, 31 July 2014, and Judy Maltz, "In 'Moderate' Jewish Settlement, Signs of Extremism Rear Their Ugly Head," *Haaretz,* 27 August 2015. On outposts, see Matt McAllester, "The Holyland's American Militants," *Details* (September 2009): 218–226.

8. See U.S. Consulate, Jerusalem Political Officer I, correspondence with the author, June 2009. I declined to name the consulate personnel I interviewed in compliance with the U.S. government's request for anonymity.

9. See U.S. Consulate, Jerusalem, Political Officer II, correspondence with the author, fall 2009. See also Adam Liptak, "Supreme Court Backs White House on Jerusalem Passport Dispute," *New York Times,* 8 June 2015.

Bibliography

Abramov, S. Zalman. *Jewish Religion in the Jewish State.* Rutherford, NJ: Fairleigh Dickinson University Press, 1976.

Abrams, Elliot. *The Influence of Faith: Religious Groups and U.S. Foreign Policy.* Lanham, MD: Rowman and Littlefield, 2001.

Abramson, Edward. *A Circle in the Square: Rabbi Shlomo Riskin Reinvents the Synagogue.* Jerusalem: Urim, 2008.

Adelman, Jeremy, and Stephen Aron. "From Borderlands to Borders: Empires, Nation-States, and the People in between in North American History." *American Historical Review* 104, no. 3 (June 1999): 814–841.

Adelson, Sheldon G. "I Didn't Leave the Democrats, They Left Me." *Wall Street Journal,* 4 November 2012.

"After 5 Years of the Intifada, Israelis Have Learned to Adjust." *Jewish Telegraphic Agency,* 9 December 1992.

Almog, Oz. *The Sabra.* Translated by Haim Watzman. Berkeley: University of California Press, 2000.

Almog, Shmuel, Jehuda Reinharz, and Anita Shapira. *Zionism and Religion.* Hanover, NH: University Press of New England, 1998.

Alsberg, P. A. *The Israel State Archives.* Jerusalem: Israel Archives Association, 1991.

"Am Yisrael, Hi!" *Nekuda,* 22 October 1982, 16–18. [Hebrew]

American Histadrut Cultural Exchange Institute. *The Impact of Israel on American Jewry: A Symposium Sponsored by the American Histadrut Cultural Exchange Institute.* New York: American Histadrut Cultural Exchange Institute, 1969.

"Americans in the Border Settlements." *AACI Bulletin* 12, no. 2 (November 1969): 19.

Amit, David. "Tmorot B-Nofei Gush Etzion." In *Gush Etzion Me-Raishito Ad TS"H,* ed. Mordechai Naor, 3–18. Jerusalem: Yad Yitzhak Ben-Tzvi, 1986. [Hebrew]

Amit, Karen, and Ilan Riss. "The Role of Social Networks in the Immigration Decision-Making Process: The Case of North American Immigration to Israel." *Immigrant Minorities* (2007): 290–313.

Amrami, Jacob. *Bibliografia Shimushit: NILI, Brit Ha-Biryonim, Ha-Tsva Ha-Leumi Lohamei Herut Yisrael.* Tel Aviv: Hadar, 1975. [Hebrew]

Anderson, Benedict. *Imagined Communities: Reflections on the Origins and Spread of Nationalism.* London: Verso, 1983.

Antonovsky, Aaron, and Abraham David Katz. *From the Golden to the Promised Land.* Darby, PA: Norwood Editions, 1979.

Appelyard, Bryon. "Israel's 50th Anniversary." *Sunday Times* (London), 14 May 1998.

Aran, Gideon. *Kukism: Shorashei Gush Emunim, Tarbut Ha-Mitnahalim, Teologia Ziyonit, Meshihut B-Zemanenu.* Jerusalem: Karmel, 2013. [Hebrew]

Arendt, Hannah. *Eichmann in Jerusalem: A Report on the Banality of Evil.* London: Penguin, 2006.

Arens, Moshe. *Broken Covenant: American Foreign Policy and the Crisis between the U.S. and Israel.* New York: Simon and Schuster, 1995.

Arenstein, Zvi. "Shifting Sands at Yamit." *Jerusalem Post Magazine,* 6 January 1978, 4.

Arian, Alan. *The Choosing People: Voting Behavior in Israel.* Cleveland: Case Western Reserve University Press, 1973.

Arian, Asher, ed. *The Elections in Israel, 1977.* Jerusalem: Jerusalem Academic Press, 1980.

———, ed. *The Elections in Israel, 1981.* Tel Aviv: Ramot, 1983.

Arian, Asher, and Michal Shamir, eds. *The Elections in Israel, 1984.* Tel Aviv: Ramot, 1986.

———, eds. *The Elections in Israel, 1988.* Boulder, CO: Westview Press, 1990.

Arnold, Michael. "Taking It to the Streets." *Jerusalem Post,* 19 December 1997, 19.

Atlas, Yedidya, Mike Altmann, and Eliyahu Tal, eds. *Israel in Medialand: A Study of the International Media's Coverage of the Uprising (Intifada) in Judea, Samaria, and the Gaza Strip—December 1987 to August 1988.* Tel Aviv: Jerusalem Post/Tal Communications, 1988.

"Attention Americans & Canadians." *Yamiton,* 16 February 1976, 8–9.

Auerbach, Jerold S. *Hebron Jews: Memory and Conflict in the Land of Israel.* Lanham, MD: Rowman and Littlefield, 2009.

Avineri, Shlomo. *The Makings of Modern Zionism: The Intellectual Origins of the Jewish State.* New York: Basic Books, 1981.

———. "Zionism and Jewish Religious Tradition: The Dialectics of Redemption and Secularization." In *Zionism and Religion,* ed. Shmuel Almog, Jehuda Reinharz, and Anita Shapira, 1–9. Hanover, NH: University Press of New England, 1998.

Avisar, Oded, ed. *Sefer Hevron: Ir Ha-Avot V-Yeshuvah B-Ireh Ha-Dorot.* Jerusalem: Keter, 1970. [Hebrew]

Avishai, Bernard. *A New Israel: Democracy in Crisis, 1973–1988: Essays.* New York: Ticknor and Fields, 1988.

Avniel, Nachum. "Ha-Seter Ha-Adom: Raayon Im Ha-Rav Menachem Fruman." *Makor Rishon,* 1 April 2011. [Hebrew]

Avruch, Kevin. *American Immigrants in Israel: Social Identities and Change.* Chicago: University of Chicago Press, 1981.

———. "Becoming Traditional: Socialization to Bureaucracy among American Immigrants in Israel." *Studies in Comparative International Development* (Fall/Winter 1981): 64–83.

Azaryahu, Maoz. *Tel Aviv: Mythography of a City.* Syracuse, NY: Syracuse University Press, 2007.

Azaryahu, Maoz, and S. Ilan Troen. *Tel Aviv, the First Century: Visions, Designs, Actualities.* Bloomington: Indiana University Press, 2012.

Bailant, Benjamin. *Running Commentary: The Contentious Magazine That Transformed the Jewish Left into the Neo-Conservative Right.* New York: Public Affairs, 2010.

Barber, David. *A Hard Rain Fell: SDS and Why It Failed.* Jackson, MS: University of Mississippi Press, 2008.

Baritz, Loren. *City on a Hill: A History of Ideas and Myths in America.* New York: Wiley, 1964.

Barkat, Amiram, and Daphna Berman. "North American Immigration to Israel to Hit 33-Year High in 2007." *Haaretz,* 7 June 2007.

Barnett, Michael N. *The Empire of Humanity: A History of Humanitarianism.* Ithaca, NY: Cornell University Press, 2011.

———, ed. *Israel in Comparative Perspective.* Albany, NY: SUNY Press, 1996.

———. *The Star and the Stripes: A History of the Foreign Policies of American Jews.* Princeton, NJ: Princeton University Press, 2016.

Barnett, Michael N., and Janice Gross Stein. *Sacred Aid: Faith and Humanitarianism.* New York: Oxford University Press, 2012.

Bar Levy, Mordechai, Yedidya Cohn, and Shlomo Rozner, eds. *B-Meshokh Ha-Yovel: Hamishim Shanot Tenuat Bnai Akiva B-Yisrael.* Tel Aviv: Tenuat Bnai Akiva B-Yisrael, 1987. [Hebrew]

Bar-On, Mordechai. *Etgar Ha-Ribonut: Yetsirah V-Hagut B-Asor Ha-Rishon L-Medinah.* Jerusalem: Yad Yitzhak Ben-Tzvi, 1999. [Hebrew]

Bass, Warren. "Borderline Schizophrenia." *Jerusalem Post,* 28 January 1994, 16.

Baumel-Schwartz, Judith. *The "Bergson Boys" and the Origins of Contemporary Zionist Militancy.* Syracuse, NY: Syracuse University Press, 2005.

Bayly, C. A., Sven Beckert, Matthew Connelley, Isabel Hofmeyr, Wendy Kozol, and Patricia See. "AHR Conversation: On Transnational History." *American Historical Review* 111, no. 5 (December 2006): 1441–1464.

Beckerman, Gal. *When They Come for Us, We'll Be Gone: The Epic Struggle to Save Soviet Jewry.* Boston: Houghton Mifflin Harcourt, 2010.

Beinart, Peter. *The Crisis of Zionism.* New York: Times Books, 2012.

Ben-Ami, Aharon, ed. *Sefer Eretz Yisrael Ha-Shlaima.* Tel Aviv: Ha-Tenuah L-Maan Eretz Yisrael Ha-Shlaima, 1977. [Hebrew]

Ben-Ami, Shlomo. *Scars of War, Wounds of Peace: The Israeli-Arab Tragedy.* Oxford: Oxford University Press, 2006.

Ben-Ari, Eyal, and Yoram Bilu. *Grasping Land: Space and Place in Contemporary Israeli Discourse and Experience.* Albany: SUNY Press, 1997.

Ben-Horin, Mikhail, ed. *Baruch Ha-Gever: Sefer Zikharon L-Kadosh Dr. Baruch Goldstein HY"D.* Jerusalem: Golan, 1995. [Hebrew]

Ben-Meir, Yehuda. *Israeli Public Opinion.* Tel Aviv: Jaffee Center for Strategic Studies, 1995.

Benson, Michael T. *Harry S. Truman and the Founding of Israel.* Westport, CT: Praeger, 1997.

Benvenisti, Meron. *The West Bank Data Project: A Survey of Israel's Policies.* Washington, DC: American Enterprise Institute for Public Policy Research, 1984.

Ben Yaakov, Yekutiel. "Jewish Underground Suspect Replies to Rabbi Bernstein— Challenges Abuse of Religious Rights in Israeli Prisons." *Jewish Press,* 21 September 1984, 56B.

———. "Letters to the Editor: Shocking Report." *Jewish Press,* 1 June 1984, 5.

Ben-Yaakov, Yohanan. "Migdal Eder: Sipuro Shel Ha-Yishuv Ha-Yehudi Ha-Rishon Bein Hevron V-Yerushalayim." In *Gush Etzion M-Raishito Ad T"SH,* ed. Mordechai Naor, 23–40. Jerusalem: Yad Yitzhak Ben-Tzvi, 1986. [Hebrew]

Berenbaum, Michael. "Letter to the Editor: Israeli West Bank Isn't Another Selma." *New York Times,* 12 August 1995, 20.

Berg, Raffi. "Settlers 'Cut Off' by West Bank Barrier." *BBC News,* 29 November 2005.

Berger, Yotam. "Secret 1970 Document Confirms First West Bank Settlements Built on a Lie." *Haaretz,* 28 July 2016.

Berman, Daphna. "Settlers Launch First Drive in U.S. to Sell Homes." *Haaretz,* 3 March 2007.

Berman, Gerald S. *The Experience of Aliyah among Recently Arrived North American Olim: The Role of the Shaliach.* Jerusalem: Hebrew University Work and Welfare Institute, 1977.

———. "Why North Americans Migrate to Israel." *Jewish Journal of Sociology* 21, no. 2 (December 1979): 135–144.

Berman, Morton Mayer. *The Bridge to Life: The Saga of Keren Ha-Yesod, 1920–1970.* Tel Aviv: Shifrin, 1970.

Biale, David. "The Threat of Messianism: An Interview with Gershom Scholem." *New York Review of Books,* 14 August 1980, 22.

Birnbaum, Eli. "Crisis or Challenge? A Guide to Bereavement, Stress, and Modern Day Terror." Unpublished manuscript, 2009.

Bishop, Carl. "A Visitor to Israel Tells of the Horrors of Visiting Cave of Machpella." *Jewish Press,* March 1994, 11–17.

Blass, Jonathan. "Only Barrier against Chaos." *Jerusalem Post,* 3 March 1994, 6.

Bloch, Linda Renee. "Communicating as an American Immigrant in Israel: The Freier Phenomenon and the Pursuit of an Alternative Value System." *Research on Language and Social Interaction* 31, no. 2 (1998): 177–208.

Borrie, W. D., ed. *The Cultural Integration of Immigrants.* Paris: UNESCO, 1959.

"Bottom Bar." *YESHA Report* 1 (April 1992): 1.

Breines, Paul. *Tough Jews: Political Fantasies and the Moral Dilemma of American Jewry.* New York: Basic Books, 1990.

Bremer, Francis J. *First Founders: American Puritans and Puritanism in an Atlantic World.* Durham: University of New Hampshire Press, 2012.

Brill, Bruce. "Justice Never Done." *Jerusalem Post,* 1 July 1994, 5A.

Brilliant, Joshua. "Tekoa Rabbi Rapped over Bi-National State Idea." *Jerusalem Post,* 7 January 1990, 2.

———. "Tekoa Rabbi's Talks with Husseini Draw Anger, Ridicule." *Jerusalem Post,* 24 September 1989, 2.

Brodkin, Karen. *How Jews Became White Folks and What That Says about Race in America.* New Brunswick, NJ: Rutgers University Press, 1998.

Brown, Bobby. "Beit Sahur." *Jerusalem Post,* 6 May 1991.

———. "Mr. Begin, We Are Coming . . ." *Jewish Press,* 16–22 September 1977.

———. "Zionist Youth Movements in the United States and Their Influence on Immigration to Israel after World War II" (interview with Zvi Fraser). Interview 178(2), 1981 Oral History Division, Avraham Harman Institute of Contemporary Jewry, Hebrew University of Jerusalem.

Brown, Michael. *The Israeli-American Connection: Its Roots in the Yishuv, 1914–1945.* Detroit: Wayne State University Press, 1996.

Buber, Martin. *On Zion.* New York: Schocken Books, 1983.

Butler, Eamonn. *Classical Liberalism: A Primer.* London: Institute of Economic Affairs, 2015.

Butler, Menachem, and Zev Nagel, eds. *My Yeshiva College: 75 Years of Memories.* New York: Yashar Books, 2006.

Canaan, Don. "Paradise Regained, Paradise Lost." *Israel Faxx,* 24 April 1995.

Carson, Claybourne. *In Struggle: SNCC and the Black Awakening of the 1960s.* Cambridge, MA: Harvard University Press, 1995.

Cashman, Greer Fay. "Efrat Protestors Vow to Struggle On." *Jerusalem Post,* 4 August 1995, 2.

———. "Newsline with Bobby Brown." *Jerusalem Post,* 12 July 1993, 2.

Casper, Bernard M. "Reshit Zemichat Geulatenu." In *Tradition and Transition: Essays Presented to Chief Rabbi Sir Emmanuel Jakobovits to Celebrate Twenty Years in Office,* ed. Rabbi Jonathan Sacks, 107–116. London: Jews' College Publications, 1986.

Chamish, Barry. "Was Baruch Goldstein Completely Innocent?"

Chandler, Doug. "Family Living in Israel Experience." *Aliyon* (Winter 1985): 31.

Chaplin, Jonathan, and Robert Joustra, eds. *God and Global Order: The Power of Religion in American Foreign Policy.* Waco, TX: Baylor University Press, 2010.

Chen, Joanna. "Rabbi with a Cause: An Interview with Rabbi Menachem Froman." *Newsweek International,* 16 April 2001.

Chenkin, Alvin. "Demographic Highlights: Facts for Planning." In *National Jewish Population Survey 1971,* ed. Fred Massarik and the Council of Jewish Federations and Welfare Funds. New York: Council of Jewish Federations and Welfare Funds, 1972.

Chernus, Ira. "Legacy of the Six Day War Still Shapes Jewish Life." *Common Dreams,* 7 June 2002.

Cheslow, Daniella. "As Mideast Talks Begin, Palestinians Find Unlikely Support from Jewish Settlers." *Christian Science Monitor,* 1 September 2010.

Clines, Francis X. "Where Ram's Horn Blew, New Fears." *New York Times,* 3 February 1998, A8.

Cohen, Aryeh Dean. "Pupils Who Write Their Own Ten Commandments." *Jerusalem Post,* 30 September 1997, 9.

Cohen, Asher. *Ha-Talit V-Ha-Degel.* Jerusalem: Yad Yitzhak Ben-Tzvi, 1998. [Hebrew]

Cohen, Eric H. *Youth Tourism to Israel: Educational Experiences of the Diaspora.* Clevedon, UK: Channel View, 2008.

Cohen, Hillel. *Tarpat: Shnat Ha-Efes B-Sikhsukh Ha-Yehudi Aravi.* Jerusalem: Keter, 2013. [Hebrew]

Cohen, Naomi W. *The Americanization of Zionism.* Hanover, NH: University Press of New England, 2003.

Cohen, Rich. *Tough Jews: Fathers, Sons, and Gangster Dreams.* New York: Vintage Books, 1999.

Cohen, Shear Yashuv, Norman Lamm, Pinchas Peli, Michael Wyschogrod, and Walter S. Wurtzburger. "The Religious Meaning of the Six Day War: A Symposium." *Tradition* 10, no. 1 (Summer 1968): 5–20.

Cohen, Steven M. *The Dimensions of American Jewish Liberalism.* New York: American Jewish Committee, 1989.

Cohen, Steven M., and Leonard J. Fein, "From Integration to Survival: American Jewish Anxieties in Transition." *Annals of the American Academy of Political and Social Science* 480 (July 1985): 75–88.

Cohen, Stuart A., and Eliezer Don-Yehiya, eds. *Comparative Jewish Politics: Conflict and Consensus in Jewish Political Life.* Ramat Gan: Bar-Ilan University Press, 1981.

Cohen-Almagor, Raphael, ed. *The Boundaries of Liberalism and Tolerance: The Struggle against Kahanism in Israel.* Gainesville: University of Florida Press, 1994.

———, ed. *Liberal Democracy and the Limits of Tolerance: Essays in Honor and Memory of Yitzhak Rabin.* Ann Arbor: University of Michigan Press, 2000.

Collingwood, R. G. *The Idea of History.* Oxford: Oxford University Press, 1993.

Collins, Liat. "Efrat Being Connected to Cable TV." *Jerusalem Post,* 18 May 1994, 3.

"Colony for U.S. Jews Approved by Israel." *New York Times,* 8 February 1979, A14.

Colp, Judith. "James Baker Doesn't Want These Children to Live in Tekoa: Life on a Jewish Settlement in the West Bank." *Washington Times,* 11 March 1991, E1.

Commission on Social Action of Reform Judaism. *Israel and American Jewry— 1967 and Beyond: A Study-Guide for Program and Action.* New York: Union of American Hebrew Congregations, 1967.

Conforti, Yitzhak. "Between Ethnic and Civic: The Realistic Utopia of Zionism." *Israel Affairs* 17, no. 4 (October 2011): 563–582.

"Contesting History: A Tale of Two Tekoas." *Ma'an News Agency,* 17
    August 2012.
Cromer, Gerald. *The Debate about Kahanism in Israeli Society, 1984–1988.*
    Occasional Paper no. 3. New York: Harry Frank Guggenheim Foundation, 1988.
———. "'The Roots of Lawlessness': The Coverage of the Jewish Underground in
    the Israeli Press." *Terrorism* 11 (1988): 43–51.
———. *A War of Words: Political Violence and Public Debate in Israel.* London:
    Frank Cass, 2004.
"Crossroads: Israelis of Differing Viewpoints Gather in Madrid for Historic Peace
    Conference." *Harrisonberg Daily News Record,* 20 October 1991, 31.
Curtius, Mary. "West Bank Settler from Boston Is Stabbed." *Boston Globe,* 25
    June 1988, 1.
Dalsheim, Joyce. "Ant/agonizing Settlers in the Colonial Present of Israel/Pales-
    tine." *Social Analysis* 49, no. 2 (Summer 2005): 122–143.
———. "Settler Nationalism, Collective Memories of Violence, and the 'Uncanny
    Other.'" *Social Identities* 10, no. 2 (2004): 151–170.
———. *Unsettling Gaza: Secular Liberalism, Radical Religion, and the Israeli
    Settlement Project.* Oxford: Oxford University Press, 2011.
"Danny Kaye to Film for Israel." *Israel Digest,* August 1967, 6.
Dashefsky, Arnold, and Bernard Lazerwitz. "The Role of Religious Identification
    in North American Migration to Israel." *Journal for the Scientific Study of
    Religion* 22, no. 3 (1985): 263–275.
Davis, Moshe, ed. *The Yom Kippur War: Israel and the Jewish People.* New York:
    Arno Press, 1974.
Davis, O. L., Elizabeth Anne Yeager, and Stuart J. Foster, eds. *Historical Empathy
    and Perspective Taking in the Social Sciences.* Lanham, MD: Rowman and
    Littlefield, 2001.
Dawes, James. *Bad Men.* Cambridge, MA: Harvard University Press, 2013.
Dawidowicz, Lucy. "American Public Opinion." *American Jewish Yearbook 1968,*
    vol. 69. New York: American Jewish Committee, 1968.
———. *The Jewish Presence: Essays on Identity and History.* New York: Holt,
    Rinehart and Winston, 1976.
Day, David. *Conquest: How Societies Overwhelm Others.* Oxford: Oxford
    University Press, 2008.
"Dayan, Sharon Face Angry Sinai Settlers." *New York Times,* 2 January 1978, 3.
Della Pergola, Sergio, Uzi Rebhun, and Rosa Perla Raicher. "The Six Day War
    and Israel-Diaspora Relations: An Analysis of Quantitative Indicators." In *The
    Six Day War and World Jewry,* ed. Eli Lederhendler, 11–51. Bethesda: Univer-
    sity Press of Maryland, 2000.
Deloitte Consulting Group. "The Economic Impact of Nefesh B'Nefesh Aliya on
    the State of Israel." Unpublished working paper, October 2009.
Demant, Peter Robert. "Ploughshares into Swords: Israeli Settlement Policy in the
    Occupied Territories, 1967–1977." PhD dissertation, Proefschrift Universiteit
    van Amsterdam, 1988.
Derfner, Larry. "Always Look on the Bright Side." *Jerusalem Post Magazine,*
    2 February 2006.

Deutsch, Gloria. "Streetwise: A Name Unshorn." *Jerusalem Post,* 24 April 2008.

Diamond, Etan. *And I Will Dwell in Their Midst: Orthodox Jews in Suburbia.* Chapel Hill: University of North Carolina Press, 2000.

Diner, Hasia. *We Remember for Reverence and Love: American Jews and the Myth of Silence after the Holocaust, 1945–1962.* New York: NYU Press, 2009.

Divine, Donna Robinson. *Exiled in the Homeland: Zionism and the Return to Mandate Palestine.* Austin: University of Texas Press, 2009.

Doar, Yair. *Lanu Ha-Magel Hu Herev.* Kerakh Bet. Tel Aviv: Yad Tabenkin, 1997. [Hebrew]

———. *Sefer Garinei Ha-NAHAL-40 Shana: 1948–1987.* Tel Aviv: Yad Tabenkin, 1989. [Hebrew]

Dolav, Aharon. "The Minister of Housing Is Destroying the Seed-Colonies for Settlement." *Maariv,* 20 July 1975, 18. [Hebrew]

Dolgin, Janet L. *Jewish Identity and the JDL.* Princeton, NJ: Princeton University Press, 1977.

Dollinger, Marc. *Quest for Inclusion: Jews and Liberalism in Modern America.* Princeton, NJ: Princeton University Press, 2000.

Dudkevitch, Margot. "Man Killed in Drive-By Shooting." *Jerusalem Post,* 24 February 2002, 1.

———. "We Are Diamonds in the Ring Protecting Jerusalem." *Jerusalem Post,* 31 May 2001, 3.

"Editorial: There Are No Jewish Terrorists, Only Defenders of Israel." *Jewish Press,* 25 May 1984, 5.

"Efrat Chief Rabbi Apologizes for Remarks about Giving to the UJA." *Jewish Telegraphic Agency,* 10 January 1995.

Eisenstadt, S. N. *The Absorption of Immigrants: A Comparative Study Based Mainly on the Jewish Community in Palestine and the State of Israel.* Glencoe, IL: Free Press, 1955.

———. *Israeli Society.* New York: Basic Books, 1967.

Elazar, Daniel. "The Rediscovered Polity: Selections from the Literature of Jewish Public Affairs, 1967–1968." *American Jewish Yearbook 69.* New York: American Jewish Committee, 1968.

Elazar, Daniel J., and Andrea S. Arbel, eds. *Understanding the Jewish Agency.* Jerusalem: Jerusalem Center for Public Affairs, 1993.

Elbaum, Jason. *Peace Now: Playing with the Facts.* Jerusalem: Foreign Desk, YESHA Council of Jewish Communities in Judea, Samaria, and Gaza, 1993.

Eliach, David, and Joel B. Wolowelsky. "Orthodox Jewish Education Doesn't Teach Killing of Innocents." *New York Times,* 18 March 1994, A28.

Elitsur, Uri. *Kera Bein Ha-Kipot: Heshbon Nefesh Shel Dor Ha-Kipot Ha-Serugot.* Jerusalem: Mercaz Sapir, 1993. [Hebrew]

Elon, Amos. *The Israelis: Founders and Sons.* New York: Holt, Rinehart and Winston, 1971.

Endacott, Jason, and Sarah Brooks. "An Updated Theoretical Model for Promoting Historical Empathy." *Social Science Research and Practice* 8, no.1 (Spring 2013): 41–58.

Ener, Zeev. "Holtzman: Ha-Ish Sh-Natan Et Shemo L-Gush Etzion." In *Gush Etzion M-Raishito Ad T"SH*, ed. Mordechai Naor, 53–62. Jerusalem: Yad Yitzhak Ben Tzvi, 1986. [Hebrew]

Engel, Gerald S. "Comparison between American Permanent Residents in Israel: Part I, American Background." *Journal of Psychology* 71, no. 1 (January 1969): 133–142.

———. "Comparison between American Permanent Residents in Israel: Part II, Israeli Background." *Journal of Psychology* 72, no. 1 (May 1969): 135–139.

———. "Comparison between American Permanent Residents in Israel: Part III, Predictions about America and Israel." *Journal of Psychology* 73, no.1 (September 1969): 33–39.

———. "Comparison between Americans Living in Israel and Those Who Returned to America: Part I, American Background." *Journal of Psychology* 74, no. 2 (March 1970): 195–204.

———. "North American Jewish Settlers in Israel." *American Jewish Yearbook* 71 (1970): 161–187.

Englard, Zahava. *Settling for More: From Jersey to Judea*. New York: Devora Publishers, 2010.

"English News." *Yamiton*, 27 February 1976, 6–7.

"English News." *Yamiton*, 12 March 1976, 6.

Ephron, Dan. *Killing a King: The Assassination of Yitzhak Rabin and the Remaking of Israel*. New York: W. W. Norton, 2015.

Epstein, Helen. "Overseas Students: Problems and Possibilities." *Midstream* 16, no. 2 (February 1970): 3–16.

Erlich, Barbie. "Yamim Rishonim B-Efrat." *Nekuda*, 13 August 1983, 26–27. [Hebrew]

Ernstroff, Sara Rivka. "Troubled Times for Tekoa." *Jerusalem Post*, 30 November 2001, 3.

Ettinger, Yair. "The Torah Doesn't Belong to Any One Denomination." *Haaretz*, 15 September 2015.

"Etzion Settlements Draw American Immigrants." *Israel Digest*, 18 September 1970, 7.

Eyal, Eli. "American Aliya Is Losing Momentum." *National Jewish Monthly*, January 1973, 36, 41–43.

———. "Yamit after the Compromise." *Aliyon* (October 1973): 6–9.

Fackenheim, Emil L. *God's Presence in History*. New York: Harper, 1970.

Fairclough, Norman. *Analysing Discourse: Textual Analysis for Social Research*. New York: Pantheon, 1977.

———. *Language and Power*. Essex: Longman Group, 1989.

Farrell, William E. "Israelis Who Farm the Sinai Fear Uncertain Future." *New York Times*, 16 February 1978, A3.

———. "Jews Settle on a 'Volcano' in the Center of Hebron." *New York Times*, 10 November 1982, A12.

Feifel, Azi. "The Muddy Waters of Yamit." *Sh'ma: A Journal of Jewish Responsibility*. N.d.

Feifel, Chaim. "Dear Friends of Yamit." *Aliyon* (December 1973): 10–11.

———. "Yamit." *Aliyon* (November 1973): 8.

———. "Yamit News." *Aliyon* (February 1974): 16.

Feifel, Sarah, and Chaim Feifel. "Garin Yamit." *Aliyon* (October 1973): 5–6.

Feige, Michael. "Jewish Ideological Killers: Religious Fundamentalism or Ethnic Marginality?" In Bruce E. Greenspahn and Arieh Bruce Saposnik, *Contemporary Israel: New Insights and Scholarship.* New York: NYU Press, 2016.

———. *Settling in the Hearts: Jewish Fundamentalism in the Occupied Territories.* Detroit: Wayne State University Press, 2009.

———. *Shtai Mapot L-Gadah: Gush Emunim, Shalom Akhshav, V- Eizuv Ha-Merhav B-Yisrael.* Jerusalem: Y. L. Magnes, 2002. [Hebrew]

Feiglin, Moshe. "God Owns Cannabis Patent." *Yediot Ahronot,* 20 September 2012.

———. *Where There Are No Men: The Struggle of the "Zo Artzeinu" Movement against the Post-Zionist Collapse.* Translated by Menachem Bloch, Jay Shapiro, and Yitzhak Sapir. Jerusalem: Jewish Leadership Institute, 1999.

Fein, Leonard. "Israel and the Universalist Ideal." *Midstream* 17, no. 1 (January 1971): 38–46.

Fendel, Hillel. "Gush Etzion Residents Protest 'Obama Intifada.'" *Israel National News,* 21 March 2010.

Ferguson, Niall. *Colossus: The Rise and Fall of the American Empire.* London: Penguin, 2005.

Finkerfeld, Anda. *Lamed-Heh.* Jerusalem: Rubin Mass, 1998. [Hebrew]

Fisher, Elli. "Portrait of an Accused Jewish Terrorist as a Young Man." *Jewish Week,* 12 February 2009.

Fishman, Aryei. *Judaism and Collective Life: Self and Community in the Religious Kibbutz.* London: Routledge, 2002.

———, ed. *The Religious Kibbutz Movement: The Revival of the Jewish Religious Community.* Jerusalem: Jewish Agency, 1957.

Fishman, Ken, and Rachel Katsman. "The Suspects." *Jewish Press,* 29 June 1984, 51.

Fishman, Tzvi. "My Incredible First Day in Israel." *Jewish Press,* 14 May 2012.

Flapan, Simha. *The Birth of Israel: Myths and Realities.* New York: Pantheon Books, 1987.

"Foreign Policy: American Jews and Israel." *Time,* 10 March 1974.

Foucault, Michel. *Power/Knowledge.* New York: Pantheon, 1977.

"Four U.S. Olim Indicted." *Jewish Telegraphic Agency,* 28 March 1984.

Foxman, Abraham H. "The Six Day War: 40 Years Later." *New Jersey Jewish Standard,* 25 May 2007.

Freeman, J. Reuben, Amiel Ungar, Yosef Templeman, Eduardo Recanati, and Avraham Walfish. "The Situation in Beit Sahur." *Jerusalem Post,* 13 October 1989.

Friedman, Robert I. *The False Prophet: Meir Kahane—From FBI Informant to Knesset Member.* Brooklyn: Lawrence Hill Books, 1990.

———. "In the Realm of Perfect Faith." *Village Voice,* 12 November 1985. Also reprinted as "Inside the Terrorist Underground." *Journal of Palestine Studies* 15, no. 2 (Winter 1986): 190–201.

———. *Zealots for Zion: Inside Israel's West Bank Settlement Movement*. New York: Random House, 1992.

Friedman, Thomas L. "How Long Can Israel Deny Its Civil War?" *New York Times,* 27 December 1987, E3.

———. "Jewish Settlers Are Convicted in Terror Cases." *New York Times,* 11 July 1985, A1.

Frisch, Dov. "The Heart of Zion." *Jewish Press,* 11 March 1977.

Frisch, Michael. *A Shared Authority: Essays on the Craft and Meaning of Oral and Public History*. Albany: SUNY Press, 1990.

Gabbai, Yoni. "Ha-Shabak Hoshed: Teitel Rasah Od Hamisha Palestinim." *Kikar Ha-Shabbat,* 3 November 2009. [Hebrew]

Gaines, James R. "The Birth of a Settlement." *People,* 15 November 1982.

Ganin, Zvi. *Truman, American Jewry, and Israel, 1945–1948*. New York: Holmes and Meier, 1979.

"Garin Lev Tzion from the West Side to the West Bank." *Aliyon* (July–August 1979).

"Garin Yamit Newsletter." *Aliyon* (September 1974): 15.

Gavizon, Ruth. *Ha-Ideologia Shel Meir Kahane V-Tomekhav*. Jerusalem: Van Leer Institute, 1986. [Hebrew]

Gavron, Daniel. *The Kibbutz: Awakening from Utopia*. Lanham, MD: Rowman and Littlefield, 2000.

———. "A Plea for Utopia." *Jerusalem Post,* 13 October 1989.

Gellman, Marc. "Israel's Six Day War Offered American Jews a Refuge from the Social Traumas of the 1960s." *Newsweek,* 6 May 2007.

Gitelman, Zvi. *Becoming Israelis: Political Resocialization of Soviet and American Immigrants*. New York: Praeger, 1982.

Gitlin, Todd, and Liel Leibovitz. *The Chosen People: America, Israel, and the Ordeals of Divine Election*. New York: Simon and Schuster, 2010.

Glazer, Nathan. "Jewish Interests and the New Left." *Midstream* 17, no. 1 (January 1971): 32–37.

Glendon, Mary Ann. *Rights Talk: The Impoverishment of Political Discourse*. New York: Free Press, 1991.

Golan, Matti. *With Friends Like You: What Israelis Really Think about American Jews*. Translated by Hillel Halkin. New York: Free Press, 1992.

Golan, Moshe, Stan Moss, and Larry Price. *Judea and Samaria: New Dimensions* (film). Directed by Stan Moss. Jerusalem: Ministry of Absorption and Moshe Golan Productions, 1983.

Goldberg, J. J. *Jewish Power: Inside the American Jewish Establishment*. Reading, MA: Addison-Wesley, 1996.

Goldberg, Jeffrey. "A Reporter at Large: Among the Settlers." *New Yorker,* 31 May 2004.

Goldman, Julia. "Remembering the Yom Kippur War: U.S. Jews Mobilized for Israel with Prayers, Money, and Lobbying." *Jewish Telegraphic Agency,* 21 September 1998, 4.

Goldscheider, Calvin. "American Aliya: Sociological and Demographic Perspectives." In *The Jew in American Society*, ed. Marshall Sklare, 335–384. New York: Behrman House, 1974.

Goldstein, Baruch. "A History of Anti-Arab Feeling." *New York Times,* 30 June 1981, 7.

Goldstein, Eric L. *The Price of Whiteness: Jews, Race, and American Identity.* Princeton, NJ: Princeton University Press, 2006.

Goodman, Nan, and Michael P. Kramer, eds. *The Turn around Religion in America: Literature, Culture, and the Work of Sacvan Bercovitch.* Burlington, VT: Ashgate, 2011.

Gordis, Daniel. *If a Place Can Make You Cry: Dispatches from an Anxious State.* New York: Crown, 1992.

Gorenberg, Gershom. *The Accidental Empire: Israel and the Birth of the Settlements, 1967–1977.* New York: Times Books, 2006.

———. *The End of Days: Fundamentalism and the Struggle for the Temple Mount.* New York: Free Press, 2000.

———. *The Unmaking of Israel.* New York: Harper, 2011.

———. "Yaakov Teitel and the Allure of Lawlessness." *American Prospect,* 5 November 2009.

Gorny, Yosef. "Thoughts on Zionism as Utopian Ideology." *Modern Judaism* 18 (1998): 241–251.

———. "Utopian Elements in Zionist Thought." *Studies in Zionism* 5, no. 1 (1984): 19–27.

Grady, David. "Friends, Family Call Chaikin Man of Strong Faith, Courage." *Boston Globe,* 25 June 1988, 4.

Grasiel, Adi. "Ha-Rishon L-Etzion." *Arutz Sheva,* 6 April 2003. [Hebrew]

Green, Abigail, and Vincent Viaene, eds. *Religious Internationals in the Modern World: Globalization and Faith Communities since 1750.* Basingstoke, UK: Palgrave-Macmillan, 2012.

Greenberg, Cheryl Lynn. *Troubling the Waters: Black–Jewish Relations in the American Century.* Princeton, NJ: Princeton University Press, 2006.

Greenberg, Joel. "Settlers Rejoice, Arabs Are Uneasy." *New York Times,* 1 June 1996, 7.

Greenwood, Naftali. "Confessions of a Co-Conspirator." *Jerusalem Post,* 4 March 1994, 5A.

"Greetings from Yamit." *Aliyon* (April 1976): 8–9.

Griffith, R. Marie and Melani McAlister. *Religion and Politics in the Contemporary United States.* Baltimore: Johns Hopkins University Press, 2008.

Gross, Jane. "Young Orthodox Jews' Quest to Blend Word and World." *New York Times,* 16 September 1999.

Gross, Peter. "After 42 Years, Jews Are Part of Hebron." *New York Times,* 24 July 1971, 3.

Grossman, David. *The Yellow Wind.* Translated by Haim Watzman. New York: Picador, 1998.

Gruber, Freddy. *For a Jew, It's Home* (film). Directed by Freddy Gruber. Jerusalem: Dept. of Immigration and Absorption, World Zionist Organization, and Moshe Golan Productions, 1985.

Grunbitz, Aharon. "Yishlakh L-Kaiz Yamit." *Yom Ha-Shishi,* 27 March 2002. [Hebrew]

Gurock, Jeffrey S., ed. *American Zionism: Mission and Politics*. New York: Routledge, 1998.

———. *The Men and Women of Yeshiva*. New York: Columbia University Press, 1988.

"Gush Emunim Gets Into Aliya." *Counterpoint*, March 1984, 7.

Gush Etzion and the Hebron Hills. Jerusalem: Jewish Agency, 1974.

Guttman, Nathan, and Noah Smith, "Anti-Defamation League Signals New Path as Jonathan Greenblatt Takes Helm." *Jewish Daily Forward*, 13 November 2014.

Guzofsky, Yaakov. "Letters to the Editor: Open Letter from the Father of an Imprisoned Settler." *Jewish Press*, 8 June 1984, 40.

Guzofsky, Yekutiel. "'Al Fajr' and Israel's Double Standard." *Jewish Press*, 5 October 1984, 41.

Haber, Jeremiah [Charles H. Manekin]. "Shlomo Riskin, Bad Moral Luck?" *The Magnes Zionist*, 10 April 2008.

Haberman, Clyde. "Israeli Curbs on Far-Right Settlers Provoke Only Scorn from Targets." *New York Times*, 4 March 1994, A10.

———. "Massacre at Hebron Exposes Anti-American Mood in Israel." *New York Times*, 20 March 1994, 1, 14.

———. "New Clashes Likely: Massacre Sets Off Riots Causing More Deaths in the Territories." *New York Times*, 26 February 1994, 1.

———. "Some Expect Violence, Others See Pressure for Peace Talks." *New York Times*, 27 February 1994, 1.

Haefeli, Evan. "A Note on the Use of American Borderlands." *American Historical Review* 104, no. 4 (October 1999): 1222–1225.

"Ha-Im Ha-NAHAL Zorem Od?" *Zeraim* 7 (Sivan 1976): 12–13. [Hebrew]

Halamish, Aviva. *Meir Ya'ari: Biografia Kibbutzit*. Tel Aviv: Am Oved, 2009. [Hebrew]

Halevi, Yossi Klein. "Culture War." *New Republic*, 20 June 2003.

———. *Like Dreamers: The Story of the Israeli Paratroopers Who Reunited Jerusalem and Divided a Nation*. New York: HarperCollins, 2013.

———. *Memoirs of a Jewish Extremist: An American Story*. Boston: Little, Brown, 1995.

———. "War and Atonement." *Jerusalem Post*, 3 October 2003.

Halkin, Hillel. "Americans in Israel." *Commentary*, May 1972, 54–63.

Hall, David D. *Puritans in the New World: A Critical Anthology*. Princeton, NJ: Princeton University Press, 2004.

Halpern, Ben. *The American Jew: A Zionist Analysis*. New York: Theodore Herzl Foundation, 1956.

———. *A Clash of Heroes: Brandeis, Weizmann, and American Zionism*. New York: Oxford University Press, 1987.

———. *The Idea of a Jewish State*. Cambridge, MA: Harvard University Press, 1961.

Halsell, Grace. "New Yorkers Turned Colonists." *Boca Raton News*, 21 January 1980, 3.

———. "'Pioneering' on the West Bank." *Worldview Magazine*, 1 December 1980.

"Ha-NAHAL M-Alef Ad Taf." *B-Mahaneh Ha-NAHAL,* issue 2–1 [309–310]
(October 1977): 27. [Hebrew]

"Ha-Pisasa Ha-Revia." *Nekuda,* 27 June 1980. [Hebrew]

Harnoi, Meir. *Ha-Mitnahalim.* Or Yehuda: Maariv, 1994. [Hebrew]

Harow, Eve. "Distorted Portrayal." *Jerusalem Post,* 18 February 1994, 2.

Harris, Ben. "War Galvanized American Jews." *Jewish Telegraphic Agency,*
30 May 2007.

Harris, Dianne, ed. *Second Suburb: Levittown, Pennsylvania.* Pittsburgh: University of Pittsburgh Press, 2010.

Harris, Thomas. *Black Sunday.* New York: G. P. Putnam and Sons, 1975.

Harris, William. *Taking Root: Israeli Settlement Policy in the West Bank, the
Golan, and Gaza-Sinai, 1967–1980.* Chichester, UK: Research Studies Press,
1980.

Hazony, David, Yoram Hazony, and Michael B. Oren. *New Essays on Zionism.*
Jerusalem: Shalem Press, 2006.

Hazony, Yoram. *The Jewish State: The Struggle for Israel's Soul.* New York: Basic
Books, 2000.

Hedges, Chris, and Joel Greenberg. "Before Killing, Final Prayers and Final
Taunt." *New York Times,* 28 February 1994, A1.

Heicksen, Martin H. "Tekoa: Excavations in 1968." *Grace Journal* 10, no. 2
(Winter 1969): 3–10.

Hein, Avram. "Ideological Migration: A Detailed Study on North American
Jewish Immigration to Israel." Unpublished working paper, Association for
Israel Studies Annual Meeting, 2007.

Heller, Aron. "Israel Nabs Serial Attacker of Arabs, Leftist Jews." *Boston Globe,* 2
November 2009.

Herman, Simon. *American Students in Israel.* Ithaca, NY: Cornell University Press,
1970.

———. *Jewish Identity: A Social Psychological Perspective.* New Brunswick, NJ:
Transaction, 1989.

Hertzberg, Arthur. "Israel and American Jewry." *Commentary* 44, no. 2 (August 1967): 69–73.

———. *A Jew in America: My Life and a People's Struggle for Identity.* San
Francisco: Harpers, 2002.

———. "Jewish Identification after the Six-Day War," *Jewish Social Studies* 31,
no. 3 (July 1969): 267–271.

———, ed. *The Zionist Idea: A Historical Analysis and Reader.* Philadelphia:
Jewish Publication Society, 1997.

Herzog, Chaim. "A Dagger in Democracy's Back." *Jerusalem Post,* 18
March 1994, 4A.

Herzog, Jonathan P. *The Spiritual-Industrial Complex: America's Religious Battle
against Communism in the Early Cold War.* New York: Oxford University
Press, 2011.

Heydermann, Steven, ed. *The Begin Era: Issues in Contemporary Israel.* Boulder,
CO: Westview Press, 1984.

Hill, Michael R. *Archival Strategies and Techniques.* Newbury Park, CA: Sage, 1993.

Himmelfarb, Milton. "In the Light of Israel's Victory." *Commentary,* 1 October 1967, 53–61.

———. "The Jewish Vote—Again." *Commentary* 55, no. 6 (June 1973): 81.

Hirschhorn, Sara Yael. "Constructing Kahane: Zionism, Judaism, and Democracy in the Religio-Political Philosophy of Rabbi Meir Kahane." MA thesis, University of Chicago, 2005.

———. "Israeli Terrorists, Born in the U.S.A." *New York Times,* 4 September 2015.

Hobsbawn, E. J. *Nations and Nationalism since 1780: Programme, Myth, and Reality.* Cambridge: Cambridge University Press, 1992.

Hoffman, Gil. "Aiming High." *Jerusalem Post,* 10 August 2012, 8.

———. "Anglo Likud Candidates Shut Out of the Knesset." *Jerusalem Post,* 10 December 2008, 3.

———. "Feiglin Adopts Obama's Fund-Raising Strategy." *Jerusalem Post,* 22 January 2012, 4.

Hoffman, Shifra. "Mother of 'Underground' Suspect Pleads for His Release." *Jewish Press,* 8–14 June 1984, backmatter.

Horovitz, David. "If We Give Back Hebron, They'll Cry in Borough Park." *Jerusalem Post,* 7 December 1989.

———. "In Tekoa, Looking Beyond the Intifada." *Jerusalem Post,* 10 December 1989, 2.

Horowitz, Elliot. *Reckless Rites: Purim and the Legacy of Jewish Violence.* Princeton, NJ: Princeton University Press, 1996.

Horowitz, Jason, and Maggie Haberman. "A Split over Israel Threatens the Democrats' Hope for Unity." *New York Times,* 25 May 2016.

Horowitz, Ruth Tamar. "Jewish Immigrants to Israel: Self-Reported Powerlessness and Alienation among Immigrants from the Soviet Union and North America." *Journal of Cross-Cultural Psychology* 10, no. 3 (September 1979): 366–374.

Hourani, Albert. *Arabic Thought in the Liberal Age: 1798–1939.* Cambridge: Cambridge University Press, 1983.

"House of David Rosenfeld's Murderer Explodes." *Haaretz,* 6 July 1982, 8. [Hebrew]

Hroub, Khalid. *Hamas: Political Thought and Practice.* Washington, DC: Institute of Palestine Studies, 2000.

Hunt, Lynn. *Inventing Human Rights: A History.* New York: W. W. Norton, 2007.

Hunt, Michael H. *Ideology and U.S. Foreign Policy.* New Haven, CT: Yale University Press, 1997.

Ibrahim, Youssef M. "In a West Bank Town, a Quiet Dialogue between Settlers and Palestinians." *New York Times,* 10 June 1990, 3.

"I Decided I Could Live Here." Oral History with Israeli and Palestinian Women—Interview with Geri Bernstein Freund, 18 June 2011.

"If You're Interested in Establishing a Kibbutz or City Commune." *Campus Aliyon* (March 1972): 1.

Ignatieff, Michael. *American Exceptionalism and Human Rights*. Princeton, NJ: Princeton University Press, 2005.

"Ignored as an Average Israeli, Confessed Assassin Fits Profile." *Jewish Telegraphic Agency,* 6 November 1995.

Ikan, Yael, ed. *The World Zionist Organization: The National Institutions—Structure and Function*. Jerusalem: World Zionist Organization, 1997.

Ilan, Tzvi. "Ha-Shotafim Shel Holtzman." In *Gush Etzion M-Raishito Ad T"SH*, ed. Mordechai Naor, 63–74. Jerusalem: Yad Yitzhak Ben Tzvi, 1986. [Hebrew]

Immanuel, Jon. "Both Sides Dig In over Disputed Hill." *Jerusalem Post,* 29 December 1994, 2.

———. "Tekoa Man Held in Death of Boy in Beit Sahur." *Jerusalem Post,* 22 February 1991.

Inbari, Motti. *Jewish Fundamentalism and the Temple Mount: Who Will Build the Third Temple?* Albany: SUNY Press, 2009.

———. *Messianic Religious Zionism Confronts Israeli Territorial Compromises*. Cambridge: Cambridge University Press, 2012.

Inboden, William. *Religion and American Foreign Policy, 1945–1960: The Soul of Containment*. Cambridge: Cambridge University Press, 2008.

"Interview with Zvi Yaron." *Zeraim* 2 (Heshvan 1975): 8. [Hebrew]

"The Intifada Is Souring Business Ventures in Judea: Trapped in Tekoa." *Jerusalem Post,* 12 September 1989, 9.

Isaacs, Charles S. *Inside Ocean-Hill Brownsville: A Teacher's Education*. Albany: SUNY Press, 2014.

Isaacs, Harold Robert. *American Jews in Israel*. New York: John Day, 1967.

"Israel." *Deseret News,* 21 April 1982, 2.

Israel Central Bureau of Statistics. *The Statistical Abstract of Israel*. 61 vols. Jerusalem: Central Bureau of Statistics, 1950–.

"Israel Said to Urge More Settlements: Security Plan Reported to Include a Major West Bank Influx." *New York Times,* 2 September 1977, 1, A4.

"Israeli Civilians Avenge Attacks with Gunfire." *Deseret News,* 25 June 1988.

"Israeli Settlers and Palestinians." *Religion & Ethics Newsweekly,* 17 September 2010.

"Israeli Settler Yaakov Teitel Goes on Trial for Murder." *BBC,* 9 December 2009.

"Israeli Trump Supporters Open Campaign Office in West Bank." *Reuters,* 5 September 2016.

Izenberg, Dan. "Peres Outraged at Supporters of Goldstein." *Jerusalem Post,* 1 March 1994, 2.

"Jack Teitel, 'Jewish Terrorist,' Appeals Verdict to Supreme Court." *Yediot Ahronot,* 21 May 2013.

Jacobs, Seth. *America's Miracle Man in Vietnam: Ngo Dinh Diem, Religion, Race, and U.S. Intervention in Southeast Asia, 1950–1957*. Durham, NC: Duke University Press, 2004.

Jacobson, Matthew Frye. *Roots Too: White Ethnic Revival in Post–Civil Rights America*. Cambridge, MA: Harvard University Press, 2006.

Jansen, Clifford J. *Readings in the Sociology of Migration*. New York: Pergamon Press, 1970.

Jewish Agency Settlement Division. *Hevel Eshkol.* Jerusalem: Jewish Agency, 1972. [Hebrew]

"Jewish Communal Services: Programs and Finances." in *American Jewish Yearbook 69.* New York: American Jewish Committee, 1968.

Jewish Defense in the Hebron Hills. Gush Etzion: Gush Etzion Field School, 1970.

"Jewish Extremism in Israel." *Jewish Action,* Spring 1985, 21.

John Chaiken and Marilyn Chaiken v. VV Publishing Corp d/b/a The Village Voice, Robert Friedman, Modiin Publishing House d/b/a Maariv and Ron Dagoni, 119 F3d 1018 U.S. Court of Appeals, 2nd Circuit, no. 292, Docket 95-9301, 21 July 1997.

Jones, Robert P., and Daniel Cox. *Chosen for What? Jewish Values in 2012.* Washington, DC: Public Religion Research Institute, 2012.

Jubas, Harry Leib. "The Adjustment Process of Americans and Canadians in Israel and Their Integration into Israeli Society." PhD dissertation, Michigan State University, 1974.

Judis, John B. *Genesis: Truman, American Jews, and the Origins of the Arab/Israeli Conflict.* New York: Farrar, Straus and Giroux, 2014.

Juergensmeyer, Mark. *Terror in the Mind of God: The Global Rise of Religious Violence.* Berkeley: University of California Press, 2000.

Kahane, Libby. *Rabbi Meir Kahane: His Life and Thought.* Jerusalem: Institute for the Publication of the Writings of Rabbi Meir Kahane, 2008.

Kahane, Meir. *Forty Years.* Miami Beach: Institute of the Jewish Idea, 1983.

———. *Israel: Revolution or Referendum?* Secaucus, NJ: Barricade Books, 1990.

———. *Listen World, Listen Jew.* Jerusalem: Institute for the Publication of the Writings of Rabbi Meir Kahane, 1995.

———. *Our Challenge: The Chosen Land.* Radnor, PA: Chilton Book Co., 1974.

———. *The Story of the Jewish Defense League.* Radnor, PA: Chilton Book Co., 1975.

———. *They Must Go.* New York: Grosset and Dunlap, 1981.

———. *Uncomfortable Questions for Comfortable Jews.* Secaucus, NJ: Lyle Stuart, 1987.

Kahane, Meir, Joseph Churba, and Michael King. *The Jewish Stake in Vietnam.* New York: Crossroads, 1967.

Kahn, Ava Fran, and Adam Mendelsohn, eds. *Transnational Traditions: New Perspectives on American Jewish History.* Detroit: Wayne State University Press, 2014.

Kalman, Matthew. "Two Israeli Teenagers Stoned to Death." *USA Today,* 20 June 2001.

Kandall, Jonathan. "Jews in Sinai Jeer, Then Applaud Begin." *New York Times,* 6 April 1979, A1.

Kaplan, Allison. "Violence Clouds Shamir's Arrival." *Jerusalem Post,* 30 October 1991, 2.

Kaplan, David E. "The View from Over There." *Jerusalem Post,* 20 July 2007, 10.

Kaplan, Edward K. *Spiritual Radical: Abraham Joshua Heschel in America, 1940–1972.* New Haven, CT: Yale University Press, 2007.

Kaplan, Eran. *The Jewish Radical Right: Revisionist Zionism and Its Ideological Legacy.* Madison: University of Wisconsin Press, 2005.

Karpin, Michael, and Ina Friedman. *Murder in the Name of God: The Plot to Kill Yitzhak Rabin.* New York: Metropolitan Books, 1998.

Katsman, Rachel. "Can an American Rabbi Make It in Israel?" *Counterpoint,* (January 1985), 2.

Katz, Pearl. "Acculturation and Social Networks of American Immigrants in Israel." PhD dissertation, SUNY at Buffalo, 1974.

Katz, Yossi. *B-Hazit Ha-Karkah: Keren Kayemet L-Yisrael B-Terem Medinah.* Jerusalem: Ha-Universita Ha-Ivrit, 2001. [Hebrew]

———. *Ha-Hityashvut Ha-Yehudit B-Harei Hevron V-Gush Etzion, 1940–1947.* Ramat Gan: Universitat Bar Ilan, 1992. [Hebrew]

———. *Torah V-Avoda B-Binyan Haaretz: Ha-Kibbutz Ha-Dati B-Tekufat Ha-Mandat.* Ramat Gan: Universitat Bar Ilan, 1996. [Hebrew]

Kaufman, David. *Shul with a Pool: The Synagogue-Center in American Jewish History.* Hanover, NH: University Press of New England, 1999.

Kaufman, Menachem. "From Philanthropy to Commitment: The Six Day War and the United Jewish Appeal." *Journal of Israeli History* 15, no. 2 (1994): 161–191.

Kaufman, Sybil. "Pioneering—1975: Come to Yamit!" *Israel Digest* 15, no. 24 (November 1974): 2.

Kaufmann, Shoshana. *American Immigrants in Israel: A Selected Annotated Bibliography, 1948–1985.* New York: Institute on American Jewish-Israeli Relations, 1987.

Kay, Avi. "Citizen Rights in Flux: The Influence of American Immigrants to Israel on Modes of Political Activism." *Jewish Political Studies Review* 13, nos. 3–4 (Fall 2004).

———. *Making Themselves Heard: The Impact of North American Olim on Israeli Protest Politics.* New York: American Jewish Committee, 1995.

Keinon, Herb. "The Army Faces Off against a Rabbinical Battalion." *Jerusalem Post,* 14 July 1995, 9.

———. "Feiglin & Co. Hit the Big Time." *Jerusalem Post,* 15 September 1995, 9.

———. "Group Plans Groundbreaking for 130 'New Settlements' Tomorrow." *Jerusalem Post,* 23 December 1993, 2.

———. "Protestors Back Zo Artzenu Leaders Going on Trial Today." *Jerusalem Post,* 17 January 1996, 2.

———. "Revived Settler Group Plans Roads Takeover." *Jerusalem Post,* 28 July 1995, 2.

———. "Settlers Choose Civil Disobedience as Their Best Shot." *Jerusalem Post,* 4 August 1995, 7.

———. "Unlikely Place for a Battle." *Jerusalem Post,* 6 January 1995, 7.

———. "Walking a Thin Line over the Green Line." *Jerusalem Post,* 18 March 1994, 3B.

———. "Zo Artzenu Leaders Guilty of Sedition." *Jerusalem Post,* 3 September 1997, 3.

Keinon, Herb, and Jacob Dallal. "Protestors Snarl Traffic All Over the Country." *Jerusalem Post,* 9 August 1995, 1.

Keinon, Herb, and Miriam Feldman. "A Perpetual Optimist." *Jerusalem Post,* 21 May 1993.

Keinon, Herb, and Bill Hutman. "Police Break Up Anti-Government Protest in Capital, 22 Arrested, 30 Injured; Shahal: We Showed Restraint." *Jerusalem Post,* 14 September 1995.

Keinon, Herb, and ITIM News Service. "Levinger Sentenced for Attacking Policemen." *Jerusalem Post,* 19 December 1995, 2.

Kellerman, Aharon. *Society and Settlement: Jewish Land of Israel in the Twentieth Century.* Albany: SUNY Press, 1993.

Kelly, Barbara M. *Expanding the American Dream: Building and Rebuilding Levittown.* Albany: SUNY Press, 1993.

Kelner, Shaul. "Ritualized Protest and Redemptive Politics: Cultural Consequences of the American Mobilization to Free Soviet Jewry." *Jewish Social Studies* 14, no. 3 (Spring/Summer 2008): 1–37.

———. *Tours That Bind: Diaspora, Pilgrimage, and Israeli Birthright Tourism.* New York: NYU Press, 2010.

Kershner, Isabel. "From an Israeli Settlement, a Rabbi's Unorthodox Plan for Peace." *New York Times,* 6 December 2008.

Kertzer, Morris. *Today's American Jews.* New York: McGraw-Hill, 1967.

Keys, Barbara J. *Reclaiming American Virtue: The Human Rights Revolution of the 1970s.* Cambridge, MA: Harvard University Press, 2014.

Khalidi, Muhammed Ali. "Utopian Zionism or Zionist Proselytism? A Reading of Herzl's Altenuland." *Journal of Palestine Studies* 30, no. 4 (Summer 2001): 55–67.

Kimmerling, Baruch. *The Israeli State and Society: Boundaries and Frontiers.* Albany: SUNY Press, 1989.

———. *Zionism and Territory: The Socio-Territorial Dimensions of Zionist Politics.* Berkeley: University of California Press, 1983.

Kimmerling, Baruch, and Joel S. Migdal. *The Palestinian People: A History.* Cambridge, MA: Harvard University Press, 2003.

Kirby, Dianne, ed. *Religion and the Cold War.* New York: Palgrave, 2003.

Klatch, Rebecca E. *A Generation Divided: The New Left, the New Right, and the 1960s.* Berkeley: University of California Press, 1999.

Klein, Menachem. *Lives in Common: Arabs and Jews in Jerusalem, Jaffa, and Hebron.* Cambridge: Cambridge University Press, 2014.

Kliot, Nurit, and Shmuel Albeck. *Sinai, Anatomiya Shel Prida.* Tel Aviv: Misrad Ha-Bitahon, 1996. [Hebrew]

Knohl, Dov. *Siege in the Hebron Hills: The Battle of the Etzion Bloc.* New York: Thomas Yoseloff, 1958.

Kohn, Hans. *The Idea of Nationalism: A Study of Its Origins and Background.* New Brunswick, NJ: Transaction, 2005.

Kolsky, Thomas A. *Jews against Zionism: The American Council for Judaism, 1942–1948.* Philadelphia: Temple University Press, 1990.

Koren, David. *Ha-NAHAL: Tsava Im Erekh Mosaf.* Tel Aviv: Yad Tabenkin, 1997. [Hebrew]

The Koren Sacks Siddur: A Hebrew-English Prayerbook. Jerusalem: Koren Publishers, 2009.

Kotler, Yair. *Heil Kahane.* Tel Aviv: Modan, 1985. [Hebrew]

Kurz, Anat. *Fatah and the Politics of Violence: The Institutionalization of a Popular Struggle.* Brighton, UK: Sussex University Press, 2005.

Kushner, David. *Levittown: Two Families, One Tycoon, and the Fight for Civil Rights in America's Legendary Suburb.* New York: Walker, 2009.

Lamar, Howard Roberts, and Leonard Monteath Thompson. *The Frontier in History: North America and South Africa Compared.* New Haven, CT: Yale University Press, 1981.

"Land Close to Bethlehem Is Seized." *New York Times,* 17 March 1980, A3.

Landau, David. "New Town Planned for Gush Etzion." *Jewish Telegraphic Agency,* 8 February 1979.

Langer, Ruth, and Steve Fine, eds. *Liturgy in the Life of the Synagogue: Studies in the History of Jewish Prayer.* Winona Lake, IN: Eisenbrauns, 2005.

Laqueur, Walter. *A History of Zionism.* New York: Schocken Books, 2003.

Lazaroff, Tova. "Gush Etzion Terror Attack Victim Dalya Lamkus Laid to Rest in Tekoa." *Jerusalem Post,* 11 November 2014.

Leavy, Patricia. *Oral History: Understanding Qualitative Research.* Oxford: Oxford University Press, 2008.

Le Burkien, Michael P. *An Israeli View of American Jewry's Reaction to the Six Day War: 1967.* Cincinnati: N.p., 1969.

Lederhendler, Eli, ed. *The Six Day War and World Jewry.* Bethesda: University Press of Maryland, 2000.

Lee, Eric. *Saigon to Jerusalem: Conversations with U.S. Veterans of the Vietnam War Who Emigrated to Israel.* Jefferson, NC: McFarland, 1992.

Leegant, Joan. *Wherever You Go.* New York: W. W. Norton, 2010.

Lehmann, Manfred F. "One Year Later . . . Purim Hebron Remembered."

Lehrman, Hal. "When Americans Emigrate to Israel: A Report on Some Latter-Day Pioneers." *Commentary* 13 (February 1, 1952), 124–133.

Leiblich, Amia. *Yalde Kfar Etzion.* Haifa: Universitat Haifa, 2007. [Hebrew]

Leibovitz, Liel. *Aliya: Three Generations of American-Jewish Immigration to Israel.* New York: St. Martin's Press, 2006.

Leibowitz, Meir. "Letter to the Editor." *New York Times,* 2 September 1984, SM46.

Leiter, Yechiel. "Children of the Opposition." *YESHA Report,* 1994.

———. *Crisis in Israel.* New York: S.P.I. Books, 1994.

———. "Hebron: A Microcosm of the Middle East." *YESHA Report* (April–May 1994): 4.

———. *Israel at the Crossroads: The View from the Hills of Judea and Samaria.* New York: One Israel Fund/YESHA Heartland Campaign, 1999.

———. *A Peace to Resist: Why the Rabin-Arafat Deal Must be Stopped, and How It Can Be Done.* Jerusalem: YESHA Council Foreign Desk, 1993.

———. "Their Unfinished Work." *YESHA Report* (February 1997): 5.

Lerner, Aaron. "Interview: Rabbi Menachem Fruman—Permanent Peace Not Possible." *IMRA,* 17 May 2001.

Leshem, Elazar, and Judith T. Shuval. *Immigration to Israel: Sociological Perspectives.* New Brunswick, NJ: Transaction, 1998.

Leshem, Rafi. "L-Maan Shituf Peula." *Yamiton* 23, 28 May 1976, 6. [Hebrew]

Lester, Eleanore. "Whose West Bank? 24 Pioneers Plan Aliyah to Form Community." *Jewish Week,* 24 July 1977.

Lev, Yehuda. "And He . . . Went and Dwelt in Nayot." *Jewish Frontier,* December 1964, 15–19.

Levinger, Miriam. "Women in the Settlements after the Six Day War" (interview with Judy Lev). Interview 247 (1), 1999. Oral History Division, Avraham Harman Institute of Contemporary Jewry, Hebrew University of Jerusalem.

Levinson, Chaim. "Israel Subsidizes West Bank Housing, Breaking Promise to U.S." *Haaretz,* 11 January 2012.

———. "Psychiatrist Rules Accused Jewish Terrorist Jack Teitel Psychotic, Unfit to Stand Trial." *Haaretz,* 5 May 2010.

———. "Who Is Suspected Jewish Terrorist Yaakov Teitel?" *Haaretz,* 1 November 2009.

Levitt, Matthew. *Hamas: Politics, Charity, and Terrorism in the Service of Jihad.* New Haven, CT: Yale University Press, 2006.

Levy, Andre, and Alex Weingrod. *Homelands and Diasporas: Holy Lands and Other Places.* Stanford, CA: Stanford University Press, 2005.

Levy, David. "Why Some American Jews Are Moving to Israel: The Aliya from Washington." *Jewish Digest* 17, no. 8 (May 1972): 31–42.

Lewis, Bernard. *History: Remembered, Recovered, Invented.* Princeton, NJ: Princeton University Press, 1975.

Liebman, Charles S. "American Students in Israel and Israel–Diaspora Relations." *Diaspora and Unity* 12 (1968).

———. "Jewish Ultra-Nationalism in Israel: Converging Strands." In *Survey of Jewish Affairs,* ed. William Frankel, 28–50. Rutherford, NJ: Farleigh-Dickinson University Press, 1985.

———. "Judaism and Vietnam: A Reply to Dr. Wyschogrod." *Tradition* 9 (Spring/Summer 1967).

———. *Religion, Democracy, and Israeli Society.* Amsterdam: Harwood Academic Press, 1997.

———. *Religious and Secular: Conflict and Accommodation between Jews in Israel.* Jerusalem: Keter, 1990.

Liebman, Charles S., and Eliezer Don-Yehiya. *Civil Religion in Israel: Traditional Judaism and Political Culture in the Jewish State.* Berkeley: University of California Press, 1983.

———. *Religion and Politics in Israel.* Bloomington: Indiana University Press, 1984.

Limerick, Patricia Nelson. *The Legacy of Conquest: The Unbroken Past of the American West.* New York: Norton, 1987.

Liphshiz, Cnaan. "Hesitating Anglo Immigrants End Up in 'Ethnic Enclaves,' Study Reveals." *Haaretz,* 23 May 2008.

Lisky, Livia. "'Lev Zion' Oleh M-Harai Catskills L-Hityashev B-Shomron." *Maariv,* 18 September 1977, 1.

Little, David, ed. *Peacemakers in Action: Profiles of Religion in Conflict Resolution.* Cambridge: Cambridge University Press, 2007.

Lowenstein, Steven M. *Frankfurt on the Hudson: The German-Jewish Community of Washington Heights, 1933–1983, Its Structure and Culture.* Detroit: Wayne State University Press, 1989.

Lumer, Hyman. *The "Jewish Defense League": A New Face for Reaction.* New York: Outlook, 1971.

Lustick, Ian S. *For the Land and the Lord: Jewish Fundamentalism in Israel.* New York: Council on Foreign Relations, 1988.

———. "Israeli State Building in the West Bank and Gaza Strip: Theory and Practice." *International Organization* 41 (1987): 151–171.

———. "Two-State Illusion." *New York Times,* 14 September 2013.

———. *Unsettled States, Disputed Lands: Britain and Ireland, France and Algeria, Israel and the West Bank–Gaza.* Ithaca, NY: Cornell University Press, 1993.

Luz, Ehud. *Parallels Meet: Religion and Nationalism in the Early Zionist Movement (1882–1904).* Translated by Lenn J. Schramm. Philadelphia: Jewish Publication Society, 1988.

MacKenzie, G. Calvin, and Robert Weisbrot. *The Liberal Hour: Washington and the Politics of Change of the 1960s.* New York: Penguin Press, 2008.

Magee, Malcolm D. *What the World Should Be: Woodrow Wilson and the Crafting of a Faith-Based Foreign Policy.* Waco, TX: Baylor University Press, 2008.

Magnezi, Aviel. "'Jewish Terrorist' Jack Teitel Convicted." *Yediot Ahronot,* 16 January 2013.

"Ma Hadash? Gush Emunim." *Zeraim* 6 (March 1975): 15. [Hebrew]

"Ma Hadash: Meahaz Tekoa." *Zeraim* 11 (Av 1975): 16. [Hebrew]

Mahler, Gregory S., ed. *Israel after Begin.* Albany: SUNY Press, 1990.

Maisels, L. Sandy, and Ira N. Forman, eds. *Jews in American Politics.* Lanham, MD: Rowman and Littlefield, 2001.

"Makom Rishon L-Harubit, Tekoa: Rishon Bein Ha-Meahazim." *B-Mahaneh Ha-NAHAL* 5 [301] (February 1977): 1. [Hebrew]

Makovsky, David. "Breaking Ranks in 'Occupied Scarsdale.'" *U.S. News and World Report,* 14 August 1995, 31.

Makovsky, David, Evelyn Gordon, and Herb Keinon. "Government Likely to Stop Efrat Construction." *Jerusalem Post,* 2 January 1995, 1.

Makovsky, David, and Herb Keinon. "Entire Cabinet to Review Settlement Expansion Plans." *Jerusalem Post,* 4 January 1995, 1.

Mallison, Thomas W., and Sally V. Mallison. *The Palestine Problem in International Law and World Order.* Essex, UK: Longman Group, 1986.

Maltz, Judy. "From the BDS Frontlines: How the On-Campus Brawl Is Turning Young Jews Off from Israel." *Haaretz,* 9 May 2016.

"Manager of the Herodian Site in the Judean Desert Murdered." *Haaretz,* 4 July 1982, 8. [Hebrew]

Mandell, Sheri. *The Blessing of a Broken Heart*. New Milford, CT: Toby Press, 2003.

Manela, Erez. *The Wilsonian Moment: Self-Determination and the International Origins of Anticolonial Nationalism*. Oxford: Oxford University Press, 2007.

Marcus, Menachem. "Raishit Geula: The Untold Story behind the Establishment of Efrat." Unpublished manuscript, January 2012.

Margalit, Elkanah. *Anatomia Shel Smol: Poalei Tsion Smol B-Eretz Yisrael*. Jerusalem: Ha-Universita Ha-Ivrit, 1976. [Hebrew]

Margolick, David. "Man Sought by Israel Is in New York." *New York Times*, 24 May 1985.

Markham, James M. "The Jolt of Losing a Dream Unsettles Settlers in Yamit." *New York Times*, 2 September 1980, A2.

Marty, Martin E., and F. Scott Appleby, eds. *The Fundamentalism Project*. 5 vols. Chicago: University of Chicago Press, 1991–1995.

Masad, Uri. "Settlers and Soldiers Face Off as Efrat Becomes Flashpoint." *JWeekly*, 4 August 1995.

Maslow, Aaron D. "Do Not Murder." *New York Times*, 9 March 1994, A15.

"Mass. Man Ruled Victim of Bias over Hat." *Lewiston Daily Sun*, 10 March 1979, 5.

Massarik, Fred, and Alvin Chenkin. "The Jewish Population of the United States in 1970: A New Estimate." In *National Jewish Population Survey 1971*, ed. Fred Massarik and the Council of Jewish Federations and Welfare Funds. New York: Council of Jewish Federations and Welfare Funds, 1972.

Massarik, Fred, and the Council of Jewish Federations and Welfare Funds, eds. *National Jewish Population Survey 1971*. New York: Council of Jewish Federations and Welfare Funds, 1972.

Matusow, Allen J. *The Unraveling of America: A History of Liberalism in the 1960s*. New York: Harper and Row, 1984.

Maynes, Mary Jo, Jennifer L. Pierce, and Barbara Laslett. *Telling Stories: The Use of Personal Narratives in the Social Sciences and History*. Ithaca, NY: Cornell University Press, 2008.

Mazal, Gedaliah. "A Letter from Yamit," *Jewish Press*, 10 February 1978, 52.

Mazower, Mark. *No Enchanted Palace: The End of Empire and the Ideological Origins of the United Nations*. Princeton, NJ: Princeton University Press, 2009.

McAlister, Melani. *Epic Encounters: Culture, Media, and U.S. Interests in the Middle East Since 1945*. Berkeley: University of California Press, 2005.

McAllester, Matt. "The Holyland's American Militants." *Details* (September 2009): 218–226.

McCarthy, Rory. "American-Israeli Settler Questioned over Terrorist Attacks." *The Guardian*, 2 November 2009.

McGeary, Johanna. "The Settlers' Lament." *Time*, 14 August 2005.

Medad, Yisrael. *"But I Saw It . . . I Read It . . . I Heard It . . .": The Activist's Guide to Monitoring Media Bias toward Israel*. Jerusalem: Israel's Media Watch, 2003.

———. "I Wasn't Invited." *My Right Word*, 11 January 2007.

————. "Nekuda B-Anglit." *Nekuda* 329 (April 2010). [Hebrew]

————. "Of Terrorists, Undergrounds, and Demonstrations: Special Report." *Counterpoint* (July 1985): 6.

————. "Waging a War for Democracy." *Jerusalem Post,* 15 October 1991, 6.

Medad, Yisrael (Winkie), and Beth Medad. "Zionist Youth Movements in the United States and Their Influence on Immigration to Israel after World War II" (interview with Zvi Fraser). Interview 178(4), 1980. Oral History Division, Avraham Harman Institute of Contemporary Jewry, Hebrew University of Jerusalem.

Medad, Yisrael, and Eli Pollack. *Israel's Electronic Broadcasting: Reporting or Managing the News?* Tel Aviv: Ariel Center for Policy Research, 1988.

"Medina Stuma." *Yediot Ahronot,* 9 August 1995, 1–4. [Hebrew]

Medoff, Rafael. "Gush Emunim and the Question of Jewish Counterterror." *Middle East Review* (Summer 1986): 17–23.

————. *Militant Zionism in America: The Rise and Impact of the Jabotinsky Movement in the United States, 1926–1948.* Tuscaloosa: University of Alabama Press, 2002.

Mendelsohn, Jane. "Yamit: Hard Work and Determined Efforts Are Building a City." *Israel Digest* 20, no. 16 (12 August 1977): 8.

Mendes-Flohr, Paul. "The Emancipation of European Jewry: Why Was It Not Self-Evident?" *Studia Rosenthaliana* 30, no. 1 (1996): 7–20.

————. "Reflections on the Ethical and Political Dialectics of Commitment." *Criterion* 47, no. 3 (Spring 2010): 11–13.

Mendes-Flohr, Paul, and Jehuda Reinharz. *The Jew in the Modern World: A Documentary History.* Oxford: Oxford University Press, 1995.

Mergui, Raphael, and Philippe Simonnot. *Israel's Ayatollahs: Meir Kahane and the Far Right in Israel.* London: Saqi Books, 1987.

Merry, Robert W. *Sands of Empire: Missionary Zeal, American Foreign Policy, and the Hazards of Global Ambition.* New York: Simon and Schuster, 2005.

Miller, Aaron David. *The PLO and the Politics of Survival.* New York: Praeger, 1983.

Miller, James. *Democracy in the Streets: From Port Huron to the Siege of Chicago.* New York: Simon and Schuster, 1987.

Miller, Richard Brian. *Terror, Religion, and Liberal Thought.* New York: Columbia University Press, 2010.

"Miriam Levinger Gets 10 Days for Contempt of Court." *Jerusalem Post,* 21 November 1995, 2.

Miron, Dan. "Teuda L-Yisrael: L-Maan Eretz Yisrael Ha-Shlaima." *Politika* 14–15 (June 1987): 37–45. [Hebrew]

Mishal, Shaul, and Avraham Sela. *The Palestinian Hamas: Vision, Violence, and Coexistence.* New York: Columbia University Press, 2000.

Mitchell, Alison. "A Killer's Path to Militancy." *New York Times,* 26 February 1994, 7.

Mitnick, Joshua. "The Two Faces of Accused Terrorist Jack Teitel." *Jewish Week,* 4 November 2009.

Mittelberg, David. *Strangers in Paradise: The Israeli Kibbutz Experience.* New Brunswick, NJ: Transaction Books, 1988.

"Mivza Elef: Hazlaha Helkit." *Nekuda,* 7 September 1983, 7. [Hebrew]

"Mivza Elef: Operation 1000; Success!" *Counterpoint* (September 1983): front cover, 4, 7.

Moore, Deborah Dash, and S. Ilan Troen, eds. *Divergent Jewish Cultures: Israel and America.* New Haven, CT: Yale University Press, 2001.

Morgan, Michael L. *Beyond Auschwitz: Post-Holocaust Thought in America.* Oxford: Oxford University Press, 2001.

Morris, Benny. *The Birth of the Palestinian Refugee Problem, 1947–1949.* Cambridge: Cambridge University Press, 1987.

——. *Righteous Victims: A History of the Zionist–Arab Conflict, 1881–2001.* New York: Vintage Books, 1999.

Morrison, David. *The Gush: Center of Modern Religious Zionism.* Jerusalem: Gefen, 2004.

Mosaic Magazine. "If American Jews and Israel Are Drifting Apart, What Is the Reason?" roundtable, April 2016.

"Moshav Naot Sinai Inaugurated." *Haaretz,* 30 September 1977, 1. [Hebrew]

Moyn, Samuel. *The Last Utopia: Human Rights in History.* Cambridge, MA: Harvard University Press, 2010.

Moyn, Samuel, and Andrew Santori, eds. *Global Intellectual History.* New York: Columbia University Press, 2013.

Nach, Yossi. "B-Hiahazut Tekoa." *Amudim* 374, no. 25, Kerakh Gimmel (Kislev 1977): 106. [Hebrew]

Naor, Mordechai. *Gush Etzion M-Raishito Ad T"SH.* Jerusalem: Yad Yitzhak Ben Tzvi, 1986. [Hebrew]

Navon, Daniel. "We Are a People, One People: How 1967 Transformed Holocaust Memory and Jewish Identity in Israel and the US." *Journal of Historical Sociology* (2014): 342–373.

Near, Henry. *Frontiersmen and Halutzim: The Image of the Pioneer in North America and Pre-state Jewish Palestine—Discussion Paper.* Haifa: University of Haifa, 1997.

"Nekuda L-Inyan Im: Era Rapaport, Shaliah 'Gush Emunim' B-New York—Shalihai Ha-Mitsvah." *Nekuda,* 16 April 1984, 8–9. [Hebrew]

Neslen, Arthur. *Occupied Minds: A Journey through the Israeli Psyche.* London: Pluto Press, 2006.

Neuman, Tamara. "Reinstating the Religious Nation: A Study of National Religious Persuasion, Settlement, and Violence in Hebron." PhD dissertation, University of Chicago, 2000.

Neumann, Boaz. *Land and Desire in Early Zionism.* Translated by Haim Watzman. Waltham, MA: Brandeis University Press, 2011.

Neusner, Jacob. "American Jews in Israel: A Special Breed—They Have Something Rarer Than Money to Contribute." *Present Tense* 1, no. 1 (Autumn 1973): 40–41.

New Dimensions: Aliyah to Judaea, Samaria, and Gaza. Jerusalem: World Zionist Organization, 1984.

Newman, David. "From Hitnachalut to Hitnatkut: The Impact of Gush Emunim and the Settlement Movement on Israeli Politics and Society." *Israel Studies* 10, no. 3 (Fall 2005): 192–247.

———. *The Impact of Gush Emunim: Politics and Settlement in the West Bank.* New York: St. Martin's Press, 1985.

———. *Jewish Settlement in the West Bank: The Role of Gush Emunim.* Durham, UK: University of Durham, 1982.

———. "The Territorial Politics of Exurbanization: Reflections on 25 Years of Jewish Settlement in the West Bank." *Israel Affairs* 3, no. 1 (August 1996): 61–85.

Newton, Michael. *Bitter Grain: Huey Newton and the Black Panther Party.* Los Angeles: Holloway House, 1991.

"1968 Tourism to Israel Tops Predictions." *Israel Digest,* 27 December 1968, 7.

Ninkovich, Frank. *The United States and Imperialism.* Malden, MA: Blackwell, 2001.

Nissenson, Hugh. *Notes from the Frontier.* New York: Dial Press, 1968.

Nobles, Gregory H. *American Frontiers: Cultural Encounters and Continental Conquest.* New York: Hill and Wang, 1997.

"Notice: We Are Planning to Build an American Suburb in Israel!" *Aliyon* (October 1972): 5.

Novick, Peter. *The Holocaust in American Life.* New York: Houghton Mifflin, 1999.

OECD. "Society at a Glance 2014—Highlights: Israel."

O'Malley, Padraig. *The Two-State Delusion: Israel and Palestine—A Tale of Two Narratives.* New York: Viking, 2015.

Oppenheimer, Mark. *Knocking on Heaven's Door: American Religion in the Age of Counterculture.* New Haven, CT: Yale University Press, 2003.

Oren, Michael B. *Ally: My Journey across the American–Israeli Divide.* New York: Random House, 2015.

———. *Power, Faith, and Fantasy: America in the Middle East, 1776 to the Present.* New York: W. W. Norton, 2007.

———. *Six Days of War: June 1967 and the Making of the Modern Middle East.* New York: Ballantine Books, 2002.

Orenstein, Amaryah. "Let My People Go! The Student Struggle for Soviet Jewry and the Rise of American Jewish Identity Politics." PhD dissertation, Brandeis University, 2014.

"OU Announces Aliyah Fund Drive." *Arutz Sheva,* 3 July 2003.

Oz, Amos. *In the Land of Israel.* Translated by Maurie Goldberg-Bartura. London: Fontana, 1983.

Paine, Robert. "Beyond the Hebron Massacre, 1994." *Anthropology Today* 11, no. 1 (February 1995): 8–15.

Pappe, Ilan. "Zionism and Colonialism: A Comparative View of Diluted Colonialism in Asia and Africa." *South Atlantic Quarterly* 107, no. 4 (2008): 611–633.

Paraszczuk, Joanna. "Court Rules Yaakov 'Jack' Teitel Fit to Stand Trial." *Jerusalem Post,* 12 July 2011.

Parker, Michael. *John Winthrop: Founding the City on the Hill.* New York: Routledge, 2014.

"Passover and Easter in the Holy Land." *Religion & Ethics Newsweekly,* 18 April 2003.

"Paterson, N.J. Adopts 'El Al.'" *Israel Digest,* 7 March 1969, 5.

Patterson, Richard North. "Israel Is the GOP's New Wedge Issue." *Boston Globe,* 28 July 2015.

Paz, Shelly. "New York–Born Likud Contender Promises to Promote Aliya and Fight a Two-State Solution." *Jerusalem Post,* 7 December 2008, 2.

"'Peace Corps for Israel' Proposed for U.S. Jewry." *Israel Digest,* April 1968, 6.

Pedahzur, Ami. *Miflegot Ha-Yamin Ha-Kitsoni B-Yisrael: M-Tzemiha L-Deikhah.* Tel Aviv: Tel Aviv University, 2000. [Hebrew]

Pedahzur, Ami, and Arie Perlinger. *Jewish Terrorism in Israel.* New York: Columbia University Press, 2009.

Peleg, Samuel. *Zealotry and Vengeance—Quest of a Religious Identity Group: A Socio-Political Account of the Rabin Assassination.* Lanham, MD: Lexington Books, 2002.

Penslar, Derek J. *Zionism and Technocracy: The Engineering of Jewish Settlement in Palestine, 1870–1918.* Bloomington: Indiana University Press, 1991.

"The People of Israel and the Land of Israel, Including Judea and Samaria." Religious Services Listings. *New York Times,* 27 February 1981, classified ad 286, D15.

Peretz, Martin. "The American Left and Israel." *Commentary* 44, no. 5 (November 1, 1967): 27–34.

Peters, Joshua Nathan. "The Origins and Development of the NAHAL Brigades of the Israeli Defense Forces, 1949–1999." MA thesis, University of Brunswick, 2008.

Petersen, William. "A General Typology of Migration." *American Sociological Review* 23, no. 3 (June 1958): 256–266.

Pew Research Center. *A Portrait of Jewish Americans: Findings from a Pew Research Center Survey of U.S. Jews.* Pew Research Center, 2013.

Pins, Arnulf L. "The Crisis in Jewish Life: The Aftermath of the Yom Kippur War." *Journal of Jewish Communal Service* 51, no. 1 (September 1974): 9–20.

Pinsky, Marc I. "613 Words: The Summer of '67." *American Jewish Life Magazine,* May/June 2007.

Podhoretz, Norman. "Neoconservativism: A Eulogy." In *The Norman Podhoretz Reader,* ed. Thomas L. Jeffers. New York: Free Press, 2004.

———. "Now, Instant Zionism." *New York Times Magazine,* 3 February 1974.

———. *Why Are Jews Liberals?* New York: Doubleday, 2009.

Poll, Solomon, and Ernest Krausz, eds. *On Ethnic and Religious Diversity in Israel.* Ramat-Gan: Bar-Ilan University, 1975.

Preston, Andrew. *Sword of the Spirit, Shield of Faith: Religion in American War and Diplomacy.* New York: Albert A. Knopf, 2012.

Preston, Andrew, Bruce J. Shulman, and Julian E. Zelitzer, eds. *Faithful Republic: Religion and Politics in Modern America.* Philadelphia: University of Pennsylvania Press, 2015.

Preuss, Teddy. "An Easy Excuse for Murder." *Jerusalem Post,* 28 February 1994, 6.

Primus, Richard A. *The American Language of Rights.* Cambridge: Cambridge University Press, 1999.

"Profile of the Yishuv: Efrat Municipality." Mayor's Office, Municipality of Efrat, summer 2011. [Hebrew]

"Project 1000: An Israel Summer Tour for the Family." *Aliyon* (Winter 1983): 17.

"Psst . . . Wanna Join a Garin?" *Aliyon* (March 1978): 14–16.

Quandt, William B. *Peace Process: American Diplomacy and the Arab–Israeli Conflict since 1967*. Washington, DC: Brookings Institution Press, 2005.

"Rabin Raps Israeli Settlers as Protestors Continue Campaign." *Jewish Telegraphic Agency*, 2 August 1995.

Rabin, Yitzhak. "168th Statement to the Knesset by Prime Minister Yitzhak Rabin: Statement in the Knesset by Prime Minister Yitzhak Rabin on the Hebron Murders" (28 February 1994). Israel Ministry of Foreign Affairs, vols. 13–14.

Rabinovich, Abraham. "Between a Rock and a Hard Place." *Jerusalem Post*, 7 July 1989, 8.

Raider, Mark A. *The Emergence of American Zionism*. New York: NYU Press, 1998.

Raider, Mark A., Jonathan D. Sarna, and Ronald W. Zweig. *Abba Hillel Silver and American Zionism*. London: Frank Cass, 1997.

Rangel, Jesus. "Man Sought in Israel for Attacks on Arabs Is Seized." *New York Times*, 16 January 1986.

Rapaport, Era. *Letters from Tel Mond Prison: An Israeli Settler Defends His Act of Terror*. Edited by William B. Helmreich. New York: Free Press, 1996.

Rappel, Joel. "The Convergence of Politics and Prayer: Jewish Prayers for the Government and the State of Israel." PhD dissertation, Boston University, 2008.

Rauzin, Alan H. "The Yesha Mission's Journey." *YESHA Report* (September–October 1997): 12.

"Rav Shel Ir O Ir Shel Rav?" *Gushpanka* 1, vo. 21 (November 1986). [Hebrew]

Ravitzsky, Aviezer. *Dat U-Medina*. Jerusalem: Israel Democracy Institute, 2005. [Hebrew]

———. *Messianism, Zionism, and Jewish Religious Radicalism*. Chicago: University of Chicago Press, 1996.

———. *Religious and Secular Jews in Israel: A Kulturkampf?* Jerusalem: Israel Democracy Institute, 1997.

Rebhun, Uzi, and Lilach Lev Ari. *American Israelis: Migration, Transnationalism, and Disaporic Identity*. Leiden: Brill, 2010.

Rebhun, Uzi, and Chaim I. Waxman. "The 'Americanization' of Israel: A Demographic, Cultural, and Political Evaluation." *Israel Studies* 5, no. 1 (Spring 2000): 65–91.

Reich, Tova. *The Jewish War: A Novel*. New York: Pantheon Books, 1995.

"Religion: The Sound of the Shofar." *Time*, 4 October 1971.

"Report of Garin Yamit Conference." *Aliyon* (May 1974): 4, 10.

Revivi, Oded. "Beyond the Lines." *Times of Israel*, 28 July 2016.

Rifkin, Ira. "Liberals Turn Right: U.S.-Born Settlers Fight for Turf as Peace Looms." *JWeekly*, 28 July 1995.

Rifkind, Gabrielle, and Giandomenico Pico. *The Fog of Peace: The Human Face of Conflict Resolution*. London: I. B. Tauris, 2014.

"The Right on the Rise." *Journal of Palestine Studies* 15, no. 1 (Autumn 1985): 163–165.

"Riskin, on U.S. Visit, Defends Civil Disobedience by Settlers." *Jewish Telegraphic Agency,* 18 July 1995.

Riskin, Shlomo. *Listening to God: A Gift for My Grandchildren.* London: Toby Press, 2010.

———. *The Living Tree: Studies in Modern Orthodoxy.* Jerusalem: Maggid Books, 2014.

———. "Retorika Shel Manhig V-Hakamat Ha-Yishuv Efrat."

Rock, Stephen R. *Faith and Foreign Policy: The Views of U.S. Christians and Christian Organizations.* New York: Continuum International, 2011.

Rodan, Steve. "Efrat Women Execute Secret Mission for the Land of Israel." *Jerusalem Post,* 4 August 1995, 8.

Rodinson, Maxime. *Israel: A Colonial-Settler State?* New York: Pathfinder, 1973.

Roei, Menachem. "Ha-Im Takum Ir Hadash Bein Gush Etzion L-Yerushalayim?" *Yediot Ahronot,* 3 June 1975, 20. [Hebrew]

Rose, Jacqueline. *The Question of Zion.* Princeton, NJ: Princeton University Press, 2005.

Rosen, Jeffrey. *Louis D. Brandeis: American Prophet.* New Haven, CT: Yale University Press, 2016.

Rosenberg, Stuart E. *America Is Different: The Search for Jewish Identity.* London: Thomas Nelson and Sons, 1964.

Rosenblatt, Carole. "Amerika, Amerika." *Yamiton* 28, 14 October 1976, 13. [Hebrew]

———. "English News." *Yamiton* 23, 28 May 1976, 10.

———. "'Sister City,' Yamit Adopted by PB [Palm Beach]." *Jewish Floridian of Palm Beach County,* 16 December 1977, 10.

Rosenblatt, Liane Sue. "Building Yamit: Relationships between Officials and Settler Representatives in Israel." PhD dissertation, University of Rochester, 1983.

Roskin, Michael, and Jeffrey L. Edelson. "The Emotional Health of English Speaking Immigrants to Israel." *Journal of Jewish Communal Service* 60, no. 2 (Winter 1983): 155–161.

———. "A Research Note on the Emotional Health of English-Speaking Immigrants in Israel." *Jewish Journal of Sociology* 26, no. 2 (December 1984): 139–144.

Ross, Dennis. *Doomed to Succeed: The U.S.–Israel Relationship from Truman to Obama.* New York: Farrar, Straus and Giroux, 2015.

———. *The Missing Peace: The Inside Story of the Fight for Middle East Peace.* New York: Farrar, Straus and Giroux, 2004.

Ross, Jack. *Rabbi Outcast: Elmer Berger and American Jewish Anti-Zionism.* Washington, DC: Potomac Books, 2011.

Rot, Nurit. "Korbanotav Shel Yaakov Teitel Tovaim Pizui B-Sakh 4 Million Shekel." *The Marker (Haaretz),* 12 November 2009. [Hebrew]

Roth, Stephen J., ed. *The Impact of the Six Day War: A Twenty Year Assessment.* Houndsmills, UK: Macmillan, 1998.

Rourke, Mary. "In Pursuit of Non-Violence." *Jerusalem Post,* 11 January 2002, 19.

Routtenberg, Aryeh, and Sandy Amichai, eds. *The Etzion Bloc in the Hills of Judea.* Kfar Etzion: Kfar Etzion Field School, 2005.

Rubenstein, Amnon. *The Zionist Dream Revisited: From Herzl to Gush Emunim and Back.* New York: Schocken Books, 1984.

Rubenstein, Danny. *Mi L-Hashem Elai: Gush Emunim.* Tel Aviv: Ha-Kibbutz Ha-Meuhad, 1982. [Hebrew]

Rubin, Barry. *Revolution until Victory? The Politics and History of the PLO.* Cambridge, MA: Harvard University Press, 1994.

Ruby, Robert. "To Extremist Arabs and Israelis, Peace Efforts Call for Increase in Violence—To Hardliners, Talks Threaten Basic Beliefs in Right to Territory." *Baltimore Sun,* 30 October 1991.

Russo, Yocheved Miriam. "Personal Encounters: The Meatman of Yamit." *Jerusalem Post,* 18 April 2007.

———. "Veterans: Carole Rosenblatt." *Jerusalem Post,* 2 October 2008.

Rutenberg, Jim, Mike McIntire, and Ethan Bronner. "Tax-Exempt Funds Aiding Settlements in the West Bank." *New York Times,* 6 July 2010, A1.

Rynhold, Jonathan. *The Arab-Israeli Conflict in American Political Culture.* Cambridge: Cambridge University Press, 2015.

———. "Re-conceptualizing Israeli Approaches to 'Land for Peace' and the Palestinian Question since 1967." *Israel Studies* 6, no. 2 (Summer 2001): 33–52.

Sackett, Shmuel. "Disappointed? Not Me." *Jerusalem Post,* 11 September 1996, 6.

Sacks, Jonathan. *Not in God's Name: Confronting Religious Violence.* London: Hodder and Stoughton, 2015.

———, ed. *Tradition and Transition: Essays Presented to Chief Rabbi Sir Emmanuel Jakobovits to Celebrate Twenty Years in Office.* London: Jews' College Publications, 1986.

Said, Edward. *Orientalism.* New York: Vintage Books, 1978.

———. *Representations of the Intellectual: The 1993 Reich Lectures.* London: Vintage, 1994.

———. "Zionism from the Standpoint of Its Victims." *Social Texts* 1 (Winter 1979): 7–58.

Sally, Razeen. *Classical Liberalism and International Economic Order: Studies in Theory and Intellectual History.* London: Routledge, 2002.

Salzman, Jack, and Cornell West. *Struggles in the Promised Land: Toward a History of Black-Jewish Relations in the United States.* New York: Oxford University Press, 1997.

Sand, Shlomo. *The Invention of the Jewish People.* London: Verso, 2009.

Sanders, Ronald. "Settling in Israel?" *Commentary* 40, no. 2 (August 1, 1965): 37–44.

Sandler, Shmuel. *The State of Israel, the Land of Israel: The Statist and Ethno-nationalist Dimensions of Foreign Policy.* Westport, CT: Greenwood Press, 1993.

Sarna, Jonathan D. *American Judaism: A History.* New Haven, CT: Yale University Press, 2004.

"Save the Dates" (special advertising section). *YESHA Report,* June 1997.

Schenker, Hillel. "'Does He Really Represent Us?' Meir Kahane and American Israelis." *Israel Horizons* 33 (January/February 1985): 20–23.

Schiff, Gary S. *Tradition and Politics: The Religious Parties of Israel.* Detroit: Wayne State University Press, 1977.

Schiff, Stacy. "The Witches of Salem." *New Yorker,* 7 September 2015.

Schiff, Ze'ev, and Ehud Ya'ari. *Israel's Lebanon War.* New York: Simon and Schuster, 1984.

Schiffman, Steve. "Pioneer Who Followed a Dream." *Israel Digest* 20, no. 16 (12 August 1977): 9.

Schmemann, Serge. "Rabbi Takes U.S.-Style Protest to Israel." *New York Times,* 7 August 1995, A5.

Schoffman, Stuart. "My Fellow Lunatics." *Jerusalem Report,* 21 April 1994, 50.

Schrag, Carl. "Flower Power." *Jerusalem Post,* 14 February 1992.

Schwartz, Joshua. "Modicum of Validity." *Jerusalem Post,* 11 February 1994, 2.

Schweid, Eliezer. *The Land of Israel: National Home or Land of Destiny.* Translated by Deborah Greniman. Cranbury, NJ: Associated University Presses, 1985.

Sedan, Gil. "Gush Demands Appear to Have Split the NRP Leadership." *Jewish Telegraphic Agency,* 9 October 1979.

———. "25 Released Terrorists to Leave Israel." *Jewish Telegraphic Agency,* 5 June 1985.

Segal, Haggai. *Dear Brothers: The West Bank Jewish Underground.* Woodmere, NY: Beit Shamai Publications, 1988.

———. *Yamit, Sof: Ha-Maavak L-Azirat Ha-Nesiga B-Sinai.* Mizrah Binyamin: Midreshet Ha-Darom, 1999. [Hebrew]

Segev, Tom. *Elvis in Jerusalem: Post-Zionism and the Americanization of Israel.* New York: Metropolitan Books, 2002.

———. *1967: Israel, the War, and the Year That Transformed the Middle East.* Translated by Jessica Cohen. New York: Metropolitan Books, 2005.

Seliktar, Ofira. *New Zionism and the Foreign Policy System of Israel.* Carbondale: Southern Illinois University Press, 1986.

"Senior Branch." *AACI Jerusalem Voice* 8, no. 1 (September 1973): 1–2.

Shadar, Rachel. "Bridge from Manhattan." *Israel Scene* (December 1982): 26.

Shafat, Gershon. *Gush Emunim: Ha-Sipur M-Ahorei Ha-Klaim.* Beit El: Sifriyat Beit El, 1995. [Hebrew]

Shafir, Gershon. "Challenging Nationalism and Israel's 'Open Frontier' on the West Bank." *Theory and Society* 13 (1984): 803–827.

———. *Land, Labor, and the Origins of the Israeli-Palestinian Conflict, 1882–1914.* Cambridge: Cambridge University Press, 1989.

———. "Zionism and Colonialism: A Comparative Approach." In *Israel in Comparative Perspective,* ed. Michael N. Barnett. Albany: SUNY Press, 1996.

Shafir, Gershon, and Yoav Peled. "Thorns in Your Eyes: The Socio-Economic Base of the Kahane Vote." In *The Elections in Israel, 1984,* ed. Asher Arian and Michal Shamir, 189–206. Jerusalem: Ramot, 1986.

Shahak, Israel, and Norton Mezvinsky. *Jewish Fundamentalism in Israel.* London: Pluto Press, 2004.

Shain, Yossi. *Marketing the American Creed Abroad: Diasporas in the U.S. and Their Homelands.* Cambridge: Cambridge University Press, 1999.

Shalman, Michael, and Menachem Hadar. *A Summer Family Experience: Operation 1000* (film). Directed by Menachem Hadar. Jerusalem: Ministry of Absorption and NZR Film Productions, 1983.

Shalom, Zaki. "Kissinger and the American Jewish Leadership after the 1973 War." *Israel Studies* 7, no. 1 (Spring 2002): 195–232.

Shapira, Anita. "Ben Gurion and the Bible: The Forging of a Historical Narrative." *Middle Eastern Studies* 33, no. 4 (October 1977): 645–674.

———. *Ha-Mavak Ha-Nikhzav: Avoda Ivrit, 1929–1939.* Tel Aviv: Universitat Tel Aviv, 1977. [Hebrew]

———, ed. *Israeli Identity in Transition.* Westport, CT: Praeger, 2004.

———. *Land and Power: The Zionist Resort to Force, 1881–1948.* Stanford, CA: Stanford University Press, 1992.

Shapiro, Edward S. *A Time for Healing: American Jewry since World War II.* Baltimore: Johns Hopkins University Press, 1992.

Shapiro, Haim. "Ben-Eliezer Says Settlers 'Almost Blew Up' His Car." *Jerusalem Post,* 5 October 1993, 4.

———. "Tell It on the Mountain." *Jerusalem Post,* 7 May 1999, 14.

Shapiro, Jay. *From Both Sides Now: An American-Israeli Odyssey.* Tel Aviv: Dvir Katzman, 1983.

Shapiro, Michael. *Divisions between Traditionalism and Liberalism in the American Jewish Community.* Lewiston, ME: Edwin Mellon, 1991.

Sharon, Jeremy. "Orthodox Woman Appointed to Serve as Communal Spiritual Leader in Efrat." *Jerusalem Post,* 18 January 2015.

Shatz, Adam. *Prophets Outcast: A Century of Dissident Jewish Writing about Israel and Zionism.* New York: Thunder's Mouth Press, 2003.

Shavit, Ari. *My Promised Land: The Triumph and Tragedy of Israel.* London: Scribe, 2014.

Shavit, Yaakov. *Jabotinsky and the Revisionist Movement, 1925–1948.* London: Frank Cass, 1988.

———. *M-Ivri Ad Kenaani.* Tel Aviv: Universitat Tel Aviv, 1984. [Hebrew]

Shelef, Nadav. *Evolving Nationalism: Homeland, Identity, and Religion in Israel, 1925–2005.* Ithaca, NY: Cornell University Press, 2010.

"Sherut Bitahon Klali: Hakirat Yaakov (Jack) Teitel—Pianuah Sharsheret Piguim." [N.d.] Shin Bet (General Security Service), Israel.

Shiloah, Zvi. *Ashmat Yerushalayim.* Tel Aviv: Karni, 1989. [Hebrew]

Shimoni, Gideon. *The Zionist Ideology.* Hanover, NH: University Press of New England, 1995.

Shindler, Colin. *The Land beyond Promise: Israel, Likud, and the Zionist Dream.* London: Tauris, 2002.

———. *The Rise of the Israeli Right: From Odessa to Hebron.* New York: Cambridge University Press, 2015.

———. *The Triumph of Military Zionism: Nationalism and the Origins of the Israeli Right.* London: I. B. Tauris, 2006.

Shipler, David K. "Israel Accuses 4 Jews of a Dozen Grenade Attacks." *New York Times,* 10 April 1984, A4.

———. "Israel Calls Jewish Terrorists Isolated." *New York Times,* 9 March 1984, A3.

———. "Israeli Cabinet Approves Payment to the Displaced Settlers in Sinai." *New York Times,* 8 January 1982, A3.

———. "Israelis to Expand Seven Settlements in the West Bank—But Cabinet, in a Unanimous Vote, Decides Not to Seize Private Arab-Held Land for Them." *New York Times,* 15 October 1979, A1.

———. "Militants Try To Reach Sinai By Boat." *New York Times,* 2 April 1982, A3.

———. "Settlers Protest Sinai Compensation Plan." *New York Times,* 12 January 1982, A3.

Shivi, Chaim. "B-Ofra Huhzara Ha-Puga, U B-Tekoa Hehala Prizat Ha-Geder L-Har Haba." *Yediot Ahronot,* 5 October 1979, 2. [Hebrew]

———. "Tokhnit Sharon Kolelet Hakamat Gush Yishuvim M-Daron L-Hevron." *Yediot Ahronot,* 4 November 1979, 4. [Hebrew]

———. "Yom Shalem Nihalu Hayalai TZHAL V-Ha-Mitnahalim Mishakai 'Tofeset V-Mehaboim' B-Rehavai Yehuda V-Shomron." *Yediot Ahronot,* 16 October 1979: 3. [Hebrew]

Shlaim, Avi. *The Iron Wall: Israel and the Arab World.* New York: W. W. Norton, 2000.

Shuval, Judith. *Immigrants on the Threshold.* New York: Antherton Press, 1963.

Sidikman, Judith. "Efrat, City of Dreams." *Jerusalem Post,* 15 August 1995, 6.

Siegman, Henry, ed. *The Religious Dimensions of Israel: The Challenge of the Six-Day War.* New York: Synagogue Council of America, 1968.

Silberman, Charles E. *A Certain People: American Jews and Their Lives Today.* New York: Summit Books, 1985.

Silberstein, Laurence J. *Jewish Fundamentalism in Comparative Perspective: Religion, Ideology, and the Crisis of Modernity.* New York: NYU Press, 1993.

———. *The Post-Zionism Debates: Knowledge and Power in Israeli Culture.* New York: Routledge, 1999.

Silver, Eric. "The Radicalization of Rabbi Riskin." *Jerusalem Report,* 23 March 1995, 16.

Silver, Matthew. *First Contact: Origins of the American-Israeli Connection—Haluzim from America during the Palestine Mandate.* West Hartford, CT: Graduate Group, 2006.

———. *Our Exodus: Leon Uris and the Americanization of Israel's Founding Story.* Detroit: Wayne State University Press, 2010.

Sim, Chaim. "Op-Ed: Baruch Goldstein and Hebron Ten Years Later." *Israel National News,* 2 March 2004.

Simmons, Erica. *Hadassah and the Zionist Project.* Lanham, MD: Rowman and Littlefield, 2006.

Simons, Jake Wallis. "Meet the Settlers: Chapter Four—The Murder of Kobi Mandell." *The Telegraph,* 2014.

Simons, Judy. "Gush Etzion: Tragedy and Rebirth." Arutz 7 Radio broadcast, 21 April 2010.

Siskin, Joshua. "From Berkeley to Beit Shean: Portrait of a Jew as a Young Man." Unpublished manuscript, Jerusalem, 1974. Cataloged at the National Library of Israel.

Sivan, Emmanuel. "The Enclave Culture." In *Fundamentalisms Comprehended,* ed. Martin E. Marty and F. Scott Appleby, 11–68. Chicago: University of Chicago Press, 1995.

"Siyur Sh-Kazeh." *B-Mahaneh Ha-NAHAL* 3 [287] (December 1975): 21. [Hebrew]

Sklare, Marshall. "Lakeville and Israel: The Six-Day War and Its Aftermath." *Midstream* 14, no. 8 (October 1968): 6.

————, ed. *The Jew in American Society.* New York: Behrman House, 1974.

————. *Observing America's Jews.* Hanover, NH: University Press of New England, 1993.

Sklare, Marshall, and Joseph Greenblum. *Jewish Identity on the Suburban Frontier: A Study of Survival in the Open Society.* Chicago: University of Chicago Press, 1979.

Slater, Robert. "Angry Settlers at 'Little Sea.'" *Time,* 30 January 1978.

Sleeper, James A., and Alan L. Mintz, eds. *The New Jews.* New York: Vintage Books, 1971.

Sluga, Glenda. *Internationalism in the Age of Nationalism.* Philadelphia: University of Pennsylvania Press, 2013.

Smith, Anthony D. *Nations and Nationalism in the Global Era.* Cambridge: Polity Press, 1995.

Smith, George H. *The System of Liberty: Themes in the History of Classical Liberalism.* Cambridge: Cambridge University Press, 2013.

Smith, Tony. *America's Mission: The United States and the Worldwide Struggle for Democracy in the Twentieth Century.* Princeton, NJ: Princeton University Press, 1995.

Smolowe, Jill. "Americans Talk of Plan for Life on West Bank." *New York Times,* 23 March 1980, 11.

Smooha, Sammy. *Israel: Pluralism and Conflict.* Berkeley: University of California Press, 1978.

Sobel, Zvi, and Benjamin Beit-Hallahmi. *Tradition, Innovation, Conflict: Jewishness and Judaism in Contemporary Israel.* Albany: SUNY Press, 1991.

"Sons of Etzion Return to Build Homes." *Israel Digest,* 20 October 1967, 1.

"Special Family and Legal Defense Fund" [advertisement]. *Jewish Press,* 8 June 1984, 41.

"Special Interview: Mayor of Shiloh Believes West Bank Is No Longer an Issue for International Negotiation." *Jewish Telegraphic Agency,* 11 March 1983.

Spiegel, Steven L. *The Other Arab-Israeli Conflict: Making America's Middle East Policy, from Truman to Reagan.* Chicago: University of Chicago Press, 1985.

Spielman, Danny. "Lamah Olim Aleinu?" *Nekuda* 71 (23 March 1984): 22–23.

Sprinzak, Ehud. *The Ascendance of Israel's Radical Right.* Oxford: Oxford University Press, 1991.

————. *Brother against Brother: Violence and Extremism in Israeli Politics from Altalena to the Rabin Assassination.* New York: Free Press, 1999.

————. "The Iceberg Model of Political Extremism." In *The Impact of Gush Emunim: Politics and Settlement in the West Bank,* ed. David Newman, 27–45. New York: St. Martin's Press, 1985.

————. *Ish Ha-Yashar B-Enav: Ilegalism B-Hevra Ha-Yisraelit.* Tel Aviv: Sifriyat Poalim, 1986. [Hebrew]

————. *The Israeli Right and the Peace Process, 1992–1996.* Jerusalem: Hebrew University of Jerusalem, 1998.

Stanislawski, Michael. *Zionism and the Fin de Siècle: Cosmopolitanism and Nationalism from Nordau to Jabotinsky.* Berkeley: University of California Press, 2001.

Starr, Joyce R. *Kissing through Glass: The Invisible Shield between Americans and Israelis.* Chicago: Contemporary Books, 1990.

State of Israel Ministry of Immigrant Absorption and Jewish Agency Department for Aliya and Absorption. *Higher Education in Israel: A Guide for Overseas Students.* Tel Aviv: Yarom Press, 1970.

"The State of Jewish Belief: A Symposium." *Commentary,* 1 August 1966, 71–160.

State of Palestine Negotiations Affairs Department. "Media Brief: Israel's Colonization in West Bethlehem and Its Policy of Destroying the Prospects for Peace." September 2014.

Staub, Michael E., ed. *The Jewish 1960s: An American Sourcebook.* Waltham, MA: Brandeis University Press, 2004.

————. *Torn at the Roots: The Crisis of Jewish Liberalism in Postwar America.* New York: Columbia University Press, 2002.

Steding, William. *Presidential Faith and Foreign Policy: Jimmy Carter the Disciple and Ronald Reagan the Alchemist.* New York: Palgrave Macmillan, 2014.

Stein, Gary. "Ex-Bostonian Calls Life in Hebron Rare Chance to Make Jewish History." *Florida Sun-Sentinel,* 24 February 1988.

Stein, Harvey. "The Peace-Seeking Settler Rabbi." *Tablet Magazine,* 12 March 2013.

Stein, Kenneth W. *Heroic Diplomacy: Sadat, Kissinger, Carter, Begin, and the Quest for Arab-Israeli Peace.* New York: Routledge, 1999.

————. *The Land Question in Palestine, 1917–1939.* Chapel Hill: University of North Carolina Press, 1984.

Stephanson, Anders. *Manifest Destiny: American Expansion and the Empire of Right.* New York: Hill and Wang, 1995.

"Stereotype of American Olim Questioned." *Counterpoint* (August 1984): 1.

Sternberg, Shlomo. "From Orthodox Jewish Education to Hebron." *New York Times,* 9 March 1994, A14.

Stock, Ernest. *Partners and Pursestrings: A History of the United Israel Appeal.* Lanham, MD: University Press of America, 1987.

Stone, I. F. "Holy War." *New York Review of Books,* 3 August 1967.

Stone, Russell A. *Social Change in Israel: Attitudes and Events, 1967–79.* New York: Praeger, 1982.

Stork, Joe, and Sharon Rose. "Zionism and American Jewry." *Journal of Palestine Studies* 3, no. 3 (Spring 1974): 39–57.

"Suspects Detained in the Murder of Herodian Manager." *Haaretz*, 5 July 1982, 6. [Hebrew]

Tabory, Joseph. "The Piety of Politics: Jewish Prayers for the State of Israel." In *Liturgy in the Life of the Synagogue: Studies in the History of Jewish Prayer*, ed. Ruth Langer and Steven Fine, 225–246. Winona Lake, IN: Eisenbrauns, 2005.

"Takanu Yeted B-Tekoa." *Zeraim* 11 (Av 1975): 3; 5. [Hebrew]

Talmi, Menachem. "Ha-Amerikanim Mistarfim L-Rusim B-Yamit." *Maariv* (Sof Shavua), Passover edition, 1975. [Hebrew]

Taub, Gadi. *The Settlers and the Struggle over the Meaning of Zionism*. New Haven, CT: Yale University Press, 2010.

Tayar, Yehudit. "Yesha Council Unveils Ambitious Tourism Campaign." *YESHA Report* (August 1997): 5.

———. "Yesha Launches Tourism Campaign." *YESHA Report* (November 1997): 5.

"Tekoa." *Zeraim* 9 (Sivan 1975): 16. [Hebrew]

"Tekoa Resident Loses Appeal in Self-Defense Shooting Case." *Israel National News*, 3 March 2002.

Temko, Ned. "West Bank's Changing Face: New Settlers Less Politicized, Arab Youth More So than Their West Bank Predecessors." *Christian Science Monitor*, 18 October 1985.

Tessler, Mark. *A History of the Israeli-Palestinian Conflict*. Bloomington: Indiana University Press, 1994.

"Thousands Stage Anti-Kahane Rally in an Arab Village." *Jewish Telegraphic Agency*, 6 August 1984.

Tilley, Virginia. *The One State Solution*. Ann Arbor: University of Michigan Press, 2005.

"Travel Agents on Study-Tour in Israel." *Israel Digest*, 15 December 1967, 7.

Troen, S. Ilan. "Frontier Myths and Their Applications in America and Israel: A Transnational Perspective." *Journal of American History* 88, no. 3 (December 1999): 1209–1230.

———. *Imaging Zion: Dreams, Designs, and Realities in a Century of Jewish Settlement*. New Haven, CT: Yale University Press, 2003.

———. "Spearheads of the Zionist Frontier: Historical Perspectives on Post-1967 Settlement Planning in Judea and Samaria." *Planning Perspectives* 7, no. 1 (January 1992): 81–100.

Tsahor, Zeev. *Hazan: Tenuat Hayim—Ha-Shomer Ha-Tsair, Ha-Kibbutz Ha-Arzi Mapam*. Jerusalem: Yad Yitzhak Ben-Zvi, 1997. [Hebrew]

Tsuda, Takeyuki, ed. *Diasporic Homecomings: Ethnic Return Migration in Comparative Perspective*. Stanford, CA: Stanford University Press, 2009.

Tsur, Bathsheva. "Gordon: Rejecting Immigrants for Their Views Is Not Acceptable." *Jerusalem Post*, 16 March 1994, 2.

———. "Tsaban: US Extremists Should Be Forbidden to Immigrate." *Jerusalem Post*, 1 March 1994, 2.

———. "Weizman: Worst Thing in Zionism." *Jerusalem Post,* 27 February 1994, 3.
Turner, Frederick Jackson. *The Significance of the Frontier in American History.* London: Penguin, 2008.
Tyrrell, Ian. *Transnational Nation: United States History in Global Perspective Since 1789.* New York: Palgrave Macmillan, 2015.
"U.J.A. Fact-Finding Mission." *Israel Digest,* November 1968, 6.
The Underground: Jewish Settlers Fight Back. Special Supplement. *Counterpoint,* August 1984.
Ungar, Beverly Anne. "Outraged." *Jerusalem Post,* 25 April 1994, 6.
Uris, Leon. *Exodus.* New York: Bantam Books, 1959.
Urofsky, Melvin I. *American Zionism from Herzl to Holocaust.* Garden City, NY: Anchor Press, 1975.
———. *Louis D. Brandeis: A Life.* New York: Pantheon Books, 2009.
———. *A Voice That Spoke for Justice: The Life and Times of Stephen S. Wise.* Albany: SUNY Press, 1982.
———. *We Are One! American Jewry and Israel.* Garden City, NY: Anchor Books, 1978.
"U.S. Group Formed to Create Settlement in the West Bank." *JTA News Bulletin,* 8 August 1977, 1.
van Dijk, Teun A. "Aims of Critical Discourse Analysis." *Japanese Discourse* 1 (1995): 17–27.
———. "Principles of Critical Discourse Analysis." *Discourse and Society* 4, no. 2 (1993): 249–283.
"V-Ata, L-Mahapeha B-Aliya." *Nekuda,* 7 September 1983, 3. [Hebrew]
Vilnay, Zev. *Legends of Judea and Samaria.* Jerusalem: Sefer V-Sefel, 2006.
Visman, Alizah. *Ha-Pinui: Sipur Akirat Ha-Yishuvim B-Hevel Yamit.* Bet-El: Sifriyat Bet El, 1990. [Hebrew]
Vorspan, Albert. "Vietnam and the Jewish Conscience." *American Judaism* 15 (1966).
Wald, Kenneth, and Samuel Shye. "Religious Influence in Electoral Behavior: The Role of Institutional and Social Forces in Israel." *Journal of Politics* 57, no. 2 (May 1995): 495–507.
Walker, Sari. "Lev Tzion—A Stronghold on Sand: An Interview with Bobby Brown." *Bechol Zot* 2, no. 1 (1978).
Wall, Harry. "The Road from Yamit." *Jerusalem Post International Edition,* 16–22 December 1979: 16.
Wallach, John, and Janet Wallach. *Still Small Voices.* New York: Citadel Press, 1989.
"Warning Reported before Hebron Massacre." *New York Times,* 13 March 1994, 19.
Waxman, Chaim I. *American Aliya: Portrait of an Innovative Migration Movement.* Detroit: Wayne State University Press, 1989.
———. "American Israelis in Judea and Samaria: An Empirical Analysis." *Middle East Review* 17, no. 2 (Winter 1984/1985): 48–54.
———. "In the End Is It Ideology? Religio-Cultural and Structural Factors in American Aliya." *Contemporary Jewry* 16 (1995): 50–67.

————. "The Limited Impact of the Six Day War on America's Jews." In *The Six Day War and World Jewry*, ed. Eli Lederhendler. Bethesda: University Press of Maryland, 2000.

————. "Political and Social Attitudes of Americans among the Settlers in the Territories." In *The Impact of Gush Emunim: Politics and Settlement in the West Bank*, ed. David Newman, 200–220. New York: St. Martin's Press, 1985.

Waxman, Chaim I., and Michael Appel. *To Israel and Back: American Aliyah and Return Migration*. New York: American Jewish Committee, 1986.

Waxman, Dov. *Trouble in the Tribe: The American Jewish Conflict over Israel*. Princeton, NJ: Princeton University Press, 2016.

"We Went Out to Tour in Tekoa." *Zeraim* 12 (Elul 1975): 2–3. [Hebrew]

Weber, Nancy. "The Truth of Tears." *Village Voice*, 15 June 1967.

Weisburd, David. *Jewish Settler Violence: Deviance as Social Reaction*. University Park: Pennsylvania State University Press, 1989.

Whartman, Eliezer. "Why So Small an Aliyah from America." *The Reconstructionist*, 7 March 1952, 19–23.

Whitehead, John. "How Have American Historians Viewed the Frontier?" Meeting of the Frontiers Conference—Library of Congress (Summary), 21 September 2010.

"Who Votes for Kahane?" *MERIP Reports*, nos. 136–137 (October/December 1985): 32.

Wiesel, Elie. *Night*. New York: Bantam Books, 1960.

Wilder, David. "I Was Baruch Goldstein's Friend." *Jewish Press*, 28 February 2014.

Williams, William Appleman. *The Tragedy of American Diplomacy*. New York: W. W. Norton, 1972.

Wise, Stephen. *Challenging Years: The Autobiography of Stephen Wise*. New York: Putnam's Sons, 1949.

Wisse, Ruth R. *If I Am Not for Myself: The Liberal Betrayal of the Jews*. New York: Free Press, 1992.

Wistrich, Robert S. "Theodore Herzl: Zionist Icon, Myth-Maker, and Social Utopian." *Israel Affairs* 1, no. 3 (1995): 1–37.

Wistrich, Robert S., and David Ohana. *The Shaping of Israeli Identity: Myth, Memory, and Trauma*. London: Frank Cass, 1995.

Wodak, Ruth, ed. *Language, Power, and Ideology*. Amsterdam: Benjamins, 1989.

Wolf, Arnold, and Jonathan S. Wolf. *The Unfinished Rabbi: Selected Writings of Arnold Jacob Wolf*. Chicago: Ivan R. Dee, 1998.

Wolfsfeld, Gadi. "Collective Political Action and Media Strategy: The Case of Yamit." *Journal of Conflict Resolution* 28, no. 3 (September 1984): 363–381.

Woocher, Jonathan S. *Sacred Survival: The Civil Religion of American Jews*. Bloomington: Indiana University Press, 1986.

"World News Briefs: U.S.-Born Killer Is Freed by Israel." *New York Times*, 27 October 1997.

Wuthnow, Robert, and John Hyde Evans, eds. *The Quiet Hand of God: Faith-Based Activism and the Public Role of Mainline Protestantism*. Berkeley: University of California Press, 2002.

Wyschgrod, Michael. "The Jewish Interest in Vietnam." *Tradition* 8 (Winter 1966).

Yahav, Dan. *Mifal Ha-Hityashvut B-Hevel Yamit: Halom Sh-Nagoz: Esrim Shana L-Hakama, Asor L-Pinui (1971–1992).* Tel Aviv: Y. Golan, 1992. [Hebrew]

Yakowicz, Will. "'V' Is for Victory: The Odyssey of Jack Teitel—An Intimate Look at the Accused Jewish Killer." *Tablet Magazine,* 14 July 2010.

"Yamit: Chalutz Aliyah of the Mid. '70s." *Aliyon* (October 1973): 4–5.

Yanovitzky, I., and G. Weinmann. "The Attitude of Jewish Settlers toward Law and Democracy in Israel: An Analysis of *Nekuda,* the Settlers' Main Publication." *Megamot* 34, no. 3 (1998): 191–215.

Yavin, Chaim, Eran Torbiner, Shai Nesher, Anat Tzom-Ayalon, Sharon Ben Ezer, and Haim Ilfman. *Eretz Ha-Mitnahalim: Yoman Masa* (film). Directed by Chaim Yavin. New York: Americans for Peace Now, 2005.

"Yediot." *Amudim* 358, 23, no. 12 (Elul 1975): 438.

Yerushalmi, Yosef. *Zakhor, Jewish History and Jewish Memory.* Seattle: University of Washington Press, 1982.

"Yesha and Washington Share Resources." *YESHA Report* (February 1995): 6.

"Yesha Attends the CJF General Assembly." *YESHA Report* (November–December 1994): 4.

"Yesha in Cyberspace." *YESHA Report* (July–August 1996): 11.

"Yesha Information Campaign Launched." *YESHA Report* 19 (February–March 1994): 5.

"Yesha News: The Yesha Tourist Authority." *YESHA Report* (March–April 2000): 12.

"Yesha's Leaders on the North America Campaign Trail." *YESHA Report* 26 (January 1995): 1.

YESHA Speaker's Bureau: Sponsored by the Jewish Communities in Judea, Samaria, and Gaza. Jerusalem: Moetzet Ha-Yishuvim Ha-Yehudiyim B-Yehuda, Shomron, V-Hevel Aza, 1992.

Yishal, Yael. *Land or Peace: Whither Israel?* Stanford, CA: Hoover Institution Press, 1987.

Yow, Valerie Raleigh. *Recording Oral History: A Practical Guide for Social Scientists.* Thousand Oaks, CA: Sage, 1994.

Zait, David. *Ziyonut B-Darkhei Ha-Shalom: Darkho Ha-Rayonit Politit Shel Ha-Shomer Ha-Tsair.* Givat Haviva: Mercaz Tiud Shel Ha-Shomer Ha-Tzair, 1985. [Hebrew]

Zeitz, Joshua Michael. "'If I Am Not for Myself . . .': The American Jewish Establishment in the Aftermath of the Six Day War." *American Jewish History* 88, no. 2 (2000): 253–286.

Zelnicker, Shimshon, and Michael Kahan. "Religion and Nascent Cleavages: The Case of Israel's National Religious Party." *Comparative Politics* 9, no. 1 (October 1976): 21–49.

Zertal, Idith, and Akiva Eldar. *Lords of the Land: The War over Israel's Settlements in the Occupied Territories, 1967–2007.* New York: Nation Books, 2007.

Zerubavel, Yael. *Recovered Roots: Collective Memory and the Making of Israeli National Tradition.* Chicago: University of Chicago Press, 1995.

Zilbersheid, Uri. "The Utopia of Theodore Herzl." *Israel Studies* 9, no. 3 (Fall 2004): 80–114.

Zimmerman, Michael. "Volunteers, Six Days Plus." *Midstream* 49, no. 4 (May–June 2003): 23–27.

"Zionist Organization Unites in Memory of David Rosenfeld." *Haaretz*, 6 June 1982, 5. [Hebrew]

Acknowledgments

Writing the acknowledgments section of your first book is one of those cherished fantasies in the dark days of revision as you draft no less than your twelfth version of the introduction. I'm not sure I dared to dream that I would ever truly reach this destination—but I have certainly had company on this long, arduous, and ultimately fulfilling journey.

If it takes a village to raise a child, it required a whole settlement of supporters to write my first book on this challenging topic.

Like most passion projects, it was a true labor of love—for scholarship, for public debate, and perhaps most importantly, for the future of Zionism—which are professional as well as personal commitments.

While the intellectual demands of writing this book were manifold, they often were eclipsed by the emotional, financial, and spiritual trials over the past ten years of living in three different countries. I could not have written this book without the learned exchange of ideas I have benefited from over the past decade, but I could not have survived this larger endeavor without the assistance, kindness, and generosity of the many individuals who inspired me along the way. Thus, my expressions of gratitude can only be inadequately brief and incomplete.

First, my hearty thanks to Harvard University Press. I especially wish to acknowledge my editor, Andrew Kinney. I benefited tremendously from our conversations and his comments on the manuscript, and I felt I had an erudite, sensitive, and compassionate co-pilot through this entire process of scholarly publishing. I also wish to thank my anonymous peer reviewers for their extensive and empathetic critiques of my manuscript and for supporting my career. I'd also like to express my appreciation to Katrina Vassallo, who assisted me with the final preparations of the book, Tim Jones, who designed the book jacket, and the HUP publicity team led by Eleanor Andrew (USA) and Emilie Ferguson (UK/Europe/Middle East/Africa), who helped promote my work. While I could hardly believe the book would reach that stage, my gratitude also to Kimberly Giambattisto and the copyeditors,

proofreaders, indexers, and typesetters at Westchester Publishing Services who prepared the manuscript for printing.

I also thank the "ancient and honorable community of scholars" at the University of Chicago. My gratitude to Paul Mendes-Flohr, Orit Bashkin, and John Woods,
a true mentor and role model who taught me what it means to join the guild of the
historians. I also recognize the efforts of Bernard Wasserstein, who helped mold this
project in earlier stages. I also thank (past and present) history department graduate coordinators Kelly Pollack and Sonja Rusnak, as well as David Goodwine,
for assisting me during my years at the university. I am indebted to the University
of Chicago Center for Middle East Studies faculty and staff, especially Rusty Rook
and Traci Lombre. I am also grateful for the assistance of the Office of Graduate
Affairs (with a special mention to Brooke Noonan) and the Division of the Social
Sciences at the University of Chicago. Further, while this list is far from complete, I
would like to thank other faculty at the University of Chicago who were involved
at various stages of this project, including Fred Donner, Holly Shissler, Robert
Pape, John Mearsheimer, Leora Auslander, Noha Forster, Ariela Finkelstein, Salim
Yaqub, Cornell Fleischer, Ralph Austin, Naama Rokem, and Richard Hellie, among
many others. A special thanks to the staff of the Regenstein Library, especially its
Interlibrary Loan department, who tirelessly assisted me in procuring obscure materials from far-flung locales.

I worked on revising my book manuscript as a fellow at the Schusterman Center
for Israel Studies at Brandeis University in 2012–2013. This very fruitful year was
a true immersion in the field of Israel studies and a profound inspiration for my
work. I am thankful to both the faculty and the many graduate student participants in the Israel Studies Seminar who contributed greatly to the reconceptualiza-
tion of this project. In particular, I must express my heartfelt thanks to Ilan Troen
and Jonathan Sarna, as well as Yehuda Mirsky, Sylvia Barack Fishman, Shai
Feldman, Rachel Fish, Shay Rabineau, and Emily McKee for their generous collaborations. I also thank the staff of the Schusterman Center, the Department of
Near Eastern and Judaic Studies, and the Judaica library for their assistance.
Thank you for making me an honorary member of the Brandeis "mishpacha."

In a wonderful twist of fate, I found myself moving to the United Kingdom in
2013 to take up a post as the new University Research Lecturer and Sidney Brichto
fellow in Israel Studies at the University of Oxford. While I fear I've had to defer
many of Oxford's greatest charms so I could return to my desk to finish this manuscript, it is difficult to imagine a more opportune environment for a scholar. It has
been a pleasure to work with Derek Penslar, the outgoing Stanley Lewis Professor
of Israel Studies, as well as Johannes Becke, Sharon Weinblum, and Roman Vater, in
building a new curriculum. My colleagues at the Oxford Centre for Hebrew and
Jewish Studies and the Faculty of Oriental Studies have certainly taught me a great
deal about tea and queueing (and patiently forgiven all of my Americanisms); most
of all, they have mentored me as a young scholar. I know we are intended to "keep
calm and carry on," but I hope I'm allowed a few emotional words for its faculty

and students during my tenure here, especially Martin Goodman, Alison Salvesen, David Rechter, Joanna Weinberg, Jan Joosten, Adriana Jacobs, Zehavit Stern, Miri Freud Kandel, Jeremy Schonfeld, Glenda Abramson, Abigail Green, Joshua Teplitsky, Laurent Mignon, Avi Shlaim, Eugene Rogan, Michael Willis, Philip Robins, Sir Fergus Miller, Rabbi Norman Solomon, Khayke Beruriah Wiegand, Stephen Herring, and Gil Zahavi. I must also mention our wonderful staff, Martine Smith-Huvers, Sue Forteath, Sheila Philips, and Liliane Morton, who have been a great support to scholars here. I also wish to acknowledge the Leopold Muller Library for their partnership with fellows of the centre, which has extended not only to procuring materials but to letting me constantly exceed my staff borrowing privileges and receive regular research pep talks! My special thanks to Cesar Merchan-Hamman, Milena Zeidler, and the many staff who have assisted me over the past several years. I'd also like to thank the staff of the Vere Harmsworth Library and the fellows of the Rothemere American Institute, the Middle East Centre, the School of Interdisciplinary Area Studies, Wolfson College, St. Antony's College, and the TORCH Centre at the University of Oxford for their encouragement in this project.

So many other scholars across the globe have generously contributed to guiding my scholarship, including Chaim I. Waxman, Colin Shindler, Motti Inbari, Ronald Zweig, Donna Robinson Divine, Orit Rozin, Ellen Lust-Okar, Ian Lustick, Michael Brenner, Steven Zipperstein, Joel Migdal, Aryeh Saposnik, Ken Stein, Gerald Steinberg, Eli Lederhendler, Michal Shamir, Adam Ferziger, Noah Efron, Jonathan Rynhold, Asher Arian (z"l), Gershom Bashkin, Yossi Klein Ha-Levi, and Gershom Gorenberg. I am also privileged to belong to a cohort of young scholars, many of whom have been hearing about this project from its earliest inception, including Liora Halperin, Shayna Weiss, Seth Anziska, Joseph Ringel, Yair Wallach, Hila Zaban, Shaul Mitelplunkt, Amy Weiss, Jaclyn Granick, Nathan Kurz, Shay Hazkani, Eric Fleisch, Randall Geller, Shira Klein, Yoav Duman, Daniel Mahla, Amaryah Orenstein, Avi Rubin, Ori Yehudai, Assaf David, and many more individuals I cannot recognize here who have contributed in bigger and smaller ways. I must also thank all those who contributed to papers and panels related to my book project over the years at the conferences of the Association of Israel Studies, the European Association of Israel Studies, the Association of Jewish Studies, the Society for Historians of American Foreign Relations, as well as the University of Chicago Middle East History and Theory Conference, the University of Chicago Jewish Studies symposium, Yale University's Jewish Studies Colloquium, the New York University Israel Studies workshop, the AICE/Schusterman Israel Scholars convention, the Fulbright-Israel Roundtable, the Brandeis University Israel Studies Workshop, the Tel Aviv University Minerva Center Settlements working group, and the University of Oxford's Israel Studies Seminar, David Patterson lectures, Summer Institute in Contemporary Judaism, and Americans Abroad conference for allowing me to present my research findings and for providing me with valuable insights into my project. I also sincerely thank Ambassadors Dennis Ross and Michael Oren for their assistance with this project, as well as the many other foreign policy experts, journalists, and lay leaders who have communicated with me both privately and publicly over the years about this book.

I could not have completed this project without the help of various archives, libraries, and other institutions that assisted me in conducting research. My special gratitude to the various research sites that hosted me during my research trips to Israel, including the Israel State Archives (especially archivist Helena Vilensky), the Jewish Agency for Israel (my special recognition of David Schmeider, manager of the warehouse document repository in Tsrifin), the Bar-Ilan University Institute for the Research of Religious Zionism, and the staff of Israel's National Library, a veritable treasure of the Jewish People and Israel and a home away from home for visiting scholars. I also extend my sincere gratitude to the many Jewish-American settlers who participated in interviews for my research and gave generously and thoughtfully of their time during and after our meeting, including (but not restricted to) Malka Chaiken, Chaim and Sarah Feifel, Carole Rosenblatt, Rabbi Jonathan and Shifra Blass, Bobby Brown, Eli Birnbaum, Gedaliah Mazal, Eve Harow, Jay Shapiro, Attorney Marc Zell, Attorney Sondra Oster-Barras, Dr. Yehuda Ben-Meir, Rabbi Shlomo Riskin, Bob Lang, Sharon Katz, Shmuel Sackett, Era Rapaport, Michael Guzofsky, Yehiel Leiter, Aliza Herbst, Mike Guzofsky, Ari Zimmerman, David Bedein, and Rabbi David Wilder. My special appreciation to Yisrael Medad, who assisted me in various aspects of this project, including oral history research.

Without the generous support of various institutions, I would not have had the financial resources to undertake the research and writing of this project. My profound gratitude goes to the Fulbright Hays fellowship committee and the Fulbright-Israel staff (especially Neal Sherman and Judy Stavsky) for allowing me to spend academic year 2008–2009 conducting research in Israel. I also express my deepest appreciation to the Schusterman Family Foundation and the American-Israeli Cooperative Enterprise (under the directorship of Mitchell Bard) for their generous funding. I also acknowledge the University of Chicago Century Fellowship and the Kunstadter and Janco fund for their support of my studies and special assistance for research trips to Jerusalem in 2010 and 2011. Last but not least, I am most grateful to the University of Oxford John Fell Fund and the Brichto fellowship for providing me with summer research assistance to complete my manuscript.

On a more personal note, I am indebted to the many friends and family who truly saw me through each step of this process. They gave of themselves, their energies, their hearts, and their interest—not to mention their couches, their food, their shoulders, their Kleenex, their caffeine supplies, and most of all their free time and love to champion me and this book. I hope you know who you are—I look forward to the opportunity to acknowledge you properly and privately and to somehow repay the favors and kindness you have shown me over the past decade.

Only months before I submitted my final manuscript to the press, I learned that my colleague and friend Michael Feige (z"l) was tragically killed in the terrorist attack at the Sarona market in Tel Aviv in June 2016. The profound influence of Michael's work and mentorship on the settler movement meant far more than I ever had a chance to tell him, which I deeply regret. I had so looked forward to collaborations and conversations we might have had once I finished this book project. He was certainly a role model as a scholar of settlements, but also as a true mensch, a family man, and an uncynical member (and now, a martyr) of the movement for peace.

Last but certainly not least a final acknowledgment: There are truly no words or gestures that could possibly suffice to thank my parents, David and Beverly Hirschhorn, for their boundless and unwavering support throughout this process. There is a Jewish parable about the footsteps in the sand—how fortunate I am that I had both my parents who walked beside me and often carried me on their shoulders every agonizing and joyful step of the way in this scholarly and personal journey. I can only pray there is a little *naches* for this *mesirut ha-nefesh* to their only daughter. With all the gratitude and love in my heart, I dedicate this work to both of you.

Index